1001

Days out with your kids

1001

Days out with your kids

p

Contents

Introduction		vi
South East		1
South West		51
Eastern		107
East Midlands		141
West Midlands		163
Wales		185
Yorkshire		203
North West		235
North East		283
Scotland		309
Index		370
Acknowledgements & picture credits		376

Introduction

Welcome to the fifth edition of *1001 Days Out with Your Kids*. Revised, with updated information and a wealth of brand-new entries, this book will equip you with fresh ideas for places to visit throughout the year no matter what the weather, as well as giving you up-to-date information on countless famous attractions.

There is an amazing variety of places in Britain that can capture a child's imagination. They can be educational, inspirational, or just plain fun!

Attractions range from crumbling castles surrounded by magnificent moats to wildlife parks teeming with fabulous creatures; from exciting river journeys and railway trips to fascinating collections of old vehicles; from beautiful country parks with children's nature trails to theme and adventure parks packed with breathtaking rides for even the biggest 'kids'. We have also included a range of museums where you will find displays on everything from children's writers to Viking warriors.

Children's imaginations are captured by the most unexpected things at times so in order to provide ideas and inspiration for even the most difficult to please we have tried to present the widest possible selection of attractions.

Whatever you choose, don't forget to telephone the venue and check the details before setting out.

Most of all, enjoy your days out with the kids!

About this guide

This guide covers England, Scotland (including the Northern and Western Islands) and Wales and is arranged in regions, shown on the national map on page viii. The counties within each region, the towns within each county and the attractions within each town are all, where possible, arranged alphabetically (we have taken the occasional licence with the running order to enable us to include the best images). Each attraction also has a reference number and this is used to identify it on the regional map at the beginning of each section.

Understanding the entries

Coloured bands at the top of each page indicate regions; the numbers in the top corners next to the regional name refer to the numbered range of attractions on the page. The nearest major town or village to the attraction is indicated above the name of the attraction.

Quick-reference icons

- an all-weather attraction
- an attraction for sunny days only
- the expected duration of your visit
- when the attraction is open

Description

Each entry has a brief description of the attraction and a flavour of what visitors may expect to find. Additional features are also highlighted beneath the description.

Facilities

- **WC** toilet facilities available
- space available for you to eat your own food
- restaurant, café or kiosk facilities available
- good access for wheelchairs   restricted access
- dogs allowed, but they may have to be kept on a lead

Disabled visitors

Visitors with mobility difficulties should look for the wheelchair symbol which shows that all or most of the attraction is accessible to wheelchair users. We strongly recommend that visitors telephone in advance of a visit to check exact details, including access to toilets and refreshment facilities. Assistance dogs are usually accepted unless stated otherwise. For the hard of hearing, please check that hearing induction loops are available by contacting the attraction itself.

Location

These are simple directions, usually for motorists (though Underground directions are given for attractions in London) and have been provided by the attraction itself.

Opening times

These times are inclusive, e.g. Apr–Oct indicates that the attraction will be open from the beginning of April to the end of October. Where an attraction has varied opening times, these are indicated, and if it is open seven days a week, this is simply referred to as 'Daily'. Bank Holiday opening is indicated where provided by the attraction.

If you are travelling a long way, please check with the attraction itself to ensure any unexpected circumstances are not going to prevent your entry.

Admission

Wherever possible, the charges quoted are for the 2006–7 season, but please note that prices are subject to change and are correct only at the time of going to print. If no price is quoted, it does not mean that a charge will not be made. Many places that do not charge admission may ask for a voluntary donation. In some instances discounts may be available to families, groups, local residents or members of certain organisations such as English Heritage and The National Trust.

Contact details

We have given details of the administrative address and telephone number for each attraction. While these are usually those of the attraction itself, some properties are administered by an area office, and in these cases relevant these details are given (several English Heritage properties fall into this category).

Telephone numbers, and email and website addresses are also included wherever possible.

colour bar indicating region

nearest town to the attraction

quick reference icons

general description

additional features

reference number on regional map

facilities available

detailed information:
location, opening times,
admission prices,
contact details

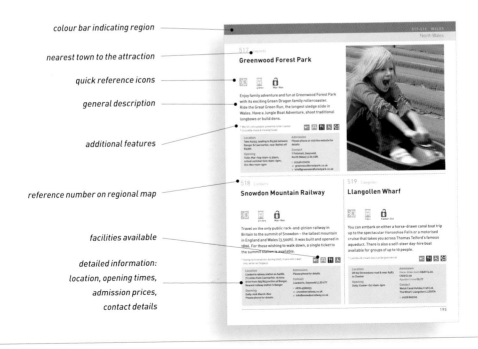

Regional colour key

- South East
- South West
- Eastern
- East Midlands
- West Midlands
- Wales
- Yorkshire
- North West
- North East
- Scotland

HIGHLANDS & ISLANDS

GRAMPIAN

CENTRAL SCOTLAND

SOUTHERN SCOTLAND

NORTHUMBERLAND

TYNE & WEAR

DURHAM

CUMBRIA

NORTH YORKSHIRE

EAST RIDING OF YORKSHIRE

LANCASHIRE

W. YORKSHIRE

MERSEY-SIDE

MANCHESTER

SOUTH YORKSHIRE

CHESHIRE

DERBYSHIRE

LINCOLNSHIRE

NORTH WALES

STAFFORD-SHIRE

NOTTING-HAMSHIRE

SHROPSHIRE

LEICESTER-SHIRE

RUT-LAND

NORFOLK

WEST MIDLANDS

CENTRAL WALES

WORCESTER-SHIRE

WARWICK-SHIRE

NORTHAMPTON-SHIRE

CAMBRIDGESHIRE

SUFFOLK

HEREFORD-SHIRE

BEDFORD-SHIRE

GLOUCESTER-SHIRE

BUCKING-HAMSHIRE

HERTFORD-SHIRE

ESSEX

SOUTH WALES

OXFORDSHIRE

LONDON

WILTSHIRE

BERKSHIRE

SURREY

KENT

SOMERSET

HAMPSHIRE

WEST SUSSEX

E. SUSSEX

DEVON

DORSET

ISLE OF WIGHT

CORNWALL

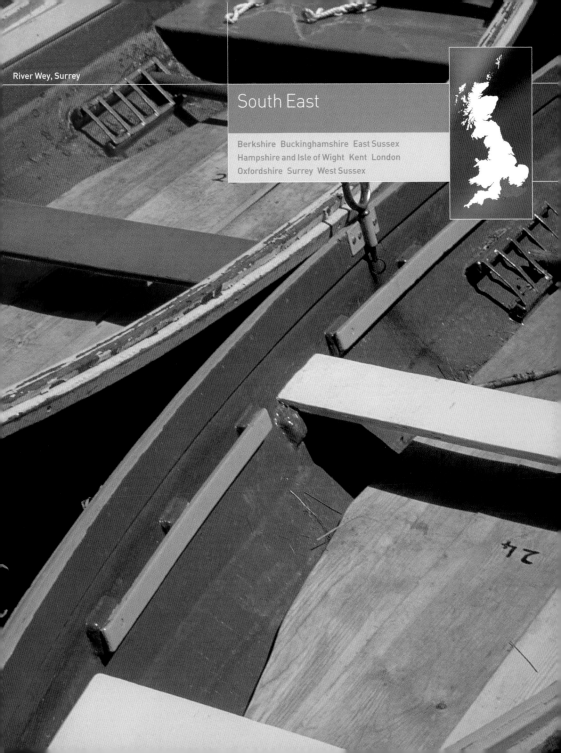

South East

Berkshire Buckinghamshire East Sussex
Hampshire and Isle of Wight Kent London
Oxfordshire Surrey West Sussex

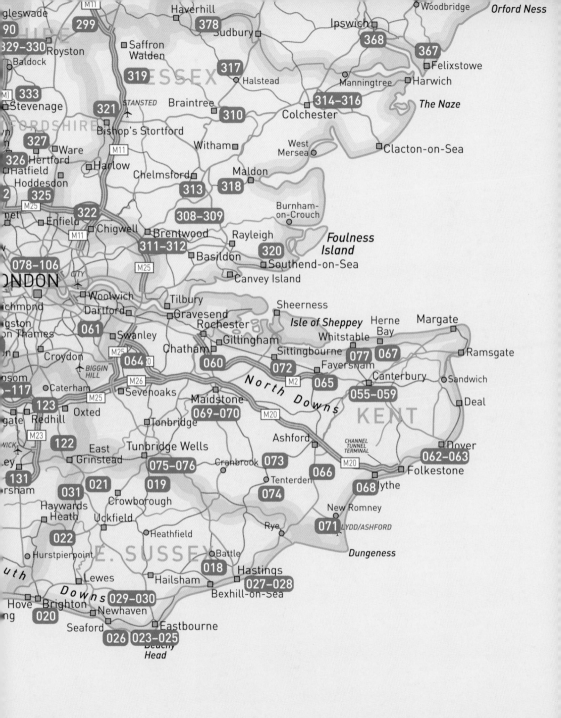

gleswade
90
299
Haverhill
378
Sudbury
Woodbridge
Orford Ness
Ipswich
368
367
329–330 Royston
Saffron Walden
Baldock
319
ESSEX
Halstead
317
Manningtree
Harwich
Felixstowe
333 Stevenage
321
STANSTED
Braintree
310
Colchester
314–316
The Naze
327 Ware
Bishop's Stortford
Witham
West Mersea
Clacton-on-Sea
HERTFORDSHIRE
326 Hertford
Hatfield
Hoddesdon
Harlow
Chelmsford
313
Maldon
318
Burnham-on-Crouch
2
325
M25
322
Enfield
M11
Chigwell
Brentwood
308–309
Rayleigh
Foulness Island
078–106
CITY
311–312
Basildon
320
Southend-on-Sea
ONDON
Woolwich
Canvey Island
ichmnd
Dartford
Tilbury
Gravesend
Sheerness
Isle of Sheppey
Herne Bay
Margate
gston on Thames
061
Swanley
Rochester
Chatham
Gillingham
Whitstable
077
067
Ramsgate
Croydon
064
M25
Sittingbourne
072
Faversham
Canterbury
Sandwich
osom
BIGGIN HILL
060
M2
065
055–059
Deal
–117
Caterham
M26
Sevenoaks
North Downs
KENT
123 Redhill
Oxted
Maidstone
069–070
M20
Ashford
CHANNEL TUNNEL TERMINAL
Dover
062–063
ate
M23
122
East Grinstead
Tunbridge Wells
075–076
Tonbridge
Cranbrook
073
M20
Folkestone
WICK
ley
131
031
021
019
Crowborough
Tenterden
074
066
068 ythe
rsham
Haywards Heath
Uckfield
New Romney
071
LYDD/ASHFORD
022
Heathfield
Rye
Dungeness
Hurstpierpoint
Downs
Battle
018
Hastings
027–028
Lewes
Hailsham
Bexhill-on-Sea
E. SUSSEX
uth
Hove
Brighton
029–030
020
Newhaven
Seaford
Eastbourne
Beachy Head
026
023–025

©MAPS IN MINUTES™ 2006. ©Crown Copyright, Ordnance Survey 2006.

BERKSHIRE
Animal Attractions
Beale Park 7
Go Ape! 6
The Living Rainforest 6

Historic Sites
Windsor Castle 8

Museums & Exhibitions
The Look Out Discovery Centre 6

Parks, Gardens & Nature
California Country Park 8
Dinton Pastures Country Park 8

Theme Parks & Adventure Playgrounds
Legoland Windsor 7

BUCKINGHAMSHIRE
Animal Attractions
Bucks Goat Centre 9
Tiggywinkles, The Wildlife Hospital Trust 9

Boat & Train Trips
Buckinghamshire Railway Centre 9

Museums & Exhibitions
Bekonscot Model Village & Railway 10
Buckinghamshire County Museum
 & Roald Dahl Gallery 9
Milton Keynes Museum 11
Wycombe Museum 10

Parks, Gardens & Nature
Emberton Country Park 11

Sport & Leisure
Xscape – Milton Keynes 11

EAST SUSSEX
Animal Attractions
Brighton Sea Life Centre 12
Drusillas Park 13
Stoneywish Nature Reserve 13

Boat & Train Trips
Bluebell Railway 16

Historic Sites
Bateman's 13
Battle Abbey & Battlefield 12
Bodiam Castle 12
Hastings Castle & 1066 Story 15
Newhaven Fort 16

Museums & Exhibitions
'How We Lived Then' Museum of Shops 14
Smuggler's Adventure 15

Parks, Gardens & Nature
Paradise Park 16
Seven Sisters Country Park 15

Theme Parks & Adventure Playgrounds
Treasure Island 14

HAMPSHIRE
Animal Attractions
Fort Victoria Marine Aquarium 25
The Hawk Conservancy Trust 17
Isle of Wight Zoo 21
Longdown Activity Farm 22
Marwell Zoological Park 24
Seaview Wildlife Encounter 21

Boat & Train Trips
Isle of Wight Steam Railway 21

Historic Sites
Calshot Castle 22
Osborne House 17
The Royal Armouries – Fort Nelson 18

Museums & Exhibitions
Beaulieu Abbey & National
 Motor Museum 17
Classic Boat Museum 20
Explosion! The Museum of Naval
 Firepower 19
Fort Victoria Model Railway 25
INTECH-Hands-on Science
 & Technology Centre 24
Museum of Army Flying 23
Spinnaker Tower 20

Parks, Gardens & Nature
Royal Victoria Country Park 23
Shanklin Chine 22
Staunton Country Park 19

Theme Parks & Adventure Playgrounds
Blackgang Chine Fantasy Park 24
The Needles Park 18
Paultons Park 20

KENT
Animal Attractions
Eagle Heights Bird of Prey Centre 28
Farming World 28
Howletts Wild Animal Park 26
Port Lympne Wild Animal Park 30
South of England Rare Breeds Centre 29
Wildwood 29

Boat & Train Trips
Bredgar & Wormshill Light Railway 32
Kent & East Sussex Railway 32
Romney, Hythe & Dymchurch Railway 31

Historic Sites
Crabble Corn Mill 27
Dover Castle 28
The Historic Dockyard, Chatham 27
Leeds Castle 30

Museums & Exhibitions
The Canterbury Tales 25
Chislehurst Caves 27
The Hop Farm 33
Museum of Canterbury with
  Rupert Bear Museum 26
Museum of Kent Life 31
Roman Museum 26

Parks, Gardens & Nature
Druidstone Park & Art Park 25
Groombridge Place Gardens
  & The Enchanted Forest 32

Theme Parks & Adventure Playgrounds
Diggerland 32
Snappy's Adventure Play Centre 33

LONDON
Animal Attractions
Deen City Farm 37
London Aquarium 34
London Zoo 38
Stepping Stones Farm 39

Guided Tours
BBC Television Centre Tours 38

Historic Sites
Buckingham Palace 35
The *Cutty Sark* 35
Houses of Parliament 41
Tower of London 40

Museums & Exhibitions
Bank of England Museum 36
The British Museum 33
Chelsea FC Museum & Tour 35
Imperial War Museum 36
Livesey Museum for Children 34

London Dungeon 37
Madame Tussaud's 37
Museum of London 34
National Gallery 41
Natural History Museum 38
Ragged School Museum 39
Royal Air Force Museum 36
Science Museum 39
Sherlock Holmes Museum 37
Thames Barrier Information
  & Learning Centre 41
Tower Bridge Exhibition 40
Winston Churchill's Britain at War
  Experience 40

Premier Site
London Eye 35

Theatre
Globe Theatre 38
Polka Theatre 41

OXFORDSHIRE
Animal Attractions
Cotswold Wildlife Park & Gardens 42

Boat & Train Trips
Chinnor & Princes Risborough Railway 42

Museums & Exhibitions
Cogges Manor Farm Museum 43
Didcot Railway Centre 42
The Oxford Story 43
The Oxfordshire Museum 43

SURREY
Animal Attractions
Bocketts' Farm Park 47
British Wildlife Centre 47
Burpham Court Farm Park 46
Godstone Farm 47
Horton Park Children's Farm 45

Historic Sites
Hampton Court Palace 45

Museums & Exhibitions
Brooklands Museum 47
River Wey & Godalming Navigations
  & Dapdune Wharf 46
Rural Life Centre 46

Parks, Gardens & Nature
Painshill Park 44

Theme Parks & Adventure Playgrounds
Chessington World of Adventures 45
Thorpe Park 44

WEST SUSSEX
Animal Attractions
Earnley Butterflies & Gardens 49
Fishers Farm Park 48
Tulleys Farm 49
WWT Arundel 48

Historic Sites
Bignor Roman Villa 50

Museums & Exhibitions
Amberley Working Museum 48
Look and Sea! 50
Military Aviation Museum 49
Weald & Downland Open-Air Museum 49

Theme Parks & Adventure Playgrounds
The Flying Fortress 50
Harbour Park 50

001 Bracknell

Go Ape!

3 hrs   Mar–Oct

Go Ape! is a network of rope bridges, trapezes and death slides that stretches for roughly a mile through the tree canopy. A unique experience that consists of an extensive cat's cradle of ropes, netting and platforms, set high above the ground in Bracknell Forest.

* 115ft aerial walkway
* Age limit is 10 & a height restriction of 1.4m applies

Location
Follow signs for Go Ape! on A322 S of Bracknell

Opening
Feb half-term & Mar–Oct 9am–5pm; Nov weekends only

Admission
Adult £21, Child £17

Contact
The Look Out, Nine Mile Ride, Swinley Forest, Bracknell RG12 7QW
t 0870 444 5562
w goape.co.uk
e info@goape.co.uk

---

002 Bracknell

The Look Out Discovery Centre

2 hrs+   All year

A hands-on science exhibition with fun for the entire family. 'Pluck' the laser beams of the Light Harp to make a little light music or put all your energy into launching the Hydrogen Rocket. Explore the wonders of the human body or try the amazing puzzles.

* Children's play area
* 2,600 acres of woodland

Location
Follow signs for Look Out Discovery Centre on A322 S of Bracknell

Opening
Daily: 10am–5pm

Admission
Please phone for details

Contact
Nine Mile Ride, Bracknell RG12 7QW
t 01344 354400
w bracknell-forest.gov.uk/be
e thelookout@bracknell-forest.gov.uk

---

003 Newbury

The Living Rainforest

1 hr+   All year

Experience the sights, sounds and smells of a rainforest under glass at this unique conservation area. There is something for everyone here including special children's activities and art workshops. Visitors can also adopt an animal.

* Endangered Goeldi's monkeys leap among branches
* Birds, butterflies & lizards roam freely as you explore

Location
Clearly signed from M4 junction 13

Opening
Daily: 10am–5.15pm (last admission 4.30pm)

Admission
Please phone or visit the wesite for details

Contact
Hampstead Norreys RG18 0TN
t 01635 202444
w livingrainforest.org
e enquiries@livingrainforest.org

004 Reading

Beale Park

4 hrs   Mar–Oct

Beale Park is dedicated to the conservation of rare birds. It is home to an amazing collection of birds including swans, owls, parrots and pheasants. There is something for everyone, ranging from gentle walks to madcap adventure play areas.

* Meerkat & wallaby enclosures & pets' corner
* Splash pool & miniature golf for children

Location
6 miles from Reading on A329 between Pangbourne & Streatley

Opening
Daily: 14 Apr–30 Sep 10am–6pm;
1 Oct–13 Apr 10am–5pm

Admission
Adult £6.50, Child £4.50, Concs £5.50

Contact
Lower Basildon,
Reading RG8 9NH

t 0870 777 7160
w bealepark.co.uk
e administration@bealepark.co.uk

005 Windsor

Legoland Windsor

6 hrs   Mar–Nov

A land where creativity meets fun, Legoland Windsor has more than 50 rides and attractions based around exhilarating activity areas and is surrounded by extensive gardens and parkland.

* Spectacular Lego models
* Daily shows

Location
2 miles from Windsor town centre on B3022 Bracknell–Windsor road

Opening
Please phone or visit the website for details

Admission
Please phone or visit the website

Contact
Winkfield Road,
Windsor SL4 4AY

t 0870 504 0404
w legoland.co.uk

006 Windsor

Windsor Castle

2 hrs+ All year

This is an official residence of the Queen and the largest occupied castle in the world. It has been a royal palace and fortress for more than 900 years. The castle and grounds cover 13 acres.

* The magnificent & beautiful St George's Chapel
* Apr–Jun, Changing of the Guard at 11am (not Sun)

Location	Contact
Follow brown tourist signs to central Windsor	Ticket Sales & Information Office, The Official Residences of The Queen, London SW1A 1AA
Opening	
Daily: Mar–Oct 9.45am–5.15pm; Nov–Feb 9.45am–4.15pm	t 0207 766 7304
	w royalcollection.org.uk
Admission	e information@royalcollection.org.uk
Please phone for details	

007 Wokingham

California Country Park

2 hrs All year

This park offers fishing and walks around a scenic lake. It contains an area of heathland and an ancient bog, which is a Site of Special Scientific Interest (SSSI). A countryside events programme runs all year.

* Conservation Award for management of SSSI 2002
* Seasonal paddling pool & playground area

Location	Contact
Join Nine Mile Ride from A321, B3016 or A3095	Nine Mile Ride, Finchampstead, Wokingham RG40 4HT
Opening	t 0118 934 2016
Daily: Please phone for details	w wokingham.gov.uk
Admission	e countryside@wokingham.gov.uk
Free. Car park £1 (weekends & hols)	

008 Wokingham

Dinton Pastures Country Park

2 hrs+ All year

Dinton Pastures Country Park is a 400-acre mosaic of rivers, lakes, meadows and wooded areas for visitors to explore. Countryside events are organised throughout the year, including guided walks, pond dips for children and activity days.

* Children's nature sessions & wildlife treasure hunt
* Join Dinton's weekly conservation volunteer group

Location	Contact
Off A329 Reading–Wokingham road. 15 min walk from Winnersh station	Davis Street, Hurst RG10 0TH
Opening	t 0118 934 2016
Daily: *summer* opening 8am (closing times vary) *winter* 8am–8pm	w wokingham.gov.uk
Admission	e countryside@wokingham.gov.uk
Free. Car park £1	

009 Aylesbury

Buckinghamshire County Museum & Roald Dahl Gallery

1 hr+   All year

Have fun with all your favourite characters at this award-winning museum, dedicated to the beloved children's author, with its innovative touchable displays and exciting programme of events. Come along and let your imagination run wild!

* Regular Roald Dahl activities & events
* Varied collections

Location
In town centre

Opening
Museum Mon–Sat 10am–5pm,
Sun 2pm–5pm
Roald Dahl Gallery Mon–Fri 3pm–5pm
(term time), 10am–5pm (hols),
Sat 10am–5pm, Sun 2pm–5pm

Admission
Museum Free
Roald Dahl Gallery Adult & Child £3.50

Contact
Church Street, Aylesbury HP20 2QP
t 01296 331441
w buckscc.gov.uk/museum
e museum@buckscc.gov.uk

010 Aylesbury

Buckinghamshire Railway Centre

2 hrs+   Apr–Oct

A working steam centre where you can ride behind full-size steam engines and on the extensive miniature railway. The museum houses a large collection of locomotives, carriages and wagons.

* See the Royal Train of 1901
* Santa Steaming on 4 weekends before Christmas

Location
Signed from A41 near Waddesdon
& A413 at Whitchurch

Opening
Apr–Oct Wed–Fri 10.30am–4.30pm,
Sat–Sun 10.30am–5.30pm

Admission
Adult £6, Child £4, Concs £5

Contact
Quainton Road Station, Quainton,
Aylesbury HP22 4BY
t 01296 655720
w bucksrailcentre.org
e abaker@bucksrailcentre.btopenworld.com

011 Aylesbury

Bucks Goat Centre

3 hrs+   All year

A centre with examples of all the British breeds of goat as well as donkeys, pets, reptiles, llamas, wallabies, pigs and poultry. Other facilities at the farm include the Naughty Nanny Café, picnic lawns and play areas with swings and slides.

* Petting pen
* Trampoline & play centre

Location
Located ½ mile S of Stoke Mandeville
on A4010

Opening
Daily: *summer* 10am–5pm
winter 10am–4pm

Admission
Adult £4, Child £3, Concs £3.50

Contact
Layby Farm, Old Risborough Road,
Stoke Mandeville,
Aylesbury HP22 5XJ
t 01296 612983
w bucksgoatcentre.co.uk
e bucksgoat@tiscali.co.uk

012 Aylesbury

Tiggywinkles, The Wildlife Hospital Trust

1½ hrs+   All year

Did you know bread and milk is bad for hedgehogs? Come to the visitor centre to find out why and learn about the hundreds of sick animals the hospital cares for. Visit the gardens and wild areas to see some of the other disabled residents (birds and badgers).

* Hedgehog history museum & baby bird viewing area
* New children's play area & CCTV link to animal hospital

Location
Signed off A418 from Aylesbury

Opening
Easter–Sep Mon–Sun 10am–4pm;
Oct–Easter Mon–Fri 10am–4pm

Admission
Adult £3.20, Child & Concs £3

Contact
Aston Road, Haddenham,
Aylesbury HP17 8AF
t 01844 292292
w sttiggywinkles.com
e mail@sttiggywinkles.org.uk

013   Beaconsfield

Bekonscot Model Village & Railway

2 hrs   Feb–Oct

The oldest model village in the world, Bekonscot is a miniature wonderland depicting rural England in the 1930s. A gauge-1 model railway winds its way through the mini-landscape among castles, thatched cottages and a cricket match on the green.

* Sit-on railway available weekends & school holidays
* Children's play area & parties in the log cabin

Location	Contact
Junction 2 off M40 (near junction 16 of M25). Follow signs to Model Village from A355	Warwick Road, Beaconsfield HP9 2PL
	t 01494 672919
Opening	w bekonscot.com
Daily: Feb–Oct 10am–5pm	e info@bekonscot.co.uk
Admission	
Family (2+2) £17.50	

014   High Wycombe

Wycombe Museum

1 hr+   All year

Explore the history of the Wycombe district in the lively modern displays in this museum. There are hands-on activities for children and special events throughout the year.

* Superb collection of Windsor chairs
* Gardens include a Norman 'castle' mound

Location	Contact
Off A404 towards Amersham	Priory Avenue, High Wycombe HP13 6PX
Opening	
Daily: Mon–Sat 10am–5pm, Sun 2pm–5pm; closed Bank Hols	t 01494 421895
	w wycombe.gov.uk/museum
	e museum@wycombe.gov.uk
Admission	
Free, donations welcomed	

015 Milton Keynes

Milton Keynes Museum

2 hrs   All year

Housed in a beautiful Victorian farmstead, attractions include room settings depicting Victorian and Edwardian domestic life, plus live demonstrations of cooking and printing from a bygone age.

* Jessie the shirehorse & historical shopping street
* Special events throughout the year

Location
Off McConnell Drive in Wolverton, just off A5 & A422

Opening
Apr–Oct Wed–Sun 11am–4.30pm;
Nov–Mar Sat–Sun 11am–4.30pm;
Christmas opening times vary.
Please phone for details

Admission
Adult £4, Concs £3, Family £10

Contact
McConnell Drive, Wolverton,
Milton Keynes MK12 5EL
t 01908 316222
w mkmuseum.org.uk
e enquiries@mkmuseum.org.uk

016 Milton Keynes

Xscape – Milton Keynes

7 hrs+   All year

Xscape is a fantastic family day out. Try indoor sky-diving in the incredible Airkix, learn to ski or snowboard on the UK's longest real-snow slope or test your nerve on Vertical Chill's 13m climbing walls. Alternatively, relax at the cinema or bowling alley.

* State-of-the-art health & fitness centre
* Wide range of restaurants & bars

Location
Junction 14 of M1 then take A509
& follow signs

Opening
Please phone for details

Admission
Please phone for details

Contact
602 Marlborough Gate,
Milton Keynes MK9 3XS
t 0871 200 3220
w xscape.co.uk
e mkevents@xscape.co.uk

017 Olney

Emberton Country Park

2 hrs+   All year

A country park with 200 acres of beautiful parkland including five lakes and various children's activities, all bordered by the River Great Ouse. The park also includes many picnic areas.

* 2 children's play areas
* Junior fishing

Location
On A509, 10 miles N of junction 14 off
M1, near Milton Keynes

Opening
Daily 24 hrs *Café* Apr–Oct open
weekends & school hols 10am–5pm

Admission
Free. Car park Apr–Oct £3;
Nov–Mar £1.80

Contact
Emberton, nr Olney MK46 5DB
t 01234 711575
w mkweb.co.uk/embertonpark
e embertonpark@milton-keynes.
gov.uk

018 Battle

Battle Abbey & Battlefield

1 hr+   All year

The site of the Battle of Hastings (1066) is now home to the Discovery Centre: a fun, activity-based exhibition open to families at weekends and during school holidays. There's also a children's themed outdoor play area, a battlefield and an audio tour of the abbey.

* Site of the most famous battle in English history
* Free interactive audio tour recreates the battle

Location
In Battle, at S end of high street. Battle is reached by turning off A21 on to A2100. 10 mins from Battle station

Opening
Daily: Apr–Sep 10am–6pm;
Oct–Mar 10am–4pm

Admission
Adult £6.30, Child £3.20, Concs £4.70

Contact
High Street, Battle TN33 0AD

t 01424 773792
w english-heritage.org.uk

019 Bodiam

Bodiam Castle

3 hrs+   All year

Bodiam Castle is one of the most famous and atmospheric castles in the country. Explore the spiral staircases, visit the medieval lavatories and watch out for the enemy from the battlements. You can even try on some medieval armour (please call in advance).

* Bat Pack Discovery fun pack for young children
* Walk the battlements

Location
Off B2244, 3 miles S of Hawkhurst & 3 miles E of A21 near Hurst Green

Opening
Nov–Feb Sat–Sun 10am–4pm;
Feb–Oct daily 10.30am–6pm (last admission 1 hr before close)

Admission
Adult £4.60, Child £2.30, Family £11.50
Car park £2

Contact
Bodiam, nr Robertsbridge,
TN32 5UA

t 01580 830436
w nationaltrust.org.uk
e bodiamcastle@nationaltrust.org.uk

020 Brighton

Brighton Sea Life Centre

2 hrs+   All year

For a fun and educational day out, visit Brighton Sea Life Centre. Walk through the Underwater Tunnel, be amazed by the fantastic Ocean Tank and get close up to sharks, rays, giant sea turtles and tropical fish. Children under 14 must be accompanied.

* One of the longest underwater tunnels in England
* More than 30 modern marine & freshwater habitats

Location
M23/A23 from London or A27 from Portsmouth & Lewes

Opening
Daily: from 10am.
Please phone for details of winter opening times

Admission
Please phone for details

Contact
Marine Parade,
Brighton BN2 1TB

t 01273 604234
w sealifeeurope.com
e slcbrighton@merlinentertainment.
biz

021 Burwash

Bateman's

2 hrs+   Mar–Oct

If you enjoyed *The Jungle Book* or the *Just So Stories*, then take a trip to the home of Rudyard Kipling. See original drawings of Mowgli and Shere Khan, and Kipling's study – just as he left it.

* Children's quiz
* Gardens & watermill

Location	Admission
Off A265 or B2096, ½ mile S of Burwash	*House & Gardens* Adult £6.20, Child £3.10, Family £15.50
Opening	**Contact**
House Mar–Oct Sat–Wed 11am–5pm	Burwash,
Wild garden Mar Sat–Sun 11am–4pm;	Etchingham TN19 7DF
Apr–Oct 11am–5pm	t 01435 882302
	w nationaltrust.org.uk
	e batemans@nationaltrust.org.uk

022 Ditchling

Stoneywish Nature Reserve

4 hrs+   All year

Stoneywish Nature Reserve is set in 52 acres of meadows and ponds. A wildlife walk enables visitors to pass through fields to a play and picnic area. There is a farm smallholding area, and free-range animals.

* Smallholding with free-range lambs, chickens, pigs & goats
* Shaker-style herb garden & shop

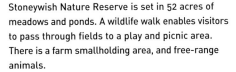

Location	Admission
Take A23 from Brighton or London, then B2116. Located ¼ mile E of Ditchling	Adult £3.75, Child £2.75, Concs £2.75
	Contact
Opening	Spatham Lane,
Mar–Oct daily 10am–5pm;	Ditchling, Hassocks BN6 8XH
Nov–Feb Sat–Sun 10am–4pm,	t 01273 843498
(last admission 30 min before close)	w stoneywish.com

023 Eastbourne

Drusillas Park

5 hrs   All year

Drusillas Park has more than 100 animal species in naturalistic environments including meerkats, otters, monkeys, penguins, bats and lemurs. The excellent children's play area includes climbing, sliding and swinging fun with the penguin slide.

* Mokomos Jungle Rock & Jungle Adventure Golf
* Explorer's Lagoon & Amazon adventure soft play area

Location	Admission
Off A27 between Lewes & Eastbourne	Please phone for details
	Contact
Opening	Alfriston BN26 5QS
Daily: *summer* 10am–6pm	t 01323 874100
winter 10am–5pm	w drusillas.co.uk
	e info@drusillas.co.uk

024 Eastbourne

'How We Lived Then' Museum of Shops

1 hr+ All year

More than 100,000 exhibits of old shops, displays and room sets depicting 100 years of shopping and social history. Stroll through Victorian-styled streets and pay a visit to the grocer, chemist and many more.

Location
Take A22 from London or A27 from Brighton

Opening
Daily: 10am–5.30pm (winter closing time subject to change)
Please phone before visiting

Admission
Adult £3, Child & Concs £3.50

Contact
20 Cornfield Terrace,
Eastbourne BN21 4NS

t 01323 737143
w how-we-lived-then.co.uk
e howwelivedthen@btconnect.com

025 Eastbourne

Treasure Island

3 hrs All year

This is a children's adventure playground filled with climbing apparatus and *Treasure Island* characters. There are also trampolines, inflatable slides and remote-control boats, cars and bikes.

* Paddling pools & sandpits
* 18-hole golf course & indoor play area

Location
Take A27 from Brighton or A22 from London. Follow signs for seafront E

Opening
Park Easter–Sep daily 10am–6pm
Golf Daily *summer* 10am–10pm
winter 10am–6pm

Admission
Park Adult £2, Child £4
Golf £4, £3.50

Contact
Royal Parade,
Eastbourne BN22 7AA

t 01323 411077
w treasure-island.info
e treasureplay@btinternet.com

Seven Sisters Country Park

2 hrs+   All year

A great location for outdoor activities, including family cycle routes, guided bike tours and canoe tuition for all abilities. Sussex Wildlife Trust offers exciting programmes for all age groups. Visit in spring to see newborn lambs on the working farm.

* Shop selling leaflets, maps & souvenirs
* Cycle & canoe hire

Location
Off A259 between Eastbourne and Seaford or 12 or 12A bus from Eastbourne

Opening
Easter–Oct daily;
Oct–Nov weekends only

Admission
Free. Car park fee

Contact
Exceat, Seaford BN25 4AD
t 01323 870280
w sevensisters.org.uk
e sevensisters@southdowns-aonb.gov.uk

Hastings Castle & 1066 Story

1 hr+   All year

Come to the first Norman castle in Britain. At Hastings you can enjoy a spectacular audio-visual show, The 1066 Story, in a medieval siege tent, and explore the dungeons carved out of solid rock beneath the North Gate.

* Discounted tickets with Smuggler's Adventure & Underwater Adventure

Location
Leave M25 at junction 5 & follow A21 to Hastings. Take A259 from Eastbourne or Rye

Opening
Daily: Easter–Sep 10am–5pm;
Oct–Easter 11am–3pm

Admission
Adult £3.65, Child £2.60, Concs £3, Family £11

Contact
Castle Hill Road, West Hill, Hastings
t 01424 781112
w discoverhastings.co.uk
e bookings@discoverhastings.co.uk

Smuggler's Adventure

1 hr   All year

A hands-on opportunity to learn more about the secrets of smugglers in a series of spooky caverns and passages. Find out what happened when the smugglers were caught and how they were punished!

Location
Junction 5 off M25 & follow A21 to Hastings. Take A259 from Eastbourne or Rye

Opening
Daily: Easter–Sep 10am–5.30pm;
Oct–Easter 11am–4.30pm

Admission
Adult £6.40, Child £4.40, Concs £5.40, Family £18.75

Contact
West Hill,
Hastings TN34 3HY
t 01424 422964
w discoverhastings.co.uk
e smugglers@discoverhastings.co.uk

Newhaven Fort

2 hrs+   Mar–Oct

The massive ramparts, gun emplacements and tunnels fire the imagination with exciting glimpses into England's wartime past.

* Quality Assured Visitor Attraction

Location
M23/A23 from London to Brighton then follow A27 towards Eastbourne. At Lewes follow A26 to Newhaven. Signed from there

Opening
Daily: Mar–end Oct 10.30am–6pm (last admission 5pm)

Admission
Adult £5.50, Child £3.60, Concs £4.60, Family £16.50

Contact
Fort Road,
Newhaven BN9 9DL

t 01273 517622
w newhavenfort.org.uk
e info@newhavenfort.org.uk

Paradise Park

3–6 hrs   All year

Discover 'Planet Earth' for an unforgettable experience. A unique Museum of Life, Dinosaur Safari, beautiful water-gardens with fish and wildfowl, planthouses, themed gardens, and Heritage Trail. The Playzone includes crazy golf and adventure play areas.

* Fantasy golf & soft play area
* Miniature railway

Location
Take A27 Brighton/Lewes bypass, then A26; or take A259

Opening
Daily: 9am–6pm

Admission
Please phone for details

Contact
Avis Road,
Newhaven BN9 0DH

t 01273 616006 (24hr info line)
   01273 512123
w paradisepark.co.uk
e promotions@paradisepark.co.uk

Bluebell Railway

1 hr+   All year

The Bluebell Railway operates standard-gauge steam trains through nine miles of scenic Sussex countryside between Sheffield Park, Horsted Keynes and Kingscote.

* Famous Terrier-class engines, *Stepney* & *Fenchurch*
* Featured in the film *The Railway Children*

Location
Sheffield Park Station

Opening
Daily: Apr–Oct 11am–4pm;
Oct–Apr Sat & Sun 11am–4pm

Admission
Adult £9.50, Child £4.70, Concs £9

Contact
Sheffield Park Station TN22 3QL

t 01825 720800
w bluebell-railway.co.uk
e info@bluebell-railway.co.uk

032 Andover

The Hawk Conservancy Trust

4 hrs+   Feb–Oct

A bird of prey park and hawk conservation centre set in 22 acres of woodland. It has more than 250 birds of prey including hawks, eagles, vultures and owls. There is also the chance to hold and fly a bird of prey. The eagles and vultures flying display is daily at 12noon, 2pm and 3.30pm.

* Flying displays & feeding times
* Duck racing

Location
4 miles W of Andover, off A303

Opening
Daily: 11 Feb–28 Oct 10.30am–5.30pm

Admission
Adult £8.75, Child £5.50, Concs £8, Family £27.50

Contact
Andover SP11 8DY

t 01264 773850
w hawk-conservancy.org
e info@hawk.conservancy.org

033 Brockenhurst

Beaulieu Abbey & National Motor Museum

3 hrs+   All year

Home of the National Motor Museum, Beaulieu has more than 250 vehicles on display. Visitors can also tour the abbey and Lord Montagu's home, as well as enjoy the many rides and drives. The unique collection includes legendary world-record breakers such as *Bluebird* and *Golden Arrow*.

* Exhibition of James Bond vehicles & props
* Secret Army exhibition: see how Army trained in WWII

Location
Going W on M27 take A326. Signed Beaulieu or National Motor Museum

Opening
Please phone for details

Admission
Please phone for details

Contact
Brockenhurst SO42 7ZN

t 01590 612123
w beaulieu.co.uk
e info@beaulieu.co.uk

034 East Cowes

Osborne House

3 hrs+   Apr–Sep

Osborne House was bought by Queen Victoria and Prince Albert in 1845 and used as a retreat from the stresses and strains of court life. Today it is one of the most important memorials to Britain's monarchy. Enjoy a horse-and-carriage ride through the grounds.

* Children's play area & interactive displays
* Glorious gardens & Swiss cottage

Location
1 mile SE of East Cowes

Opening
Daily: Apr–Sep 10am–4pm

Admission
Please phone for details

Contact
East Cowes, Isle of Wight PO32 6JY

t 01983 200022
w english-heritage.org.uk
e customer@english-heritage.org.uk

035 Fareham

The Royal Armouries – Fort Nelson

3-4 hrs   All year

Fort Nelson, a Victorian fortress overlooking Portsmouth Harbour, is home to the Royal Armouries' collection of more than 350 historic big guns. Children can explore the massive fort with its secret underground chambers, tunnels and grass ramparts.

* Big-gun salutes every day & historical performances
* Expert guided tours for the family

Location
Leave M27 at junction 11, taking A27 towards Portchester from Delme Arms roundabout. Left at 2nd traffic lights

Opening
Daily: Apr–Oct 10am–5pm; Nov–Mar 10.30am–4pm; salutes in summer at 12noon & 3pm, in winter at 1pm only. Tue opening 1 hr later

Admission
Free
Special events Adult £2.50, Child free

Contact
Down End Road, Fareham PO17 6AN

t 01329 233734
w armouries.org.uk
e fnenquiries@armouries.org.uk

036 Freshwater

The Needles Park

4 hrs+   All year

Overlooking the famous Needles, the park has attractions and rides for all the family. The chairlift boasts the most famous view on the Isle of Wight of the uniquely coloured sand cliffs.

* Magic in the Skies firework finale (on selected dates)
* Boat trips

Location
Reached via B3322

Opening
Easter–early Nov daily 10am–5pm;
Aug late-night opening on Thu;
Nov–Mar open partially.
Please phone for details

Admission
Free (plus paying attractions/rides)
Car park £3 per vehicle

Contact
Alum Bay,
Isle of Wight PO39 0JD

t 0870 458 0022
w theneedles.co.uk
e info@theneedles.co.uk

037 Gosport

Explosion! The Museum of Naval Firepower

2 hrs+   All year

Everything you've ever wanted to know about naval firepower is here: from gunpowder, cannons, guns, shells and munitions to mines, torpedoes, modern missiles and even an atom bomb. Learn, too, about the 2,500 women who worked here during WWII.

* Trafalgar Gunpowder Trail in main museum
* Café with great views of Portsmouth Harbour

Location
M27 to junction 11. Follow A32 to Gosport & brown tourist signs

Opening
Daily: Apr–Oct 10am–5.30pm;
Nov–Mar Thu, Sat & Sun
10am–4.30pm

Admission
Adult £5.50, Child £3.50, Concs £4.50

Contact
Priddy's Hard, Gosport PO12 4LE

t 02392 505600
w explosion.org.uk
e info@explosion.org.uk

038 Havant

Staunton Country Park

3–4 hrs   All year

Explore 1,000 acres of parkland with huge glasshouses, walled gardens and follies. This park also has the only remaining ornamental farm in England, with horses, pigs, sheep, llamas, peacocks and waterfowl.

* 1-hour walks on Sundays (book at visitor centre)
* Trails, play area & special events

Location
On B2149 between Havant & Horndean, easily accessible by A27 & A3. Follow brown tourist signs

Opening
Daily: 10am–5pm (closes 4pm in winter)

Admission
Adult £5, Child £3.60, Concs £4.10

Contact
Middle Park Way,
Havant PO9 5HB

t 02392 453405
w hants.gov.uk/staunton
e staunton.park@hants.gov.uk

039   Newport

Classic Boat Museum

1 hr   Mar–Nov

A great indoor collection of lovingly restored sailing and motorised classic boats from the C19. Highlights include the ultimate sailing boat, HRH Prince Philip's *Flying 15 Cowslip*, WWII airborne lifeboats and a *Cockleshell Heroes* canoe. Displays of engines, equipment and memorabilia.

* Displays & boats change annually
* Items from *Gypsy Moth IV* on view

Location	Contact
Through Seaclose Park	Seaclose Wharf, Newport, Isle of Wight PO30 2EF
Opening	
Daily: Mar–Nov 10am–4.30pm	t 01983 533493
	w classicboatmuseum.org
Admission	e cbmiow@fsmail.net
Adult £3, Child £1, Concs £2	

040   Portsmouth

Spinnaker Tower

1 hr   All year

A contemporary national icon on the South coast, providing a unique 'window on the sea'. The Spinnaker Tower is a striking new seamark, soaring 170m above Portsmouth Harbour, offering visitors spectacular views from a great height.

* Lift to upper levels
* Cross Europe's largest glass floor on Level 1

Location	Admission
Come in to Portsmouth on M275 and follow the brown tourist signs to Historic Waterfront, then Spinnaker Tower	Adult £5.95, Child £4.80, Concs £5.40
	Contact
	Gunwharf Quays, Portsmouth PO1 3TT
Opening	
Jun–Sep daily 10am–10pm;	t 02392 857520
Oct–May Sun–Fri 10am–5pm;	w spinnakertower.co.uk
Sat 10am–10pm	e info@spinnakertower.co.uk

041   Romsey

Paultons Park

5 hrs+   Feb–Dec

A family leisure park with more than 50 attractions for all ages, including big rides, little rides, play areas, museums and entertainment.

* Voted best family theme park in 2003
* Ride The Cobra, our longest rollercoaster

Location	Admission
Off M27 at junction 2	Adult £15.50, Child £14.50, Family £56
Opening	**Contact**
Daily: 18 Mar–29 Oct 10am–6.30pm (last admission 4.30pm); Closed Mon–Fri Nov–Dec	Ower, Romsey SO51 6AL
	t 02380 81 4442
	w paultonspark.co.uk
	e info@paultons.co.uk

042 Ryde

Isle of Wight Steam Railway

2 hrs+   Mar–Oct

A 5-mile steam railway that uses Victorian and Edwardian locomotives and carriages. New carriages and wagon works, adapted to be wheelchair-friendly.

* Children's playground, woodland walks
* Selected events throughout the year

Location
3 miles SW of Ryde by road

Opening
Mar–Oct selected days;
Jun–mid-Sep daily;
Dec selected days
Please phone for details

Admission
Adult £8.50–£12.50 Child £4.50–£8.50,
Family £22–£34

Contact
Railway Station, Havenstreet,
Ryde PO33 4DS

t 01983 882204
w iwsteamrailway.co.uk
e havenstreet@iwsteamrailway.co.uk

043 Sandown

Isle of Wight Zoo

2 hrs+   Apr–Oct

Situated on Sandown's beautiful seafront, this zoo is renowned for its collection of magnificent tigers and big cats. See also the rare lemurs and the Nightmares of Nature exhibit.

Location
On B3395

Opening
Apr–Oct daily 10am–6pm
Please phone to confirm

Admission
Adult £5.95, Child & Concs £4.95,
Family £19.25

Contact
Granite Fort, Yaverland Seafront,
Sandown PO36 8QB

t 01983 403883
w isleofwightzoo.com
e enquiries@isleofwightzoo.
  freeserve.co.uk

044 Seaview

Seaview Wildlife Encounter

3–4 hrs   Mar–Oct

Set in acres of landscaped gardens overlooking the Solent, this wildlife park has penguins, pelicans, flamingos, parrots, beavers and fish, and a Discovery Zone where visitors can learn all about animal conservation today.

* New tropical plant house with free-flying birds
* Events such as feeding the animals are run regularly

Location
Off B3330 between Ryde & Seaview.
Well signposted from Ryde

Opening
Daily: Mar–Oct 10am–5pm (last admission 4pm)

Admission
Adult £7.25, Child £5.25, Concs £6.25,
Family £23

Contact
Springvale, Seaview,
Isle of Wight PO34 5AP

t 01983 612153
w flamingoparkiw.com
e flamingo.park@virgin.net

045 Shanklin

Shanklin Chine

1 hr   Easter–Oct

A natural scenic gorge with a 45ft waterfall and stream leading to a beach. Shanklin Chine was once a site for shipwrecks and smuggling. It was later used for training Commandos during WWII.

* More than 150 varieties of wild plants
* The Chine drops 105ft to sea level

Location
Enter via old village, off A3055 or through W of Shanklin Esplanade, off Chine Hill

Opening
31 March–25 May 10am–5pm;
26 May–10 Sep 10am–10pm;
11 Sep–29 Oct 10am–5pm

Admission
Adult £3.75, Child £2, Concs £2.75

Contact
12 Ponona Road, Shanklin,
Isle of Wight PO37 6PF

t 01983 866432
w shanklinchine.co.uk
e jillshanklinchine@hotmail.co.uk

---

046 Southampton

Calshot Castle

2 hrs   Apr–Oct

Calshot Castle formed part of the chain of coastal forts built by Henry VIII in 1539. Its strategic importance, alongside the deep-water channel between Southampton and Portsmouth, led to it being manned throughout the centuries.

* Best known as a flying boat & RAF base in the C20
* Played a key support role in WWII

Location
From M27 (junction 2) take A326 to Fawley & Calshot

Opening
Daily: Apr–Oct 10am–4pm

Admission
Adult £2.50, Child £1.50, Concs £1.80

Contact
Calshot Spit, Fawley,
Southampton SO45 1BR

t 02380 892023
w calshot.com
e calshot.ac@hants.gov.uk

---

047 Southampton

Longdown Activity Farm

3 hrs+   Feb–Dec

There is fun for all the family at Longdown Activity Farm, with a variety of hands-on activities every day, including small animal handling and bottle-feeding of young animals. Excellent indoor and outdoor play areas, with trampolines and ball pools.

* Bottle-feeding & hand-feeding calves & goat kids
* Great for school visits, playgroups & birthday parties

Location
Just off A35 from Southampton to Lyndhurst

Opening
Daily: Feb–Dec 10am–5pm

Admission
Adult £6, Child & Concs £5, Family £21

Contact
Deerleap Lane, Longdown,
Ashurst, Southampton SO40 7EH

t 02380 293326
w longdownfarm.co.uk
e enquiries@longdownfarm.co.uk

048 Southampton

Royal Victoria Country Park

5 hrs+   All year

There are more than 240 acres of parkland, woodland and foreshore to be explored. The park is in the grounds of an old military hospital that now houses a fascinating exhibition depicting its history, with superb views and a shop.

* Miniature railway & activity sheets
* Programme of events, play area & sensory garden

Location
Take junction 8 off M27 & follow tourist signs

Opening
Park Daily: Apr–Oct 8am–9pm; Nov–Mar 8am–5pm
Exhibition, Tower & Shop Daily: Apr–Sep 12pm–4.30pm

Admission
Adult 70p, Child & Concs 35p

Contact
Netley Abbey,
Southampton SO31 5GA

t 02380 455157
w hants.gov.uk/rvcp
e rvcp@hants.gov.uk

---

049 Stockbridge

Museum of Army Flying

2 hrs+   All year

This award-winning museum traces the development of army flying, from balloons and kites through both world wars up to the present day. It houses a fine collection of aircraft and helicopters that include a Sopwith Pup, a Miles Magister and a collection of WWII gliders.

* 1940s house, children's centre, rifle range & flight simulator
* Viewing gallery overlooking airfield

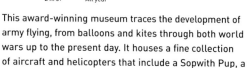

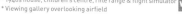

Location
A343 6 miles from Andover & 12 miles from Salisbury. Accessible from A30, A303 & M3

Opening
Daily: 10am–4.30pm

Admission
Adult £6, Child & Concs £4

Contact
Middle Wallop, Stockbridge SO20 8DY

t 01264 784421
w flying-museum.org.uk
e enquiries@flying-museum.org.uk

050 Ventnor

Blackgang Chine Fantasy Park

4 hrs   Mar–Oct

This park, originally Victorian gardens, has been developed into a family-friendly theme park, water-gardens and maze. The fun-themed areas include Frontierland, Smugglerland, Fantasyland and Nurseryland.

* New Cliffhanger rollercoaster
* High-speed family watercoaster

Location
On A3005 Chale–Ventnor road

Opening
End Mar–end Oct daily 10am–5pm;
Jul & Aug daily 10am–10pm (floodlit until 10pm)

Admission
Please phone for details

Contact
Chale, Ventnor,
Isle of Wight PO38 2HN

t 01983 730330
w blackgangchine.com
e info@blackgangchine.com

051 Winchester

INTECH-Hands-on Science & Technology Centre

2 hrs+   All year

This unique hands-on interactive science and technology centre houses more than 100 exhibits designed to amuse and enthuse. Here you will understand how to bend light, create your own tornado spout and vortex and work out how much energy it takes to power a lightbulb.

* Regularly changing exhibitions
* Gift shop with unusual & educational items

Location
Junction 10S & junction 9N on M3,
then take A31 & follow signs

Opening
Daily: 10am–4pm

Admission
Adult £6.50, Child £4, Concs £5

Contact
INTECH, Telegraph Way,
Morn Hill, Winchester SO21 1HX

t 01962 863791
w intech-uk.com
e htct@intech-uk.com

052 Winchester

Marwell Zoological Park

4 hrs+   All year

A 100-acre park with more than 200 species of animals in large paddocks and thoughtfully designed enclosures. Come face to face with an Amur tiger and hear the jungle call of the gibbons.

*Children's adventure playground

Location
On B2177 Winchester–Bishops
Waltham road. Signed from M27 & M3

Opening
Daily: *summer* 10am–6pm
winter 10am–5pm

Admission
Please phone for details

Contact
Colden Common,
Winchester SO21 1JH

t 01962 777407
w marwell.org.uk
e marwell@marwell.org.uk

053 Yarmouth

Fort Victoria Marine Aquarium

1 hr   Easter–Oct

See poisonous weever fish, graceful rays, beautiful anemones and amazing cuttlefish that change colour before your eyes. Extraordinary tropical fish and much more can be seen at this aquarium.

Location
W from Yarmouth on A3054

Opening
Daily: Easter–31 Oct 10am–6pm

Admission
Adult £2.50, Child (5–16) £1.50, Concs £2.50, Family £7

Contact
Fort Victoria Country Park
off Westhill Lane, Yarmouth,
Isle of Wight PO41 0RR
t 01983 760283
w fortvictoria.co.uk
e pfblake@tiscali.co.uk

054 Yarmouth

Fort Victoria Model Railway

1 hr+   Easter–Oct

This is the largest and most technically advanced model railway in Britain. It is entirely computer-controlled and has more than 450 model buildings, 800 model people and 180 vehicles.

Location
Take Alum Bay/Freshwater road out of Yarmouth. Take 1st turning right at brown tourist sign, then follow Westhill Lane to the end

Opening
Easter–Oct daily 10am–5pm;
Nov–Dec Sat–Sun only 10.30am–4pm

Admission
Adult £4, Child & Concs £3

Contact
Westhill Lane, Yarmouth,
Isle of Wight PO41 0RR
t 01983 761553
w wight-attractions.co.uk

055 Canterbury

The Canterbury Tales

1 hr+   All year

This fascinating audio-visual experience, sited in the centre of Canterbury, is one of the town's most popular visitor attractions. Step back in time to experience the sights, sounds and smells of the Middle Ages in this stunning reconstruction of C14 England.

* Uses headsets with earphones
* Recreates the pilgrimages of Chaucerian England

Location
In city centre, off high street

Opening
Daily: Mar–Jun 10am–5pm; Jul–Aug 9.30am–5.30pm; Sep–Oct 10am–5pm; Nov–Jan 10am–4pm

Admission
Adult £7.25, Child £5.25, Concs £6.25

Contact
St Margaret's Street,
Canterbury CT1 2TG
t 01227 479227
w canterburytales.org.uk
e info@canterburytales.org.uk

056 Canterbury

Druidstone Park & Art Park

2 hrs+   Mar–Nov

Set in attractive gardens and woodland, Druidstone caters for imaginations of all ages. Go on a discovery trail through the enchanted woodland, and enjoy hands-on experiences in the farmyard.

* Farm animals
* Play areas for all ages

Location
On A290, between Canterbury & Whitstable

Opening
Daily: Mar–Nov 10am–5.30pm

Admission
Adult £5.10, Child £3.80, Concs £4.30, Family £15

Contact
Honey Hill, Blean,
Canterbury CT2 9JR
t 01227 765168
w druidstone.net

057 Canterbury

Howletts Wild Animal Park

2–3 hrs   All year

Howletts Wild Animal Park is set in mature parkland and contains John Aspinall's collection of animals. See one of the largest collections of tigers in the world and the largest breeding colony of gorillas in captivity. Other animals include deer, leopards and elephants.

* 2 new gorillas & 2 new baby elephants
* Jurassic Mine & dinosaur & fossil shop

Location
On A2, 3 miles S of Canterbury

Opening
Daily: 10am–dusk

Admission
Adult £13.95, Child £10.95,
Concs £11.95, Family £42–£49

Contact
Bekesbourne,
Canterbury CT4 5EL

t 01303 264647
w totallywild.net
e info@howletts.net

058 Canterbury

Museum of Canterbury with Rupert Bear Museum

1 hr   All year

This museum offers new and exciting interactive displays including a Medieval Discovery Gallery, the Blitz Gallery and the Rupert Bear Museum. They're all set in one of the city's finest medieval buildings.

Location
Follow M2/A2 from London; take A28
from Ashford. Located in city centre,
on Stour Street

Opening
Mon–Sat 10.30am–5pm;
Jun–Sep 1.30pm–5pm on Sun
(last admission 4pm)

Admission
Adult £3.20, Child & Concs £2.20

Contact
Stour Street,
Canterbury CT1 2NR

t 01227 475202
w canterbury-museum.co.uk

059 Canterbury

Roman Museum

1 hr   All year

This underground museum of the Roman town is an exciting mix of excavated real objects, authentic reconstructions, and the remains of a Roman town house with mosaics. Reconstructions also include a Roman market place, shoemaker's workshop and fruit and vegetable stall.

* Computer reconstruction shows the Roman house
* Touch–screen computer game on Roman technology

Location
Butchery Lane, close to cathedral

Opening
Mon–Sat 10am–5pm (last admission
4pm); Jun–Oct also open Sun
1.30pm–5pm

Admission
Adult £3, Child & Concs £1.85

Contact
Longmarket, Butchery Lane,
Canterbury CT1 2JE

t 01227 785575
w canterburymuseums.co.uk
e museums@canterbury.gov.uk

060 Chatham

The Historic Dockyard, Chatham

4 hrs+   Feb–Nov

Visitors can enjoy 400 years of exciting naval history and architecture set in an 80-acre site. Explore HMS *Cavalier*, Britain's last WWII destroyer, the submarine *Ocelot* and the Victorian sloop *Gannet*, now fully restored.

* Wooden Walls exhibit with animatronic adventure
* Nelson's flagship HMS *Victory* was built here

Location	Admission
Leave M2 at junction 1 or 4 & follow signs	Adult £11.50, Child £6.50, Concs £9
Opening	**Contact**
Daily: 10 Feb–24 Mar 10am–4pm; 25 Mar–28 Oct 10am–6pm (last admission 4pm); Nov Sat–Sun 10am–4pm	Chatham ME4 4TZ
	t 01634 823807
	w thedockyard.co.uk
	e info@chdt.org.uk

061 Chislehurst

Chislehurst Caves

1 hr   All year

Grab a lantern and get ready for an amazing adventure! In these caves your whole family can travel back in time as you explore the maze of passageways deep beneath Chislehurst. During a 45-minute guided tour, visit the Caves Church, Druid Altar and Haunted Pool.

* Facilities for children's parties
* Private tours of the caves

Location	Admission
Take A222 between A20 & A21. At railway bridge turn into Station Approach then right again to Caveside Close	Adult £5, Child & Concs £3
	Contact
	Old Hill, Chislehurst BR7 5NB
Opening	
School hols daily 10am–4pm (except Christmas). Rest of year Wed–Sun 10am–4pm	t 020 8467 3264
	w chislehurstcaves.co.uk
	e enquiries@chislehurstcaves.co.uk

062 Dover

Crabble Corn Mill

1 hr+   All year

A restored watermill dating from 1812 and in full working order with devices not seen elsewhere. Demonstrations of flour milling take place and there is a programme of craft and art exhibitions.

Location	Admission
M2/A2 from London to Canterbury then A256 to River. From Folkestone follow B2060	Adult £4, Child & Concs £3, Family £11
	Contact
	Lower Road, River, Dover CT17 0UY
Opening	
Easter–Sep Tue–Sun 11am–5pm; *winter* Sat–Sun 11am–5pm	t 01304 823292
	w ccmt.org.uk
	e miller@ccmt.org.uk

063 Dover

Dover Castle

4 hrs+   All year

Commanding the shortest Channel sea crossing, this site has been the UK's most important defence against invasion since the Iron Age. It was built in the C12 and reinforced by Henry VIII in the 1530s. Underneath the nearby white cliffs is a series of underground tunnels.

* Reconstruction of Henry VIII's visit in 1539
* Visit the Dunkirk command room

Location
Clearly signed to E of city, on the white cliffs

Opening
Mar–Sep daily 10am–6pm; Oct daily 10am–5pm; Nov–Jan Thu–Mon 10am–4pm; Feb–Mar daily 10am–4pm

Admission
Please phone for details

Contact
Dover CT16 1HU

t 01304 211067
w english–heritage.org.uk

---

064 Eynsford

Eagle Heights Bird of Prey Centre

4 hrs+   Jan–Nov

Home to birds of prey (eagles, falcons and vultures) and reptiles (pythons, crocodiles and iguanas), the centre offers daily flying displays, indoor demonstrations of owls and reptiles, falconry courses, and Bird of Prey Experience days. It also operates as a sanctuary.

* 5-day falconry courses available
* Now housing otters

Location
Off M25 at junction 3 on to A20, or off M20 at junction 1

Opening
Daily Mar–Oct 10.30am–5pm;
Nov & Jan–Feb weekends 11am–4pm

Admission
Adult £6.95, Child £4.95, Concs £5.95

Contact
Lullingstone Lane, Eynsford DA4 0JB

t 01322 866466
w eagleheights.co.uk
e office@eagleheights.co.uk

---

065 Faversham

Farming World

4 hrs   Mar–Oct

There are more than 100 traditional breeds of farm animals to meet in this safe environment. In the Hawking Centre visitors can see many indigenous birds of prey in spectacular displays. There are also indoor play and craft areas.

* Only indoor play, crafts & animal barn open in winter
* 4 times winner of Tourism for All Award

Location
Off A299, ¼ mile E of M2 junction 7

Opening
Daily: Mar–Oct 9.30am–5.30pm

Admission
Adult £6, Child £5, Concs £5.50

Contact
Nash Court, Boughton, Faversham ME13 9SW

t 01227 751144
w farming-world.com
e enquiries@farming-world.co.uk

066 Hamstreet

South of England Rare Breeds Centre

3 hrs   All year

Here's a chance to meet and pet all your favourite friendly farm animals as you wander around a farm trail. The centre is also home to many endangered and rare British animals. Set in acres of beautiful woodland, there are plenty of places to picnic while the kids play.

* Woodland activity quiz trail
* Piglet racing in season & trailer rides

Location
Leave M20 at junction 10, follow signs to Brenzett and Hamstreet. Situated between Hamstreet & Woodchurch

Opening
Daily: Apr–Sep 10.30am–5.30pm; Oct–Mar Tue–Sun 10.30am–4.30pm

Admission
Adult £6.60, Child £6.60, Concs £5.50

Contact
Woodchurch, Ashford TN26 3RJ

t 01233 861493
w rarebreeds.org.uk
e visit@rarebreeds.org.uk

---

067 Herne Bay

Wildwood

2 hrs   All year

Set in 40 acres of ancient woodland, this beautiful discovery park is home to more than 300 animals from more than 50 species. See owls and otters, bees and beavers, wild boar and wolves – plus many more.

* Quality Assured Visitor Attraction
* Conservation programmes & woodland play area

Location
Close to Canterbury, just off A291, near Herne Bay

Opening
Daily: Apr–Sep 10am–6pm; Oct–Mar 10am–5pm

Admission
Adult £8.50, Child £7, Concs £7.50, Family £28

Contact
Herne Common, Herne Bay CT6 7LQ

t 01227 712111
w wildwoodtrust.org
e info@wildwoodtrust.org

Port Lympne Wild Animal Park

4 hrs   All year

A 600-acre wild animal park situated in the gardens of historic Port Lympne Mansion. The collection includes the largest herd of captive-bred black rhino outside Africa, plus elephants, tigers and many more. Don't miss the newly added education centre.

* Barbary lions & cubs, extinct in wild
* 2 baby rhino

Location
Leave M20 at junction 11 & follow brown tourist signs to Lympne

Opening
Daily: *summer* 10am–6pm (last admission 4.30pm) *winter* 10am–dusk (last admission 3pm)

Admission
Adult £13.95, Child £10.95, Concs £11.95, Family £42–£49

Contact
Lympne, Hythe CT21 4PD

t 01303 264647
w totallywild.net
e info@howletts.net

Leeds Castle

3 hrs   All year

This medieval castle, situated on two islands in a lake set in 500 acres of parkland, is a popular attraction. Once a Norman stronghold, the castle has since been a residence for six of England's medieval queens, a palace for Henry VIII, and a retreat for the powerful.

* Open-air concert programme
* Grand Firework spectacular

Location
Leave M20 at junction 8. Castle is 7 miles E of Maidstone

Opening
Daily: Apr–Sep 10am–5pm; Oct–Mar 10am–3pm

Admission
Adult £13.50, Child £8, Concs £11

Contact
Maidstone ME17 1PL

t 01622 765400
w leeds-castle.com
e enquiries@leeds-castle.co.uk

070 Maidstone

Museum of Kent Life

2 hrs+   Feb–Nov

A unique open-air living museum that celebrates 300 years of Kentish history. Traditional crafts are demonstrated on a working farm. This is one of the few places in England where hops are grown, harvested, dried and packed using time-honoured techniques.

* Calendar of events throughout the year
* Hop-picking festival in Sep

Location
Off M20 at junction 6. Follow signs

Opening
Daily: Feb–Nov 10am–5pm

Admission
Adult £7, Child £5, Concs £5.20

Contact
Cobtree, Lock Lane, Sandling,
Maidstone ME14 3AU
t 01622 763936
w museum-kentlife.co.uk
e enquiries@museum-kentlife.co.uk

071 New Romney

Romney, Hythe & Dymchurch Railway

2 hrs   All year

This was the world's smallest public railway when it opened in July 1927. It now runs regular passenger services covering a distance of 13½ miles from the picturesque Cinque Port of Hythe to the fishermen's cottages and lighthouses at Dungeness.

* Thomas the Tank Engine & Santa specials
* Dining-train specials

Location
The stations at New Romney,
Dungeness and Hythe are all
on or near A259 trunk road

Opening
Trains run daily Apr–Sep & weekends
Oct & Mar. Please phone or visit the
website for timetable

Admission
Adult £5–£11, Child half-fare

Contact
New Romney TN28 8PL
t 01797 362353
w rhdr.org.uk
e info@rhdr.org.uk

072 Sittingbourne

Bredgar & Wormshill Light Railway

3–4 hrs   May–Oct

One of the best narrow-gauge railways in the UK, this steam-train service runs along the line between Warren Wood and Stony Shaw, through attractive Kent countryside. There are 11 restored steam locomotives, plus steam traction engines.

* Woodland walks
* Vintage cars, a beam engine & a model railway

Location
4½ miles N of M20 (junction 8/ Leeds Castle exit) on B2163. 1 mile S of Bredgar

Opening
1 May–2 Oct open 1st Sun of month 11am–5pm

Admission
Adult £6, Child £3

Contact
The Warren, Bredgar, Sittingbourne ME9 8AT

t 01622 884254
w bwlr.co.uk
e thewarren@prquis.net

073 Strood

Diggerland

4 hrs+   All year

A truly unique adventure park based on the world of construction machinery, where children and adults can ride and drive real diggers and dumpers in safety.

* ROSPA Award for safety
* Suitable for adults & children

Location
Exit M2 at junction 2 on to the A228; follow signs to Strood. Turn right at roundabout & park is on right

Opening
Feb–Nov Sat–Sun, Bank Hols & school hols 10am–5pm
Dec–Jan daily 10am–5pm

Admission
Adult & Child £12.50, Concs £6.25

Contact
Medway Valley Leisure Park, Strood ME2 2NU

t 08700 344437
w diggerland.com
e mail@diggerland.com

074 Tenterden

Kent & East Sussex Railway

2 hrs   Mar–Oct

Take a nostalgic trip behind a full-size steam engine on Britain's first light railway. Journey through 10½ miles of unspoilt countryside between Tenterden and the Sussex village of Bodiam and be thrilled by the sights and sounds of steam engines.

* Children's play area & museum
* Quality Assured Visitor Attraction

Location
Follow A28 from Ashford or Hastings

Opening
Mar–April & Oct Sat–Sun; May–Sep Mon & Fri, daily in Aug. Please phone for details of times

Admission
Adult £10.50, Child £5.50, Concs £9.50, Family £27

Contact
Tenterden Town Station, Tenterden TN30 6HE

t 01580 765155
w kesr.org.uk
e enquiries@kesr.org.uk

075 Tunbridge Wells

Groombridge Place Gardens & The Enchanted Forest

4 hrs+   Apr–Nov

In addition to the formal gardens, visit the Enchanted Forest and enjoy exciting playgrounds, huge swings, strange plants, giant rabbits and shy deer. Don't miss the raised wooden adventure boardwalk, the Dinosaur and Dragon Valley and the Serpent's Lair.

* Home to one of only 2 zeedonks (zebra-donkeys) in the UK
* Largest centre for birds of prey in the South East

Location
A26 towards Tunbridge Wells, turn right on to B2176 towards Penshurst. 3 miles past Penshurst village turn left at T junction with A264. Follow signs

Opening
Daily: Apr–Nov 10am–5.30pm

Admission
Adult £8.70, Child & Concs £7.20

Contact
The Estate Office, Groombridge Place, Groombridge, Royal Tunbridge Wells TN3 9QG

t 01892 861444
w groombridge.co.uk
e office@groombridge.co.uk

076 Tunbridge Wells

The Hop Farm

3 hrs+   All year

Spread among a collection of Victorian oast houses, there is a multitude of attractions for all the family. Create your own work of art in our pottery and craft centre, explore our extensive indoor and outdoor play areas or meet the shire horses and other animals at our farm.

* Special events throughout the year
* 4 permanent museums and exhibitions

Location
Located on A228 near Paddock Wood, Kent. Follow brown tourist signs from junction 4 of M20 or junction 5 of M25 on to A21 S

Opening
Daily: 10am–5pm (last admission 4pm)

Admission
Adults £7.50, Child (3–15yrs) £6.50, under-3s free
(prices will vary on event days)

Contact
Paddock Wood TN12 6PY

t 0870 0274166
w thehopfarm.co.uk

077 Whitstable

Snappy's Adventure Play Centre

2 hrs+   All year

Snappy's is a large indoor adventure play centre with an extensive range of approved play equipment all designed around an exciting dinosaur theme. There is a dedicated area for under-fours, a twin wavy-board slide, and a Game Zone for older children.

Location
From Whitstable take A290 up Borstal Hill & turn left on to A2990. At next roundabout turn right then right again

Opening
Daily: 10am–6.30pm

Admission
Mon–Fri Under-4s £2.95, over-4s £3.95; Sat–Sun £3.50, £4.50

Contact
45b Joseph Wilson Estate, Millstrood Road, Whitstable CT5 3PS

t 01227 282100
w snappysadventureplay.co.uk

078 Bloomsbury

The British Museum

2 hrs+   All year

Far more than a collection of arts and antiquities, the British Museum offers virtual tours for children of all ages, family activities and events, plus exhibitions of games and toys – a marvellous cultural day out for the whole family.

* Spectacular covered courtyard

Location
Underground Tottenham Court Road

Opening
Daily: Sat–Wed 10am–5.30pm, Thu–Fri 10am–8.30pm (selected galleries 5.30pm–8.30pm)

Admission
Free, exhibitions may charge

Contact
Great Russell Street, London WC1B 3DG

t 020 7323 8299
w thebritishmuseum.ac.uk
e information@thebritishmuseum.ac.uk

079 Camberwell

Livesey Museum for Children

1 hr+   All year

The Livesey Museum runs a changing programme of lively, unusual, fully hands-on exhibitions for children up to the age of 12. An all-new interactive exhibition is shown every year.

* New Numbers exhibition opens Nov 2006

Location
Underground **London Bridge**, then 21 bus

Opening
During exhibitions open only Tue–Sat 10am–5pm; closed Bank Hols

Admission
Free

Contact
682 Old Kent Road, London SE15 1JF

t 020 7635 5829
w liveseymuseum.org.uk
e livesey.museum@southwark.gov.uk

080 City

Museum of London

2 hrs+   All year

Experience London as you've never seen it before. The Museum of London is the world's largest urban museum and presents a quarter of a million years of history. Meet the Romans, take a walk down a Victorian street, or hear a cockney tale of London life.

* Covers the history of the city since it began
* Regular calendar of exhibitions & special events

Location
Underground **Barbican & St Paul's**

Opening
Mon–Sat 10am–5.50pm, Sun 12noon–5.50pm

Admission
Free

Contact
London Wall, London EC2Y 5HN

t 0870 444 3852
w museumoflondon.org.uk
e info@museumoflondon.org.uk

081 County Hall

London Aquarium

2 hrs   All year

London Aquarium is home to more than 350 species from oceans, lakes, rivers and streams around the world. Visitors can stand face to face with spectacular sharks in a two-storey tank, get hands-on with a ray at the touchpool or spot animals in the coral reef.

* Late-night opening times in summer
* Themed activity weeks

Location
Inside County Hall on South Bank of the Thames by Westminster Bridge
Underground **Westminster**

Opening
Daily: 10am–6pm (7pm on selected summer evenings)

Admission
Please phone for details

Contact
County Hall, Westminster Bridge Road, London SE1 7PB

t 020 7967 8000
w londonaquarium.co.uk
e info@londonaquarium.co.uk

082 County Hall

London Eye

½ hr   All year

This is the most popular paid-for tourist attraction in the UK. The 443ft observation wheel provides the most spectacular views of one of the biggest cities in the world. On a clear day you can see 25 miles in every direction from a fully enclosed capsule.

* More than 15,000 people a day travel on the Eye
* Views are breathtaking in virtually all conditions

Location
On South Bank of the Thames by County Hall
Underground Waterloo

Opening
Daily: May–Sep 9.30am–9pm;
Oct–Apr 9.30am–8pm

Admission
Adult £13, Child £6.50, Concs £10

Contact
BA London Eye, Riverside Building, County Hall, London SE1 7PB

t 0870 5000 600
w ba-londoneye.com
e customer.services@ba-londoneye.com

083 Fulham

Chelsea FC Museum & Tour

1 hr+   All year

Visit the home of the Champions! Take the behind-the-scenes tour of London's premier club and view the magnificent Chelsea FC dressing rooms, the manager's dug-out, the press room and much, much more! All tours include a visit to the centenary museum.

* Visit the Chelsea Megastore and have your photograph taken with the world-famous Premiership trophy!

Location
Underground Fulham Broadway

Opening
Tours Mon–Fri 11am, 1pm & 3pm,
Sat & Sun 12noon & 2pm
Museum Mon–Fri 10.30am–4.30pm,
Sat–Sun 11.30am–3.30pm

Admission
Adult £13, Child & Concs £7

Contact
100 Fulham Broadway,
London SW6 1HS

t *Enquiries* 0207 957 8278
Booking 0870 603 0005
w chelseafc.com
e tours@chelseafc.com

084 Green Park

Buckingham Palace

1 hr+   Aug–Sep

Do you fancy being Queen for a day? Take a trip around the official residence of the Royal Family with audio tours introduced by HRH Prince Charles. Enjoy a walk in the palace grounds or take part in an activity trail and catch the Changing of the Guard.

* The state rooms form the heart of the working palace
* Furnished with treasures from the Royal Collection

Location
Mainline Victoria
Underground Victoria, Green Park & Hyde Park Corner

Opening
Daily: Aug–Sep 9.45am–6pm (last admission 3.45pm)

Admission
Adult £14, Child £8, Concs £12

Contact
Ticket Sales & Information Office, The Official Residences of The Queen, London SW1A 1AA

t 020 7766 7300
w royalcollection.org.uk
e bookinginfo@royalcollection.org.uk

085 Greenwich

The *Cutty Sark*

1 hr   Jan–Sep

It's 1880 and the *Cutty Sark*'s Captain has just jumped overboard, you're 1,000 miles from home and there is a 100ft wave in front of you! Actually, you're in Maritime Greenwich overlooking the River Thames, holding the wheel of the fastest tea clipper ever built.

* Experience life on board one of the world's most famous ships
* £25m conservation programme begins in Oct 2006

Location
Mainline Docklands Light Railway
Cutty Sark Station
Underground Canary Wharf
By boat from Westminster Pier

Opening
Daily: 10am–5pm (last admission 4.30pm)

Admission
Adult £4.50, Child £3.25, Concs £3.75

Contact
King William Walk, Greenwich, London SE10 9HT

t 020 8858 3445
w cuttysark.org.uk
e enquiries@cuttysark.org.uk

086 Hendon

Royal Air Force Museum

4 hrs   All year

Soar through the history of aviation for an aerodynamic day of fun. With a brand-new interactive gallery, film shows and more than 80 legendary aircraft on display, this is the place to land for a great family day out.

Location
Easy access from M25. Signed from M1, A41, A5 & A406
Underground Colindale
Mainline Mill Hill Broadway

Opening
Daily: 10am–6pm

Admission
Free. Under 16s must be accompanied by an adult

Contact
Grahame Park Way, London NW9 5LL
t 020 8358 4849
w rafmuseum.org
e london@rafmuseum.org

---

087 Lambeth

Imperial War Museum

3 hrs+   All year

Come and relive life during WWI and WWII. Walk through the WWI trenches and share the dramatic WWII Blitz experience, complete with the sounds and smells of London during an air raid. Find out about spies in the Secret War exhibition.

* Special Holocaust exhibition
* Cinema shows museum's collection of film & video

Location
Mainline Waterloo & Elephant & Castle
Underground Lambeth North
5 min walk

Opening
Daily: 10am–6pm

Admission
Free, exhibitions may charge

Contact
Lambeth Road, London SE1 6HZ
t 020 7416 5320
w iwm.org.uk
e mail@iwm.org.uk

088 Liverpool Street

Bank of England Museum

1 hr+   All year

This museum, housed within the Bank of England, traces the history of the bank. Visitors can view gold bars dating from ancient to modern times, as well as coins, a unique collection of bank notes and more.

* Audio tours cost £1
* Special events & activities & try to lift a real gold bar

Location
Underground Bank & Liverpool Street

Opening
Weekdays 10am–5pm; also open on day of Lord Mayor's Show; closed Sat, Sun & Bank Hols

Admission
Free

Contact
Threadneedle Street, London EC2R 8AH
t 020 7601 5491
w bankofengland.co.uk/museum
e museum@bankofengland.co.uk

089   London

Deen City Farm

½ hr+   All year

Hiding in the heart of South London, this extensive city farm covers 5 acres. Come and visit our wide range of farm animals from Magic the Dexter cow to our unusual alpacas Milo and Kimby. Pet the guinea pigs and rabbits and on certain days take a pony ride.

* Animal Encounter birthday parties available
* Café and farm shop

Location	Contact
Underground Colliers Wood & South Wimbledon	39 Windsor Avenue, Merton Abbey SW19 2RR
Opening	t 020 8543 5300
Tue–Sun 10am–4.30pm	w deencityfarm.co.uk
Admission	e information@deencityfarm.co.uk
Free	

090   London Bridge

London Dungeon

1 hr+   All year

The London Dungeon is an interactive historic horror attraction that dispenses fear and fun in equal doses. Visitors encounter The Great Fire of London, Jack the Ripper and the Judgement Day boat ride.

* Traitor boat ride to hell, visit Sweeney Todd the demon barber
* The terrible truth about Jack the Ripper

Location	Contact
Underground London Bridge	28–34 Tooley Street, London SE1 2SZ
Opening	t 020 7403 7221
Daily: 10am–5.30pm	w thedungeons.com
Admission	e londondungeon@ merlinentertainments.biz
Adult £16.95, Child £11.95, Concs £13.95	

091   Marylebone

Madame Tussaud's

2 hrs+   All year

Dance like a diva and take to the stage with Beyoncé, Britney and Kylie, see if you can bend it like David Beckham or have a dinner date with George Clooney. Also try out as a Pop Idol, be photographed by the paparazzi, have your DNA checked and explore the galaxy.

* Spectacular hardman attraction
* World At Your Feet football attraction

Location	Admission
Underground Baker Street	Adult from £19.99, Child from £16.99, Concs from £18.99
Opening	
Daily: Mon–Fri 9.30am–5.30pm, Sat–Sun 9am–6pm, extended hrs during school hols	Contact
	Marylebone Road, London NW1 5LR
	t 0870 400 3000
	w madame-tussauds.com
	e csc@madame-tussauds.com

092   Marylebone

Sherlock Holmes Museum

  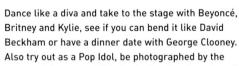
1 hr   All year

The museum consists of Holmes's apartment on the first floor, plus the entire second, third and fourth floors, which contain the new exhibition area. It features several life-size wax figures from the best-known Sherlock Holmes adventures.

* Shop selling all kinds of Sherlock Holmes novelty goods

Location	Contact
Underground Baker Street	221b Baker Street London NW1 6XE
Opening	t 020 7935 8866
Daily: 9.30am–6pm	w sherlock-holmes.co.uk
Admission	e londonlinks@btconnect.com
Adult £6, Child £4	

093 Regent's Park

London Zoo

4 hrs   All year

Come face to face with some of the hairiest, scariest, tallest and smallest animals on the planet. See our Animals in Action presentation and watch some of our finest flying, leaping and climbing animals showing off their skills. Don't miss a visit to B.U.G.S!

* Regular programme of feeding times & special shows
* New komodo dragon

Location
At NE corner of Regent's Park on Outer Circle
Underground **Camden Town**

Opening
Daily: 7 Mar–23 Oct 10am–5.30pm ;
24 Oct–31 Oct 10am–4.30pm; Nov–Feb
10am–4pm

Admission
Adult £14.50, Child £11.50,
Concs £12.70

Contact
Regent's Park, London NW1 4RY

t 020 7722 3333
w zsl.org

094 Shepherd's Bush

BBC Television Centre Tours

2 hrs   All year

On this tour you will see behind the scenes of the BBC TV Centre. You may visit areas such as the News Centre, dressing rooms and studios. No two tours are ever the same. All tours must be prebooked and visitors must be ten years and over.

* Winner of the 2003 Group Travel Awards
* Also new CBBC tours

Location
Underground **White City**

Opening
Tours run 9 times a day Mon–Sat;
booking essential

Admission
Adult £8.95, Child £6.50

Contact
BBC Television Centre,
Wood Lane,
London W12 7RJ

t 0870 603 0304 (bookings)
w bbc.co.uk/tours
e bbctours@bbc.co.uk

095 South Bank

Globe Theatre

1–3 hrs   All year

This museum is an exciting, engaging introduction to the life, works and theatre of Shakespeare's time. Experience a performance in a replica Elizabethan theatre, or enjoy the interactive exhibits about Shakespeare's life.

* Annual programme of Shakespeare's plays
* Permanent exhibition & theatre tours

Location
Mainline **London Bridge & Waterloo**
Underground **Southwark**

Opening
Theatre Daily: May–Sep 10am–7.30pm
Exhibition Daily: May–Sep 9am–5pm;
Oct–Apr 10am–5pm (tours available)

Admission
Exhibition Adult £9, Child £6.50,
Concs £7.50

Contact
21 New Globe Walk, London SE1 9DT

t *Enquiries* 020 7902 1400
   Box office 020 7401 9919
w shakespeares-globe.org
e info@shakespearesglobe.com

096 South Kensington

Natural History Museum

2 hrs+   All year

The Natural History Museum has hundreds of exciting interactive exhibits. Highlights include Dinosaurs, Creepy-Crawlies, Human Biology, the must-see exhibition about humans, and Mammals, with its unforgettable huge blue whale.

* Investigate the wildlife garden
*Special exhibitions throughout the year

Location
Underground **South Kensington**

Opening
Mon–Sat & Bank Hols 10am–5.50pm,
Sun 11am–5.50pm (last admission
5.30pm)

Admission
Free

Contact
Cromwell Road, London SW7 5BD

t 020 7942 5000
w nhm.ac.uk
e info@nhm.ac.uk

097 South Kensington

Science Museum

3 hrs+   All year

Come and see more than 40 galleries and 2,000 hands-on imaginative exhibits at this amazing museum. You can step into the future in the Wellcome Wing, change your sex, age 30 years in 30 seconds and create your own identity profile – all in a day!

* Range of interactive exhibits, including new Energy Gallery
* IMAX® cinema

Location
Underground South Kensington

Opening
Daily: 10am–6pm

Admission
Free, donations welcomed, exhibitions may charge

Contact
Exhibition Road, South Kensington, London SW7 2DD
t 0870 870 4868
w sciencemuseum.org.uk
e sciencemuseum@nmsi.ac.uk

098 Stepney

Ragged School Museum

1 hr   All year

This museum is dedicated to London's East End. On the old site of Barnardo's ragged school, the museum has a reconstructed Victorian classroom, along with exhibits on housing, education and work in the East End from the 1880s to 1900.

Location
Underground Mile End
Mainline Limehouse

Opening
Wed & Thu 10am–5pm; 1st Sun of month 2pm–5pm

Admission
Free

Contact
46–50 Copperfield Road, London E3 4RR
t 020 8980 6405
w raggedschoolmuseum.org.uk

099 Stepney

Stepping Stones Farm

2 hrs+   All year

This is an urban working farm with a full range of livestock. Educational sessions and structured demonstrations, such as sheep shearing, can be arranged for groups, according to season.

* Play area & activity room
* Farm trail

Location
Corner of Stepney Way & Stepney High Street
Underground Stepney Green

Opening
Tue–Sun 10am–4pm; closed Mon except Bank Hols; open Easter

Admission
Free, small charges for special events

Contact
Stepney Way, London E1 3DG
t 020 7790 8204
e lynne.rosie@btconnect.com

100   Tower Bridge

Tower Bridge Exhibition

1 hr   All year

Inside the Tower Bridge Exhibition you will learn how one of the world's most famous bridges works and discover the history of its construction. Enjoy panoramic views from the walkways high above the River Thames and visit the original Victorian engines.

* New interactive computer displays
* Special ticket rate for Tower Bridge & Monument

Location
Underground Tower Hill & London Bridge
Boat from Tower Pier

Opening
Daily: *summer* 10am–6.30pm *winter* 9.30am–5.30pm (last admission 1 hr before close)

Admission
Adult £5.50, Child £3, Concs £4.25

Contact
Tower Bridge, London SE1 2UP
t 020 7403 3761
w towerbridge.org.uk
e enquiries@towerbridge.org.uk

101   Tower Bridge

Winston Churchill's Britain at War Experience

1 hr+   All year

An educational adventure about the home front of WWII Britain. Special effects and original artefacts recreate everyday life for ordinary people – the Blitz, rationing, blackouts and evacuation. See it, feel it, breathe it.

Location
Underground London Bridge

Opening
Daily: Oct–Mar 10am–4pm; Apr–Sep 10am–5pm

Admission
Adult £9.50, Child £4.85, Concs £5.75, Family £25

Contact
64–66 Tooley Street, London SE1 2TF
t 020 7403 3171
w britainatwar.co.uk
e info@britainatwar.org.uk

102   Tower Hill

Tower of London

3 hrs   All year

A visit to the Tower of London's 11 towers encompasses 1,000 years of history – some of it bloody. Far more than just a trip to see the Crown Jewels, there are talks, tours, holiday events and family trails, all included in the basic ticket price.

* Beefeater tours all day; see the Crown Jewels
* Constant calendar of special events

Location
Underground Tower Hill

Opening
Mar–Oct Tue–Sat 9am–6pm, Sun–Mon 10am–6pm;
Nov–Feb Tue–Sat 9am–5pm, Sun–Mon 10am–5pm
(last admission 1 hr before close)

Admission
Adult £15, Child £9.50, Concs £12

Contact
Tower Hill, London EC3N 4AB
t 0870 756 6060
w hrp.org.uk

103 Trafalgar Square

National Gallery

1 hr+   All year

The National Gallery holds one of the finest permanent collections of Western European art. It includes all the greats, and is sure to please even the most reluctant gallerygoer.

* Selection of courses & lectures available
* Weekend & school holiday family events

Location
Trafalgar Square
Underground Leicester Square & Charing Cross

Opening
Daily: 10am–6pm, Wed 10am–9pm

Admission
Free, donations welcomed, exhibitions may charge

Contact
Trafalgar Square, London WC2N 5DN
t 020 7747 2885
w nationalgallery.org.uk
e information@ng-london.org.uk

104 Westminster

Houses of Parliament

2 hrs   Aug–Sep

Take a trip through the history and politics of our country – sit on the backbenches, or become a Lord. A visit to the historic seat of democracy is an invaluable introduction to politics and a great insight into citizenship.

* See & hear debates
* When Parliament is sitting, tours must be booked

Location
Underground Westminster

Opening
Tours available during summer recess Aug–Sep
Please phone for details

Admission
Please phone for details

Contact
House of Commons Information Office, Westminster, London SW1A 0AA
t 020 7219 4272
w parliament.uk
e hcinfo@parliament.uk

105 Wimbledon

Polka Theatre

2 hrs   Oct–Aug

Polka is one of the few theatre buildings in Britain producing and presenting work just for children. Shows range from classic and contemporary book adaptations to new work for the stage. Children's workshops are also available throughout the year.

* Playground
* Exhibits of costumes & props

Location
Underground Wimbledon. Turn left down the Broadway & theatre is on left

Opening
Oct–Aug Tue–Sat 9.30am–4.30pm
Please phone for performance times

Admission
Please phone for details

Contact
240 The Broadway, London SW19 1SB
t 020 8543 4888
w polkatheatre.com

106 Woolwich

Thames Barrier Information & Learning Centre

1 hr+   All year

The £500 million Thames Barrier spans the river at Woolwich Reach. There is an exhibition with a video and a working model. Please phone or check the website for dates of the monthly test gate closures. There are also riverside walkways and a children's play area.

Location
On A206. On S side of the Thames between S exit of Blackwall Tunnel & Woolwich Ferry

Opening
Daily: Apr–Sep 10.30am–4.30pm; Oct–Mar 11.30am–3.30pm

Admission
Adult £2, Child £1, Concs £1.50

Contact
1 Unity Way, London SE18 5NJ
t 020 8305 4188
w environment-agency.gov.uk
e learningcentre@environment-agency. gov.uk

107 Burford

Cotswold Wildlife Park & Gardens

3 hrs+   All year

The park, which comprises 160 acres of land and gardens around a listed Victorian manor house, has been open to the public since 1970. It's home to a collection of mammals, birds, reptiles and invertebrates, from ants to white rhinos and bats to big cats.

* Insect & reptile houses
* Tikki the 7-year-old, 19¾ft python

Location
On A361, 2 miles S of Burford

Opening
Daily: Mar–Sep 10am–5.30pm;
Oct–Feb 10am–4.30pm (last admission 1 hr before close)

Admission
Adult £9, Child & Concs £6.50

Contact
Burford OX18 4JP

t 01993 823006
w cotswoldwildlifepark.co.uk

108 Chinnor

Chinnor & Princes Risborough Railway

1 hr   Mar–Dec

Hop aboard a steam or heritage diesel train at Chinnor, then sit back and enjoy the 7-mile round trip as it heads into the country, past a stud farm, the former site of a Roman villa and the local cricket grounds. Enjoy a journey with Thomas the Tank Engine on special weekends.

* Learn how to drive a train on special training days
* Themed days throughout the year

Location
Station Road just off B4009

Opening
Mar–end Oct 10am–5.30pm;
Dec Sat–Sun
Please phone for timetable details

Admission
Adult £7.50, Child £3.75, Concs £6.50

Contact
Chinnor Station, Station Road,
Chinnor OX39 4ER

t 01844 353535/354117
w cprra.co.uk

109 Didcot

Didcot Railway Centre

2 hrs+   All year

A living museum of the Great Western Railway, based around the original depot, and now housing a collection of steam locomotives, carriages and wagons. On steam days the locomotives come to life and visitors can ride in the 1930s trains.

* Broad-gauge locomotive engine recently launched

Location
Signed from M4 (junction 13) & A34

Opening
Sat–Sun 10am–5pm; 24 Jun–3 Sep &
school hols daily 10am–4pm
Please phone or visit the website

Admission
Adult £4–£9.50, Child £3–£9.50,
Concs £3.50–£8.50, Family £12–£28

Contact
Great Western Society, Didcot
OX11 7NJ

t 01235 817200
w didcotrailwaycentre.org.uk
e didrlyc@globalnet.co.uk

110 Oxford

The Oxford Story

1 hr+   All year

Climb aboard this amazing ride and travel through 900 years of history, complete with sights, sounds and smells of the Middle Ages. Discover the link between *Alice in Wonderland* and the University.

Location
By road via A44. Follow city centre signs. A Park & Ride service is available

Opening
Daily: Jul–Aug 9.30am–5pm;
Jan–Jun & Sep–Dec Mon–Sat 10am–4.30pm, Sun 11am–4.30pm

Admission
Adult £7.25, Child £5.25, Concs £5.95

Contact
6 Broad Street, Oxford OX1 3AJ

t 01865 728822
w oxfordstory.co.uk
e info@oxfordstory.co.uk

111 Witney

Cogges Manor Farm Museum

2 hrs   Apr–Oct

Find out what life was like for the Victorians of rural Oxfordshire. The manor house includes a new Victorian schoolroom display, and the farm has original Cotswold buildings, traditional animal breeds, a walled garden and a riverside walk.

* Programme of special events
* Audio tours included in admission price

Location
½ mile SE of Witney, off A40

Opening
Apr–Oct Tue–Fri & Bank Hols 10.30am–5.30pm, Sat–Sun 12noon–5.30pm

Admission
Adult £5.40, Child £2.30, Concs £3.85, Family £13.90

Contact
Church Lane, Witney OX28 3LA

t 01993 772602
w westoxon.gov.uk

112 Woodstock

The Oxfordshire Museum

2–3 hrs   All year

This award-winning redevelopment of Fletcher's House provides a home for the new county museum celebrating Oxfordshire. It features local history, art and archaeology, as well as innovative industries.

* Interactive exhibits offer new learning experiences
* Café and large garden

Location
On A44

Opening
Tue–Sat 10am–5pm, Sun & Bank Hols 2pm–5pm (last admission 4.45pm)

Admission
Free

Contact
Fletcher's House, Park Street, Woodstock OX20 1SN

t 01993 811456
w oxfordshire.gov.uk/museums
e oxon.museum@oxfordshire.gov.uk

113 Chertsey

Thorpe Park

8 hrs   Mar–Nov

With more than 25 rides and attractions, families and thrillseekers will gasp at Thorpe Park – home to some of the most exciting rollercoaster experiences in Europe, including Stealth, the fastest, tallest launch rollercoaster in Europe. You are guaranteed to leave on a high.

* Stealth, reaching 80mph in 2.3 seconds.
* Colossus, the world's first ten looping rollercoaster

Location
Take junctions 11 or 13 off M25 &
follow signs via A320

Opening
Please phone or visit the website

Admission
Adult from £28.50, Child from £20
Save money by booking in advance

Contact
Staines Road,
Chertsey KT16 8PN

t 01932 569393
   0870 444 4466 (tickets)
w thorpepark.com

114 Cobham

Painshill Park

2 hrs+   All year

Within its 160 acres created by Charles Hamilton as a series of subtle and surprising vistas, the park's landscapes include authentic 18th-century plantings, a working vineyard, Gothic Temple, Chinese Bridge, Crystal Grotto, Turkish Tent, newly restored Hermitage and Gothic Tower.

* Historic vineyard now replanted for production
* 14–acre lake fed by a spectacular waterwheel

Location
Off A3 & A245 at Cobham

Opening
Daily: Apr–Oct 10.30am–6pm;
Nov–Mar 10.30am–4pm or dusk

Admission
Adult £6.60, Child £3.85, Concs £5.80

Contact
Portsmouth Road, Cobham KT11 1JE

t 01932 868113
w painshill.co.uk
e info@painshill.co.uk

115 East Molesey

Hampton Court Palace

3 hrs+   All year

Embark on a magical journey back through 500 years of royal history. Discover the magnificent state apartments of Henry VIII and William III, explore 60 acres of immaculate riverside gardens and enjoy the free tours and presentations.

* Horse-drawn carriages through gardens in summer
* World-famous maze in which to get lost

Location
From M25, junction 10 to A307 or junction 12 to A308

Opening
Daily: 24 Mar–27 Oct 10am–6pm;
28 Oct–25 Mar 10am–4.30pm

Admission
Adult £12.30, Child £8, Concs £10

Contact
East Molesey KT8 9AU

t 0870 752 7777
w hamptoncourtpalace.org.uk
e hamptoncourt@hrp.org.uk

116 Epsom

Chessington World of Adventures

8 hrs   Mar–Oct

An exciting range of themed attractions, games, rides and adventures. There are special Halloween events, and rides and attractions include Beanoland, Trail of the Kings and Toytown & Vampire.

* New Land of the Dragons
* Toadie's Crazy Cars

Location
Just 12 miles from London on A243, 2 miles from A3 & M25 (junction 9 or 10)

Opening
Mar–Oct; opening times vary. Please phone or visit the website for details

Admission
Please phone or visit the website for details

Contact
Leatherhead Road, Chessington KT9 2NE

t 0870 999 0045
w chessington.com

117 Epsom

Horton Park Children's Farm

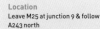

4 hrs+   All year

A friendly children's farm set up for the under-nines. There are lots of different farm animals including cows, sheep, pigs, goats, ponies, a donkey, a llama, poultry, alpacas, rheas, rabbits, guinea pigs, gerbils, mice, birds – and even a friendly snake! There is also a play barn.

* Indoor soft play barn
* Adventure park; water play in summer

Location
Leave M25 at junction 9 & follow A243 north

Opening
Daily: summer 10am–6pm
winter 10am–5pm

Admission
Adult & Child £5.75, Concs £4.75
1 adult free with each paying child

Contact
Horton Lane,
Epsom KT19 8PT

t 01372 743984
w hortonpark.co.uk
e childrensfarm@hortonpark.co.uk

118 Farnham

Rural Life Centre

2 hrs+   All year

The Rural Life Centre is a museum of past village life covering the years from 1750 to 1960. It is set in more than 10 acres of garden and woodland and housed in purpose-built and reconstructed buildings including a chapel, village hall and cricket pavilion.

* Displays show village crafts & trades
* Arboretum with more than 100 species of trees

Location
Off A287, 3 miles S of Farnham

Opening
Mar–Oct Wed–Sun & Bank Hol Mon
10am–5pm;
Nov–Feb Wed & Sun 11am–4pm

Admission
Adult £5.50, Child £3.50, Concs £4.50

Contact
Reeds Road, Tilford,
Farnham GU10 2DL

t 01252 795571
w rural-life.org.uk
e rural.life@lineone.net

119 Guildford

Burpham Court Farm Park

2 hrs   All year

A 76-acre conservation centre for endangered breeds of farm livestock including cattle, sheep, pigs, goats, llamas, poultry and ponies. Explore the nature trail and enjoy the many opportunities for hands-on contact with the animals including collecting eggs with the farmer at 3.30pm.

*Feed the friendly sheep & poultry & help the farmer
*Angling day-tickets available for owners of a rod licence

Location
From A3 southbound take Burpham & Merrow exit; signed from A3100, or from A320 at Jacobs Well

Opening
Daily: 10am–6pm (or dusk if earlier);
feeding time 3.30pm in summer, 3pm in winter

Admission
Adult £4.75, Child £3.95, Concs £4.35

Contact
Clay Lane, Jacobs Well,
Guildford GU4 7NA

t 01483 576089
w burphamcourtfarm.com

120 Guildford

River Wey & Godalming Navigations & Dapdune Wharf

2 hrs+   Mar–Oct

Discover the story of Surrey's oldest waterway and the people who lived and worked on it. Climb aboard a Wey barge and enjoy the interactive exhibits or take a boat trip.

* Boat trips available
* The entire 19-mile towpath is open to walkers

Location
Wharf Road is behind Surrey County Cricket Ground, off Woodbridge Road

Opening
End Mar–end Oct Mon & Thu–Sun
11am–5pm

Admission
Adult £3.50, Child £2

Contact
Wharf Road, Guildford GU1 4RR

t 01483 561389
w nationaltrust.org.uk
e riverwey@nationaltrust.org.uk

121 Leatherhead

Bocketts' Farm Park

3 hrs+   All year

This is a working family farm set in beautiful downland countryside with many friendly farm animals who enjoy being fed and handled. The farm boasts tractor and pony rides, a 70ft slide and daily pig races.

* Surrey Farm Diversification Award 2002
* Play barn & trampolines

Location
Just off A246 Epsom–Guildford road,
S of Leatherhead

Opening
Daily: 10am–6pm

Admission
Adult £5.95, Child & Concs £5.40

Contact
Young Street, Fetcham,
Leatherhead KT22 9BF

t 01372 363764
w bockettsfarm.co.uk
e jane@bockettsfarm.co.uk

122 Lingfield

British Wildlife Centre

2 hrs+   Mar–Oct

The British Wildlife Centre is home to one of the finest collections of native mammals, reptiles and birds in the country, with more than 40 species inhabiting 30 acres. Many are rare in the wild but at the centre you have the chance to observe them close-up.

* Keeper talks every 30 minutes
* Café, gift shop & picnic area

Location
Leave M25 at junction 6, then follow
A22 S to Newchapel

Opening
Mar–Oct Sat, Sun, Bank
Hols & daily during school
hols 10am–5pm

Admission
Adult £7, Child £5, Family £22

Contact
Newchapel,
Lingfield RH7 6LF

t 01342 834658
w britishwildlifecentre.co.uk
e info@britishwildlifecentre.co.uk

123 Redhill

Godstone Farm

6 hrs+   All year

Set in 40 acres of wooded farmland, Godstone Farm is home to cows, sheep, pigs, horses, ponies, goats, llamas, ducks, chickens, rabbits and more. Children can hold the smaller animals.

* Large indoor soft play area & outdoor play barn
* Toboggan run

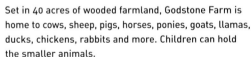

Location
From M25 (junction 6) follow road to
Godstone. Signposted from village

Opening
Daily: 10am–6pm

Admission
Adult & Child £5.80
1 adult free with each paying child

Contact
Tilburstow Hill Road,
Godstone RH9 8LX

t 01883 742546
w godstonefarm.co.uk
e havefun@godstonefarm.co.uk

124 Weybridge

Brooklands Museum

3 hrs+   All year

A family-friendly motorsport and aviation museum with walk-on exhibits, a hands-on discovery centre and regular family activities. There are motorsport events and fly-ins throughout the year. Come and see inside Concorde and experience a virtual flight in the Concorde Experience.

* Extensive programme of motoring events
* Large display of cars, bikes & aircraft

Location
Off B374, A3 to A245. Follow signs

Opening
Daily: summer 10am–5pm
winter 10am–4pm

Admission
Adult £7, Child £5, Concs £6

Contact
Brooklands Road,
Weybridge KT13 0QN

t 01932 857381
w brooklandsmuseum.com
e info@brooklandsmuseum.com

125 Arundel

Amberley Working Museum

3 hrs+   Mar–Oct

Amberley is a 36-acre open-air museum on the South Downs. With its historic buildings, working exhibits and demonstrations, the museum aims to show how science, technology and industry have affected people's lives. The railway exhibition hall is now open.

* Variety of crafts demonstrated daily
* Trips on vintage bus & narrow-gauge railway

Location
Off B2139 between Arundel & Storrington

Opening
Mar–Oct Wed–Sun 10am–5.30pm (last admission 4.30pm)

Admission
Adult £8.20, Child £5, Concs £7.20

Contact
Amberley, Arundel BN18 9LT
t 01798 831370
w amberleymuseum.co.uk
e office@amberleymuseum.co.uk

126 Arundel

WWT Arundel

2 hrs+   All year

The new visitor centre at Arundel is surrounded by ancient woodland and overlooked by the town's historic castle. The wetlands are home to many rare species of wetland wildlife. Learn more about them in the Eye-of-the-Wind wildlife art gallery.

* Programme of educational activities & events
* Many rare birds regularly sighted

Location
Close to A27 & A29. Follow brown duck signs on approaching Arundel

Opening
Daily: 9.30am–5.30pm; 4.30pm in winter

Admission
Adult £6.95, Child £3.75, Concs £5.25

Contact
Mill Road, Arundel BN18 9PB
t 01903 883355
w wwt.org.uk/visit/arundel
e sarah.fraser@wwt.org.uk

127 Billingshurst

Fishers Farm Park

4 hrs   All year

A mixture of rural farmyard and dynamic adventure playground, Fishers Farm Park has a combine-harvester ride and tractor, and pony and horse rides. There are also quad bikes, bumper boats, climbing walls, a mega bouncy slide, a theatre and shows.

* Quality Assured Visitor Attraction

Location
Near village of Wisborough Green. Follow signs on A272 & B2133

Opening
Daily: 10am–5pm

Admission
High season Adult £10.75, Child £10.25, Concs £9.25 Mid-season £9.75, £9.25, £8.25 Low season £7.75, £7.25, £6.25

Contact
Newpound Lane, Wisborough Green RH14 0EG
t 01403 700063
w fishersfarmpark.co.uk
e info@fishersfarmpark.co.uk

128 Chichester

Earnley Butterflies & Gardens

3 hrs+   Mar–Nov

At Earnley Gardens visitors can see the ornamental butterfly house and covered theme gardens from around the world. The gardens also house Noah's Ark – a rescue centre for small animals, including reptiles. There is a Shipwreck Museum and exotic birds garden.

* Rejectamenta – British C20 nostalgia museum
* 15-hole crazy golf course & animal handling

Location
Follow A286 from Chichester to the Witterings. After 3 miles turn left & follow signs

Opening
Daily: End Mar–early Nov 10am–6pm

Admission
Adult £7, Child £4, Concs £6

Contact
133 Almodington Lane, Earnley, Chichester PO20 7JR
t 01243 512637
e willprid@hotmail.com

129 Chichester

Military Aviation Museum

4 hrs+   Feb–Nov

Learn about 70 years of military aviation in Sussex, in particular the air war over southern England from 1939 to 1945. Meet the friendly volunteers, many of whom were wartime RAF pilots, navigators and groundcrew. On display are aircraft, uniforms and other memorabilia.

* Opportunity to 'fly' a fighter simulator
* Direct 55 bus service from Chichester to museum

Location
3 miles E of Chichester off A27

Opening
Daily: Feb & Nov 10am–4.30pm;
Mar–Oct 10am–5.30pm

Admission
Adult £5, Child £1.50, Concs £4

Contact
Military Aviation Museum, Tangmere, Chichester PO20 6ES
t 01243 775223
w tangmere-museum.org.uk
e tangmeretrust@aol.com

130 Chichester

Weald & Downland Open-Air Museum

2 hrs+   All year

This museum, in 50 acres of beautiful Sussex countryside, offers a chance to wander through a collection of nearly 50 historic buildings dating from the C13 to the C19. Many have period gardens and farm animals. Enjoy also the woodland walks, and the lake.

* The leading museum of historic buildings in England
* See food prepared in the working Tudor kitchen

Location
7 miles N of Chichester on A286

Opening
3 Jan–18 Feb Wed–Sun 10.30am– 4pm;
19 Feb–31 Mar & Nov–23 Dec daily 10.30am–4pm;
Apr–Oct daily 10.30am–6pm

Admission
Adult £7.75, Child £4.25, Concs £6.95

Contact
Singleton, Chichester PO18 0EU
t 01243 811348
w wealddown.co.uk
e office@wealddown.co.uk

131 Crawley

Tulleys Farm

3 hrs+   All year

A farm with pick-your-own soft fruit and vegetables and a 7-acre Maize Maze to entertain all the family. The farm also hosts special events, including the Halloween Spooktacular festival. Animals include goats, pigs, chipmunks, rabbits and guinea pigs.

* Play area & pets' corner

Location
Take B2110 from East Grinstead to Turners Hill. Signed from there

Opening
Tearoom 9.30am–4.30pm
Farm shop 9am–6pm; 5pm in winter
Maize Maze Daily: Jul–early Sep 10am–6pm

Admission
Maize Maze Adult £7, Child £6

Contact
Turners Hill, Crawley RH10 4PE
t 01342 718472
w tulleysfarm.com

132 Ford

The Flying Fortress

2 hrs+   All year

The newest family entertainment centre on the South coast boasts an enormous plane-shaped playframe with loads of activities and games to keep all age groups happy – from toddlers to teens. The 300+ seat café serves a wide range of freshly prepared food and drinks.

* Special events programme for holidays
* Also available for private functions

Location
Just off A259 going towards Yapton. Look out for blue RAC signs or follow signs to Ford Airfield Industrial Estate

Opening
Daily: Mon–Thu 9.30am–6.30pm, Fri 9.30am–6pm Sat & Sun 10am–6.30pm

Admission
Adults £1, Babies free, Under-4s £3.50, Over-4s £4.50, Teen club £4.50 Mon–Tue term time ½ price entry

Contact
Ford Airfield, Ford BN18 0HY

t 01903 733550
w flying-fortress.co.uk
e captain@flying-fortress.co.uk

133 Littlehampton

Harbour Park

3 hrs+   All year

A family amusement park right by the beach, with traditional attractions – dodgems, waltzer, arcade – plus a host of other rides and activities for all ages.

* Log flume
* Indoor skating rink

Location
A27, then follow A280 or A284 to Littlehampton

Opening
Arcade, skating rink, play area & food bar 10am–6pm (later in summer)
Outside attractions Easter–Oct from 12noon; limited opening in winter Please phone for details

Admission
Free, charges for individual rides

Contact
Sea Front, Littlehampton BN17 5LL

t 01903 721200
w harbourpark.com
e fun@harbourpark.com

134 Littlehampton

Look and Sea!

1 hr+   All year

Explore the geology, geography and history of Littlehampton, finishing in the stunning glass-walled viewing tower with fantastic views across the River Arun out to sea and to Arundel. The attractions include an interactive maritime exhibition and a variety of displays.

* Riverside walks
* Café overlooking the river & out to the sea

Location
By the river, 300 yrds from railway station

Opening
Daily: 9am–5pm

Admission
Adult £1.95, Child & Concs £1.50

Contact
63 Surrey Street, Littlehampton BN17 5AW

t 01903 718984
w lookandsea.co.uk
e info@lookandsea.co.uk

135 Pulborough

Bignor Roman Villa

1 hr+   Mar–Oct

Discovered in 1811, this site, probably dating from the C3, is one of the largest Roman villas in Britain and boasts amazing mosaics of gladiators in combat. It has 65 rooms in the main complex and nine outbuildings, including a bath house and summer and winter dining rooms.

* Spectacular mosaics depicting Venus & Medusa
* One of the largest Roman villas in Britain

Location
6 miles N of Arundel, signed from A29 (Bignor-Billingshurst) and A285 (Chichester–Petworth)

Opening
Mar–Apr Tue–Sun & Bank Hols 10am–5pm; May & Oct daily 10am–5pm; Jun–Sep daily 10am–6pm

Admission
Adult £4.35, Child £1.85, Concs £3.10

Contact
Bignor Lane, Pulborough RH20 1PH

t 01798 869259
w pyrrha.demon.co.uk
e bignorromanvilla@care4free.net

Burton Bradstock, Dorset

South West

Bristol Cornwall Devon Dorset
Gloucestershire Somerset Wiltshire

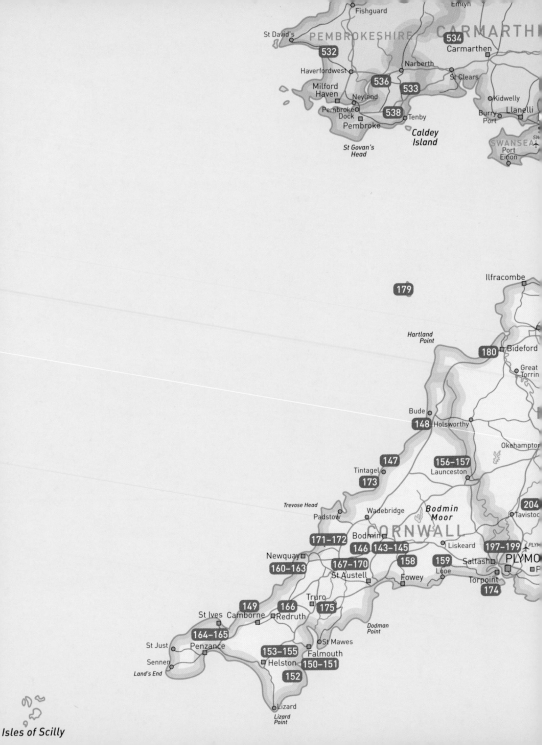

Fishguard

St David's

PEMBROKESHIRE

CARMARTHI

532

534

Carmarthen

Haverfordwest

Narberth

536

533

St Clears

Milford
Haven

Neyland

Kidwelly

Pembroke
Dock

538

Tenby

Burry
Port

Llanelli

Pembroke

SWANSEA

Caldey
Island

Port
Einon

St Govan's
Head

Ilfracombe

179

Hartland
Point

180

Bideford

Great
Torrin

Bude

148

Holsworthy

Okehampton

147

156–157

Tintagel

173

Launceston

204

Trevose Head

Bodmin
Moor

Tavistoc

Padstow

Wadebridge

CORNWALL

Bodmin

171–172

PLYM

Newquay

146

143–145

Liskeard

197–199

160–163

167–170

158

159

Sattash

PLYMO

St Austell

Fowey

Looe

P

Truro

Torpoint

149

166

175

174

St Ives

Camborne

Redruth

Dodman
Point

164–165

St Just

Penzance

St Mawes

Sennen

153–155

Falmouth

Land's End

Helston

150–151

152

Lizard

Isles of Scilly

Lizard
Point

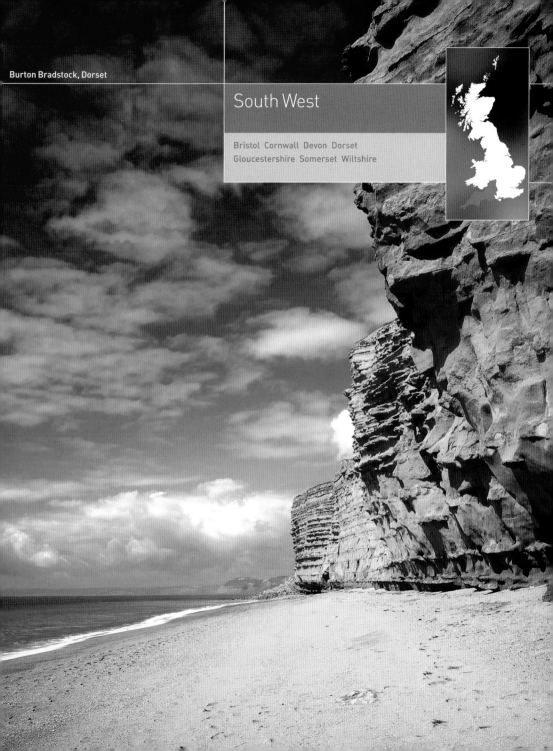

Burton Bradstock, Dorset

South West

Bristol Cornwall Devon Dorset
Gloucestershire Somerset Wiltshire

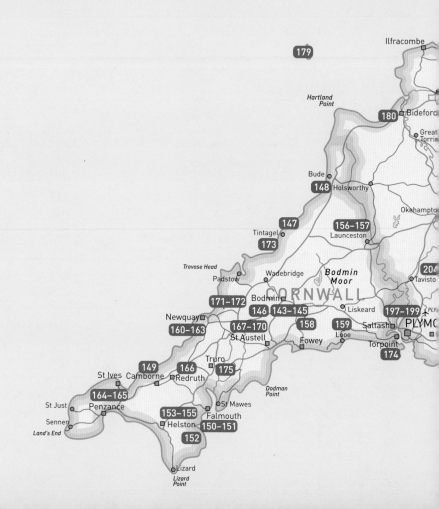

BRISTOL

Animal Attractions
Bristol Zoo Gardens 56
Horseworld 58
Noah's Ark Zoo Farm 58

Historic Sites
SS *Great Britain* 57

Museums & Exhibitions
City Museum & Art Gallery 57

Sport & Leisure
@Bristol 56
Bristol Ice Rink 56

CORNWALL

Animal Attractions
Dairyland Farm World 63
The Monkey Sanctuary Trust 63
National Seal Sanctuary 61
Newquay Zoo 64
Porfell Animal Land Wildlife Park 62
Springfields Fun Park & Pony Centre 66
The Tamar Otter & Wildlife Centre 62
Trethorne Leisure Farm 62

Boat & Train Trips
Bodmin & Wenford Railway 58
Lappa Valley Steam Railway 64

Historic Sites
Cornish Mines & Engines 65
Goonhilly Satellite Earth Station 61
Isles of Scilly Steamship Company 64
Lanhydrock House 59
Poldark Mine & Heritage Complex 62
Tintagel Castle 67

Museums & Exhibitions
Charlestown Shipwreck
 & Heritage Centre 65
Museum of Witchcraft 59
National Maritime Museum Cornwall 60
Royal Cornwall Museum 67

Parks, Gardens & Nature
Camel Trail 59
Colliford Lake Park 59
The Eden Project 65
Glendurgan Gardens 60
Lost Gardens of Heligan 66
Mount Edgcumbe House & Park 67
Tehidy Country Park 60

Sport & Leisure
Land's End Visitor Centre 65
Polkyth Leisure Centre 66

Theme Parks & Adventure Playgrounds
Brocklands Adventure Park 60
Flambards Theme Park 61
Holywell Bay Fun Park 63
Spirit of the West American
 Theme Park 66

DEVON

Animal Attractions
Buckfast Butterfly Farm
 & Dartmoor Otter Sanctuary 70
The Donkey Sanctuary 77
Living Coasts 79
The National Marine Aquarium 75
Paignton Zoo Environmental Park 74
Pennywell Farm & Wildlife Centre 70

Boat & Train Trips
Paignton & Dartmouth Steam
 Railway 74
Seaton Tramway 76
Sound Cruising 75
South Devon Railway 70
Stuart Line Cruises & Boat Trips 73

Historic Sites
Barnstaple Heritage Centre 68
Beer Quarry Caves 68
Bygones 79

Crownhill Fort 75
Grand Pier 77
The Golden Hind 70
House of Marbles 73
Killerton House 72
Knightshayes Court 78
Lundy Island 69
Morwellham Quay 77
Tuckers Maltings 74

Museums & Exhibitions
Pecorama Pleasure Gardens
 & Exhibition 76
Tiverton Museum of Mid Devon Life 78
Totnes Elizabethan House Museum 80

Parks, Gardens & Nature
Arlington Court 68
Bicton Park Botanical Gardens 71
Blackpool Sands 72
Norman Lockyer Observatory
 & James Lockyer Planetarium 77
Woodlands Leisure Park 80

Sport & Leisure
Babbacombe Model Village 78
Diggerland 71
Exmouth Model Railway 73
The Riviera International Centre
 & Waves Leisure Pool 80

Theme Parks & Adventure Playgrounds
Crealy Adventure Park   72
The Milky Way Adventure Park   69
Wonderland & The Cardew Tea Pottery   69

DORSET
Animal Attractions
Farmer Palmer's Farm Park   84
Monkey World   87
Oceanarium Bournemouth   81

Boat & Train Trips
Dorset Belle Cruises   81
Swanage Railway   86

Historic Sites
Abbotsbury Swannery   87
Brewers Quay   87
Corfe Castle   86
Lulworth Castle   86

Museums & Exhibitions
The Dinosaur Museum   82
Dorset County Museum   82
The Dorset Teddy Bear Museum   83
Tank Museum   82
The Tutankhamun Exhibition   83

Parks, Gardens & Nature
Avon Heath Country Park   85
Brownsea Island National Trust   84
Durlston Country Park   85
Kingston Maurward Gardens   83
Stapehill Abbey, Crafts & Gardens   88
Studland Beach & Nature Reserve   85
Upton Country Park   85
Wimborne Model Town & Gardens   88

Theme Parks & Adventure Playgrounds
Zorb South UK   84

GLOUCESTERSHIRE
Animal Attractions
Birdland Park   89
Cattle Country Adventure Park   89
Cotswold Farm Park   90
Prinknash Bird & Deer Park   92

Historic Sites
Berkeley Castle   88
Chedworth Roman Villa   90
WWT Slimbridge Wildfowl
 & Wetlands Trust   93

Museums & Exhibitions
Cotswold Motor Museum
 & Toy Collection   89
Museum in the Park   93
National Waterways Museum   91
Soldiers of Gloucestershire Museum   92

Parks, Gardens & Nature
Dyrham Park   91
Puzzle Wood   91
Robinswood Hill Country Park   92
Woodchester Park & Mansion   92

Sport & Leisure
Sandford Parks Lido   90

SOMERSET
Animal Attractions
Alstone Wildlife Park   99
Animal Farm Adventure Park   96
Ferne Animal Sanctuary   96
Seaquarium, Weston-super-Mare   101
Viaduct Fishery   101
The Wildlife Park at Cricket St Thomas   96

Boat & Train Trips
Bath Balloons   94
West Somerset Railway   99

Historic Sites
Cheddar Gorge & Caves   97

Dunster Castle   97
Farleigh Hungerford Castle   98
Glastonbury Abbey   98
Roman Baths & Pump Rooms   95
Wookey Hole Caves & Papermill   102

Museums & Exhibitions
Fleet Air Arm Museum   102
Haynes Motor Museum   100
The Helicopter Museum   101
The Jane Austen Centre   95
Radstock Museum   100
Somerset County Museum   101
West Somerset Rural Life Museum   99

Parks, Gardens & Nature
Barrington Court   94
Prior Park Landscape Garden   95

WILTSHIRE
Animal Attractions
Cholderton Rare Breeds Farm Park   104
Longleat   106
Westbury White Horse
 & Bratton Camp   106

Historic Sites
Avebury   102
Bowood House   103
Oasis Leisure Centre   105
Old Sarum   104
Stonehenge   102

Museums & Exhibitions
Athelstan Museum   103
Lacock Abbey & Fox Talbot Museum   103
STEAM – Museum of the
 Great Western Railway   105

Parks, Gardens & Nature
Stourhead Gardens   104

Sport & Leisure
Link Centre   105

136 Bristol

@Bristol

3 hrs+   All year

In Explore you can play virtual volleyball, test your memory and run in a giant hamster wheel. Wildwalk takes you on a journey through life on earth using botanical houses, animals and multimedia. The IMAX® Theatre is the biggest cinema screen in the region.

* Tropical forest with free-flying birds & butterflies
* Bristol's very own planetarium

Location	Contact
Off Anchor Road in central Bristol	Harbourside, Bristol BS1 5DB
Opening	t 0845 345 1235
Daily: 10am–5pm, Sat–Sun & school hols 10am–6pm	w at–bristol.org.uk
	e information@at–bristol.org.uk
Admission	
Explore Adult £8, Child £5.50, Concs £6.50	
Wildwalk & IMAX® £6.50, £4.50, £5.50	

137 Bristol

Bristol Ice Rink

2 hrs   All year

Bristol Ice Rink offers a variety of family and disco skating sessions every day. 'Learn to ice-skate' courses are available throughout the year.

* Birthday parties
* Refreshments available

Location	Contact
In city centre	Frogmore Street, Bristol BS1 5NA
Opening	t 0117 929 2148
Daily: 10am–10.30pm	w jnll.co.uk
Admission	e jnlbristol@nikegroup.co.uk
Adult £6.50, Child £2.75	
Please phone for details	

138 Bristol

Bristol Zoo Gardens

3 hrs   All year

Bristol Zoo Gardens has more than 400 endangered and exotic species. Visit the Seal & Penguin Coasts, Bug World, Twilight World, the Monkey House, Livingstone's fruit bats, Asiatic lions, the Reptile House and Gorilla Island. Or simply relax in the stunning gardens.

* Voted Zoo of the Year 2004 by the Good Britain Guide

Location	Admission
From M5 (junction 17 or 18) follow brown elephant signs	Adult £11, Child £7, Concs £9.70, Family £33
Opening	**Contact**
Daily: 9am–5.30pm in high season, 5pm in low season (animal houses close at 4.30pm in winter)	Clifton, Bristol BS8 3HA
	t 0117 974 7399
	w bristolzoo.org.uk
	e information@ bristolzoo.org.uk

Theme Parks & Adventure Playgrounds
Crealy Adventure Park 72
The Milky Way Adventure Park 69
Wonderland & The Cardew Tea Pottery 69

DORSET
Animal Attractions
Farmer Palmer's Farm Park 84
Monkey World 87
Oceanarium Bournemouth 81

Boat & Train Trips
Dorset Belle Cruises 81
Swanage Railway 86

Historic Sites
Abbotsbury Swannery 87
Brewers Quay 87
Corfe Castle 86
Lulworth Castle 86

Museums & Exhibitions
The Dinosaur Museum 82
Dorset County Museum 82
The Dorset Teddy Bear Museum 83
Tank Museum 82
The Tutankhamun Exhibition 83

Parks, Gardens & Nature
Avon Heath Country Park 85
Brownsea Island National Trust 84
Durlston Country Park 85
Kingston Maurward Gardens 83
Stapehill Abbey, Crafts & Gardens 88
Studland Beach & Nature Reserve 85
Upton Country Park 85
Wimborne Model Town & Gardens 88

Theme Parks & Adventure Playgrounds
Zorb South UK 84

GLOUCESTERSHIRE
Animal Attractions
Birdland Park 89
Cattle Country Adventure Park 89
Cotswold Farm Park 90
Prinknash Bird & Deer Park 92

Historic Sites
Berkeley Castle 88
Chedworth Roman Villa 90
WWT Slimbridge Wildfowl
 & Wetlands Trust 93

Museums & Exhibitions
Cotswold Motor Museum
 & Toy Collection 89
Museum in the Park 93
National Waterways Museum 91
Soldiers of Gloucestershire Museum 92

Parks, Gardens & Nature
Dyrham Park 91
Puzzle Wood 91
Robinswood Hill Country Park 92
Woodchester Park & Mansion 92

Sport & Leisure
Sandford Parks Lido 90

SOMERSET
Animal Attractions
Alstone Wildlife Park 99
Animal Farm Adventure Park 96
Ferne Animal Sanctuary 96
Seaquarium, Weston-super-Mare 101
Viaduct Fishery 101
The Wildlife Park at Cricket St Thomas 96

Boat & Train Trips
Bath Balloons 94
West Somerset Railway 99

Historic Sites
Cheddar Gorge & Caves 97

Dunster Castle 97
Farleigh Hungerford Castle 98
Glastonbury Abbey 98
Roman Baths & Pump Rooms 95
Wookey Hole Caves & Papermill 102

Museums & Exhibitions
Fleet Air Arm Museum 102
Haynes Motor Museum 100
The Helicopter Museum 101
The Jane Austen Centre 95
Radstock Museum 100
Somerset County Museum 101
West Somerset Rural Life Museum 99

Parks, Gardens & Nature
Barrington Court 94
Prior Park Landscape Garden 95

WILTSHIRE
Animal Attractions
Cholderton Rare Breeds Farm Park 104
Longleat 106
Westbury White Horse
 & Bratton Camp 106

Historic Sites
Avebury 102
Bowood House 103
Oasis Leisure Centre 105
Old Sarum 104
Stonehenge 102

Museums & Exhibitions
Athelstan Museum 103
Lacock Abbey & Fox Talbot Museum 103
STEAM – Museum of the
 Great Western Railway 105

Parks, Gardens & Nature
Stourhead Gardens 104

Sport & Leisure
Link Centre 105

136 Bristol

@Bristol

3 hrs+   All year

In Explore you can play virtual volleyball, test your memory and run in a giant hamster wheel. Wildwalk takes you on a journey through life on earth using botanical houses, animals and multimedia. The IMAX® Theatre is the biggest cinema screen in the region.

* Tropical forest with free-flying birds & butterflies
* Bristol's very own planetarium

Location	Contact
Off Anchor Road in central Bristol	Harbourside, Bristol BS1 5DB
Opening	t 0845 345 1235
Daily: 10am–5pm, Sat–Sun & school hols 10am–6pm	w at-bristol.org.uk
	e information@at-bristol.org.uk
Admission	
Explore Adult £8, Child £5.50, Concs £6.50	
Wildwalk & IMAX® £6.50, £4.50, £5.50	

137 Bristol

Bristol Ice Rink

2 hrs   All year

Bristol Ice Rink offers a variety of family and disco skating sessions every day. 'Learn to ice-skate' courses are available throughout the year.

* Birthday parties
* Refreshments available

Location	Contact
In city centre	Frogmore Street, Bristol BS1 5NA
Opening	
Daily: 10am–10.30pm	t 0117 929 2148
	w jnll.co.uk
Admission	e jnlbristol@nikegroup.co.uk
Adult £6.50, Child £2.75	
Please phone for details	

138 Bristol

Bristol Zoo Gardens

3 hrs   All year

Bristol Zoo Gardens has more than 400 endangered and exotic species. Visit the Seal & Penguin Coasts, Bug World, Twilight World, the Monkey House, Livingstone's fruit bats, Asiatic lions, the Reptile House and Gorilla Island. Or simply relax in the stunning gardens.

* Voted Zoo of the Year 2004 by the Good Britain Guide

Location	Admission
From M5 (junction 17 or 18) follow brown elephant signs	Adult £11, Child £7, Concs £9.70, Family £33
Opening	**Contact**
Daily: 9am–5.30pm in high season, 5pm in low season (animal houses close at 4.30pm in winter)	Clifton, Bristol BS8 3HA
	t 0117 974 7399
	w bristolzoo.org.uk
	e information@ bristolzoo.org.uk

139 Bristol

City Museum & Art Gallery

2 hrs+   All year

Bristol's premier museum and art gallery. This magnificent building houses important collections of minerals and fossils, natural history, Eastern art, archaeology, seven galleries of fine and applied art and ever-changing temporary exhibitions.

* World Wildlife Gallery

Location
In Clifton; follow brown signs from town centre

Opening
Daily: 10am–5pm

Admission
Free

Contact
t 0117 922 3571
w bristol-city.gov.uk/museums
e general_museum@bristol-city.
   gov.uk

140 Bristol

SS *Great Britain*

2 hrs   All year

Visit the world's first great ocean liner, the pinnacle of Victorian engineering and luxury. Take a hard-hat tour and witness the conservation of this historically important iron ship.

* Designed by Isambard Kingdom Brunel
* Descend under the sea into the dry dock

Location
Follow anchor signs in Bristol Historic Dockyard

Opening
Daily: Apr–Oct 10am–5.30pm;
Nov–Mar 10am–4.30pm

Admission
Adult £8.95, Child £4.95, Concs £6.95

Contact
Great Western Dockyard,
Gas Ferry Road, Bristol BS1 6TY
t 0117 926 0680
w ssgreatbritain.org
e admin@ss-great-britain.com

141 Whitchurch

HorseWorld

3 hrs+   All year

HorseWorld Visitor Centre is a great day out for all the family. Support the South West's leading horse welfare charity and meet the rescued horses, ponies and donkeys. There are interactive museums and nature trails as well as pony rides and pet handling.

* Twice-daily presentations
* Indoor & outdoor play areas

Location
Take A37 from Bristol & follow brown signs. Through Whitchurch – HorseWorld is on left

Opening
Mar–Sep daily 10am–5pm; Sep–Mar Tue–Sun 10am–4pm

Admission
Please phone for details

Contact
Staunton Manor Farm,
Staunton Lane, Whitchurch,
Bristol BS14 0QJ

t 01275 540173
w horseworld.org.uk
e visitorcentre@horseworld.org.uk

142 Wraxall

Noah's Ark Zoo Farm

4 hrs+   Feb–Oct

There is plenty to entertain children – water buffalo, rhinos, yaks, monkeys, giraffes, rhinos, reptiles and 80 other species. There are indoor and outdoor adventure play areas and scenic tractor rides, plus the chance to bottle-feed lambs, handle baby chicks and milk a bionic cow!

* Quality Assured Visitor Attraction
* World's longest hedge maze & shop

Location
On B3128 Bristol-Clevedon road

Opening
Feb half-term–Oct Tue-Sat
10.30am–5pm & Bank Hols;
school hols Mon–Sat 10.30am–5pm

Admission Adult £8, Child £6,
Concs £7, Family £25

Contact
Failand Road, Wraxall,
Bristol BS48 1PG

t 01275 852606
w noahsarkzoofarm.co.uk
e info@noahsarkzoofarm.co.uk

143 Bodmin

Bodmin & Wenford Railway

3 hrs   Mar–Oct

A trip on this standard-gauge railway, operating mainly steam engines, covers 6½ miles from Bodmin town to Bodmin Parkway. You'll pass through the beautiful River Fowey valley and stop at Boscarne Junction for the Camel Trail.

* Quizzes available for children

Location
On B3268 in central Bodmin

Opening
Please phone for details

Admission
Adult £10, Child £6, Family £28

Contact
Bodmin General Station,
Lostwithiel Road,
Bodmin PL31 1AQ

t 0845 125 9678
w bodminandwenfordrailway.co.uk
e enquiries@bodminandwenfordrailway.
co.uk

144 Bodmin

Camel Trail

All day   All year

Take a whole day to explore this way-marked path, which runs along 17 miles of the Camel Estuary and Camel Valley from Padstow to Poley's Bridge. The route is suitable for pedestrians, cyclists and horses.

*Local bike hire

Location
Accessible from Wadebridge town, or A389 from Bodmin or main car park in Padstow

Opening
Please phone for details

Admission
Free

Contact
3–5 Barn Lane,
Bodmin PL31 1LZ
t 01208 265644
w ncdc.gov.uk

145 Bodmin

Lanhydrock House

3 hrs+   Apr–Oct

One of the finest houses in Cornwall, built in the late C19. It is set in wooded parkland and surrounded by a garden with rare shrubs and trees. 'Below stairs' has a huge kitchen, larder, dairy and bake house.

* Children's guide & quizzes
* Organised activities in school holidays

Location
2 miles E of Bodmin. Follow signs off either A30 or A38

Opening
Apr–Oct Tue–Sun & Bank Hol Mon
11am–5.30pm (5pm in Oct)

Admission
Please phone for details

Contact
Lanhydrock, Bodmin PL30 5AD
t 01208 265950
w nationaltrust.org.uk
e lanhydrock@nationaltrust.org.uk

146 Bolventor

Colliford Lake Park

3 hrs+   Easter–Oct

Colliford Lake Park is a farm-based attraction set in the spectacular Bodmin Moor. Overlooking Colliford Lake, this 40-acre park combines natural beauty with an action-packed day out. There are pedal-karts, challenging agility trails and a target range.

* Extensive indoor & outdoor play areas
* Nature trails around Colliford Lake

Location
500 yards off A30 between Launceston & Bodmin

Opening
Daily: Easter–Oct 10.30am–5.30pm

Admission
Adult £6, Child & Concs £6

Contact
Bolventor, Bodmin Moor PL14 6PZ
t 01208 821469
w collifordlakepark.com
e info@collifordlakepark.com

147 Boscastle

Museum of Witchcraft

1 hr   Easter–Oct

The museum contains the world's largest collection of witchcraft-related artefacts and regalia. With a series of fascinating displays covering everything from stone circles and sacred sites to ritual magic, charms and spells, it is a unique and memorable collection.

* Library with 3,000 books on witchcraft (by appointment only)
* Fresh new displays since the floods of 2004

Location
Located by the Harbour in Boscastle. Boscastle is on N coast of Cornwall between Tintagel & Bude

Opening
Daily: Easter–Oct Mon–Sat
10.30am–6pm, Sun 11.30am–6pm

Admission
Adults £2.50, Child & Concs £1.50

Contact
The Harbour, Boscastle PL35 0HD
t 01840 250111
w museumofwitchcraft.com
e museumwitchcraft@aol.com

148 Bude

Brocklands Adventure Park

4 hrs+ Apr–Oct

Younger children will enjoy the sandpit, swings and slides at this activity-packed park. For older kids there is a mini assault course and Aqua Blaster, plus pony rides, bumper boats, two-seater Supakarts, a new tenpin bowling centre and much more.

* Quality Assured Visitor Attraction
* Fully licensed bar

Location
On A39 Atlantic Highway between Bude & Bideford

Opening
Please phone for details

Admission
Adult & Child £6, Concs £4

Contact
West Street, Kilkhampton, Bude EX23 9QW

t 01288 321920
w brocklands.com

149 Camborne

Tehidy Country Park

4 hrs+ All year

Enjoy an active day at this country park comprising 345 acres of woodland, lakes and ponds, with 9 miles of footpaths to explore. There is also the opportunity to follow horse, cycle and woodland trails.

* Sensory trail for visually impaired visitors
* Redesigned orienteering course

Location
Access on B3301 from Portreath to North Cliffs

Opening
Please phone for details

Admission
Free

Contact
Tehidy, Camborne TR14 0HA

t 01209 714494
w cornwall.gov.uk
e enquiries@cornwall.gov.uk

150 Falmouth

Glendurgan Gardens

2 hrs Feb–Nov

These delightful subtropical gardens include an extensive laurel maze, the Giant's Stride swing and a reconstructed C19 schoolroom. The gardens run down to the sandy beach of Durgan, which offers good swimming and rock pools.

Location
4 miles SW of Falmouth, ½ mile SW of Mawnan Smith on road to Helford Passage

Opening
Feb–Nov Tue–Sat 10.30am–5.30pm (last admission 4.30pm); open Bank Hol Mon

Admission
Adult £5, Child £2.50, Concs £4.25

Contact
Mawnan Smith, nr Falmouth TR11 5JZ

t 01326 250906
e glendurgan@nationaltrust.org.uk

151 Falmouth

National Maritime Museum Cornwall

2 hrs All year

One of only three natural underwater viewing locations in the world. Enjoy hands-on interactives, audio-visual immersive experiences, talks, special exhibitions and the opportunity to get out on to the water and discover the marine life around our coastline.

* Climb to the top of the tower for views over the harbour
* Display of Cornish maritime artefacts

Location
At SE end of harbourside. Or follow signs from A39 for Park & Float

Opening
Daily: 10am–5pm

Admission
Adult £7, Child & Concs £4.80

Contact
Discovery Quay, Falmouth TR11 3QY

t 01326 313388
w nmmc.co.uk
e enquiries@nmmc.co.uk

Goonhilly Satellite Earth Station

2 hrs+   All year

Visit Goonhilly, the largest satellite station on earth, to learn about space and modern communications. There are interactive exhibits, film shows and high-speed touch-screen internet terminals. And don't miss the absorbing multimedia visitor centre.

* Fastest internet cafe in the world
* Send email to an alien, 3D virtual head creation

Location
Follow brown tourist signs from Helston

Opening
Tue–Thu & Sat–Sun from 10am
Closing times vary, please phone for details

Admission
Adult £6.50, Child £4.50, Concs £5

Contact
Goonhilly, Helston TR12 6LQ
t 0800 679593
w goonhilly.bt.com
e goonhilly.visitorscentre@bt.com

Flambards Theme Park

4 hrs+   Easter–Nov

Set in glorious gardens, this Cornish theme park combines internationally acclaimed exhibitions such as Britain in the Blitz with thrilling playground rides and family shows.

* Firework displays during Aug

Location
On A3083 Lizard road. Signed from A394 Truro–Helston road & A394 Penzance–Helston road

Opening
Easter–Nov 10.30am–5pm;
peak season 10am–5.30pm

Admission
Super Family Saver tickets available, please phone for details

Contact
Helston TR13 0QA
t 0845 6018684 (24hr info line)
w flambards.co.uk
e info@flambards.co.uk

National Seal Sanctuary

2 hrs+   All year

Get to know the seals at this leading marine mammal rescue centre. Watch them at feeding time and learn about their characteristics from informative staff. The centre also has other rescued animals such as ponies and goats.

* Barbecues in summer
* See the otters in Otter Creek

Location
Follow A3083 from Helston towards the Lizard. Turn left on to B3291 & into Gweek

Opening
Daily from 10am
Please phone for last admission

Admission
Adult £10.50, Child £6.95, Concs £7.95, Family £28.95

Contact
Gweek, Helston TR12 6UG
t 01326 221361
w sealsanctuary.co.uk
e slcgweek@merlinentertainments.biz

155 Helston

Poldark Mine & Heritage Complex

3 hrs   Easter–Oct

Enjoy a guided tour of a genuine C18 Cornish tin mine, with a museum, gardens, children's play areas and craft demonstrations. Pan for real gold, throw a pot or try your hand at woodturning.

* Entry to the site itself is free
* Family attractions in addition to the mine

Location
2 miles from Helston on B3297

Opening
Daily:10am–5.30pm (last tours 4pm)

Admission
Adult £7.50, Child £4.90, Concs £7

Contact
Wendron, Helston TR13 0ES

t 01326 573173
w poldark-mine.co.uk
e info@poldark-mine.co.uk

156 Launceston

The Tamar Otter & Wildlife Centre

2 hrs+   Apr–Oct

Situated on the banks of the River Waveney, the centre gives visitors a rare chance to see otters at close quarters, along with other wetland wildlife. The informative visitor centre explores the lives and habits of otters and the conservation issues surrounding them.

* Children's play area
* Beautiful riverbank walks

Location
Situated at North Petherwin, 5 miles NW of Launceston off the B3254 road to Bude, Cornwall

Opening
Daily: Apr–Oct 10.30am–6pm
Otters 12noon & 3pm
Waterfowl 2.30pm

Admission
Adult £6, Child £3.50, Concs £5, Family £17

Contact
Nr Launceston PL15 8LW

t 01566 785646
w tamarotters.co.uk
e info@tamarotters.co.uk

157 Launceston

Trethorne Leisure Farm

4–7 hrs   All year

This farm and leisure park offers more than 45,000 square feet of indoor attractions. They include a virtual climbing wall, Jolly Roger Ball Blaster, ball pools, assault course, crazy golf, tenpin bowling and pony rides. Visitors can also pet and hold the animals.

* Ride on electric cars
* Bars & gift shop

Location
On A395, 3 miles W of Launceston, just off A30

Opening
Daily: Leisure park 10am–6pm
Tenpin bowling 10am–11pm
Please phone for details of winter opening

Admission
Adult £6.80, Child £6.25, Concs £5

Contact
Kennards House,
Launceston PL15 8QE

t 01566 86324
w trethorne.co.uk
e trethorneleisure@btconnect.com

158 Liskeard

Porfell Animal Land Wildlife Park

2 hrs+   Apr–Oct

A place where families can enjoy close contact with domestic, exotic and wild animals. Discovery and surprise are all part of the fun as you feed the ducks, chickens, goats and deer. There are also zebras, lemurs, raccoons, wallabies and many more.

* Children's farm
* Small children's play area

Location
Take A38 from Liskeard to Dobwalls. Turn on to A390 & at East Taphouse turn left on to B3359. First turning on the right

Opening
Daily: 1 Apr–31 Oct 10am–6pm

Admission
Adult £5, Child (3–13) £4, Concs £4.50

Contact
Trecangate, nr Lanreath
Liskeard PL14 4RE

t 01503 220211
w porfellanimalland.co.uk

159 Looe

The Monkey Sanctuary Trust

2 hrs   Easter–Sep

See Amazon woolly monkeys in their own spacious territory at this environmentally aware centre. Talks are given throughout the day about the monkeys and their threatened rainforest habitat. There is also an opportunity to see a colony of lesser horseshoe bats.

* Wildlife gardens
* Children's activity rooms & play area

Location
Signed on B387 Looe–Plymouth road at No Man's Land. 4 miles from Looe, 18 miles from Plymouth

Opening
1st Sun before Easter–Sep & autumn half-term Sun–Thu 11am–4.30pm

Admission
Adult £6, Child £3.50, Concs £4.50, Family £16, Wheelchair users ½ price

Contact
Looe PL13 1NZ

t 01503 262532
w monkeysanctuary.org
e info@monkeysanctuary.org

160 Newquay

Dairyland Farm World

5 hrs   Easter–Oct

One of the UK's leading working farm attractions, Dairyland has a wealth of animals that children love to pet. Included in the menagerie are kittens, kids, lambs, rabbits, donkeys, chipmunks and chinchillas. You can even have a go at milking Clarabelle, the cyber cow.

* Pony rides
* Cornish Board Attraction of the Year 2005

Location
On A3058, 4 miles from Newquay

Opening
Daily: Easter–Oct 10am–5pm

Admission
Adult £7.75, Child £6.75, Concs £5.75, Family £27

Contact
Tresillian Barton, Summercourt, Newquay TR8 5AA

t 01872 510246
w dairylandfarmworld.com
e farmworld@yahoo.com

161 Newquay

Holywell Bay Fun Park

3 hrs   Easter–Oct

Great rides, go-karts, crazy golf and a maze are just a few of the attractions at this fun park. Others include bumper boats, children's fun rides, a climbing wall and a beach nearby.

* Quality Assured Visitor Attraction

Location
Follow A3075 Newquay–Perranporth road; turn right to Cubert. Located on the right, 1 mile past Cubert

Opening
Daily: Easter–Oct from 10.30am

Admission
'Pay as you play' token system

Contact
Holywell Bay, Newquay TR8 5PW

t 01637 830531
w holywellbay.co.uk
e info@trevornick.co.uk

162 Newquay

Lappa Valley Steam Railway

3–4 hrs   Easter–Oct

Enjoy a 2-mile steam train journey, boating, crazy golf, a maze and woodland walks in scenic countryside. Included in the admission price is entry to the viewing platform of the largest mine-engine house in Cornwall.

Location	Admission
Follow A3075 to Newquay. Just past Newquay turn E to St Newlyn East & follow tourist signs to railway	Please phone for details
	Contact
Opening	St Newlyn East,
Mid-Apr–Oct	Newquay TR8 5HZ
Please phone for details	t 01872 510317
	w lappavalley.co.uk

163 Newquay

Newquay Zoo

2 hrs+   All year

Home to many of the world's endangered species, Newquay Zoo is set in beautiful subtropical gardens. Explore the rainforest and its fascinating wildlife in the Tropical Zone. Events run throughout the year, and group bookings are welcome.

* Quality Assured Visitor Attraction
* Winner of many awards

Location	Admission
Off A3075 Edgcumbe Avenue in Trenance Park, Newquay	Please phone or visit the website for details
Opening	Contact
Daily: Apr–Sep 9.30am–6pm (last admission 5pm);	Trenance Park, Newquay TR7 2LZ
Oct–Mar 10am–dusk	t 01637 873342
	w newquayzoo.org.uk
	e info@newquayzoo.org.uk

164 Penzance

Isles of Scilly Steamship Company

10 hrs   All year

Fly or cruise to the Isles of Scilly on a comfortable passenger ferry with a bar, buffet and comfy seating all available. During the journey you can see an interesting exhibition about the islands and listen to a commentary by the ship's captain.

* Chairlift available between main and 2nd decks
* Family tickets available throughout the year– please phone

Location	Contact
On the A30 or A394 to Penzance	Steamship House, Quay Street Penzance TR18 4BZ
Opening	
Mon–Fri 8am–5pm, Sat 8am–4pm	t 08457 105555
	w ios-travel.co.uk
Admission	e sales@islesofscilly-travel.co.uk
Day trip Adult £36, Child (2–15) £18, Family £88	

165 Penzance

Land's End Visitor Centre

2 hrs+   All year

This heritage centre is set amid the breathtaking scenery of Land's End, one of Britain's most famous sites. The centre has exhibitions and shows including the Air Sea Rescue Theatre Experience. There is also a playground.

* Land's End sweet factory
* Stunning scenery

Location
At end of A30, 12 miles from Penzance

Opening
Daily: from 10am (closing times vary)
Please phone for details

Admission
Adult £9.95, Child £5.95, Concs £7.95

Contact
Land's End, Sennen,
Penzance TR19 7AA

t 01736 871501
w landsend-landmark.co.uk
e info@landsend.landmark.co.uk

166 Redruth

Cornish Mines & Engines

2 hrs   Easter–Oct

Learn the story of Cornwall's industrial heritage, and find out what life was like for the miners of tin, copper and china clay. You can also see the enormous working beam engine and find out about the fascinating geology of the area.

* National Trust property

Location
At Pool, 2 miles W of Redruth on either side of A3047. Midway between Redruth and Camborne

Opening
Easter–Oct 11am–5pm (closed Sat)

Admission
Adult £5, Child £2.50, Family £12.50

Contact
Pool, nr Redruth TR15 3NP

t 01209 315027
w nationaltrust.org.uk

167 St Austell

Charlestown Shipwreck & Heritage Centre

2 hrs   Mar–Oct

Learn about diving, rescues and shipwrecks in this major display of maritime history, the largest shipwreck artefact collection in the British Isles. There is also an exhibition about the *Titanic*.

Location
Reached via A390

Opening
Daily: Mar–Oct 10am–5pm

Admission
Adult £5.95, Child £2.95,
Under-10s free, Concs £3.95

Contact
Quay Road, Charlestown,
St Austell PL25 3NJ

t 01726 69897
w shipwreckcharlestown.com
e admin@shipwreckcharlestown.com

168 St Austell

The Eden Project

4 hrs+   All year

Visit the largest greenhouses in the world with plants from many diverse habitats such as the tropical rainforest, Mediterranean fruit groves and the fields of California. There are also free events throughout the year.

* Project has 2 million visitors a year
* See coffee plants, palm trees & pineapples

Location
Follow signs from A390 at St Austell & A30 Bodmin bypass

Opening
Daily: *summer* 9.30am–6pm
(last admission 4.30pm)
winter 10am–4.30pm
(last admission 3.30pm)

Admission
Adult £13.80, Child £5, Concs £10

Contact
Bodelva, St Austell PL24 2SG

t 01726 811900
w edenproject.com
e info@edenproject.com

169 St Austell

Lost Gardens of Heligan

4 hrs+   All year

These world-renowned gardens comprise 80 acres of pleasure grounds plus a complex of walled gardens. Many spectacular subtropical species thrive in this frost-free Cornish valley. Heligan has undergone one of the largest restoration projects of its kind in Europe.

* Stunning collection of plants from all over the world
* Featured in major Channel 4 series

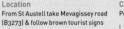

Location
From St Austell take Mevagissey road (B3273) & follow brown tourist signs

Opening
Mar–Oct 10am–6pm; Nov–Feb 10am–5pm

Admission
Adult £7.50, Child £4, Concs £7

Contact
Pentewan, St Austell PL26 6EN
t 01726 845100
w heligan.com
e info@heligan.com

170 St Austell

Polkyth Leisure Centre

2 hrs+   All year

Exercise to your heart's content in this well-equipped sports hall, with badminton courts, squash courts, tennis courts and swimming pools. A hoist is available for disabled visitors.

* Hydrotherapy pool
* Fitness room & new state-of-the-art gym & dance studio

Location
Accessible via A390 & A391. Follow brown tourist signs

Opening
Daily: Mon–Fri 9am–10pm, Sat & Sun 9am–5pm

Admission
Please phone for details

Contact
Carlyon Road, St Austell PL25 4DB
t 01726 223344
w polkythleisure.co.uk
e polkythmanagement@restormel.gov.uk

171 St Columb

Spirit of the West American Theme Park

3 hrs+   May–Sep

A theme park dedicated to the Wild West with Native American artefacts and live street-action shows. There are two themed towns, spanning 100 acres. Pan for gold, fish at Retallack and visit the museums. There's also a Western store and a photographic parlour.

* Westworld auto raceway
* Shooting gallery & pony trail rides

Location
On A39 St Columb–Wadebridge road, just off Winnards Perch roundabout on B3274

Opening
Theme Park May–Sep Sun–Fri from 10.30am (last admission 4pm)
Fishery All year

Admission
Adult £7, Child & Concs £5, Family £22

Contact
Retallack Park, Winnards Perch, nr St Columb TR9 6DE
t 01637 881160
w wildwestthemepark.co.uk
e sheriffjaybee@aol.com

172 St Columb

Springfields Fun Park & Pony Centre

   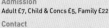

5 hrs+   Easter–Oct

Have fun along the nature walk, try pond-dipping, then sample the indoor and outdoor play zones, free-fall slides, trampolines and more.

* Farm animals & bottle-feeding
* Pony, cart & train rides

Location
nr Newquay. Follow brown signs off the A30 or A39. From the SW follow the signs from the A30 for the Airport.

Opening
Daily: Easter–Sep 10am–6pm (last admission 4pm); Oct Sat–Sun & half-term only

Admission
Adult £6.95, Child £5.95, Concs £4.95, Family £22

Contact
Ruthvoes, St Columb TR9 6HU
t 01637 881224
w springfieldsponycentre.co.uk
e info.springfieldsponycentre@btconnect.com

173 Tintagel

Tintagel Castle

1 hr+   All year

This is the legendary home of King Arthur and Merlin, and its awesome setting with the crashing waves on three sides adds fuel to the story. The ruins that stand today are the remnants of a castle built by Earl Richard of Cornwall, brother of Henry III.

* Short film about the castle
* Put your foot in 'Arthur's Footprint'

Location
Take ½-mile track from village (no vehicles beyond village)

Opening
Daily: Apr–Sep 10am–6pm; Oct 10am–5pm; Nov–Mar 10am–4pm

Admission
Adult £4.30, Child £2.20, Concs £3.20

Contact
Tintagel PL34 0HE

t 01840 770328
w english-heritage.org.uk/membership
e tintagel.castle@english-heritage.org.uk

---

174 Torpoint

Mount Edgcumbe House & Park

2 hrs+   All year

For 400 years this was home to the Earls of Mount Edgcumbe. Its landscaped park overlooking Plymouth Sound has fallow deer, and woodland and coastal walks. Mount Edgcumbe offers the opportunity to experience life as a Victorian, including trying on costumes.

* Landscaped gardens of Mount Edgcumbe
* Ferry cruise on River Tamar

Location
Take Torpoint ferry or Cremyll foot ferry from Plymouth, then A374 & B3247

Opening
House Apr–Sep Sun–Thu 11am–4.30pm; *Park* All year daily

Admission
House & Earl's Garden Adult £4.50, Child £2.25, Concs £3.50
Combined ticket Adult £7, Child £4.50

Contact
Cremyll, Torpoint PL10 1HZ

t 01752 822236
w mountedgcumbe.gov.uk
e mt.edgcumbe@plymouth.gov.uk

---

175 Truro

Royal Cornwall Museum

2 hrs   All year

See a myriad of minerals, view our naked mummy, and discover Cornwall's unique culture. Admire the collection of Newlyn School paintings in the decorative arts gallery. The museum presents a range of changing exhibitions from textiles to contemporary art.

* Diverse range of children's activities

Location
In town centre

Opening
Mon–Sat 10am–5pm (last admission 4.30pm) (closed Sun & Bank Hols)

Admission
Free

Contact
River Street, Truro TR1 2SJ

t 01872 272205
w royalcornwallmuseum.org.uk
e enquiries@royalcornwallmuseum.org.uk

176 Barnstaple

Arlington Court

3 hrs+   Easter–Oct

The Victorian home of Miss Rosalie Chichester, Arlington Court is full of fascinating artefacts that she collected. In the basement, from May to September, visitors can follow the activities of Devon's largest colony of lesser horseshoe bats.

* 'Batcam' films bat colony from May to Sep
* Carriage rides around the grounds

Location
Follow signs off A39, 8 miles N of Barnstaple

Opening
House Easter–Oct Sun–Fri 11am–5pm
Gardens Jul–Aug daily 10.30am–5.30pm

Admission
House & Gardens Adult £7, Child £3.50
Gardens & Parkland £5, £2.50

Contact
Arlington, Barnstaple EX31 4LP
t 01271 850296
w nationaltrust.org.uk
e arlingtoncourt@nationaltrust.org.uk

© NTPL/Nadia Mackenzie

177 Barnstaple

Barnstaple Heritage Centre

1 hr+   All year

More than 1,000 years of Barnstaple's history is on show here, with hands-on visual and audio displays and life-size models and reconstructions.

* Exhibition has been refurbished and improved

Location
In town centre, on quayside

Opening
Apr–Oct Mon–Sat 10am–5pm;
Nov–Mar Mon–Fri 10am–4.30pm,
Sat 10am–3.30pm

Admission
Adult £3.50, Child £2, Concs £2.50,
Family £10

Contact
Queen Anne's Walk, The Strand, Barnstaple EX31 1EU
t 01271 373003
w devonmuseums.net/barnstable heritage
e dteague.barumheritage@ btconnect.com

178 Beer

Beer Quarry Caves

1 hr+   Easter–Oct

Take an eerie tour of this vast underground quarry with a long and eventful history, from the Romans to the Victorians. Beer Quarry stone was used in 24 cathedrals, plus Hampton Court, Windsor Castle and the Tower of London.

* Used for secret Roman Catholic worship in the past
* A hiding place for contraband

Location
Take B3174 to Beer & follow brown tourist signs from there

Opening
Daily: Mon before Easter–30 Sep 10am–5pm; Oct 11am–4pm

Admission
Adult £5.50, Child & Concs £3.95, Family £16.50

Contact
Quarry Lane, Beer, Seaton EX12 3AS
t 01297 625830
w beerquarrycaves.fsnet.co.uk
e john@beerquarrycaves.fsnet.co.uk

179 Bideford

Lundy Island

4 hrs+   All year

Spend a day walking on this beautiful island, 3 miles
long and only 24 miles out into the Bristol Channel.
It has a lighthouse and castle and is ideal for bird-
watching. It is a great place to take children, not least
because there are no roads or cars.

* Lots of wildlife can be seen on the island

Location	Admission
Take A361 to Ilfracombe & A386 to Bideford for MS *Oldenburg* to Lundy Island	Adult £29, Child £14, Concs £26, Family £67 (included in MS *Oldenburg* fare)
Opening	**Contact**
Please phone for details	Bideford EX39 2LY
	t 01271 863636
	w lundyisland.co.uk
	e info@lundyisland.co.uk

180 Bideford

The Milky Way Adventure Park

4 hrs   All year

Set in 18 acres of landscaped grounds, this is an
all-weather attraction with rides and slides for
all age groups. The North Devon Bird of Prey Centre
is also located here.

* Clone Zone Alien Encounter
* Dodgems

Location	Admission
On A39 Bideford–Bude road, 2 miles from Clovelly	Adult £8, Child £8, Concs £6, Family £26.50
Opening	**Contact**
Daily: Apr–Nov 10.30am–6pm; Nov–Mar Sat–Sun & school hols 11am–5pm	Downland Farm, Clovelly, Bideford EX39 5RY
	t 01237 431255
	w themilkyway.co.uk
	e info@themilkyway.co.uk

181 Bovey Tracey

Wonderland & The Cardew Tea Pottery

2 hrs   All year

This venue includes 10 acres of woodland filled with
activities, plus the Tea Pottery, where visitors can
paint their own pottery to take home. There is also
the Cheshire Cat's aerial walkway, duck-feeding, an
adventure play area and a tour of a working pottery.

* Sit at a potter's wheel & have a go!

Location	Contact
On A382 Bovey Tracey–Newton Abbot road, just off A38	Newton Road, Bovey Tracey TQ13 9DX
Opening	t 01626 832172 ext 235
Daily: 10am–5.30pm	e enquires@craftsatcardew.co.uk
Admission	
Free	

182 Brixham

The Golden Hind

1 hr   Mar–Oct

This full-size replica of Sir Francis Drake's original Tudor galleon offers a unique insight into life aboard a C16 sailing ship. Explore the cramped decks and learn about all aspects of a sailor's life from his food and health to pay and punishment.

* Re-enactments & special exhibitions
* Tours for groups & schools

Location	Contact
Follow A3022 to town centre. Ship moored in harbour	Brixham Harbour, Brixham TQ5 8AW
	t 01803 856223
Opening	w goldenhind.co.uk
Daily: Mar–Jun & Sep–Oct	e info@goldenhinde.co.uk
9.30am–4pm; Jul–Aug 9am–8pm	
Admission	
Adult £3, Child & Concs £2	

183 Buckfastleigh

Buckfast Butterfly Farm & Dartmoor Otter Sanctuary

2 hrs   Easter–Oct

Walk among some of the most beautiful butterflies in the world, flying free in a tropical garden with waterfalls, ponds and bridges. At the otter sanctuary visitors can see the playful otters from above and below the water, and at feeding time.

* Butterfly habitat constructed to maximise viewing
* British, Asian & North American otters on show

Location	Contact
Follow signs from A38 at A384 to Buckfastleigh	Buckfastleigh TQ11 0DZ
	t 01364 642916
Opening	w ottersandbutterflies.co.uk
Easter–Oct 10am–5.30pm	e contact@ottersandbutterflies.co.uk
Admission	
Adult £6.25, Child £4.75, Concs £5.75	

184 Buckfastleigh

Pennywell Farm & Wildlife Centre

5 hrs+   Feb–Oct

With a different hands-on activity, show or display every 30 minutes, children won't get bored at this fun farm. From feeding the animals to egg-collecting, this is also a great educational experience. Ride on our miniature railway and quad bikes.

* Visitor Attraction of the Year 2004
* Pony & donkey rides & go-karts

Location	Contact
Head for Buckfastleigh on A38 between Plymouth & Exeter	Buckfastleigh TQ11 0LT
	t 01364 642023
Opening	w pennywellfarmcentre.co.uk
Daily: Feb half-term–Oct 10am–5pm	e info@pennywellfarmcentre.co.uk
Admission	
Adult £8.95, Child £6.95, Concs £7.95, Family £29.95	

185 Buckfastleigh

South Devon Railway

4 hrs   Apr–Oct

All aboard for a traditional steam-train journey through a beautiful stretch of Devon countryside. There is a free vintage bus service around town on many days.

* Play area
* Small museum

Location	Contact
Between Exeter & Plymouth on A38 Expressway	The Station, Buckfastleigh TQ11 0DZ
	t 0845 345 1420
Opening	w southdevonrailway.org
Daily: Apr–Oct 10am–5pm	e info@southdevonrailway.org
Admission	
Adult £8.80 return ticket, Child £5.30 return ticket, Family £25.40	

186 Budleigh Salterton

Bicton Park Botanical Gardens

3 hrs+   All year

Gardeners, young or old, will be absorbed by this historic garden with its C19 palm house, glasshouses and Italian garden. There are also indoor and outdoor play areas and train rides on offer.

* Exhibition of traction engines & vintage machinery
* Children's play area & narrow-gauge railway

Location
Off M5 at junction 30. Follow signs via Newton Poppleford

Opening
Daily: *summer* 10am–6pm
winter 10am–5pm

Admission
Adult £5.95, Child & Concs £4.95

Contact
East Budleigh,
Budleigh Salterton EX9 7BJ

t 01395 568465
w bictongardens.co.uk
e info@bictongardens.co.uk

187 Cullompton

Diggerland

4 hrs   Feb–Nov

Based on the world of construction machinery, this is a unique adventure park where children and adults can experience the thrill of riding and driving real diggers and dumpers in safety.

Location
Exit M5 (junction 27), head E on A38, turn right at roundabout on to B3181 & park is 3 miles on the left

Opening
Feb–Nov Sat–Sun, Bank Hols & school hols 10am–5pm

Admission
All-inclusive (rides & entry) £12.50

Contact
Verbeer Manor,
Cullompton EX15 2PE

t 08700 344437
w diggerland.com
e mail@diggerland.com

188 Dartmouth

Blackpool Sands

1 hr+   Apr–Oct

Blackpool Sands is an award-winning beach in an unspoilt sheltered bay among evergreens and pines. There is also a watersports centre for kayaking, surfing, snorkelling and more.

* Quality Assured Visitor Attraction
* Dogs allowed Nov–Mar only

Location
On A379, 3 miles from Dartmouth

Opening
Daily: Apr–Oct 9am–7pm

Admission
Free
Car park charges apply Apr–Oct £2–£5

Contact
Blackpool, Dartmouth TQ6 0RG

t 01803 770606
w blackpoolsands.co.uk
e info@blackpoolsands.co.uk

189 Exeter

Crealy Adventure Park

4 hrs+   All year

Visit Crealy for maximum fun in each of its exciting activity realms. Meet Devon's friendliest pets in the Animal Realm, try out the Dino Blasters and techno race-karts in the Action Realm, experience the rides in the Adventure Realm and much more.

* Explore the Natural, Farming & Magical Realms
* Special events throughout the year

Location
Take junction 30 of M5 on to
A3052. Follow signs to Crealy

Opening
Daily: *summer* 10am–6pm
winter (dates limited) 10am–5pm

Admission
Please phone for details

Contact
Clyst St Mary, Sidmouth Road,
Exeter EX5 1DR

t 0870 1163333
w crealy.co.uk
e fun@crealy.co.uk

190 Exeter

Killerton House

2 hrs+   Mar–Oct

Built in the C18, Killerton House offers a display of costumes and has period room sets, a laundry, stable yard and chapel. It is set in delightful gardens and parkland, filled with many exotic plants and trees. Children can find the ice house and rustic Bear's Hut.

* Discovery centre
* Family events & extensive woodland walk

Location
6 miles from Exeter off B3181

Opening
Mid-Mar–Jul & Sep Wed–Mon
11am–5pm; Aug daily 11am–5pm;
Oct Wed–Sun 11am–5pm

Admission
House & Gardens
Adult £7.30, Child £3.50

Contact
Broadclyst, Exeter EX5 3LE

t 01392 881345
w nationaltrust.org.uk

191 Exmouth

Exmouth Model Railway

1 hr   Apr–Sep

With more than 7,500ft of track, this is one of the world's largest scenic 00-gauge model railways. It runs through villages and towns, all exquisitely modelled in great detail. A must for all model railway buffs.

* Model railway accessories for sale

Location
On Exmouth seafront, via A376

Opening
Daily: Easter–Sep 10am–5pm

Admission
Adult £2.25, Child £1.25, Concs £1.75

Contact
Seafront, Exmouth EX8 2AY

t 01395 278383

192 Exmouth

Stuart Line Cruises & Boat Trips

1 hr+   All year

Go on a pleasureboat cruise along the beautiful River Exe or a sea trip along the South Devon coast (known for the fossils exposed in its rocks and now an official World Heritage Site). There are also day trips to Torquay, Brixham and Sidmouth.

* Guided tours for individuals
* Mackerel & deep-sea fishing trips

Location
Exmouth Marina on seafront

Opening
Daily: Please phone for details

Admission
Adult from £4.50, Child from £2.50
Fares depend on trip

Contact
Exmouth Marina, Exmouth Docks, Exmouth EX8 1DU

t 01395 279693/222144
w stuartlinecruises.co.uk
e info@stuartlinecruises.co.uk

193 Newton Abbot

House of Marbles

1 hr   All year

A working glass-blowing factory that also has a museum of glass artefacts, including toys and marbles. We probably have the largest marble runs in the world! Visitors can watch glass-blowing when this centuries-old work is in progress.

Location
On A382 from Newton Abbot to Bovey Tracey & A38 from Exeter

Opening
Daily: Mon–Sat 9am–5pm,
Sun 11am–5pm

Admission
Free

Contact
The Old Pottery, Pottery Road,
Bovey Tracey, Newton Abbot TQ13 9DS

t 01626 835285
w houseofmarbles.com
e uk@houseofmarbles.com

194 Newton Abbott

Tuckers Maltings

2 hrs+   Easter–Oct

Take a guided tour of England's only working malt house open to the public and watch Victorian machinery producing malt from barley. Visitors of all ages can see, touch, smell and taste, while video and audio guides explain Tuckers Maltings in an educational but fun way.

* Guided tours last 1 hour
* Video & hands-on discovery centre

Location
3 min walk from Newton Abbot railway station

Opening
Easter–Oct 10am–5pm, closed Sun
Please phone for tour times

Admission
Adult £5.75, Child £3.45, Concs £4.95

Contact
Teign Road,
Newton Abbott TQ12 4AA

t 01626 334734
w tuckersmaltings.com
e info@tuckersmaltings.com

195 Paignton

Paignton & Dartmouth Steam Railway

2 hrs+   Apr–Oct

Travel Torbay's spectacular coast and the beautiful River Dart by steam train from Paignton to Kingswear. The trip can be combined with river excursions to picturesque Dartmouth.

* Thomas the Tank Engine weekend
* Santa Specials in December

Location
Follow brown tourist signs to centre of Paignton. Situated next to mainline trains

Opening
Jun–Sep daily; Apr, May & Oct open on selected dates
Please phone for details

Admission
Please phone for details

Contact
Queens Park Station, Torbay Road, Paignton TQ4 6AF

t 01803 555872
w paignton-steamrailway.co.uk

196 Paignton

Paignton Zoo Environmental Park

3 hrs+   All year

Home to some of the world's most endangered plants and animals, the zoo has hundreds of different animals and birds, including tigers, rhinos and giant tortoises. They are grouped into different climate zones that reflect the world's major habitats.

* 1,500 different plants from around the world
* Starred in the BBC programme *Zoo Keepers*

Location
On A3022 Totnes Road, 1 mile from Paignton town centre

Opening
summer 10am–6pm
winter 10am–dusk

Admission
Please phone for details

Contact
Totnes Road, Paignton TQ4 7EU

t 01803 697500
w paigntonzoo.org.uk
e info@paigntonzoo.org.uk

197 Plymouth

Crownhill Fort

2 hrs   Apr–Oct

At the largest of Plymouth's great Victorian forts, visitors can discover the underground tunnels, explore the ramparts, marvel at Victorian architecture and view the historic guns, including the 'disappearing' Moncrieff.

* Special bookings available for schools & conferences
* Also available for children's parties

Location	Contact
Just off A386 Plymouth–Tavistock road	Crownhill Fort Road, Plymouth PL6 5BX
Opening	
Daily: Apr–Oct 10am–5pm	t 01752 793754
Open all year to prebooked groups	w crownhillfort.co.uk
	e info@crownhillfort.co.uk
Admission	
Adult £5, Child £3, Concs £4	

198 Plymouth

The National Marine Aquarium

1 hr   All year

Explore the world's oceans from the shallows to the deep in a series of fascinating galleries. Get a cinema screen-sized window on an Atlantic reef, see circling sharks and morays in Europe's deepest tank and gaze at the beautiful colours of a coral reef.

* 'Meet the expert' sessions in the Discovery Theatre
* Café with panoramic views of the harbour

Location	Admission
Take A38 to Marsh Mills then along A374 Embankment Road. Follow brown & white fish signs	Adult £9.50, Child £5.75, Concs £8
	Contact
Opening	Rope Walk, Coxside, Plymouth PL4 0LF
Daily: Nov–Mar 10am–5pm; Apr–Oct 10am–6pm	t 01752 600 301
	w national-aquarium.co.uk

199 Plymouth

Sound Cruising

1 hr+   Feb–Nov

Sound Cruising offers daily cruises around Plymouth's naval harbour, as well as regular cruises to Calstock on the River Tamar.

Location	Contact
Follow signs to Plymouth city centre, via Plymouth Hoe, then through Barbican to Phoenix Wharf	Phoenix Wharf, Barbican, Plymouth PL1 1NZ
	t 01752 671166
Opening	w soundcruising.com
Daily: Feb–Nov 10am–3pm	e soundcruising@btinternet.com
Admission	
Please phone for details	

200   Seaton

Pecorama Pleasure Gardens & Exhibition

3 hrs   All year

On a visit to these pleasure gardens, visitors can enjoy a gentle stroll around the Peco Millennium Celebration Garden, which has five linked and themed gardens, and a 1-mile miniature steam locomotive journey on the Beer Heights Light Railway.

* Daily children's entertainment
* Children's activity areas & crazy golf

Location
Follow A3052 W from Lyme Regis or E from Exeter then B3174 to Beer

Opening
Model exhibition & Shop All year daily
Outdoor facilities Easter–Oct Mon–Fri 10am–5.30pm, Sat 10am–1pm

Admission
Please phone for details

Contact
Underleys, Beer, Seaton EX12 3NA

t 01297 21542
w peco-uk.com
e pecorama@btconnect.com

---

201   Seaton

Seaton Tramway

2 hrs   Feb–Nov

Take a leisurely journey through the glorious Axe Valley in a unique narrow-gauge tramcar. Enjoy panoramic views of the estuary's wading birds and the beautiful countryside from an open-topper. In poorer weather, take shelter in the elegant, enclosed saloon cars.

* Small Visitor Attraction of the Year
* Quality Assured Visitor Attraction

Location
Follow brown tourist signs on A3052 Exeter–Lyme Regis road, or A358 from Taunton, Chard & Axminster

Opening
1 Apr–5 Nov daily;
11 Nov–24 Dec Sat–Sun only

Admission
Adult £6.95, Child £4.85, Concs £6.25, Family £14.10

Contact
Harbour Road, Seaton EX12 2NQ

t 01297 20375
w tram.co.uk
e info@tram.co.uk

202 Sidmouth

The Donkey Sanctuary

2 hrs   All year

This famous donkey sanctuary is home to more than 400 rescued donkeys. There are five walks to choose from, winding through beautiful surroundings. Meet the donkeys in the main yard or ramble down to the sea visiting our nature centre along the way.

• Donkey quiz for children

Location
On A3052 just outside Sidford, towards Lyme Regis. Follow brown tourist signs

Opening
Daily: 9am–dusk

Admission
Free

Contact
Sidmouth EX10 0NU

t 01395 578222
w thedonkeysanctuary.org.uk
e enquiries@thedonkeysanctuary.com

203 Sidmouth

Norman Lockyer Observatory & James Lockyer Planetarium

2 hrs   All year

The solar system, space travel, communications and the weather are all explained and explored in fascinating exhibitions, models and hands-on activities. Visitors can talk to people all over the world in the radio room.

* Exhibition hall with models of the solar system
* Satellite station producing weather pictures

Location
Take A3052 Exeter–Seaton road, turn right after Sidford & follow signs

Opening
Please phone for details

Admission
Adult £4, Child £2

Contact
Salcombe Hill Road, Sidmouth EX10 0NY

t 01395 579941
w ex.ac.uk/nlo/
e g.e.white@exeter.ac.uk

204 Tavistock

Morwellham Quay

4 hrs+   All year

Despite being 23 miles from the sea, Morwellham Quay was the Empire's greatest copper port in the time of Queen Victoria. Today the 1860s are recreated with a Tamar ketch moored at the quay, shops, cottages and costumed staff to act as guides.

* Take a tram underground through a copper mine
* Explore the farm, wildlife reserve & parkland

  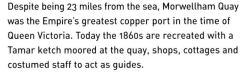

Location
4 miles from Tavistock on River Tamar

Opening
Daily: Easter–Oct 10am–5.30pm; Nov–Easter 10am–4.30pm

Admission
Adult £8.90, Child £6, Concs £7.80
Reduced prices in winter

Contact
Morwellham, Tavistock PL19 8JL

t 01822 832766
w morwellham-quay.co.uk
e enquiries@morwellham-quay.co.uk

205 Teignmouth

Grand Pier

1 hr+   All year

Have a few hours of simple fun on this traditional pier, with many family amusements and games, including the thrills and spills of a rollercoaster.

* Mini-railway
* Pirate ship

Location
Via A379

Opening
Daily: Easter–Sep 10am–9pm; Nov–Mar 11am–5pm

Admission
Free. Charges for individual attractions

Contact
The Seafront, Teignmouth TQ14 8BB

t 01626 774367

206 Tiverton

Knightshayes Court

3 hrs   Mar–Oct

This lavish house was built around 1870 by William Burges. Its much-admired garden features a waterlily pond, topiary and a newly restored walled garden.

* National Trust property
* Woodland walks & children's quizzes

Location
2 miles N of Tiverton, turn off A396 (Bampton Road) at Bolham

Opening
House Mar–Oct Sat–Thu 11am–5pm (closes 4pm in Oct)
Gardens Mar Sat–Sun 11am–4pm; mid-Mar–Oct daily 11am–5pm

Admission
Please phone for details

Contact
Bolham, Tiverton EX16 7RQ
t 01884 254665
w nationaltrust.org.uk

207 Tiverton

Tiverton Museum of Mid Devon Life

2 hrs   Feb–Dec

This is a comprehensive regional museum that has a Heathcote lace machine gallery. Also on show are agricultural and domestic implements and a collection of Devon farm wagons.

* Transport gallery reopened; includes Tivvy Bumper steam engine

Location
Via A396, A373 or A361

Opening
Feb–Dec Mon–Fri 10.30am–4.30pm, Sat 10am–1pm; closed 22 Dec–end Jan

Admission
Adult £4, Child £1, Concs £3

Contact
Beck's Square, Tiverton EX16 6PJ
t 01884 256295
w tivertonmuseum.org.uk
e curator04@tivertonmuseum.org.uk

208 Torquay

Babbacombe Model Village

2 hrs   All year

There are hundreds of 1:12 scale models set in award-winning gardens at this model village. Marvel at villages, farms and rural areas, beautiful lakes and waterfalls, railways and details of everyday life.

* Illuminations show in summer
* Summer evening opening

Location
Take A380 to Torquay, then follow brown tourist signs

Opening
Daily: From 10am. Also open summer evenings, please phone for details

Admission
Adult £6.90, Child £4.50, Cons £5.90, Family £21

Contact
Hampton Avenue, Babbacombe, Torquay TQ1 3LA
t 01803 315315
w modelvillage.co.uk
e sw@modelvillage.co.uk

202 Sidmouth

The Donkey Sanctuary

2 hrs   All year

This famous donkey sanctuary is home to more than 400 rescued donkeys. There are five walks to choose from, winding through beautiful surroundings. Meet the donkeys in the main yard or ramble down to the sea visiting our nature centre along the way.

• Donkey quiz for children

Location
On A3052 just outside Sidford, towards Lyme Regis. Follow brown tourist signs

Opening
Daily: 9am–dusk

Admission
Free

Contact
Sidmouth EX10 0NU

t 01395 578222
w thedonkeysanctuary.org.uk
e enquiries@thedonkeysanctuary.com

203 Sidmouth

Norman Lockyer Observatory & James Lockyer Planetarium

2 hrs   All year

The solar system, space travel, communications and the weather are all explained and explored in fascinating exhibitions, models and hands-on activities. Visitors can talk to people all over the world in the radio room.

* Exhibition hall with models of the solar system
* Satellite station producing weather pictures

Location
Take A3052 Exeter–Seaton road, turn right after Sidford & follow signs

Opening
Please phone for details

Admission
Adult £4, Child £2

Contact
Salcombe Hill Road, Sidmouth EX10 0NY

t 01395 579941
w ex.ac.uk/nlo/
e g.e.white@exeter.ac.uk

204 Tavistock

Morwellham Quay

4 hrs+   All year

Despite being 23 miles from the sea, Morwellham Quay was the Empire's greatest copper port in the time of Queen Victoria. Today the 1860s are recreated with a Tamar ketch moored at the quay, shops, cottages and costumed staff to act as guides.

* Take a tram underground through a copper mine
* Explore the farm, wildlife reserve & parkland

Location
4 miles from Tavistock on River Tamar

Opening
Daily: Easter–Oct 10am–5.30pm;
Nov–Easter 10am–4.30pm

Admission
Adult £8.90, Child £6, Concs £7.80
Reduced prices in winter

Contact
Morwellham, Tavistock PL19 8JL

t 01822 832766
w morwellham-quay.co.uk
e enquiries@morwellham-quay.co.uk

205 Teignmouth

Grand Pier

1 hr+   All year

Have a few hours of simple fun on this traditional pier, with many family amusements and games, including the thrills and spills of a rollercoaster.

* Mini-railway
* Pirate ship

Location
Via A379

Opening
Daily: Easter–Sep 10am–9pm;
Nov–Mar 11am–5pm

Admission
Free. Charges for individual attractions

Contact
The Seafront, Teignmouth TQ14 8BB

t 01626 774367

206 Tiverton

Knightshayes Court

3 hrs   Mar–Oct

This lavish house was built around 1870 by William Burges. Its much-admired garden features a waterlily pond, topiary and a newly restored walled garden.

* National Trust property
* Woodland walks & children's quizzes

Location
2 miles N of Tiverton, turn off A396 (Bampton Road) at Bolham

Opening
House Mar–Oct Sat–Thu 11am–5pm (closes 4pm in Oct)
Gardens Mar Sat–Sun 11am–4pm; mid-Mar–Oct daily 11am–5pm

Admission
Please phone for details

Contact
Bolham, Tiverton EX16 7RQ
t 01884 254665
w nationaltrust.org.uk

207 Tiverton

Tiverton Museum of Mid Devon Life

2 hrs   Feb–Dec

This is a comprehensive regional museum that has a Heathcote lace machine gallery. Also on show are agricultural and domestic implements and a collection of Devon farm wagons.

* Transport gallery reopened; includes Tivvy Bumper steam engine

Location
Via A396, A373 or A361

Opening
Feb–Dec Mon–Fri 10.30am–4.30pm, Sat 10am–1pm; closed 22 Dec–end Jan

Admission
Adult £4, Child £1, Concs £3

Contact
Beck's Square, Tiverton EX16 6PJ
t 01884 256295
w tivertonmuseum.org.uk
e curator04@tivertonmuseum.org.uk

208 Torquay

Babbacombe Model Village

2 hrs   All year

There are hundreds of 1:12 scale models set in award-winning gardens at this model village. Marvel at villages, farms and rural areas, beautiful lakes and waterfalls, railways and details of everyday life.

* Illuminations show in summer
* Summer evening opening

Location
Take A380 to Torquay, then follow brown tourist signs

Opening
Daily: From 10am. Also open summer evenings, please phone for details

Admission
Adult £6.90, Child £4.50, Cons £5.90, Family £21

Contact
Hampton Avenue, Babbacombe, Torquay TQ1 3LA
t 01803 315315
w modelvillage.co.uk
e sw@modelvillage.co.uk

202 Sidmouth

The Donkey Sanctuary

2 hrs   All year

This famous donkey sanctuary is home to more than 400 rescued donkeys. There are five walks to choose from, winding through beautiful surroundings. Meet the donkeys in the main yard or ramble down to the sea visiting our nature centre along the way.

• Donkey quiz for children

Location
On A3052 just outside Sidford, towards Lyme Regis. Follow brown tourist signs

Opening
Daily: 9am–dusk

Admission
Free

Contact
Sidmouth EX10 0NU

t 01395 578222
w thedonkeysanctuary.org.uk
e enquiries@thedonkeysanctuary.com

203 Sidmouth

Norman Lockyer Observatory & James Lockyer Planetarium

2 hrs   All year

The solar system, space travel, communications and the weather are all explained and explored in fascinating exhibitions, models and hands-on activities. Visitors can talk to people all over the world in the radio room.

* Exhibition hall with models of the solar system
* Satellite station producing weather pictures

Location
Take A3052 Exeter–Seaton road, turn right after Sidford & follow signs

Opening
Please phone for details

Admission
Adult £4, Child £2

Contact
Salcombe Hill Road, Sidmouth EX10 0NY

t 01395 579941
w ex.ac.uk/nlo/
e g.e.white@exeter.ac.uk

204 Tavistock

Morwellham Quay

4 hrs+   All year

Despite being 23 miles from the sea, Morwellham Quay was the Empire's greatest copper port in the time of Queen Victoria. Today the 1860s are recreated with a Tamar ketch moored at the quay, shops, cottages and costumed staff to act as guides.

* Take a tram underground through a copper mine
* Explore the farm, wildlife reserve & parkland

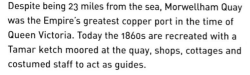

Location
4 miles from Tavistock on River Tamar

Opening
Daily: Easter–Oct 10am–5.30pm; Nov–Easter 10am–4.30pm

Admission
Adult £8.90, Child £6, Concs £7.80
Reduced prices in winter

Contact
Morwellham, Tavistock PL19 8JL

t 01822 832766
w morwellham-quay.co.uk
e enquiries@morwellham-quay.co.uk

205 Teignmouth

Grand Pier

1 hr+   All year

Have a few hours of simple fun on this traditional pier, with many family amusements and games, including the thrills and spills of a rollercoaster.

* Mini-railway
* Pirate ship

Location
Via A379

Opening
Daily: Easter–Sep 10am–9pm; Nov–Mar 11am–5pm

Admission
Free. Charges for individual attractions

Contact
The Seafront, Teignmouth TQ14 8BB

t 01626 774367

206 Tiverton

Knightshayes Court

3 hrs   Mar–Oct

This lavish house was built around 1870 by William Burges. Its much-admired garden features a waterlily pond, topiary and a newly restored walled garden.

* National Trust property
* Woodland walks & children's quizzes

Location
2 miles N of Tiverton, turn off A396 (Bampton Road) at Bolham

Opening
House Mar–Oct Sat–Thu 11am–5pm (closes 4pm in Oct)
Gardens Mar Sat–Sun 11am–4pm; mid-Mar–Oct daily 11am–5pm

Admission
Please phone for details

Contact
Bolham, Tiverton EX16 7RQ
t 01884 254665
w nationaltrust.org.uk

207 Tiverton

Tiverton Museum of Mid Devon Life

2 hrs   Feb–Dec

This is a comprehensive regional museum that has a Heathcote lace machine gallery. Also on show are agricultural and domestic implements and a collection of Devon farm wagons.

* Transport gallery reopened; includes Tivvy Bumper steam engine

Location
Via A396, A373 or A361

Opening
Feb–Dec Mon–Fri 10.30am–4.30pm, Sat 10am–1pm; closed 22 Dec–end Jan

Admission
Adult £4, Child £1, Concs £3

Contact
Beck's Square, Tiverton EX16 6PJ
t 01884 256295
w tivertonmuseum.org.uk
e curator04@tivertonmuseum.org.uk

208 Torquay

Babbacombe Model Village

2 hrs   All year

There are hundreds of 1:12 scale models set in award-winning gardens at this model village. Marvel at villages, farms and rural areas, beautiful lakes and waterfalls, railways and details of everyday life.

* Illuminations show in summer
* Summer evening opening

Location
Take A380 to Torquay, then follow brown tourist signs

Opening
Daily: From 10am. Also open summer evenings, please phone for details

Admission
Adult £6.90, Child £4.50, Cons £5.90, Family £21

Contact
Hampton Avenue, Babbacombe, Torquay TQ1 3LA
t 01803 315315
w modelvillage.co.uk
e sw@modelvillage.co.uk

209 Torquay

Bygones

2 hrs+   All year

Bygones has a life-size Victorian street with period rooms. Children will enjoy the large Hornby railway layouts, medals and militaria and the illuminated 'fantasyland'.

* Housed in a former cinema
* Christmas winter wonderland in a Victorian setting

Location
Well signed from Torquay harbour

Opening
Daily: Apr–Jun & Sep 10am–6pm;
Nov–Mar 10am–5pm;
Jul–Aug Wed–Thu 10am–9.30pm,
Fri–Tue 10am–6pm

Admission
Adult £5.50, Child £3.50, Concs £4.95

Contact
Fore Street, St Mary Church,
Torquay TQ1 4PR

t 01803 326108
w bygones.co.uk

210 Torquay

Living Coasts

2 hrs+   All year

A unique aquatic visitor attraction, focusing on the conservation of coastal and marine life around the globe. The spacious interior of the meshed aviary allows free flight for the birds and access for visitors, enabling an intimacy unusual in seabird exhibits in this country.

* Adopt an animal & underwater viewing
* Special events throughout the year

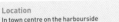

Location
In town centre on the harbourside

Opening
Mar–Sep 10am–6pm;
Oct–Feb 10am–5pm

Admission
Adult £6.75, Child £4.70, Concs £5.25

Contact
Torquay Harbourside, Beacon Quay,
Torquay TQ1 2BG

t 01803 202470
w livingcoasts.org.uk
e info@livingcoasts.org.uk

211 Torquay

The Riviera International Centre & Waves Leisure Pool

   2 hrs **All year**

There is something for children of all ages at this leisure complex. It has a health and fitness centre, a choice of leisure pools, restaurants and cafés.

* Children's water spray area
* Leisure pool, flume & wave machine

Location	Contact
2 min walk from Torquay seafront	Chestnut Avenue, Torquay TQ2 5LZ
Opening	
Please phone for details	t 01803 299992
	w rivieracentre.co.uk
Admission	e enquiries@rivieracentre.co.uk
Family swim £11.25	
Please phone for details	

212 Totnes

Totnes Elizabethan House Museum

   1 hr **Mar–Oct**

This Elizabethan house, built in 1575, features an Elizabethan herb garden, a Tudor bedroom, a kitchen and a Victorian nursery. It displays more than 5,000 years of local history, and there is a special exhibition about Charles Babbage, father of the modern computer.

Location	Contact
On main street in front of East Gate Arch in Totnes	70 Fore Street, Totnes TQ9 5RU
	t 01803 863821
Opening	w devonmuseums.net/totnes
Mid-Mar–Oct Mon–Fri 10.30am–5pm (last admission 4.30pm)	e totnesmuseum@btconnect.com
Admission	
Adult £1.50, Child 50p, Concs £1	

213 Totnes

Woodlands Leisure Park

   3 hrs+ **All year**

You'll be spoilt for choice here by an excellent combination of indoor and outdoor attractions for all ages. Some of the attractions include three watercoasters, a toboggan run, 15 play zones, massive indoor centres and animals.

* UK's biggest indoor venture centre
* Falconry centre with flying displays

Location	Contact
On A3122 between Totnes & Dartmouth	Blackawton, Totnes TQ9 7DQ
	t 01803 712598
Opening	w woodlandspark.com
Mar–Nov & school hols daily; Nov–Mar Sat–Sun	e fun@woodlandspark.com
Admission	
Please phone for details	

209 Torquay

Bygones

2 hrs+   All year

Bygones has a life-size Victorian street with period rooms. Children will enjoy the large Hornby railway layouts, medals and militaria and the illuminated 'fantasyland'.

* Housed in a former cinema
* Christmas winter wonderland in a Victorian setting

Location	Admission
Well signed from Torquay harbour	Adult £5.50, Child £3.50, Concs £4.95
Opening	**Contact**
Daily: Apr–Jun & Sep 10am–6pm;	Fore Street, St Mary Church,
Nov–Mar 10am–5pm;	Torquay TQ1 4PR
Jul–Aug Wed–Thu 10am–9.30pm,	
Fri–Tue 10am–6pm	t 01803 326108
	w bygones.co.uk

210 Torquay

Living Coasts

2 hrs+   All year

A unique aquatic visitor attraction, focusing on the conservation of coastal and marine life around the globe. The spacious interior of the meshed aviary allows free flight for the birds and access for visitors, enabling an intimacy unusual in seabird exhibits in this country.

* Adopt an animal & underwater viewing
* Special events throughout the year

Location	Contact
In town centre on the harbourside	Torquay Harbourside, Beacon Quay,
Opening	Torquay TQ1 2BG
Mar–Sep 10am–6pm;	
Oct–Feb 10am–5pm	t 01803 202470
Admission	w livingcoasts.org.uk
Adult £6.75, Child £4.70, Concs £5.25	e info@livingcoasts.org.uk

211 Torquay

The Riviera International Centre & Waves Leisure Pool

2 hrs   All year

There is something for children of all ages at this leisure complex. It has a health and fitness centre, a choice of leisure pools, restaurants and cafés.

* Children's water spray area
* Leisure pool, flume & wave machine

Location
2 min walk from Torquay seafront

Opening
Please phone for details

Admission
Family swim £11.25
Please phone for details

Contact
Chestnut Avenue,
Torquay TQ2 5LZ

t 01803 299992
w rivieracentre.co.uk
e enquiries@rivieracentre.co.uk

212 Totnes

Totnes Elizabethan House Museum

1 hr   Mar–Oct

This Elizabethan house, built in 1575, features an Elizabethan herb garden, a Tudor bedroom, a kitchen and a Victorian nursery. It displays more than 5,000 years of local history, and there is a special exhibition about Charles Babbage, father of the modern computer.

Location
On main street in front of East Gate
Arch in Totnes

Opening
Mid-Mar–Oct Mon–Fri 10.30am–5pm
(last admission 4.30pm)

Admission
Adult £1.50, Child 50p, Concs £1

Contact
70 Fore Street, Totnes TQ9 5RU

t 01803 863821
w devonmuseums.net/totnes
e totnesmuseum@btconnect.com

213 Totnes

Woodlands Leisure Park

3 hrs+   All year

You'll be spoilt for choice here by an excellent combination of indoor and outdoor attractions for all ages. Some of the attractions include three watercoasters, a toboggan run, 15 play zones, massive indoor centres and animals.

* UK's biggest indoor venture centre
* Falconry centre with flying displays

Location
On A3122 between Totnes
& Dartmouth

Opening
Mar–Nov & school hols daily;
Nov–Mar Sat–Sun

Admission
Please phone for details

Contact
Blackawton, Totnes TQ9 7DQ

t 01803 712598
w woodlandspark.com
e fun@woodlandspark.com

214 Bournemouth

Dorset Belle Cruises

1 hr+   All year

Take a glorious coastal and harbour cruise on any number of routes linking Bournemouth, Swanage, Poole Quay and the Isle of Wight, or explore Brownsea Island. Specialist cruises are also available along this stunning coastline.

* Boats available for charter & evening cruises
* Fireworks & magnificent sunset cruises

Location
Boats depart from Bournemouth pier, Swanage or Poole

Opening
Daily: Apr–Oct, please phone for details of trips; Nov–Mar 10.30am–6pm

Admission
Adult from £7, Child from £2

Contact
Pier Approach,
Bournemouth BH2 5AA

t 01202 558550
w dorsetcruises.co.uk
e thedorsetbelle@aol.com

215 Bournemouth

Oceanarium Bournemouth

2 hrs   All year

Discover the secrets of the ocean and some of the world's most amazing waters. Come face to face with a vast array of colourful creatures – from stingrays, sharks and exotic fish to piranhas, chameleons, green turtles and tortoises.

* Gift shop
* Great café

Location
Follow signs to Bournemouth beaches & piers

Opening
Please phone for details

Admission
Adult £7.50, Child £5, Concs £6.50

Contact
Pier Approach,
Bournemouth BH2 5AA

t 01202 311993
w oceanarium.co.uk
e info@oceanarium.co.uk

216 Bovington

Tank Museum

3 hrs+   All year

The Tank Museum houses the world's finest indoor collection of armoured fighting vehicles, including a WWII tank that visitors can touch. Tanks in Action displays are held throughout the summer.

* Indoor collection of 150 vehicles from 26 countries
* Vehicle rides & live demonstrations

Location
Off A352, between Dorchester & Wareham, near Wool. Follow signs from Bere Regis

Opening
Daily: 10am–5pm

Admission
Adult £10, Child £7, Concs £9

Contact
Bovington BH20 6JG

t 01929 405096
w tankmuseum.org
e info@tankmuseum.org

217 Dorchester

The Dinosaur Museum

1 hr+   All year

The award-winning Dinosaur Museum combines fossils, skeletons and life-size dinosaur reconstructions with videos, hands-on and computer displays. This is fascinating fun for all the family.

* Winner of Dorset Family Attraction Award
* Top 10 Hands-on Museum

Location
In town centre

Opening
Daily: Easter–Oct 9.30am–5.30pm;
Nov–Mar 10am–4.30pm

Admission
Adult £6.50, Child £4.75, Concs £5.50

Contact
Icen Way, Dorchester DT1 1EW

t 01305 269880
w thedinosaurmuseum.org
e info@thedinosaurmuseum.com

218 Dorchester

Dorset County Museum

1 hr+   All year

Encounter Dorset's wildlife, geology and social history in interactive exhibitions and audio-visual displays. Galleries to visit include one devoted to Dorset writers such as Thomas Hardy, and the archaeology gallery.

* Interactive audio guide
* Film on Roman invasion of Maiden Castle

Location
In town centre; follow museum signs

Opening
Oct–Jun Mon–Sat 10am–5pm;
Jul–Sep daily 10am–5pm

Admission
Adult £6, Child free, Concs £5

Contact
High West Street,
Dorchester DT1 1XA

t 01305 262735
w dorsetcountymuseum.org
e secretary@dor-mus.demon.co.uk

219 Dorchester

The Dorset Teddy Bear Museum

1 hr — All year

This is a delightfully unusual museum where the teddy bears are life-size. See the teddy bear family at work, rest and play. A large selection of teddy bears can be bought at the period shop.

Location
In town centre

Opening
Daily: 10am–5.30pm

Admission
Adult £5.50, Child £3.75, Family £17

Contact
Eastgate, corner of High East Street & Salisbury Street,
Dorchester DT1 1JU

t 01305 266040
w teddybearhouse.co.uk
e info@teddybearhouse.co.uk

---

220 Dorchester

Kingston Maurward Gardens

2 hrs+ — All year

A formal Edwardian garden with a stunning ornamental lake in front of the C18 mansion house. The animal park has a collection of miniature Shetland ponies, as well as donkeys, rabbits and guinea pigs.

* National Collections of penstemons & salvias
* Edwardian formal & walled demonstration gardens

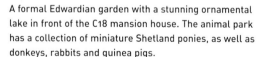

Location
1 mile E of Dorchester off A35

Opening
Daily: 5 Jan–21 Dec 10am–5.30pm or dusk if earlier

Admission
Adult £5, Child £3, Concs £4.50

Contact
Dorchester DT2 8PY

t 01305 215003
w kmc.ac.uk
e administration@kmc.ac.uk

---

221 Dorchester

The Tutankhamun Exhibition

1 hr — All year

This exhibition recreates the original Tutankhamun artefacts found when the pharaoh's tomb was reopened. The artefacts are displayed in a model of the tomb chamber as it looked in 1922 when local archaeologist Howard Carter unearthed it.

* A permanent exhibition of the World Heritage Organisation
* Death of Tutankhamun exhibition

Location
3 min walk from town centre

Opening
Daily: Easter–Oct 9.30am–5.30pm;
Nov–Easter Mon–Fri 9.30am–5pm,
Sat 10am–5pm, Sun 10am–4.30pm

Admission
Adult £6.50, Child £4.75, Concs £5.50

Contact
High West Street,
Dorchester DT1 1UW

t 01305 269571
w tutankhamun-exhibition.co.uk
e info@tutankhamun-exhibition.co.uk

222 Dorchester

Zorb South UK

1 hr   Apr–Oct

Zorbing is the latest adrenaline-surging fix of fun. Ride within the gigantic 3m high PVC ball down the 200-metre run – the world's longest. Options include tandem and triple-harnessed rides and hydro-zorbing in a water-filled zorb.

* Booking essential
* Under-6 age restriction

Location
Follow A35 NE of Dorchester & at Stinsford roundabout take road signed Bockhampton/Tincleton. Situated approximately 1 mile on the left

Opening
Please phone for details

Admission
Please phone for details

Contact
Pine Lodge Farm, Bockhampton, Dorchester DT2 8QL

t 01929 426595
w zorbsouth.co.uk
e info@zorbsouth.co.uk

223 Poole

Brownsea Island National Trust

3 hrs+   Mar–Oct

Just a short boat journey (not National Trust) from Poole or Sandbanks, the island offers spectacular views, a peaceful setting for walks and picnics, a rich variety of habitats for wildlife (including the rare red squirrel) and a varied and colourful history.

* Family events throughout the year
* Guided walk in nature reserve (summer only)

Location
By boat from Poole, Sandbanks, Bournemouth or Swanage

Opening
25 Mar–Oct from 10am (closing time varies)

Admission
Adult £4.40, Child £2.20

Contact
Poole Harbour, BH13 7EE

t 01202 707744
w nationaltrust.org.uk/brownsea
e brownseaisland@nationaltrust.org.uk

224 Poole

Farmer Palmer's Farm Park

6 hrs   Feb–Dec

A delightful farm designed for children up to eight years old, where they can enjoy lots of hands-on fun with animals and ride a tractor trailer. There is also an undercover straw mountain, bouncy castles, pedal tractors and a new indoor soft play area.

* Maize maze (in summer)
* Large play area

Location
Off A35 Poole–Dorchester road

Opening
10 Feb–30 Oct daily;
Nov–Dec Fri–Sun
Please phone for details of times

Admission
Adult £4.95, Child £4.75, Concs £4.50, Family £16

Contact
Organford, Poole BH16 6EU

t 01202 622022
w farmerpalmer.co.uk
e info@farmerpalmers.co.uk

225 Poole

Upton Country Park

  2 hrs All year

Upton House, on the edge of Poole harbour, has pretty, formal gardens that lead into woodland, meadow and a saltmarsh teeming with wildlife.

* Nature trails
* Cycling allowed on way-marked cycle route

Location
On S side of A35/A3409, 4 miles
W of Poole town centre

Opening
Daily: 9am–dusk

Admission
Free

Contact
Upton Road, Upton,
Poole BH17 7BJ

t 01202 672625

226 St Leonards

Avon Heath Country Park

  4 hrs+ All year

Enjoy a day at Dorset's largest country park, walking or cycling in the beautiful heathland and woods. Special events include pond-dipping, Easter egg trails, bug hunts, den-building, orienteering, animal tracks and signs, and dawn-chorus walks.

* Barbecue hire available
* Birthday parties & school visits

Location
On A31, 2 miles W of Ringwood

Opening
Park Daily: Apr–Sep 8am–7.30pm;
Oct–Mar 8.30am–5.30pm
Visitor centre Daily: 11am–4pm

Admission
Free. Car park fee

Contact
Brocks Pine, St Leonards,
Ringwood BH24 2DA

t 01425 478470

227 Studland

Studland Beach
& Nature Reserve

  3 hrs+ All year

There are miles of golden sands at Studland. The shallow waters are perfect for bathing, and the heathland behind the beach is a National Nature Reserve. This haven for birds and wildlife can be enjoyed from several public paths and two nature trails, plus bird hides at Little Sea.

* Guided discovery walks & storytelling (summer)
* Dogs allowed on beach Sep–Jun only

Location
Across Bournemouth & Swanage
motor road ferry or via Corfe Castle on
B3351

Opening
Daily; Please phone for details

Admission
Parking charges vary through seasons
Please phone for details

Contact
Countryside Office, Studland,
Swanage BH19 3AX

t 01929 450259
w nationaltrust.org.uk
e studlandbeach@nationaltrust.org.uk

228 Swanage

Durlston Country Park

 3 hrs+ All year

A country park with wildflower meadows, downland, cliffs, sea and a wealth of wildlife. There is also a visitor centre for local information.

* Theme trails & ranger-guided walks
* Education service

Location
Take A351 to Swanage & follow brown
tourist signs

Opening
Park Daily: dawn–dusk
Visitor centre & Café Apr–Oct daily
10am–5pm; Nov–Mar Sat–Sun &
school hols 10.30am–4pm

Admission
Free. Car park fee

Contact
Durlston, Swanage BH19 2JL

t 01929 424443
w durlston.co.uk
e info@durlston.co.uk

229 Swanage

Swanage Railway

2 hrs+   All year

Take a nostalgic steam-train journey through magnificent countryside and the village of Corfe Castle, offering good views of the historic ruins. Pass through the eastern gateway to the World Heritage Jurassic Coast.

Location
Station is in centre of Swanage, a few min walk from the beach

Opening
Trains daily Apr–Oct & 26–31 Dec; Sat–Sun only rest of the year

Admission
Adult £7.50, Child & Concs £5.50

Contact
Station House, Swanage BH19 1HB

t 01929 425800
w swanagerailway.co.uk
e general@swanrail.freeserve.co.uk

230 Wareham

Corfe Castle

1 hr+   All year

Explore this ruined castle with a long and fascinating history as a fortress, prison and home. The Castle View Visitor Centre has hands-on displays and children are encouraged to touch castle artefacts and try on replica medieval clothing.

* Special events including historical re-enactments
* Guided tours available

Location
On A351 Wareham–Swanage road

Opening
Daily: Mar & Oct 10am–5pm; Apr–Sep 10am–6pm; Nov–Feb 10am–4pm

Admission
Adult £5, Child £2.50

Contact
The National Trust, The Square, Corfe Castle, Wareham BH20 5EZ

t 01929 481294
w nationaltrust.org.uk
e corfecastle@nationaltrust.org.uk

231 Wareham

Lulworth Castle

3 hrs+   All year

There's plenty to entertain children at this historic building. After viewing the house, which has lots of new exhibitions, take a woodland walk and feed the animals at a nearby farm.

* Adventure playground & indoor activity room
* In Aug jousting shows Mon–Fri

Location
3 miles SW of Wareham. Follow signs

Opening
summer Sun–Fri 10.30am–6pm
winter Sun–Fri 10.30am–4pm
(closed Sat)

Admission
Adult £7, Child £4, Concs £6

Contact
East Lulworth, Wareham BH20 5QS

t 01929 400352
w lulworth.com
e estate.office@lulworth.com

232 Wareham

Monkey World

2 hrs+   All year

At this sanctuary for more than 160 primates including chimpanzees, orang-utans and gibbons, learn how they are looked after and live in social groups. Other attractions include a bird pond, a pets' corner with donkeys, and an adventure play area.

* Largest group of chimpanzees outside Africa
* Featured in many TV programmes, including *Animal Hospital*

Location	Contact
Between Bere Regis & Wool, 1 mile from Wool railway station	Longthorns, Wareham BH20 6HH
	t 01929 462537
Opening	w monkeyworld.org
Daily: 10am–5pm (6pm in Jul–Aug)	e apes@monkeyworld.org
Admission	
Adult £9, Child & Concs £6.50	

233 Weymouth

Abbotsbury Swannery

2 hrs   Mar–Oct

Visitors can walk among the only colony of free-flying mute swans in the world that can be visited. During the hatching period (mid-May to end June), you can watch the eggs hatch.

* Feeding of up to 1,000 swans daily at 12noon & 4pm
* Children's play area & bail maze

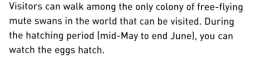

Location	Admission
On B3157 between Bridport and Weymouth	Adult £7.50, Child £4.50, Concs £7
	Car park free
Opening	**Contact**
Daily: mid-Mar–29 Oct 10am–6pm;	New Barn Road, Abbotsbury,
11 Sep–29 Oct 10am–6pm	Weymouth DT3 4JG
(last admission 1 hr before close)	t 01305 871858
	w abbotsbury-tourism.co.uk
	e info@abbotsbury-tourism.co.uk

234 Weymouth

Brewers Quay

3 hrs+   All year

Visit this redeveloped Victorian brewery in the Old Harbour to enjoy the shops and café, and to see an award-winning exhibition that takes you on a voyage with Miss Paws, the brewery cat, through 19 life-size scenes, recreating 600 years of local history.

Location	Contact
On harbour, 5 min from town centre	Hope Square, Weymouth DT4 8TR
Opening	t 01305 777622
Daily: 10am–5.30pm	w brewers-quay.co.uk
Admission	e brewersquay@yahoo.co.uk
Free entry to complex	
Timewalk attraction Adult £4.75,	
Child £3.50, Concs £4.25	

235 Wimborne

Stapehill Abbey, Crafts & Gardens

3 hrs   All year

Award-winning gardens and woodland surround this C19 Cistercian abbey. It has a craft centre, countryside museum, Japanese garden and home farm, where a range of domestic animals can be seen at close quarters.

* Special events throughout the year including
  Steam weekend

Location
8 miles from Ringwood on A31

Opening
Apr–Sep daily 10am–5pm;
Oct–Mar Wed–Sun 10am–4pm

Admission
Adult £7.50, Child £4.50, Concs £7,
Family from £12
Please phone for winter rates

Contact
Wimborne Road West, Stapehill,
Wimborne BH21 2EB

t 01202 861686

236 Wimborne

Wimborne Model Town & Gardens

2 hrs   Mar–Oct

Set in award-winning gardens, the models are exact 1:10 scale replicas of the town of Wimborne Minster as it was in the 1950s. Children will enjoy the play houses in Wendy Street.

* Interactive model railway new in 2006
* Putting lawn

Location
Accessible via A31

Opening
Daily: 26 Mar–29 Oct 10am–5pm

Admission
Adult £3.50, Child £2.50, Concs £3

Contact
16 King Street,
Wimborne Minster BH21 1DY

t 01202 881924
w wimborne-modeltown.com
e wimbornemodeltown@hotmail.com

237 Berkeley

Berkeley Castle

4 hrs   Apr–Oct

This stunning medieval castle, stately home of the Berkeley family for 900 years, was the scene of Edward II's murder. It is filled with treasures and is set in beautiful Elizabethan terraced gardens. There is a programme of events, with lots of fun activities for children.

* Programme of events throughout the year

Location
On A38 (M5, exit 13 or 14)
W of Dursley

Opening
Apr–Oct Tue–Sat & Bank Hol Mon
11am–4pm, Sun 2pm–5pm;
Oct Sun only

Admission
Adult £7.50, Child £4.50, Concs £6

Contact
Berkeley GL13 9BQ

t 01453 810332
w berkeley-castle.com
e info@berkeley-castle.com

238 Berkeley

Cattle Country Adventure Park

3 hrs   Mar–Oct

A farm park with exotic cattle such as American bison. It also has Gloucester Old Spot pigs and a large adventure playground with big slides and an outdoor paddling pool (in summer) and miniature railway.

* Ideal for private parties

Location
On B4066, near Berkeley

Opening
School hols (except Christmas)
Daily: Mar–Oct 10am–5pm
Please phone for other opening hours

Admission
summer £6.50 *winter* £5
group discounts available

Contact
Berkeley Heath Farm, Berkeley
Heath, Berkeley GL13 9EW

t 01453 810510
w cattlecountry.co.uk
e info@cattlecountry.co.uk

239 Bourton-on-the-Water

Cotswold Motor Museum & Toy Collection

1 hr   Feb–Nov

Although the main focus here is on motoring, the museum has a toy collection that includes teddy bears, aeroplanes and rare pedal cars. It's also home to Brum, the little yellow car from the hit children's BBC TV series, which was filmed here.

* Britain's largest collection of historic motoring signs

Location
Bourton town centre at junction with Sherbourne Street

Opening
Daily: Feb–Nov 10am–6pm

Admission
Adult £2.95, Child £1.95;
Please phone for family details

Contact
The Old Mill, Sherbourne Street, Bourton-on-the-Water, Cheltenham GL54 2BY

t 01451 821255
w cotswold-motor-museum.com
e motormuseum@csma-netlink.co.uk

240 Cheltenham

Birdland Park

3 hrs +   All year

There are more than 500 birds and 50 aviaries in this beautiful centre set in woodlands and gardens. See the penguins, flamingos, storks, cranes, parrots, ibis, hornbills and many other rare birds at this centre for all things feathered.

* Children's play area
* Dogs allowed as long as they are kept on their leads

Location
Follow A436 to Bourton-on-the-Water

Opening
Daily: 1 Apr–31 Oct 10am–6pm;
1 Nov–31 Mar 10am–4pm
(last admission 1 hr before close)

Admission
Adult £5.20, Child (4–14) £3
Concs £4.20, Family £15

Contact
Rissington Road, Bourton-on-the-Water, Cheltenham GL54 2BN

t 01451 820480
w birdland.co.uk
e simonb@birdland.co.uk

241 Cheltenham

Chedworth Roman Villa

2 hrs   Mar–Nov

See the remains of one of the largest Romano-British villas in the country. The site comprises more than a mile of walls, several fine mosaics, two bath houses, hypocausts, a water-shrine and a latrine. The museum houses objects from the villa.

* National Trust property
* Audio-visual presentation

Location
3 miles NW of Fossebridge on the Cirencester-Northleach road (A429). Approach from A429 via Yanworth or from A436 via Withington

Opening
Mar & 1 Nov-mid-Nov Tue–Sun 11am–4pm; Apr–Oct Tue–Sun 10am–5pm; Bank Hol Mon 10am–5pm

Admission
Adult £5.50, Child £3

Contact
Yanworth, nr Cheltenham GL54 3LJ

t 01242 890256
w nationaltrust.org.uk
e chedworth@nationaltrust.org.uk

242 Cheltenham

Cotswold Farm Park

3 hrs   Mar–Oct

Meet more than 50 flocks and herds of British rare breeds. Enjoy seasonal demonstrations and children's activities, including adventure playgrounds, an indoor tractor school, farm safari rides and a rare breeds maze.

* Camping site & children's birthday parties
* Lambing, shearing & milking during the year

Location
Follow B4077 from Stow for 5 miles. Signed

Opening
Mar–Sep daily 10.30am–5pm; Oct weekends & autumn half-term 10.30am–4pm

Admission
Adult £5.50, Child £4.50, Concs £5

Contact
Guiting Power, Cheltenham GL54 5UG

t 01451 850307
w cotswoldfarmpark.co.uk
e info@cotswoldfarmpark.co.uk

243 Cheltenham

Sandford Parks Lido

2 hrs+   Apr–Oct

Set in beautiful grounds, Sandford Parks Lido tempts the whole family to take the plunge in the 50m heated outdoor pool.

* Playground
* Children's pool

Location
Off A40, near town centre

Opening
Daily: 20 Apr-3 Sep 11am-7.30pm. Early morning swims, please phone for details

Admission
Adult £3.50, Child & Concs £1.80

Contact
Keynsham Road, Cheltenham GL53 7PU

t 01242 524430
w sandfordparkslido.org.uk
e swim@sandfordparkslido.org.uk

244 Chipping Sodbury

Dyrham Park

2 hrs All year

Dyrham Park was built from 1691 to 1702 for William Blathwayt, and its rooms have changed little since they were first furnished. There are restored Victorian domestic rooms, including kitchen, bells passage, bake house, larders, tenants' hall and a Delft-tiled dairy.

* National Trust property
* Peacocks & fallow deer in the park

Location
8 miles N of Bath & 12 miles E of Bristol, off A46

Opening
House Mar–Oct Fri–Tue
12noon–4.45pm (last admission 4pm)
Gardens Mar–Oct Fri–Tue 11am–5pm
Park All year daily 11am–5.45pm

Admission
Adult £9, Child £4.50, Family £22.50
Gardens & Park only: £3.50, £1.80, £8

Contact
Dyrham, nr Bath SN14 8ER

t 0117 937 2501
e dyrhampark@nationaltrust.org.uk

245 Coleford

Puzzle Wood

1 hr+ Easter–Oct

This pre-Roman open-cast iron-ore mine is set in 14 acres of spectacular scenery. Pathways take you through deep ravines and passageways between moss-covered rocks, forming a very unusual maze. There is also an opportunity to meet the farm animals.

* Quality Assured Visitor Attraction
* Indoor wood puzzle with secret doorways

Location
Take B4228 from Coleford to Chepstow. Puzzle Wood is ½ mile from Coleford

Opening
Easter–Sep Tue–Sun 11am–5.30pm
(last admission 4.30pm);
Oct & Feb half-term 11am–4pm
(last admission 3pm)

Admission
Adult £3.95, Child £2.80

Contact
Lower Perrygrove Farm, Coleford GL16 8RB

t 01594 833187

246 Gloucester

National Waterways Museum

2 hrs All year

Take a journey through Britain in this award-winning museum, telling the 200-year story of inland waterways. Investigate interactive displays, historic craft, a traditional blacksmith's and an activities room. You enter through a replica lock complete with running water.

* Learn about Gloucester's role as an important dock
* For boat trips please phone for availability

Location
Follow signs for Historic Docks

Opening
Daily: 10am–5pm

Admission
Adult £5.95, Child & Concs £4.75
Occasionally subject to change, please phone for details

Contact
Llanthony Warehouse, Gloucester Docks GL1 2EH

t 01452 318200
w nwm.org.uk
e bookingsnwml@thewater waystrust.org

247 Gloucester

Prinknash Bird & Deer Park

1 hr   All year

Relish a wildlife experience walking in this bird park with fallow deer and pygmy goats, peacocks and cranes. There are bird pavilions and a reputedly haunted fish pond teeming with large trout! You can also see a wild range of waterfowl and exotic pheasants.

* Tame deer
* Tudor-style Wendy house

Location
Exit M5 at junction 11a then take A46 towards Stroud

Opening
Daily: summer 10am–5pm
winter 10am–4pm

Admission
Adult £5, Child £3.50, Concs £4.50

Contact
Cranham, Gloucester GL4 8EU

t 01452 812727
w prinknash-bird-and-deerpark.com

248 Gloucester

Robinswood Hill Country Park

1 hr+   All year

Explore 250 acres of open countryside with way-marked nature trails and a visitor centre. Pay a free visit to the new rare breeds farm and see traditional breeds of farm animals.

Location
Take Gloucester outer ring road, S of the city road

Opening
Daily: dawn–dusk

Admission
Free

Contact
Reservoir Road, Gloucester GL4 6SX

t 01452 303206

249 Gloucester

Soldiers of Gloucestershire Museum

1 hr+   All year

The story of Gloucestershire's soldiers and their families in times of peace and war over the past 300 years is told in this award-winning museum.

* Archive film & computer animations
* Life-size displays & sound effects

Location
Follow signs to Historic Docks

Opening
Daily: 10am–5pm; closed winter Mons & Christmas (last admission 4.30pm)

Admission
Adult £4.25, Child £2.25, Concs £3.25

Contact
Gloucester Docks GL1 2HE

t 01452 522682
w glosters.org.uk
e regimental-secretary@rgbw.army.mod.uk

250 Nympsfield

Woodchester Park & Mansion

2 hrs+   Easter –Oct

Known as 'The Secret Valley', this park was formerly an C18 park with five lakes and it is now virtually covered with trees. It contains an unfinished Victorian Gothic mansion and there are way-marked walks and trails through the woods.

* Dogs in park only

Location
1 mile NW of Nailsworth; 4 miles SW of Stroud

Opening
Mansion Easter–Oct Sat–Sun
11am–4pm Park Daily

Admission
Mansion Adult £5, Child free, Concs £4
Park Free

Contact
Nympsfield, Stonehouse GL10 3TS

t 01453 861541
w woodchestermansion.org.uk
e visitor@woodchestermansion.org.uk

251 Nympsfield

WWT Slimbridge Wildfowl & Wetlands Trust

3 hrs+   All year

Visit a large collection of exotic, rare and endangered ducks, geese, swans and flamingos in this important reserve vital for many migrating birds. The Discovery Centre has hands-on displays.

* Face-painting & badge-making
* Special activities during school holidays

Location	Contact
Between Bristol & Gloucester, just off A38, signed from M5 (junction 13 or 14)	Slimbridge GL2 7BT
	t 01453 891900
Opening	w wwt.org.uk/visit/slimbridge
Daily: 9.30am–5pm; Nov–Mar closes 4pm	e info.slimbridge@wwt.org.uk
Admission	
Adult £6.75, Child £4, Concs £5.50, Family £18.50	

252 Stroud

Museum in the Park

1 hr+   Jan–Nov

An innovative museum set in a park, its imaginative displays include dinosaur bones, a Roman temple and the world's first lawnmower. There are also family activity packs, special events and exhibitions.

* Quiz trails

Location	Contact
From junction 13 of M5 take A419 Ebley bypass towards Stroud	Stratford Park, Stratford Road, Stroud GL5 4AF
Opening	t 01453 763394
Please phone or visit the website for details	w stroud.gov.uk
	e museum@stroud.gov.uk
Admission	
Free	

Barrington Court

2 hrs+   Mar–Oct

An enchanting garden laid out in a sequence of walled rooms, with a working kitchen garden. The Tudor manor house is an antique furniture showroom.

* Children's activities
* Nature trail

Location
5 miles NE of Ilminster in village of Barrington

Opening
Mar & Oct Thu–Tue 11am–4.30pm;
Apr–Sep Thu–Tue 11am–5pm;
weekends in Dec 11am–4pm

Admission
Please phone for details

Contact
Barrington TA19 0NQ

t 01460 241938
w nationaltrust.org.uk
e barringtoncourt@
  nationaltrust.org.uk

Bath Balloons

3–4 hrs   Apr–Oct

Ever wanted to fly over rooftops? You can – in a hot-air balloon! You'll ascend as high as 3,000 feet and travel up to 10 miles during the one-hour flight, depending on the weather conditions. Good stout shoes are recommended in case the balloon lands in a field.

* Fantastic views of the city
* No 2 trips are the same

Location
Royal Victoria Park is 5 min walk from city centre

Opening
Apr–Oct (office open all year)

Admission
Please phone for details

Contact
8 Lambridge, London Road,
Bath BA1 6BJ

t 01225 466888
w balnet.co.uk
e sales@balnet.co.uk

The Jane Austen Centre

1 hr   All year

Jane Austen lived in this street from 1801 to 1806.
This exciting and informative centre tells the story
of her time in Bath and of the influence the city had
on her novels *Northanger Abbey* and *Persuasion*.

* New Regency tea room

Location
In city centre N of Queen Square

Opening
Daily: Apr–Oct 10am–5.30pm;
Nov–Mar 10am–4.30pm, Sat
10am–5.30pm

Admission
Adult £5.95, Child £2.95, Concs £4.50

Contact
40 Gay Street, Bath BA1 2NT

t 01225 443000
w janeausten.co.uk
e info@janeausten.co.uk

Prior Park Landscape Garden

1 hr+   All year

Enjoy an exhilarating walk through this stunning garden
set in a sweeping valley with magnificent views of the city
of Bath. This unique C18 garden is in the final stages of
restoration and includes a Gothic Temple, Serpentine
Lake, Cascades and Palladian Bridge.

* National Trust property
* Access to skyline walk

Location
There is no parking (except
prebooked disabled) at the
gardens. Please phone for details
of public transport connections

Opening
Feb–Nov Wed–Mon 11am–4.30pm;
Dec–Jan Fri–Sun 11am–dusk
(closed Tue)

Admission
Adult £4.50, Child £2.50, Family £11.50
NT Free

Contact
Ralph Allen Drive,
Bath BA2 5AH

t 01225 833422
w nationaltrust.org.uk
e priorpark@nationaltrust.org.uk

Roman Baths & Pump Rooms

2 hrs   All year

The Roman Baths are one of the best-preserved
Roman sites north of the Alps. Below the streets of
Bath are the Sacred Spring, a Roman temple and the
Roman bath house, while the Georgian pump house
stands at street level.

* Taste the water in the C18 Pump Rooms above the Temple
* Displays include sculpture, coins & jewellery

Location
In city centre near the abbey

Opening
Nov–Feb 9.30am–4.30pm;
Mar–June & Sep–Oct 9am–5pm;
July–Aug 9am–9pm (last exit 1 hr after
close)

Admission
Adult £10, Child £6, Concs £8.50
Jul–Aug: £11, £6, £8.50

Contact
Abbey Church Yard, Bath BA1 1LZ

t 01225 477785
w romanbaths.co.uk
e romanbath_bookings@bathnes.
gov.uk

© NTPL

258 Berrow

Animal Farm Adventure Park

4 hrs+   All year

Children can pet and feed many of the friendly animals at this farm. There is a play barn with big indoor slides and a large play park to explore, plus free train rides for visitors to enjoy.

* Phone for details of special events
* Delightful walks

Location	Admission
10 min from junction 22 of M5. Head for Berrow & follow signs	Adult & Child £5.50, Concs £4.50, Family £21
Opening	**Contact**
Daily: *summer* 10am–5.30pm	Red Road, Berrow TA8 2RW
winter 10am–4.30pm	t 01278 751628
	w animal-farm.co.uk
	e mike@afap.fsnet.co.uk

259 Chard

Ferne Animal Sanctuary

3 hrs   All year

Take your time as you stroll around 51 acres of tranquil surroundings, home to 300 unwanted and retired animals, ranging from horses to chipmunks.

Location	Contact
3 miles W of Chard in Somerset, signed from A30	Chard TA20 3DH
	t 01460 65214
Opening	w ferneanimalsanctuary.org
Daily 10am–5pm	e info@ferneanimalsanctuary.org
Admission	
Free, donations appreciated	

260 Chard

The Wildlife Park at Cricket St Thomas

3–5 hrs   All year

This park is home to more than 600 animals, including lemurs, monkeys, leopards, oryx, zebra, camels, wallabies, cheetahs and birds. Through its captive breeding programmes, it plays an important part in the conservation of rare and endangered species.

* Licensed for civil marriages
* New meerkat enclosure

     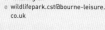

Location	Contact
3 miles from Chard on A30. Signed from M5 junction 25 & A303	Chard, Somerset TA20 4DD
	t 01460 30111
Opening	w wild.org.uk
summer Mon–Sun 10am–6pm	e wildlifepark.cst@bourne-leisure.
winter Mon–Sun 10am–4.30pm	co.uk
Admission	
Please phone for details	

© NTPL

261 Cheddar

Cheddar Gorge & Caves

3 hrs+   All year

The fascinating caves at Cheddar Gorge have long been popular attractions. Wonder at the mysterious stalagmites and stalactites in Gough's Cave and enjoy the Crystal Quest Challenge in the underground fantasy adventure game. There are explorer audio-guide tours.

* New Cheddar Man & the Cannibals attraction
* Open-top bus tour runs through gorge Apr–Sep

Location
Follow signs from junction 22 of M5 & A38 or take B3135 from A37 & follow brown tourist signs

Opening
Jul–Aug 10am–5pm;
Sep–Jun 10.30am–4.30pm

Admission
Explorer ticket for all attractions
Adult £11.50, Child £8.50

Contact
Cheddar BS27 3QF

t 01934 742343
w cheddarcaves.co.uk
e info@cheddarcaves.co.uk

262 Dunster

Dunster Castle

2 hrs   Mar–Nov

The fortified home of the Luttrels for 600 years, this castle is set in beautiful parkland and has a terraced garden of rare shrubs. Attic and basement tours with a below-stairs exhibition are popular; a children's guide, trail and activity sheets are available.

* C13 gate house survives
* Surrounded by beautiful parkland for walking

Location
Off A39, 3 miles SE of Minehead

Opening
Castle 4 Mar–4 Nov Sat–Wed
11am–5pm
Gardens & Park Daily 10am–5pm

Admission
Castle Adult £7.20, Child £3.60
Gardens & Park £3.90, £1.70

Contact
Dunster, nr Minehead TA24 6SL

t 01643 821314
w nationaltrust.org.uk
e dunstercastle@nationaltrust.org.uk

263 Farleigh Hungerford

Farleigh Hungerford Castle

2 hrs   All year

In 1370 Sir Thomas Hungerford began the fortification of the original Farleigh Manor, transforming it into what became Farleigh Hungerford Castle. The two south towers still remain, as do parts of the curtain wall, the outer gate house, and the C14 chapel and crypt.

* Important collection of death masks in chapel crypt
* Programme of living history throughout the year

Location
9 miles SE of Bath off A36

Opening
Daily: Apr–Jun & Sep–Oct 10am–5pm;
Jul–Aug 10am–6pm;
Nov–Mar Sat–Sun 10am–4pm

Admission
Adult £3.50, Child £1.80, Concs £2.60

Contact
Farleigh Hungerford,
nr Trowbridge BA2 7RS
t 01225 754026
w english-heritage.org.uk/farleigh
hungerford
e customers@english-heritage.org.uk

264 Glastonbury

Glastonbury Abbey

2 hrs   All year

Steeped in history and legend, this ancient abbey, though now ruined, is still a Christian sanctuary and an oasis of peace and quiet set in parkland with ponds and wildlife areas. The whole family can relax in its tranquil surroundings.

* Visitor centre with award-winning museum
* Period-dressed guides in summer months

Location
Take A39 from junction 23 of M5.
Follow signs once in Glastonbury

Opening
Daily: Jun–Aug 9am–6pm; Mar–May
& Sep–Nov 9.30am–6pm or dusk if
earlier; Dec–Feb 10am–dusk

Admission
Adult £4.50, Child £3, Concs £4

Contact
Abbey Gatehouse, Magdalene Street,
Glastonbury BA6 9EL
t 01458 832267
w glastonburyabbey.com
e info@glastonburyabbey.com

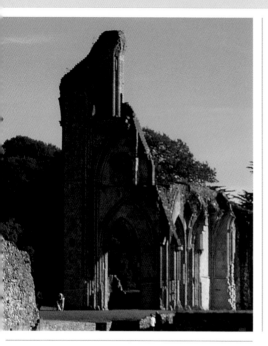

Alstone Wildlife Park

1 hr+   Easter–Nov

A small, noncommercial family-run park and licensed zoo with camels, pigs, deer, ponies, emu, owls and llama. Special features include Theodore the friendly camel, tame red deer and a pets' corner.

* Highland steer

Location
A38 Highbridge–Bridgwater road, signed turning on the right ¹/₂ mile from Highbridge

Contact
Alstone Road, Highbridge TA9 3DT

t 01278 782405

Opening
Daily: Easter–mid-Nov 10am–5.30pm

Admission
Adult £4, Child £3, Concs £3.50

West Somerset Railway

3 hrs   Feb–Dec

This wonderfully preserved railway recaptures perfectly the atmosphere of a country branchline during the age of steam. Operating between Minehead and Bishop's Lydeard, near Taunton, its 20 miles of track make it the longest independent railway in Britain.

* Visitor centres & museums
* Model railway

Location
Reached via A39 & A358

Contact
The Station, Minehead TA24 5BG

Opening
Feb–Dec (daily late May–late Sep)
Please phone for details

t 01643 704996
w west-somerset-railway.co.uk
e info@west-somerset-railway.co.uk

Admission
Adult £12.40, Child £6.20, Concs £10.60

West Somerset Rural Life Museum

1 hr+   May–Sep

Visit the schools of the past in this museum, housed in an old school building, with a thatched roof and riverside garden. Children can dress up in Victorian clothes, write on slates and play with traditional toys.

Location
On A39 from Minehead

Contact
The Old School, Allerford, Minehead TA24 8HN

Opening
Easter & May–Sep Wed–Fri
10.30am–4pm

t 01643 862529
w allerfordwebsite.ic24.net

Admission
Adult £1.50, Child 50p

268 Radstock

Radstock Museum

1 hr   Feb–Nov

This award-winning museum depicts the social and industrial heritage of the former North Somerset coalfield. It offers a unique insight into life in the region since the C19.

* Interactive & hands-on displays
* Heritage trail

Location
10 miles S of Bath

Opening
Feb–Nov Tue–Sat 11am–5pm, Sun 2pm–5pm; Bank Hols 2pm–5pm

Admission
Adult £3, Child & Concs £2

Contact
The Market Hall, Waterloo Road, Radstock BA3 3EP
t 01761 437722
w radstockmuseum.co.uk

269 Sparkford

Haynes Motor Museum

3 hrs   All year

Haynes Motor Museum is the UK's largest exhibition of the greatest cars from around the world. Travel through 100 years of motoring history with more than 350 amazing cars and motorcycles, from nostalgic classics of the 1950s and 1960s, to exciting supercars of today.

* Fabulous collection of American sports cars
* 70-seat video theatre

Location
½ mile N of Sparkford on A359

Opening
Daily: Apr–Oct 9.30am–5.30pm; Nov–Mar 10am–4.30pm

Admission
Adult £7.50, Child £4.50, Concs £6.50

Contact
Sparkford BA22 7LH
t 01963 440804
w haynesmotormuseum.co.uk
e info@haynesmotormuseum.co.uk

270 Street

Viaduct Fishery

5 hrs   All year

Set in the beautiful Cary Valley, this fishery offers six coarse fishing lakes spread out over a peaceful 25-acre site. Tuition is available for beginners.

* Tackle shop

Location	Contact
On N outskirts of Somerton	Cary Valley, Somerton TA11 6LJ
Opening	t 01458 274022
Daily: Dawn–dusk	
Admission	
Adult £6, Child & Concs £4	

271 Taunton

Somerset County Museum

2–3 hrs   All year

A fascinating museum housed in Taunton Castle, the Somerset County Museum has costumes, silver and a C16 alms house on display. Recent additions include the Shapwick coin hoard – the largest hoard of Roman silver coins found in Britain.

Location	Contact
Reached via A38 & M5	Taunton Castle, Castle Green, Taunton TA1 4AA
Opening	t 01823 320201
Tue–Sat 10am–5pm	w somerset.gov.uk
Admission	e county-museums@somerset.
Free	gov.uk

272 Weston-super-Mare

The Helicopter Museum

2 hrs   All year

More than 80 helicopters dating from 1931 to the present day are diplayed here in hangars. There are open-cockpit days, and Helicopter Experience or Air Experience flights are available. The museum organises special events throughout the year.

* World's largest helicopter museum
* Weston-super-Mare's largest all-weather attraction

Location	Admission
On A371, off M5 (junction 21)	Adult £5.30, Child £3.30, Concs £4.30
Opening	**Contact**
Apr–Oct Wed–Sun 10am–5.30pm;	The Heliport, Locking Moor Road,
Nov–Mar 10am–4.30pm;	Weston-super-Mare BS24 8PP
Easter & summer school hols daily	
10am–5.30pm	t 01934 635227
	w helicoptermuseum.co.uk

273 Weston-super-Mare

Seaquarium, Weston-super-Mare

2 hrs   All year

Walk through the underwater tunnel to view hundreds of fascinating fish, including sharks and rays, in 30 naturally themed marine habitats. There are interactive touchscreens as well.

* Discovery trail

Location	Contact
On seafront. Take junction 21 or 22 off M5 & follow brown tourist signs	Marine Parade, Weston-super-Mare BS23 1BE
Opening	t 01934 641603
Daily: *summer* 10am–5pm	w seaquarium.co.uk
winter 10am–4pm	e weston@seaquarium.co.uk
(last admission 4pm)	
Admission	
Please phone for details	

Somerset | Wiltshire

274 Wookey Hole

Wookey Hole Caves & Papermill

4 hrs   All year

It is said that the infamous Witch of Wookey lived in these spectacular caves. Guided tours of the caves are amazing. Visitors can also watch demonstrations of traditional papermaking at a 400-year-old papermill. There are also numerous activities for children.

* Magical mirror maze & penny arcade
* New Haunted Witches ghost train

Location	Contact
Junction 22 of M5 & then follow signs A39 from Bath to Wells	Wookey Hole, nr Wells BA5 1BB
	t 01749 672243
Opening	w wookey.co.uk
Daily: Apr–Oct 10am–5pm; Nov–Mar 10am–4pm	e witch@wookey.co.uk
Admission	
Adult £10.90, Child & Concs £8.50	

275 Yeovil

Fleet Air Arm Museum

3 hrs+   All year

The Fleet Air Arm Museum is one of the 'must-see' attractions when in the South West. Among Europe's largest collection of naval aircraft, see Concorde, Harriers, helicopters and the award-winning Aircraft Carrier Experience. There is even a nuclear bomb.

* *Ark Royal* Aircraft Carrier Experience
* Many events throughout the year

Location	Admission
1 mile off A303/A37 roundabout	Adult £10, Child £7, Concs £8
Opening	Contact
Apr–Oct daily 10am–5.30pm; Nov–Mar Wed–Sun 10am–4.30pm; open Bank Hols & school hols	PO Box D6, RNAS, Yeovilton, Ilchester BA22 8HT
	t 01935 840565
	w fleetairarm.com
	e info@fleetairarm.com

276 Amesbury

Stonehenge

1 hr   All year

Now a World Heritage Site, Stonehenge is a powerful witness to the Stone and Bronze Ages. These monolithic stones – whether they were part of a sun-worshipping religion or formed a giant astronomical calendar – are a tribute to their architects and builders.

* World Heritage Site
* Audio tours in 9 languages

Location	Contact
2 miles W of Amesbury on junction of A303 & A360	Stonehenge Information Line
	t 0870 333 1181
Opening	w english-heritage.org.uk/stonehenge
Daily: Please phone for details	e customers@english-heritage.org.uk
Admission	
Adult £5.90, Child £3, Concs £4.40	

277 Avebury

Avebury

2 hrs+   All year

This great stone circle, encompassing part of the village of Avebury, is roughly ¼ mile across. It encloses an area of about 28 acres and contains two smaller circles within. It is believed to be an ancient religious and ceremonial centre.

* World Heritage Site
* World's biggest megalithic monument

Location	Admission
6 miles W of Marlborough, 1 mile N of Bath road (A4) on A4361 & B4003	Adult £4.20, Child £2.1o
Opening	Contact
Daily: Apr–Oct 10am–6pm; Nov–Mar 10am–4pm	nr Marlborough SN8 1RF
	t 01672 539250
	w nationaltrust.org.uk
	e avebury.estateoff@nationaltrust.org.uk

278 Calne

Bowood House

3 hrs   Apr–Nov

Fun, beauty and history are all on offer at the magnificent family home of the Marquis and Marchioness of Lansdowne. The house is set in beautiful Capability Brown parkland, and there is an adventure playground, plus the Soft Play Palace, to entertain children.

Location	Contact
Off A4 Chippenham–Calne road in Derry Hill village	Derry Hill, Calne SN11 0LZ
	t 01249 812102
Opening	w bowood.org
Daily: Apr–31 Oct 11am–6pm (last admission 5pm)	e houseandgardens@bowood.org
Admission	
Adult £7.50, Child (5–16) £5, Child (2–4) £3.50, Family £22.50	

280 Malmesbury

Athelstan Museum

½ hr   All year

This museum has local history exhibits such as costumes, an early fire engine, photographs of the town and an educational hands-on activity called the Mini Museum Detective. There are regular special exhibitions throughout the year for visitors to enjoy.

*No WC facilities on site, but some are situated very close to the building

Location	Admission
Off A429, 5 miles from M4 (junction 17)	Free
	Contact
Opening	Town Hall, Cross Hayes, Malmesbury SN16 9BZ
Apr–Oct daily 10.30am–4.30pm Please phone for details of winter opening times	t 01666 829258
	w northwilts.gov.uk
	e athelstanmuseum@northwilts.gov.uk

279 Chippenham

Lacock Abbey & Fox Talbot Museum

2 hrs+   Mar–Oct

This fine medieval abbey and house, set in gardens and woodland, is home to a museum dedicated to former resident William Henry Fox Talbot, inventor of the positive/negative photographic process.

* Harry Potter films filmed here
* Beautiful Victorian woodland garden

Location	Admission
3 miles S of Chippenham, just E of A350	Adult £7.80, Child £3.90
Opening	**Contact**
Abbey Mar–Oct Wed–Mon 1pm–5.30pm	Chippenham SN15 2LG
Museum Mar–Oct 11am–5.30pm; Nov–Feb weekends only	t 01249 730141
	w nationaltrust.org.uk

© NTPL

281 Salisbury

Cholderton Rare Breeds Farm Park

4 hrs+   All year

This park for rare farm animals has a wealth of things to see and do, and is home to one of Britain's largest collections of rabbit breeds. There is a replica Iron Age roundhouse farm and nature trail. Also at the farm park is an undercover soft-play barn and climbing wall.

* Toddlers' play area & adventure playground
* Pig-racing & tractor rides (in season)

Location
Reached by A303 from Andover or A338 from Salisbury or Marlborough

Opening
Daily: 10am–6pm; *winter* weekends only. Please phone for details

Admission
Adult £5.50, Child (2–16) £4.95, Concs £4.50

Contact
Amesbury Road, Cholderton, Salisbury SP4 0EW

t 01980 629438
w rabbitworld.co.uk
e group@rabbitworld.co.uk

282 Salisbury

Old Sarum

1½ hrs   All year

This great earthwork, with more than 2,000 years of history and its huge banks and ditches, was created by Iron Age people around 500BC, and later occupied by Romans, Saxons and the Normans. See the remains of the prehistoric fortress, the palace, castle and cathedral.

* William the Conqueror paid off his army here in 1070
* Beautiful views of surrounding chalk downs

Location
2 miles N of Salisbury off A345

Opening
Daily: Apr–Jun & Sep 10am–5pm; Jul–Aug 9am–6pm; May & Oct 10am–4pm; Nov–Feb 11am–3pm

Admission
Adult £2.90, Child £1.50, Concs £2.20

Contact
English Heritage, Castle Road, Salisbury SP1 3SD

t 01722 335398
w english-heritage.org.uk/oldsarum
e old_sarum.castle@english-heritage.org.uk

283 Stourhead

Stourhead Gardens

3 hrs+   All year

Stourhead's magnificent landscaped gardens offer space to let off steam and there's plenty to discover and explore. Discover the mini-temples and a spooky grotto and climb Alfred's Tower to enjoy the spectacular views. The house has fine interiors, paintings and furnishings.

* Palladian mansion & gift shop
* King Alfred's Tower, a 50m redbrick folly

Location
Just off A303 at Mere

Opening
House Mar–Oct (closed Wed–Thu)
Gardens Daily

Admission
Gardens or House Adult £6.20, Child £6.40 *Both* £10.40, £5.20

Contact
Stourhead Gardens, nr Warminster BA12 6QD

t 01747 842020
w nationaltrust.org.uk
e stourhead@nationaltrust.org.uk

284 Swindon

Link Centre

2 hrs+   All year

This multipurpose sports centre could keep you occupied all day. The Link offers an ice rink, swimming pool, badminton and squash courts, snooker and even a climbing wall. When you need a break, relax in the cafeteria or bar.

Location
In W Swindon, 1½ miles from town centre. Follow brown tourist signs from M4 (junction 16)

Opening
Please phone or visit the website for details

Admission
Please phone or visit the website for details

Contact
Whitehill Way, Westlea, Swindon SN5 7DL

t 01793 445566
w swindon.gov.uk/link

285 Swindon

Oasis Leisure Centre

2 hrs+   All year

This leisure centre has activities for all age groups. The lagoon pool has a new pirate ship for the under-eights, three giant water slides, a wave machine and a water cannon. There are also squash courts, a gym and an indoor bowling green.

* Outdoor multiplay pitches

Location
Follow brown tourist signs on all major roads to Swindon

Opening
Please phone for details

Admission
Please phone for details

Contact
North Star Avenue, Swindon SN2 1EP

t 01793 445401
w swindon.gov.uk/oasis

286 Swindon

STEAM – Museum of the Great Western Railway

2 hrs   All year

STEAM tells the story of workers on the Great Western Railway. Housed in beautiful railway buildings, this award-winning museum has hands-on exhibits and famous locomotives and makes a great day out for all the family.

* Day out with Thomas the Tank Engine
* World-famous GWR locomotives

Location
Follow signs from Swindon town centre

Opening
Daily: 10am–5pm

Admission
Adult £5.95, Child & Concs £3.95

Contact
Kemble Drive, Swindon SN2 2TA

t 01793 466646
w swindon.gov.uk/steam
e steampostbox@swindon.gov.uk

287 Warminster

Longleat

4 hrs+   Feb–Nov

From safari to stately home and from miniature trains to mazes and safari boat rides, there is always something to enjoy at Longleat. Encounter some of the world's most exotic animals, then visit King Arthur's mirror maze and the pets' corner.

* Longleat hedge maze
* Featured in the BBC programme *Animal Park*

Location
Off A36 between Bath & Salisbury
(A362 Warminster–Frome road)

Opening
Daily: Feb–Nov
Times vary; please phone for details

Admission
Please phone for details

Contact
The Estate Office, Longleat,
Warminster BA12 7NW

t 01985 844400
w longleat.co.uk
e enquiries@longleat.co.uk

288 Westbury

Westbury White Horse & Bratton Camp

3 hrs+   All year

The 300-year-old Westbury White Horse is the oldest in Wiltshire. Located on a very steep slope, just below the Iron Age fort of Bratton camp, it's an ideal spot for kite-flying and hang-gliding. There are marvellous views for miles around.

*Neolithic barrow or burial mound

Location
Between Westbury & B3098

Opening
Daily: Please phone for details

Admission
Free

Contact
Westbury Tourist Information Centre

t 01373 827158
w english-heritage.org.uk

Tollesbury, Essex

Eastern

Bedfordshire Cambridgeshire Essex
Hertfordshire Norfolk Suffolk

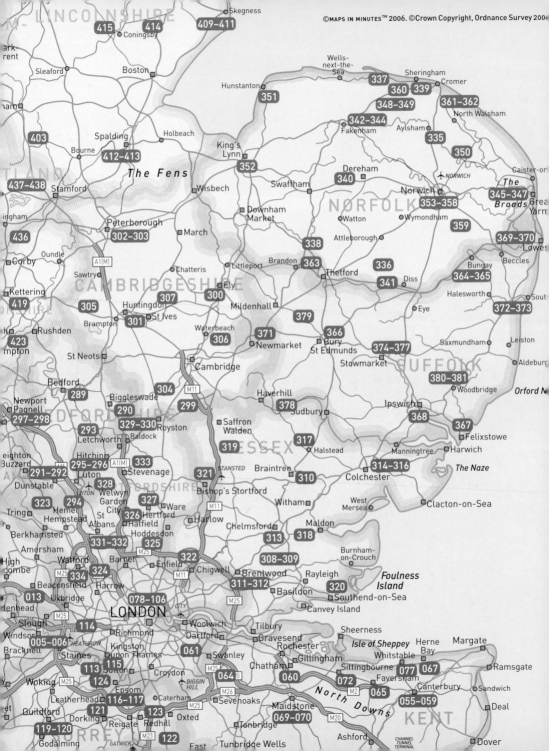

M. LINCOLNSHIRE
Skegness
415 **414** **409–411**
Coningsby
ark-
rent
Sleaford
Boston
403
Spalding
Holbeach
Bourne
412–413
ham
The Fens
King's Lynn
Wisbech
351
Hunstanton
Wells-next-the-Sea
337
Sheringham
Cromer
360 **339**
348–349
361–362
North Walsham
342–344
Fakenham
Aylsham
335
437–438
Stamford
Downham Market
Swaffham
352
Dereham
340
NORWICH
350
NORFOLK
Norwich
353–358
The Broads
345–347
Grea Yarm
ingham
436
Peterborough
302–303
March
Watton
Wymondham
359
369–370
Lowe
Corby
Oundle
A1(M)
Chatteris
Littleport
Ely
307
300
Mildenhall
Attleborough
Beccles
305
Huntingdon
St Ives
301
338
363
Thetford
336
Bungay
364–365
Halesworth
Sout
372–373
Kettering
419
SHIRE
Brampton
Waterbeach
306
Newmarket
379
Diss
341
Eye
Rushden
423
mpton
St Neots
Cambridge
304
306
371
366
Bury St Edmunds
374–377
Stowmarket
SUFFOLK
Saxmundham
Leiston
Aldebur
Bedford
289
Biggleswade
290
329–330
Royston
Saffron Walden
Haverhill
378
Sudbury
380–381
Woodbridge
Orford N
Newport Pagnell
297–298
DFORD
293
Letchworth
Baldock
319
317
Halstead
Ipswich
368
367
Felixstowe
eighton
Buzzard
291–292
Hitchin
A1(M)
295–296
Luton
333
Stevenage
321
STANSTED
Bishop's Stortford
Braintree
310
314–316
Colchester
Manningtree
Harwich
The Naze
Dunstable
328
LUTON
Tring
323
294
Hemel Hempstead
Welwyn Garden City
327
Ware
326
Hertford
M11
Harlow
Witham
West Mersea
Clacton-on-Sea
Berkhamsted
Amersham
St Albans
Hatfield
Hoddesdon
331–332
325
Chelmsford
313
318
Maldon
Burnham-on-Crouch
High
combe
013
Watford
334
324
Barnet
M25
322
Enfield
Chigwell
M11
308–309
311–312
Brentwood
Basildon
Rayleigh
320
Foulness Island
Beaconsfield
Harrow
Southend-on-Sea
Uxbridge
denhead
M25
078–106
LONDON
CITY
Canvey Island
Slough
Windsor
005–006
HEATHROW
114
Richmond
Kingston upon Thames
Woolwich
Tilbury
Sheerness
Margate
Bracknell
Staines
113
115
Sutton
Dartford
Gravesend
Rochester
Gillingham
Isle of Sheppey
Whitstable
Herne Bay
Ramsgate
Woking
M25
124
Epsom
061
Swanley
Chatham
060
Sittingbourne
Faversham
077 **067**
072
Canterbury
Sandwich
Leatherhead
116–117
Caterham
064
065
055–059
Deal
Guildford
121
Dorking
123
Oxted
Sevenoaks
M26
Maidstone
069–070
North Downs
KENT
119–120
Godalming
Reigate
Redhill
M23
122
East
Tunbridge Wells
Tonbridge
Ashford
M20
CHANNEL TUNNEL TERMINAL
Dover
REY
GATWICK

BEDFORDSHIRE
Animal Attractions
Bedford Butterfly Park ... 111
The English School of Falconry ... 111
HULA Animal Rescue: South Midlands
 Animal Sanctuary ... 113
Whipsnade Wild Animal Park ... 112
Woburn Safari Park ... 113

Boat & Train Trips
Leighton Buzzard Railway ... 111

Historic Sites
Dunstable Downs Countryside Centre
 & Whipsnade Estate ... 112

Museums & Exhibitions
Stockwood Craft Museum & Gardens ... 113
Stondon Motor Museum ... 112

Parks, Gardens & Nature
John Dony Field Centre ... 112

CAMBRIDGESHIRE
Animal Attractions
Hamerton Zoo Park ... 116
The Raptor Foundation ... 117
Wimpole Home Farm ... 116

Boat & Train Trips
Nene Valley Railway ... 116

Historic Sites
Houghton Mill ... 115
Oliver Cromwell's House ... 114

Museums & Exhibitions
Denny Abbey & The Farmland Museum ... 117
Flag Fen Bronze Age Centre ... 115
Imperial War Museum Duxford ... 114

ESSEX
Animal Attractions
Barleylands Craft Village & Farm Centre ... 117
Colchester Zoo ... 119
Hanningfield Reservoir Visitor Centre ... 117
Mole Hall Wildlife Park ... 121
Old MacDonald's Educational Farm Park ... 118

Historic Sites
Hedingham Castle ... 120
Kelvedon Hatch Secret Nuclear Bunker ... 118
Royal Gunpowder Mills ... 121

Museums & Exhibitions
Chelmsford Museum & Essex Regiment
 Museum ... 119
Combined Military Services Museum ... 120
The House on the Hill Toy Museum ... 121

Parks, Gardens & Nature
High Woods Country Park ... 119

Sport & Leisure
Adventure Island ... 121
The Original Great Maze ... 118
Quasar at Rollerworld ... 120

HERTFORDSHIRE
Animal Attractions
Paradise Wildlife Park ... 122
Shepreth Wildlife Park ... 124
Waterhall Farm & Craft Centre ... 123
Willows Farm Village ... 125

Historic Sites
Ashridge Estate ... 122

Museums & Exhibitions
Hertford Museum ... 123
Maple Street British Museum of
 Miniatures ... 124
Mill Green Museum & Mill ... 123
Verulamium Museum ... 124

Sport & Leisure
Topsy Turvy World ... 125

Parks, Gardens & Nature
Aldenham Country Park ... 122
Fairlands Valley Park ... 125

NORFOLK

Animal Attractions
Banham Zoo 126
Blakeney Point 127
Great Yarmouth Sealife Centre 128
Hunstanton Sea Life Centre 130
Norfolk Shire Horse Centre 127
Thrigby Hall Wildlife Gardens 129
Wroxham Barns 130

Boat & Train Trips
Bank Boats 131
Barton House Railway 132
Bishop's Boats Seal Trips 130
Bure Valley Railway 126

Historic Sites
Baconsthorpe Castle 130
Horsey Windpump 129
Langham Glass 128

Museums & Exhibitions
Caithness Crystal Visitor Centre 131
Gressenhall Museum & Workhouse 127
Grimes Graves 127
Norfolk Motor Cycle Museum 134
The Muckleburgh Collection 134

Parks, Gardens & Nature
Bressingham Steam Experience
  & Gardens 128
Fairhaven Woodland & Water Garden 132
Felbrigg Hall, Garden & Park 133
ILPH Hall Farm 133

Theme Parks & Adventure Playgrounds
Dinosaur Adventure Park 132
Elephant Playbarn 134
The Play Barn 134
Pleasure Beach, Great Yarmouth 129
South Creake Maize Maze 128

SUFFOLK

Animal Attractions
National Stud 137
Redwings Rescue Centre 139
Suffolk Owl Sanctuary 138

Boat & Train Trips
Coastal Voyager 138
Deben Cruises 140

Historic Sites
Bungay Castle 135
Bury St Edmunds Abbey Gardens 136
Southwold Pier 138

Museums & Exhibitions
Ipswich Transport Museum 136
Lowestoft Maritime Museum 136
Mid-Suffolk Light Railway Museum 138
Norfolk & Suffolk Aviation Museum 135
Sutton Hoo 140
West Stow Country Park 140
  & Anglo-Saxon Village

Parks, Gardens & Nature
Clare Castle Country Park 139
High Lodge Forest Centre 135

Sport & Leisure
Southwold Pier 138

Theme Parks & Adventure Playgrounds
Manning's Amusement Park 136
Pleasurewood Hills Theme Park 137
Xcite Playworld 139

289 Bedford

Bedford Butterfly Park

2 hrs+   All year

Set in a landscape of wildflower hay meadows, this fascinating conservation park features a tropical glasshouse. Visitors walk through a wonderful scene of waterfalls, ponds and lush foliage, with spectacular butterflies flying around.

* Quality Assured Visitor Attraction
* Nature trails & mini-farm

Location
Off A421, near Bedford. From Bedford town centre follow signs for Cambridge. As you leave Bedford, turn left for Renhold & Wilden; follow signs for Wilden

Opening
Jan–Feb Thu–Sun 10am–4pm; Feb–Oct daily 10am–5pm; Nov–Dec Thu–Sun 10am–4pm

Admission
Adult £4.75, Child £3.90, Concs £4.25, Family £16

Contact
Renhold Road, Wilden, Bedford MK44 2PX

t 01234 772770
w bedford-butterflies.co.uk
e enquiries@bedford-butterflies.co.uk

290 Biggleswade

The English School of Falconry

3 hrs+   Feb–Oct

Located in woodland, this family-run centre has recreated an environment close to the birds' natural habitat. Here you can see more than 300 birds, including falcons, hawks, eagles, vultures and owls, some of which you can handle or watch fly during the daily displays.

* 3 flying displays daily
* New reptile house

Location
Old Warden is 2 miles W of A1 where it bypasses Biggleswade

Opening
Daily: Feb–Oct 10am–5pm

Admission
Adult £8, Child £5, Concs £7

Contact
Old Warden Park, Biggleswade SG18 9EX

t 01767 627527
w birdsofpreycentre.co.uk
e falconry.centre@virgin.net

291 Dunstable

Leighton Buzzard Railway

2 hrs   Mar–Oct

Take a journey into the world of the English light railway – experience sharp curves, steep gradients and level crossings. Passengers can now make a 70-minute round trip from Page's Park to Stonehenge Works.

* Children's play area
* Explore the Guntry terminus

Location
Off A4146 on edge of Leighton Buzzard, close to junction with A505 Dunstable–Aylesbury road

Opening
Please phone for timetable details

Admission
Adult £6, Child (2–15) £3, Concs £5

Contact
Billington Road, Leighton Buzzard LU7 4TN

t 01525 373888
w buzzrail.co.uk
e info@buzzrail.co.uk

292 Dunstable

Whipsnade Wild Animal Park

3–5 hrs   All year

Whipsnade Wild Animal Park is home to more than 2,500 rare and exotic animals. Seize the chance to see tigers, elephants, hippos, giraffes, rhinos and more in their huge outdoor enclosures. See the 'Lions of the Serengeti' and the park's two baby elephants, Euan and Aneena.

* Children's farm & adventure playground
* Free-flying bird display & penguin feeding

Location
Follow brown elephant signs from M1 junction 9 or 12. Just 20 mins from M25 junction 21

Opening
Daily: from 10am (closing times vary) Please visit the website for details

Admission
Adult £15, Child (3–15) £11.50, Concs £13, Family £48. Car park £3.50. Book online up to 24 hours in advance and receive a 10% discount

Contact
Dunstable LU6 2LF

t 01582 872171
w whipsnade.co.uk

---

293 Henlow

Stondon Motor Museum

2 hrs   All year

Travel back in time to discover vehicles from the beginning of the last century to modern-day classics. The 400 vehicles are housed in five halls and include Rolls-Royce and Bentley cars. Outside the museum is an exact replica of Captain Cook's ship HM *Endeavour*.

* Full-size replica of Captain Cook's *Endeavour*
* Large free car park

Location
At Lower Stondon near Henlow off A600

Opening
Daily: 10am–5pm

Admission
Adult £6, Child £3, Concs £5

Contact
Station Road, Lower Stondon, Henlow SG16 6JN

t 01462 850339
w transportmuseum.co.uk
e info@transportmuseum.co.uk

---

294 Kensworth

Dunstable Downs Countryside Centre & Whipsnade Estate

2 hrs+   All year

A great place to learn all about flora and fauna, walk, cycle along designated routes, fly kites or watch paragliders. Visit in July to see spectacular displays during the annual kite-flying festival. The centre also has exhibitions and a wide range of kites for sale.

* New visitor facility & annual kite festival
* Designated Area of Outstanding Natural Beauty

Location
4 miles NE of Ashridge between B4540 & B4541

Opening
Downs All year
Centre Apr–Oct daily 10am–5pm; Nov–Apr Sat–Sun 10am–4pm

Admission
Free

Contact
Whipsnade Road, Kensworth, Dunstable LU6 2TA

t 01582 608489
w nationaltrust.org.uk
e dunstabledowns@nationaltrust.org.uk

---

295 Luton

John Dony Field Centre

1 hr+   All year

The Field Centre is located close to a number of important sites of natural history interest in north-east Luton. There are displays featuring local and natural history, conservation and archaeology.

* Wildlife garden

Location
In Bushmead Estate, near A6, in N Luton. Signed from roundabout at Barnfield College on A6

Opening
Please phone for details

Admission
Free

Contact
Hancock Drive, Bushmead, Luton LU2 7SF

t 01582 486983
w luton.gov.uk
e tweent@luton.gov.uk

296 Luton

Stockwood Craft Museum & Gardens

1 hr+   Apr–Oct

This award-winning museum covers nine centuries of garden history and rural life. Its collection of vehicles, (on which visitors can ride) illustrates the development of horse-drawn road transport in Britain from Roman times to the 1930s. Events and activities run all year.

* Conservatory tearoom set in C18 walled garden
* Largest display of horse-drawn carriages in the UK

Location
2 miles S of town centre, close to junction 10 of M1

Opening
Daily: Apr–Oct 10am–5pm

Admission
Free, donations welcomed

Contact
Farley Hill, Luton LU1 4BH

t 01582 738714
w lutononline.gov.uk
e museum.gallery@luton.gov.uk

297 Milton Keynes

HULA Animal Rescue: South Midlands Animal Sanctuary

1 hr+   All year

HULA Animal Rescue is the headquarters of the charity founded in 1972 and houses rescued and abandoned animals. Ponies, donkeys, cattle, chickens, ducks, sheep and pigs are residents; dogs, cats, rabbits and small rodents await adoption into new homes.

* Café & shop open on monthly open days
* Animal houses

Location
From village square in Aspley Guise turn into Church Road, then into Salford Road & entrance to Glebe Farm is on the right

Opening
Fri & Sat–Sun 1pm–3pm
Please phone for details of monthly open days & Bank Hols opening times

Admission
Adult £1, Child 50p

Contact
Glebe Farm, Salford Road, Aspley Guise, Milton Keynes MK17 8HZ

t 01908 584000 (1pm–3pm)
w hularescue.org
e hularescue@yahoo.co.uk

298 Milton Keynes

Woburn Safari Park

6 hrs   All year

Enjoy a Safari Adventure! Experience the thrill of being alongside rhinos, lions, giraffes and more. The excitement continues with close encounters in walkthroughs with wallabies, squirrel monkeys and lemurs, playgrounds, trains, boats, keeper talks and demonstrations.

* Tour the animal reserves as often as you wish
* See bears & wolves running together

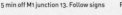

Location
5 min off M1 junction 13. Follow signs

Opening
Daily: Feb half-term & Mar–Oct 10am–5pm; Nov–Feb Sat–Sun 11am–3pm

Admission
Please phone for details

Contact
Woburn MK17 9QN

t 01525 290407
w discoverwoburn.co.uk
e info@woburnsafari.co.uk

299 Duxford

Imperial War Museum Duxford

3 hrs+   All year

With its air shows, unique history and atmosphere, nowhere else combines the sights, sounds and power of aircraft quite like Duxford. It is home to 200 historic aircaft including biplanes, Spitfires, Concorde and Gulf War jets – many of which still fly regularly.

* Normandy Experience complete with video story
* Flying displays held throughout summer

Location
Off junction 10 of M11

Opening
Daily: mid-Mar–mid-Oct 10am–6pm;
winter 10am–4pm

Admission
Adult £13, Child free, Concs £11

Contact
Duxford CB2 4QR

t 01223 835000
w iwm.org.uk/duxford
e duxford@iwm.org.uk

300 Ely

Oliver Cromwell's House

1 hr+   All year

Home of Ely's most famous former resident, Cromwell's carefully restored house now contains Civil War exhibitions including weapons and armour. It also has illustrations of everyday C17 life and a history of the Fenlands and its transformation from marsh to farmland.

* C15 inglenook fireplace restored to working order
* Kitchen area has display of C17 recipes & ingredients

Location
In town centre next to St Mary's church

Opening
Apr–Oct daily 10am–5.30pm;
Nov–Mar Sun–Fri 11am–4pm,
Sat 10am–5pm

Admission
Adult £3.95, Child £2.70, Concs £3.45

Contact
29 St Mary's Street, Ely CB7 4HF

t 01353 662062
w ecambs.gov.uk
e tic@ely.org.uk

Stockwood Craft Museum & Gardens

1 hr+   Apr–Oct

This award-winning museum covers nine centuries of garden history and rural life. Its collection of vehicles, (on which visitors can ride) illustrates the development of horse-drawn road transport in Britain from Roman times to the 1930s. Events and activities run all year.

* Conservatory tearoom set in C18 walled garden
* Largest display of horse-drawn carriages in the UK

Location
2 miles S of town centre, close to junction 10 of M1

Opening
Daily: Apr–Oct 10am–5pm

Admission
Free, donations welcomed

Contact
Farley Hill, Luton LU1 4BH

t 01582 738714
w lutonline.gov.uk
e museum.gallery@luton.gov.uk

HULA Animal Rescue: South Midlands Animal Sanctuary

1 hr+   All year

HULA Animal Rescue is the headquarters of the charity founded in 1972 and houses rescued and abandoned animals. Ponies, donkeys, cattle, chickens, ducks, sheep and pigs are residents; dogs, cats, rabbits and small rodents await adoption into new homes.

* Café & shop open on monthly open days
* Animal houses

Location
From village square in Aspley Guise turn into Church Road, then into Salford Road & entrance to Glebe Farm is on the right

Opening
Fri & Sat–Sun 1pm–3pm
Please phone for details of monthly open days & Bank Hols opening times

Admission
Adult £1, Child 50p

Contact
Glebe Farm, Salford Road, Aspley Guise, Milton Keynes MK17 8HZ

t 01908 584000 (1pm–3pm)
w hularescue.org
e hularescue@yahoo.co.uk

Woburn Safari Park

6 hrs   All year

Enjoy a Safari Adventure! Experience the thrill of being alongside rhinos, lions, giraffes and more. The excitement continues with close encounters in walkthroughs with wallabies, squirrel monkeys and lemurs, playgrounds, trains, boats, keeper talks and demonstrations.

* Tour the animal reserves as often as you wish
* See bears & wolves running together

Location
5 min off M1 junction 13. Follow signs

Opening
Daily: Feb half-term & Mar–Oct 10am–5pm; Nov–Feb Sat–Sun 11am–3pm

Admission
Please phone for details

Contact
Woburn MK17 9QN

t 01525 290407
w discoverwoburn.co.uk
e info@woburnsafari.co.uk

299 Duxford

Imperial War Museum Duxford

3 hrs+   All year

With its air shows, unique history and atmosphere, nowhere else combines the sights, sounds and power of aircraft quite like Duxford. It is home to 200 historic aircaft including biplanes, Spitfires, Concorde and Gulf War jets – many of which still fly regularly.

* Normandy Experience complete with video story
* Flying displays held throughout summer

Location
Off junction 10 of M11

Opening
Daily: mid-Mar–mid-Oct 10am–6pm; *winter* 10am–4pm

Admission
Adult £13, Child free, Concs £11

Contact
Duxford CB2 4QR

t 01223 835000
w iwm.org.uk/duxford
e duxford@iwm.org.uk

300 Ely

Oliver Cromwell's House

1 hr+   All year

Home of Ely's most famous former resident, Cromwell's carefully restored house now contains Civil War exhibitions including weapons and armour. It also has illustrations of everyday C17 life and a history of the Fenlands and its transformation from marsh to farmland.

* C15 inglenook fireplace restored to working order
* Kitchen area has display of C17 recipes & ingredients

Location
In town centre next to St Mary's church

Opening
Apr–Oct daily 10am–5.30pm;
Nov–Mar Sun–Fri 11am–4pm,
Sat 10am–5pm

Admission
Adult £3.95, Child £2.70, Concs £3.45

Contact
29 St Mary's Street, Ely CB7 4HF

t 01353 662062
w ecambs.gov.uk
e tic@ely.org.uk

Houghton Mill

1 hrs   Apr–Oct

Discover how flour is made at this working watermill on an island on the Great Ouse. Have a go at turning the millstone and pull on a rope to lift the bags of flour. There has been a mill on this site since AD 974. The flour is for sale and there are family and children's guides.

* National Trust property
* Hands-on activities & children's quiz & trail

Location
In Houghton village, signed from A1123 Huntingdon–St Ives road

Opening
Apr & Oct Sat–Sun 1pm–5pm;
May–Sep Sat–Wed 1pm–5pm
Open to groups at other times by arrangement

Admission
Adult £3.20, Child £1.50, Family £7

Contact
Houghton, nr Huntingdon PE28 2AZ

t 01480 301494
w nationaltrust.org.uk
e sally.newton@nationaltrust.org.uk

Flag Fen Bronze Age Centre

4 hrs   All year

Travel back in time to the Bronze Age and see how people lived more than 3,000 years ago. Discover tools, technology, clothes and food from 1000BC. The museum displays artefacts including swords, daggers and axes, and the earliest wheel ever discovered in England.

* Featured on the Channel 4 programme *Time Team*
* Set within a 20-acre park

Location
NE of Peterborough, off A1139 or A605

Opening
Daily: 10am–5pm (last admission 4pm)

Admission
Adult £4.75, Child £3.50, Concs £4.25

Contact
The Droveway, Northey Road,
Peterborough PE6 7QJ

t 01733 313414
w flagfen.com
e office@flagfen.co.uk

©NTPL

303 Peterborough

Nene Valley Railway

3 hrs+ All year

Home to a real Thomas the Tank Engine, Nene Valley Railway provides an exciting day out for train enthusiasts young and old. Travel on a 15-mile round trip through the beautiful Nene Park and enjoy one of Britain's leading collections of engines and carriages, both steam and diesel.

* Children's play area
* Talking Timetable 01780 784404

Location
Off southbound A1 at Stibbington between A47 & A605 junctions

Opening
Daily: 9am–4.30pm

Admission
Adult £10.50, Child £5.50, Concs £8

Contact
Wansford Station, Stibbington, Peterborough PE8 6LR

t 01780 784444
w nvr.org.uk
e nvrorg@aol.com

304 Royston

Wimpole Home Farm

2–4 hrs All year

Built in 1794, Wimpole is a working farm and home to a number of rare farmyard breeds. Children can feed and handle many of the animals, and enjoy the adventure playground with pedal tractors.

* Parkland includes restored lakes & Gothic tower
* Walks available through woodland & rolling hills

Location
8 miles SW of Cambridge. Junction 12 of M11/junction 9 of A1(M)

Opening
Sat–Wed 10.30am–5pm (11am–4pm in winter); open Bank Hols & extra days in school hols, please phone for details

Admission
Adult £6, Child £4

Contact
Wimpole Hall, Arrington, Royston SG8 0BW

t 01223 206000
w wimpole.org
e wimpolehall@nationaltrust.org.uk

305 Sawtry

Hamerton Zoo Park

2 hrs+ All year

Do you know what a curassow, a seriema or a binturong is? Find out by visiting the zoo's fascinating array of beautiful creatures from around the world. There are special enclosures with low windows to give children thrilling views of the most popular animals.

* Spacious indoor-outdoor enclosures for monkeys
* Opportunity to handle many different animals

Location
On A14, turn off to B660 at junction 15 on to A1M. Follow signs

Opening
Daily: 10.30am–6pm (4pm in winter)

Admission
Please phone for details

Contact
Hamerton, nr Sawtry PE28 5RE

t 01832 293362
w hamertonzoopark.com
e office@hamertonzoopark.com

Waterbeach

Denny Abbey & The Farmland Museum

1 hr+   Apr–Oct

Learn about local rural life at the Farmland Museum with hands-on displays and interactive exhibits. Visit a traditional farmer's cottage and discover the story of the Benedictine monks, Knights Templar and Franciscan nuns who lived in Denny Abbey.

* Farmland Museum Trust
* Café open at weekends

Location	Contact
6 miles N of Cambridge on A10	Ely Road, Waterbeach CB5 9PQ
Opening	t 01223 860489
Daily: Apr–Oct 12noon–5pm	w dennyfarmlandmuseum.org.uk
Admission	
Adult £3.80, Child £1.70, Concs £3, Family £9.60	

Woodhurst

The Raptor Foundation

2 hrs+   All year

Home to more than 300 birds of prey and more than 40 species, the Raptor Foundation is a unique and exciting place for children and adults alike. Pay a visit to meet and learn about owls, falcons, hawks and buzzards.

* Quality Assured Visitor Centre
* Junior Raptors Club

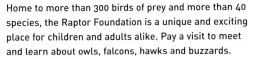

Location	Contact
Off A14 St Ives exit. Turn on to B1040 to Somersham & follow brown tourist signs	The Heath, St Ives Road, Woodhurst PE28 3BT
	t 01487 741140
Opening	w raptorfoundation.org.uk
Daily: 10am–5pm	e heleowl@aol.com
Admission	
Adult £4, Child £2.75, Concs £3	

Billericay

Barleylands Craft Village & Farm Centre

2 hrs   All year

A unique attraction with probably the largest collection of working crafts in East Anglia and an impressive farm museum. Children can meet and feed the friendly pigs, cows, goats and sheep in the animal centre. There is also an adventure play area.

* Indoor sand pit & trampolines

Location	Admission
Follow brown tourist signs from A127 or A129	*Craft Village* Free *Farm Centre* £3
Opening	**Contact**
Craft village All year (closed Mon) *Farm centre* Daily: Mar–Oct 10am–5pm; Nov–Feb 10am–4pm	Barleylands Road, Billericay CM11 2UD
	t 01268 290229
	w barleylands.co.uk
	e info@barleylands.co.uk

Billericay

Hanningfield Reservoir Visitor Centre

2–3 hrs   All year

The visitor centre is the gateway to the 100-acre nature reserve on the shores of Hanningfield Reservoir. As a breeding site for overwintering birds, this reserve has been designated a Site of Special Scientific Interest.

* Events throughout the year
* Children's activities throughout the year

Location	Admission
Turn off B1007 on to Downham Road & turn left on to Hawkswood Road. Centre is just beyond causeway, opposite Crowsheath	Free, donations requested
	Contact
	Hawkswood Road, Downham, Billericay CM11 1WT
Opening	t 01268 711001
Please phone for details	w essexwt.org.uk
	e hanningfield@essexwt.org.uk

The Original Great Maze

3 hrs+   Jul–Sep

The Great Maze offers more than 5 miles of pathway cut from 10 acres of maize and sunflowers, which reach a height of almost 10 feet. A new maze is designed every year, so enthusiasts can return time and time again to find their way through each new creation.

* Viewing platform & Lost Souls map available
* Shopping at Blake House Craft Centre

Location	Contact
On B1256 between Great Dunmow & Braintree; follow brown tourist signs	Blake House Craft Centre, Blake End, Braintree CM77 6RA
Opening	t 01376 553146
Please phone for details	w greatmaze.info
Admission	e info@lazydaisy.biz
Please phone for details	

Kelvedon Hatch Secret Nuclear Bunker

2 hrs+   All year

Explore the biggest and deepest bunker in South-East England, designed as a shelter for more than 600 people in the event of nuclear attack. Explore the labyrinth of rooms deep within the earth, hidden behind the massive 1.5 tonne blast doors.

* Try out authentic military uniforms & gasmasks

Location	Admission
Access is from A128 Chipping Ongar–Brentwood road at Kelvedon Hatch	Adults £6, Child £4
Opening	**Contact**
Mar–Oct Mon–Fri 10am–4pm, Sat–Sun & Bank Hols 10am–5pm; Nov–Feb Thu–Fri 10am–4pm, Sat–Sun 10am–5pm	Crown Buildings, Kelvedon Hall Lane, Brentwood CM14 5TL
	t 01277 364883
	w secretnuclearbunker.co.uk
	e bunkerInfo@japar.demon.co.uk

Old MacDonald's Educational Farm Park

3 hrs+   All year

This educational farm park was created to provide a greater understanding of British farm livestock, wildlife and the countryside. There are 17 acres of pasture and woodland, with hard paths to ensure dry feet and wheelchair access and opportunities to get close to the animals.

* Playground, soft play area & amusements
* Otters, red squirrels & owls

Location	Admission
Off M25 at junction 28 on to A1023. Left at 1st lights into Wigley Bush Lane, left at junction with Weald Road, 2 miles on Weald Road. Farm is on the left	Adult £5.75, Child £4.50, Concs £5.25
Opening	**Contact**
Daily: *summer* 10am, please phone for details of closing times *winter* 10am–dusk	Weald Road, South Weald, Brentwood CM14 5AY
	t 01277 375177/375393
	w oldmacdonaldsfarm.org.uk
	e info@oldmacdonaldsfarm.org.uk

Denny Abbey & The Farmland Museum

1 hr+   Apr–Oct

Learn about local rural life at the Farmland Museum with hands-on displays and interactive exhibits. Visit a traditional farmer's cottage and discover the story of the Benedictine monks, Knights Templar and Franciscan nuns who lived in Denny Abbey.

* Farmland Museum Trust
* Café open at weekends

Location	Contact
6 miles N of Cambridge on A10	Ely Road, Waterbeach CB5 9PQ
Opening	t 01223 860489
Daily: Apr–Oct 12noon–5pm	w dennyfarmlandmuseum.org.uk
Admission	
Adult £3.80, Child £1.70, Concs £3, Family £9.60	

The Raptor Foundation

2 hrs+   All year

Home to more than 300 birds of prey and more than 40 species, the Raptor Foundation is a unique and exciting place for children and adults alike. Pay a visit to meet and learn about owls, falcons, hawks and buzzards.

* Quality Assured Visitor Centre
* Junior Raptors Club

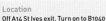

Location	Contact
Off A14 St Ives exit. Turn on to B1040 to Somersham & follow brown tourist signs	The Heath, St Ives Road, Woodhurst PE28 3BT
Opening	t 01487 741140
Daily: 10am–5pm	w raptorfoundation.org.uk
Admission	e heleowl@aol.com
Adult £4, Child £2.75, Concs £3	

Barleylands Craft Village & Farm Centre

2 hrs   All year

A unique attraction with probably the largest collection of working crafts in East Anglia and an impressive farm museum. Children can meet and feed the friendly pigs, cows, goats and sheep in the animal centre. There is also an adventure play area.

* Indoor sand pit & trampolines

Location	Admission
Follow brown tourist signs from A127 or A129	*Craft Village* **Free** *Farm Centre* **£3**
Opening	**Contact**
Craft village **All year** (closed Mon)	Barleylands Road, Billericay CM11 2UD
Farm centre **Daily: Mar–Oct** 10am–5pm; Nov–Feb 10am–4pm	t 01268 290229
	w barleylands.co.uk
	e info@barleylands.co.uk

Hanningfield Reservoir Visitor Centre

2–3 hrs   All year

The visitor centre is the gateway to the 100-acre nature reserve on the shores of Hanningfield Reservoir. As a breeding site for overwintering birds, this reserve has been designated a Site of Special Scientific Interest.

* Events throughout the year
* Children's activities throughout the year

Location	Admission
Turn off B1007 on to Downham Road & turn left on to Hawkswood Road. Centre is just beyond causeway, opposite Crowsheath	Free, donations requested
	Contact
Opening	Hawkswood Road, Downham, Billericay CM11 1WT
Please phone for details	t 01268 711001
	w essexwt.org.uk
	e hanningfield@essexwt.org.uk

310 Braintree

The Original Great Maze

3 hrs+   Jul–Sep

The Great Maze offers more than 5 miles of pathway cut from 10 acres of maize and sunflowers, which reach a height of almost 10 feet. A new maze is designed every year, so enthusiasts can return time and time again to find their way through each new creation.

* Viewing platform & Lost Souls map available
* Shopping at Blake House Craft Centre

Location
On B1256 between Great Dunmow & Braintree; follow brown tourist signs

Opening
Please phone for details

Admission
Please phone for details

Contact
Blake House Craft Centre, Blake End, Braintree CM77 6RA

t 01376 553146
w greatmaze.info
e info@lazydaisy.biz

311 Brentwood

Kelvedon Hatch Secret Nuclear Bunker

2 hrs+   All year

Explore the biggest and deepest bunker in South-East England, designed as a shelter for more than 600 people in the event of nuclear attack. Explore the labyrinth of rooms deep within the earth, hidden behind the massive 1.5 tonne blast doors.

* Try out authentic military uniforms & gasmasks

Location
Access is from A128 Chipping Ongar–Brentwood road at Kelvedon Hatch

Opening
Mar–Oct Mon–Fri 10am–4pm,
Sat–Sun & Bank Hols 10am–5pm;
Nov–Feb Thu–Fri 10am–4pm,
Sat–Sun 10am–5pm

Admission
Adults £6, Child £4

Contact
Crown Buildings, Kelvedon Hall Lane, Brentwood CM14 5TL

t 01277 364883
w secretnuclearbunker.co.uk
e bunkerInfo@japar.demon.co.uk

312 Brentwood

Old MacDonald's Educational Farm Park

3 hrs+   All year

This educational farm park was created to provide a greater understanding of British farm livestock, wildlife and the countryside. There are 17 acres of pasture and woodland, with hard paths to ensure dry feet and wheel-chair access and opportunities to get close to the animals.

* Playground, soft play area & amusements
* Otters, red squirrels & owls

Location
Off M25 at junction 28 on to A1023. Left at 1st lights into Wigley Bush Lane, left at junction with Weald Road, 2 miles on Weald Road. Farm is on the left

Opening
Daily: *summer* 10am, please phone for details of closing times
winter 10am–dusk

Admission
Adult £5.75, Child £4.50, Concs £5.25

Contact
Weald Road, South Weald, Brentwood CM14 5AY

t 01277 375177/375393
w oldmacdonaldsfarm.org.uk
e info@oldmacdonaldsfarm.org.uk

313 Chelmsford

Chelmsford Museum & Essex Regiment Museum

1 hr+   All year

Chelmsford museum houses three exhibitions telling the story of Chelmsford from the Ice Ages, via the Roman town, to the present day. Also visit the superb Essex Regiment Museum which houses many military artefacts as well.

* Bright & colourful Victorian pottery from Hedingham
* Regiment Museum houses many military artefacts

Location	Contact
In Oaklands Park, off Moulsham Street	Oaklands Park, Chelmsford CM2 9AQ
Opening	
Daily: Mon–Sat 10am–5pm, Sun 2pm–5pm (winter 1pm–4pm)	t 01245 605700
	w chelmsfordmuseums.co.uk
Admission	e oaklands@chelmsfordbc.gov.uk
Free, donations welcomed	

314 Colchester

Colchester Zoo

6 hrs   All year

Colchester Zoo has some of the best cat and primate collections in Europe. Come face-to-face with a white tiger in White Tiger Valley, or get closer to the zoo's chimpanzees at Chimp World. Other enclosures include Penguin Shores and Lion's Rock.

* Playa Patagonia – sealion underwater experience
* Spirit of Africa, elephants, giraffes, rhinos etc

Location	Contact
Take A1124 exit from A12	Maldon Road, Stanway, Colchester CO3 0SL
Opening	
Daily: from 9.30am, (closing times vary)	t 01206 331292
	w colchester-zoo.co.uk
Admission	e enquiries@colchester-zoo.co.uk
Please phone or visit the website for details.	

315 Colchester

High Woods Country Park

2hrs+   All year

This country park boasts areas of woodland, wetland, grassland and farmland. Numerous footpaths provide an opportunity to see a wide range of wildlife. A visitor centre houses exhibits of local and natural history.

* Quality Assured Visitor Attraction
* Award-winning Green Flag park

Location	Admission
Accessible from Mile End Road & Ipswich Road, travelling N from Colchester	Free
	Contact
Opening	Turner Road, Colchester CO4 5JR
Visitor centre 1 Apr–30 Sep daily Mon–Sat 10am–4.30pm, Sun & Bank Hols 11am–5.30pm; 1 Oct–31 Mar Sat–Sun only 10am–4pm	t 01206 853588
	w colchester.gov.uk
	e countryside@colchester.gov.uk

316 Colchester

Quasar at Rollerworld

1 hr+   All year

In this futuristic laser game each player is armed with a laser gun and shoots the opposition to win points. Players have unlimited lives and the Game Marshal instructs you on how to play. Under-12s must be accompanied by a playing adult.

* Suitable for ages 8–80
* Supervised by Game Marshal

Location
From A12 take turn-off to Harwich & Colchester. Continue straight over roundabouts & follow brown tourist signs

Opening
Please phone for details

Admission
Please phone for details

Contact
Eastgates,
Colchester CO1 2TJ

t 01206 868868
w rollerworld.co.uk

317 Halstead

Hedingham Castle

1 hr+   Apr–Sep

Built in 1140 by the Earls of Oxford, this is one of the best-preserved Norman keeps in England. The castle is set in beautiful parkland and holds special events such as jousts throughout the summer.

* Special events weekends, including jousting tournaments
* 1920s bog garden contains camellias & azaleas

Location
In Castle Hedingham, ½ mile from A1017 between Cambridge & Colchester

Opening
Apr–Sep Sun 10am–5pm

Admission
Adult £4.50, Child £3.50, Concs £4

Contact
Halstead CO9 3DJ

t 01787 460261
w hedinghamcastle.co.uk
e hedinghamcastle@aspects.net.co.uk

318 Maldon

Combined Military Services Museum

2 hrs   All year

The museum has a fascinating array of equipment and weaponry used by soldiers from the Civil War to the present day. Find out about James Bond-style espionage gadgets and even try on some of the uniforms yourself.

* See rare RAF escape & survival equipment
* Captured Iraqi personnel carrier

Location
Half a mile from Maldon's High Street, it is most easily reached via A130/A414, then follow Maldon's ringroad

Opening
Wed–Sun 10.30am–5pm

Admission
Adult £3.50, Child £2, Concs £2.75, Family £10

Contact
Station Road, Maldon CM9 4LQ

t 01621 841826
w cmsm.co.uk
e cmsm@btopenworld.com

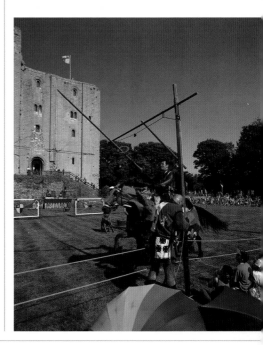

Chelmsford Museum & Essex Regiment Museum

1 hr+   All year

Chelmsford museum houses three exhibitions telling the story of Chelmsford from the Ice Ages, via the Roman town, to the present day. Also visit the superb Essex Regiment Museum which houses many military artefacts as well.

* Bright & colourful Victorian pottery from Hedingham
* Regiment Museum houses many military artefacts

Location
In Oaklands Park, off Moulsham Street

Opening
Daily: Mon–Sat 10am–5pm,
Sun 2pm–5pm (winter 1pm–4pm)

Admission
Free, donations welcomed

Contact
Oaklands Park,
Chelmsford CM2 9AQ

t 01245 605700
w chelmsfordmuseums.co.uk
e oaklands@chelmsfordbc.gov.uk

Colchester Zoo

6 hrs   All year

Colchester Zoo has some of the best cat and primate collections in Europe. Come face-to-face with a white tiger in White Tiger Valley, or get closer to the zoo's chimpanzees at Chimp World. Other enclosures include Penguin Shores and Lion's Rock.

* Playa Patagonia – sealion underwater experience
* Spirit of Africa, elephants, giraffes, rhinos etc

Location
Take A1124 exit from A12

Opening
Daily: from 9.30am, (closing times vary)

Admission
Please phone or visit the website
for details.

Contact
Maldon Road, Stanway, Colchester
CO3 0SL

t 01206 331292
w colchester-zoo.co.uk
e enquiries@colchester-zoo.co.uk

High Woods Country Park

2hrs+   All year

This country park boasts areas of woodland, wetland, grassland and farmland. Numerous footpaths provide an opportunity to see a wide range of wildlife. A visitor centre houses exhibits of local and natural history.

* Quality Assured Visitor Attraction
* Award-winning Green Flag park

Location
Accessible from Mile End Road &
Ipswich Road, travelling N from
Colchester

Opening
Visitor centre 1 Apr–30 Sep daily
Mon–Sat 10am–4.30pm, Sun & Bank
Hols 11am–5.30pm; 1 Oct–31 Mar
Sat–Sun only 10am–4pm

Admission
Free

Contact
Turner Road,
Colchester CO4 5JR

t 01206 853588
w colchester.gov.uk
e countryside@colchester.gov.uk

316 Colchester

Quasar at Rollerworld

1 hr+   All year

In this futuristic laser game each player is armed with a laser gun and shoots the opposition to win points. Players have unlimited lives and the Game Marshal instructs you on how to play. Under-12s must be accompanied by a playing adult.

* Suitable for ages 8–80
* Supervised by Game Marshal

Location
From A12 take turn-off to Harwich & Colchester. Continue straight over roundabouts & follow brown tourist signs

Opening
Please phone for details

Admission
Please phone for details

Contact
Eastgates,
Colchester CO1 2TJ

t 01206 868868
w rollerworld.co.uk

317 Halstead

Hedingham Castle

1 hr+   Apr–Sep

Built in 1140 by the Earls of Oxford, this is one of the best-preserved Norman keeps in England. The castle is set in beautiful parkland and holds special events such as jousts throughout the summer.

* Special events weekends, including jousting tournaments
* 1920s bog garden contains camellias & azaleas

Location
In Castle Hedingham, ½ mile from A1017 between Cambridge & Colchester

Opening
Apr–Sep Sun 10am–5pm

Admission
Adult £4.50, Child £3.50, Concs £4

Contact
Halstead CO9 3DJ

t 01787 460261
w hedinghamcastle.co.uk
e hedinghamcastle@aspects.net.co.uk

318 Maldon

Combined Military Services Museum

2 hrs   All year

The museum has a fascinating array of equipment and weaponry used by soldiers from the Civil War to the present day. Find out about James Bond-style espionage gadgets and even try on some of the uniforms yourself.

* See rare RAF escape & survival equipment
* Captured Iraqi personnel carrier

Location
Half a mile from Maldon's High Street, it is most easily reached via A130/A414, then follow Maldon's ringroad

Opening
Wed–Sun 10.30am–5pm

Admission
Adult £3.50, Child £2, Concs £2.75, Family £10

Contact
Station Road, Maldon CM9 4LQ

t 01621 841826
w cmsm.co.uk
e cmsm@btopenworld.com

319 Saffron Walden

Mole Hall Wildlife Park

2 hrs   All year

The park is in gardens adjoining a fully moated manor (not open to the public) and has otters, chimps, guanaco, lemurs, wallabies, deer and owls. Refreshments are available in the café.

* Tropical butterfly pavilion & animal adoption scheme

Location
Signed from B1383 & junction 8 of M11

Opening
Daily: Easter–Oct 10.30am–5.30pm;
Nov–Spring 10.30am–4pm (or dusk if earlier)
Please note: not all attractions are available during winter. Please phone for details.

Admission
Adult £6.30, Child £4.30, Concs £5

Contact
Widdington,
nr Saffron Walden CB11 3SS
t 01799 540400
w molehall.co.uk
e enquiries@molehall.co.uk

320 Southend-on-Sea

Adventure Island

6 hrs+   All year

Gasp at the dazzling array of rides at Adventure Island. Get soaked in the Water Wars, or brave the Green Scream Roller Coaster and the all new Sky Drop. Tiny tots will love the many rides and the themed Jungle Jive café.

* Fireball ride new in 2006
* Climb the Southend Rock

Location
From M25 take junction 29 or 30E towards Southend-on-Sea. Follow brown tourist signs marked 'Adventure Island'

Opening
Please phone for details

Admission
Free, Ultra Save Bands £14, Super Saver Wristband £19

Contact
Sunken Gardens, Western Esplanade,
Southend-on-Sea SS1 1EE
t 01702 443400
w adventureisland.co.uk
e bookings@stockvale.co.uk

321 Stansted Mountfitchet

The House on the Hill Toy Museum

2 hrs   All year

With more than 80,000 items on display, the museum will delight children and be a nostalgic trip for adults. The display covers toys from Victorian times to the present day, with everything from vintage slot machines to modern Barbie and Cindy dolls.

* Large collection of rock 'n' roll memorabilia
* Shop selling reproduction wall machines   WC

Location
In Stansted Mountfitchet village,
3½ miles from junction 8 of M11

Opening
Daily: Apr–Oct 10am–5pm;
Nov–Mar 10am–4pm

Admission
Adult £4, Child £3.30, Concs £3.50

Contact
Stansted, Essex CM24 8SP
t 01279 813237
w stanstedtoymuseum.com
e info@stanstedtoymuseum.com

322 Waltham Abbey

Royal Gunpowder Mills

3 hrs+   Apr–Sep

The world of explosives is uncovered with a range of interactive and static displays that follow the trail back to the C17. This unique museum traces the evolution of gunpowder technology and reveals the impact it has had on the history of Great Britain.

* Muskets, rifles, pistols & machine guns
* Munitionettes – photo exhibits of women workers in WWII

Location
1 mile from junction 26 of M25 & A121

Opening
Sat–Sun & Bank Hols only 11am–5pm
(last admission 3.30pm)

Admission
Adult £6, Child £3.25, Concs £5

Contact
Beaulieu Drive, Waltham Abbey,
EN9 1JY
t 01992 707370
w royalgunpowdermills.com
e info@royalgunpowdermills.com

323 Berkhamsted

Ashridge Estate

1 hr+   All year

There's plenty to see and do at Ashridge, no matter what season it is. Enjoy the spring bluebells, a picnic on a sunny day, or a woodland walk in autumn. Make sure you keep your eyes peeled, as Ashridge is a wildlife haven – if you're lucky, you might spot a badger or a woodpecker.

* Splendid views from Ivinghoe Beacon
* Visitor centre with exhibition room

Location
Between Northchurch & Ringshall just off B4506

Opening
All year
Visitor centre **17 Mar–16 Dec 12noon–5pm**
Duke of Bridgewater monument
17 Mar–28 Oct 12noon–5pm

Admission
Estate **Free**
Monument **Adult £1.30, Child 60p**

Contact
Ringshall, Berkhamsted HP4 1LT

t **01442 851227**
w **nationaltrust.org.uk**
e **ashridge@nationaltrust.org.uk**

324 Borehamwood

Aldenham Country Park

2 hrs+   All year

With a 65-acre reservoir, circular footpath and 175 acres of woods and meadowland, Aldenham Country Park has a range of activities and interests for the whole family, from nature trails to Winnie the Pooh features. There are also rare breeds including cattle and sheep.

* Adventure playground
* Day tickets – 0208 953 4978

Location
Approach via A5, A41, A1(M) or M1 junction 5 & park is just off A5183, N of Elstree on Aldenham road

Opening
Daily: Nov–Feb 9am–4pm; Mar–Apr & Sep–Oct 9am–5pm; May–Aug 9am–6pm

Admission
Free. Car park £4 on exit

Contact
Park Office, Dagger Lane, Elstree, Borehamwood WD6 3AT

t **0208 953 9602**
w **hertsdirect.org/aldenham**

325 Broxbourne

Paradise Wildlife Park

2 hrs+   All year

A friendly, family-run leisure park that offers excitement and enjoyment for all the family. Visitors can touch and feed paddock animals, including zebras and camels, shadow a keeper, and meet wolves and meerkats. Kids can also enjoy the play areas and funfair.

* Paradise Lagoon, the new paddling pool
* On Safari crazy golf and Wild West parrot show

Location
Junction 25 of M25 on to A10, signed from Broxbourne

Opening
Daily: Mar–Oct 9.30am–6pm; Nov–Feb 10am–5pm

Admission
Adult £11, Child & Concs £8

Contact
White Stubbs Lane, Broxbourne EN10 7QA

t **01992 470490**
w **pwpark.com**
e **info@pwpark.com**

326 Hatfield

Mill Green Museum & Mill

1 hr+   All year

A visit to this fully restored C18 working watermill, which is still producing flour, is interesting and educational. The adjacent miller's house is now the local history museum for the district. There are events throughout the year for all to enjoy.

* Waterwheel in action every day
* Watch milling of organic flour on Tue, Wed & Sun

Location
In Mill Green, between Hatfield & Welwyn Garden City

Opening
Tue–Fri 10am–5pm,
Sat–Sun & Bank Hols 2pm–5pm

Admission
Free

Contact
Mill Green, Hatfield AL9 5PD

t 01707 271362
w hertsmuseums.org.uk/millgreen
e museum@welhat.gov.uk

327 Hertford

Hertford Museum

1 hr+   All year

A local history museum in an old town house with a recreated Jacobean knot garden. There are changing temporary exhibitions to cater for all ages, with related activities for children.

* Special drop-in events in school holidays
* Tea served on Sat until Sep

Location
Just off A414 in centre of Hertford, a short walk from multistorey car park & within walking distance of railway station

Opening
Tue–Sat 10am–5pm
Please phone for details of Bank Hols opening times

Admission
Free

Contact
18 Bull Plain, Hertford SG14 1DT

t 01992 582686
w hertfordmuseum.org
e hertfordmuseum@btconnect.com

328 Hitchin

Waterhall Farm & Craft Centre

2 hrs+   All year

A small open farm featuring rare breeds and offering a hands-on experience for visitors. There is also a play area featuring a slide and an old tractor.

* Country walks, garden & tearoom
* Dogs permitted only in car park

Location
Off B651 Hitchin–St Albans road, in Whitwell village

Opening
Sat–Sun & school hols
summer 10am–5pm
winter 10am–4pm

Admission
Adult £2.75, Child (2–16) & Concs £1.75

Contact
Whitwell, Hitchin SG4 8BN

t 01438 871256

329 Royston

Maple Street British Museum of Miniatures

2 hrs   All year

Visit the Museum of Miniatures to explore the world of doll's houses and all things miniature. Its displays include the largest doll's house in the world, and the shop is the largest doll's house shop in Europe.

Location
Take A603 from Cambridge & A1198 to Royston

Opening
Daily: Mon–Sat 9.30am–5pm, Sun 12noon–4pm
Please phone for details of Bank Hols opening times

Admission
Adult £2.50, Child £1.50

Contact
Maple Street, Wendy, Royston SG8 0AB

t 01223 207025
w maplestreet.co.uk
e info@maplestreet.co.uk

330 Royston

Shepreth Wildlife Park

2–4 hrs   All year

Shepreth offers a fun and interactive day out for the whole family. It's home to animals including tigers, meerkats, wolves, deer and farmyard livestock. Children can also visit Waterworld and Bug City, where they'll come face to face with scorpions and giant spiders.

* Pirate ship adventure area
* Soft play area & sandpit for toddlers, & children's playroom

Location
Easily reached from A10 Cambridge–Royston road & A1198 Royston–Huntingdon road. Good access by train from London King's Cross to Shepreth railway station

Opening
Daily: Apr–Sep 10am–6pm; Oct–Mar 10am–dusk

Admission
Adult £7.50, Child £5.50, Concs £5.95
Bug City/Waterworld £1.90, £1.30, £1.50

Contact
Willersmill, Station Road, Shepreth, nr Royston SG8 6PZ

t 09066 800031 (info line – 25p/min)
01763 262226 (group bookings)
w sheprethwildlifepark.co.uk

331 St Albans

Verulamium Museum

1–2 hrs   All year

Verulamium Museum is a museum of everyday life in Roman Britain. Award-winning displays include recreations of Roman interiors, collections of glass, pottery and jewellery, coins and magnificent mosaics, and stunning wall-paintings.

* Quality Assured Visitor Attraction
* Hands-on discovery areas

Location
Approach via M1 junction 6 or M25 junction 21A. Museum is just off A4147, 1 mile from St Albans centre

Opening
Daily: Mon–Sat 10am–5.30pm, Sun 2pm–5.30pm (last admission 30 min before close)

Admission
Adult £3.30, Child & Concs £2

Contact
St Michaels, St Albans AL3 4SW

t 01727 751810
w stalbansmuseums.org.uk
e museum@stalbans.gov.uk

326 Hatfield

Mill Green Museum & Mill

1 hr+   All year

A visit to this fully restored C18 working watermill, which is still producing flour, is interesting and educational. The adjacent miller's house is now the local history museum for the district. There are events throughout the year for all to enjoy.

* Waterwheel in action every day
* Watch milling of organic flour on Tue, Wed & Sun

Location
In Mill Green, between Hatfield & Welwyn Garden City

Opening
Tue–Fri 10am–5pm,
Sat–Sun & Bank Hols 2pm–5pm

Admission
Free

Contact
Mill Green, Hatfield AL9 5PD

t 01707 271362
w hertsmuseums.org.uk/millgreen
e museum@welhat.gov.uk

327 Hertford

Hertford Museum

1 hr+   All year

A local history museum in an old town house with a recreated Jacobean knot garden. There are changing temporary exhibitions to cater for all ages, with related activities for children.

* Special drop-in events in school holidays
* Tea served on Sat until Sep

Location
Just off A414 in centre of Hertford, a short walk from multistorey car park & within walking distance of railway station

Opening
Tue–Sat 10am–5pm
Please phone for details of Bank Hols opening times

Admission
Free

Contact
18 Bull Plain, Hertford SG14 1DT

t 01992 582686
w hertfordmuseum.org
e hertfordmuseum@btconnect.com

328 Hitchin

Waterhall Farm & Craft Centre

2 hrs+   All year

A small open farm featuring rare breeds and offering a hands-on experience for visitors. There is also a play area featuring a slide and an old tractor.

* Country walks, garden & tearoom
* Dogs permitted only in car park

Location
Off B651 Hitchin–St Albans road, in Whitwell village

Opening
Sat–Sun & school hols
summer 10am–5pm
winter 10am–4pm

Admission
Adult £2.75, Child (2–16) & Concs £1.75

Contact
Whitwell, Hitchin SG4 8BN

t 01438 871256

329 Royston

Maple Street British Museum of Miniatures

2 hrs   All year

Visit the Museum of Miniatures to explore the world of doll's houses and all things miniature. Its displays include the largest doll's house in the world, and the shop is the largest doll's house shop in Europe.

Location	Admission
Take A603 from Cambridge & A1198 to Royston	Adult £2.50, Child £1.50
	Contact
Opening	Maple Street, Wendy,
Daily: Mon–Sat 9.30am–5pm, Sun 12noon–4pm	Royston SG8 0AB
Please phone for details of Bank Hols opening times	t 01223 207025
	w maplestreet.co.uk
	e info@maplestreet.co.uk

330 Royston

Shepreth Wildlife Park

2–4 hrs   All year

Shepreth offers a fun and interactive day out for the whole family. It's home to animals including tigers, meerkats, wolves, deer and farmyard livestock. Children can also visit Waterworld and Bug City, where they'll come face to face with scorpions and giant spiders.

* Pirate ship adventure area
* Soft play area & sandpit for toddlers, & children's playroom

Location	Admission
Easily reached from A10 Cambridge–Royston road & A1198 Royston–Huntingdon road. Good access by train from London King's Cross to Shepreth railway station	Adult £7.50, Child £5.50, Concs £5.95
	Bug City/Waterworld £1.90, £1.30, £1.50
	Contact
	Willersmill, Station Road, Shepreth, nr Royston SG8 6PZ
Opening	
Daily: Apr–Sep 10am–6pm; Oct–Mar 10am–dusk	t 09066 800031 (info line – 25p/min)
	01763 262226 (group bookings)
	w sheprethwildlifepark.co.uk

331 St Albans

Verulamium Museum

1–2 hrs   All year

Verulamium Museum is a museum of everyday life in Roman Britain. Award-winning displays include recreations of Roman interiors, collections of glass, pottery and jewellery, coins and magnificent mosaics, and stunning wall-paintings.

* Quality Assured Visitor Attraction
* Hands-on discovery areas

Location	Admission
Approach via M1 junction 6 or M25 junction 21A. Museum is just off A4147, 1 mile from St Albans centre	Adult £3.30, Child & Concs £2
	Contact
Opening	St Michaels, St Albans AL3 4SW
Daily: Mon–Sat 10am–5.30pm, Sun 2pm–5.30pm (last admission 30 min before close)	t 01727 751810
	w stalbansmuseums.org.uk
	e museum@stalbans.gov.uk

332 St Albans

Willows Farm Village

3 hrs+   Apr–Oct

Children love this farm village where they can get to know the farm animals in a countryside setting. Attractions include a bouncy haystack, Daft Duck trails, a guinea pig village, a children's show and a tractor trek.

* Falconry display
* Maze (summer holidays only)

Location
300 m from M25 junction 22

Opening
Daily: Apr–Oct 10am–5.30pm

Admission
Please phone for details

Contact
Coursers Road, London Colney, St Albans AL2 1BB

t 0870 123 3718
w willowsfarmvillage.com
e info@willowsfarmvillage.com

333 Stevenage

Fairlands Valley Park

4 hrs+   All year

This beautiful 120-acre park contains an 11-acre lake used for a range of watersport courses; its waters are kept well stocked for anglers. There is a kids' area with paddling pool and play equipment. The park is also home to a wide selection of wildlife and wildfowl.

* Children's play area
* Paddling pools open during summer

Location
On Six Hills Way, 1 mile E of Stevenage

Opening
Daily: 8am–dusk

Admission
Park Free
Charges for water sports, boat hire, etc.

Contact
Six Hills Way, Stevenage SG2 0BL

t 01438 353241
w stevenage-leisure.co.uk/fairlands
e fairlands@stevenage-leisure.co.uk

334 Watford

Topsy Turvy World

2 hrs   All year

This indoor adventure playground has a baby play pool and a separate area for toddlers – a whole new way to party and play. Children can enjoy playing amid an extreme maze of tunnels, vertical drops and slides. An integrated toddlers' area and ball cannons are also on offer.

Location
5 min from M1 junction 5 & 10 min from M25 junction 19 on Aldenham road

Opening
Daily: *Activity World* 10am–6pm

Admission
Adult free, Child (2–5) £4.50, Child (over 5) £5.95

Contact
Lincolnsfield Centre, Bushey Hall Drive, Bushey, Watford WD23 2ES

t 01923 219902
w topsyturvyworld.com
e general@topsyturvyworld.com

335 Aylsham

Bure Valley Railway

2 hrs+   All year

Bure Valley Railway is one of England's premier narrow-gauge railways serving enthusiasts, travellers and tourists. Its steam and diesel trains pass through scenery that is as varied, interesting and beautiful as any to be found on a railway journey in England.

* 2 main stations at Aylsham & Wroxham
* Easy to combine with a cruise on the Norfolk Broads

Location
Aylsham railway station is situated mid-way between Norwich & Cromer on A140

Opening
Railway Mar–Sep 10am–5.30pm plus school hols
Please phone for details of other opening times

Admission
Please phone for details

Contact
Norwich Road, Aylsham, Norfolk NR11 6BW

t 01263 733858
w bvrw.co.uk
e info@bvrw.co.uk

336 Banham

Banham Zoo

3–5 hrs   All year

Set in 35 acres of countryside and landscaped gardens, Banham Zoo is home to some of the world's most exotic and endangered animals, ranging from big cats to birds of prey, and siamangs to shire horses.

* Free safari roadtrain
* All-weather activity centre

Location
Between Attleborough & Diss; signed from A11 & A140

Opening
Daily: 10am (seasonal closing times, please phone for details)

Admission
Varies according to season, please phone for details

Contact
The Grove, Banham NR16 2HE

t 01953 887771
w banhamzoo.co.uk

337 Blakeney

Blakeney Point

4 hrs+   All year

One of Britain's foremost bird sanctuaries, the Point is noted for its colonies of breeding terns and for the rare migrants that pass through in spring and autumn. Common and grey seals can also be seen. Dogs are allowed April–August.

* Information centre at Morston Quay provides further details
* Restricted access during main bird breeding season

Location	Contact
Morston Quay, Blakeney & Cley are all off A149 Cromer–Hunstanton road	Friary Farm, Cley Road, Blakeney, Holt NR25 7NW
Opening	t 01263 740241
Daily: all reasonable times	w nationaltrust.org.uk
Admission	e blakeneypoint@nationaltrust.org.uk
Free	

338 Brandon

Grimes Graves

1 hr   Mar–Oct

At Grimes Graves there is a site exhibition displaying remarkable Neolithic flint mines. These mines first excavated in the 1870s, are 4,000 years old, and contain more than 433 pits and shafts. One of these pits is open to the public.

* No children under 5 allowed down shaft owing to 30ft drop
* Site of Special Scientific Interest

Location	Contact
Located 7 miles NW of Thetford off A134	Brandon, Lynford IP26 5DE
Opening	t 01842 810656
Please phone for details	w english-heritage.org.uk
Admission	
Adult £2.70, Child £1.40, Concs £2, Family £6.80	

339 Cromer

Norfolk Shire Horse Centre

2 hrs+   Apr–Oct

See magnificent heavy shire horses working on the land just as they did in days gone by. Take time to look around the rural museum and at the video show, see the small farm animals and the mares with their foals, and join in with feeding times.

* Children's farm & riding school
* Special events include blacksmith demonstrations

Location	Contact
Off A148 & A149	West Runton Stables, West Runton, nr Cromer NR27 9QH
Opening	t 01263 837339
Apr–Oct Sun–Fri 10am–5pm (closed Sat except Bank Hols)	w norfolk-shirehorse-centre.co.uk
Admission	e bakewell@norfolkshirehorse.
Adult £6, Child £4, Concs £5	fsnet.co.uk

340 Dereham

Gressenhall Museum & Workhouse

4 hrs+   Mar–Oct

This is a remarkable museum housed in a former workhouse and in an idyllic rural setting. It has displays on village and rural life plus a farm worked with horses and stocked with rare breeds.

* Exciting woodland playground
* Family-friendly displays

Location	Contact
3 miles NW of Dereham. Follow signs	Gressenhall, Dereham NR20 4DR
Opening	t 01362 860563
Daily: Mar–Oct 10am–5pm	w museums.norfolk.gov.uk
Admission	e gressenhall.museum@norfolk.gov.uk
Adult £7, Child £4.65, Concs £5.95	

341 Diss

Bressingham Steam Experience & Gardens

4 hrs Easter–Oct

A working steam experience in a nationally known garden setting with narrow-gauge railway rides, a Victorian steam roundabout, locomotive sheds, stationary engine displays, royal coaches, traction engines and gardens. There are miniature steam-hauled trains, too.

* Dad's Army National Collection
* Friends of Thomas the Tank Engine

Location
3 miles W of Diss on A1066 Diss–Thetford road

Opening
Daily: Easter–Oct 10.30am–5.30pm
Please phone for details

Admission
Please phone for details

Contact
Bressingham, Diss IP22 2AB
t 01379 686900
w bressingham.co.uk
e info@bressingham.co.uk

342 Fakenham

Langham Glass

3 hrs+ All year

Langham Glass is based in a large, old, pantiled and flint-faced barn in Norfolk. Teams of glassmakers can be seen working with molten glass using blowing irons and hand tools in the traditional way used for hundreds of years.

* Quality Assured Visitor Attraction
* Museum & video, plus play area

Location
Follow A148 from Holt to Fakenham for 3 miles, turn right on to B1156 & follow brown tourist signs from A148 Fakenham–King's Lynn road

Opening
Daily: 10am–5pm

Admission
Glassmaking Adult £3.95, Child & Concs £2.95

Contact
Scunthorpe Boulevard, Tattersett Business Park, Fakenham NR21 7RL
t 01485 529111
w langhamglass.co.uk
e enquiries@langhamglass.co.uk

343 Fakenham

South Creake Maize Maze

2 hrs+ Jul–Sep

Looking for excitement and adventure? Then take the challenge of a 7-acre maze in a maize field. Set in 18 acres of unspoilt Norfolk countryside, this is a chance to literally lose yourself in nature.

* Crazy golf
* Panning for gold

Location
Between Fakenham & Burnham Market on B1355, just off A148 King's Lynn–Fakenham road

Opening
Daily: Jul–Sep 10am–6pm
(last admission 5pm)

Admission
Adult £4, Child £3, Concs £3

Contact
Compton Hall, South Creake, Fakenham NR21 9JD
t 01328 823224
w amazingmaizemaze.co.uk
e info@amazingmaizemaze.co.uk

344 Great Yarmouth

Great Yarmouth Sealife Centre

3 hrs All year

Experience spectacular eye-to-eye views of everything from shrimps and starfish to sharks and stingrays. The City of Atlantis has an underwater tunnel allowing visitors to walk on the seabed and encounter sharks and multicoloured fish. Look out for Medusa's head!

* Soft play area
* Seahorse breeding centre

Location
Take A47 from Norwich, A143 from Beccles or A12 from Lowestoft

Opening
Daily: from 10am

Admission
Please phone for details

Contact
Marine Parade, Great Yarmouth NR30 3AH
t 01493 330631
w sealife.co.uk

345 Great Yarmouth

Horsey Windpump

2 hrs   Mar–Oct

Horsey Windpump is a drainage windmill built in 1912 and is the only National Trust property open to the public in the Norfolk Broads. The mill offers striking views across Horsey Mere.

* National Trust property

Location	Contact
Off B1159, 15 miles N of Great Yarmouth, between Martham & Sea Palling	Horsey, Great Yarmouth NR29 4EF
	t 01493 393904
	w nationaltrust.org.uk
Opening	e horseywindpump@nationaltrust.
Please phone or see website for details	org.uk
Admission	
Adult £2, Child £1	

347 Great Yarmouth

Thrigby Hall Wildlife Gardens

3 hrs+   All year

Meet a wide selection of Asian mammals, birds and reptiles, including tigers, storks and crocodiles. Enjoy the superb willow-pattern gardens and let off steam in the play area. There is also a dramatic swamp house for crocodiles and other tropical swamp dwellers.

* Lime Tree Lookout
* Tiger Tree Walk

Location	Contact
Off A1064 Caister–Acle road	Filby, Great Yarmouth NR29 3DR
Opening	t 01493 369477
Daily: 10am–5pm	w thrigbyhall.co.uk
Admission	
Adult £7.90, Child (4–14) £5.90, Concs £6.90	

346 Great Yarmouth

Pleasure Beach, Great Yarmouth

2 hrs+   Mar–Oct

The Pleasure Beach is on the seafront at the southern end of Great Yarmouth's Golden Mile and covers 9 acres. As well as a main ride area with more than 70 rides and attractions and the awe-inspiring Ejector Seat, there are two crazy golf courses and gardens.

* 70 rides & attractions
* New ride – Evolution

Location	Contact
Take A12 from Lowestoft or A47 from Norwich	Great Yarmouth NR30 3EH
Opening	t 01493 844585
Please phone for details	w pleasure-beach.co.uk
Admission	e GYPBeach@aol.com
Free. Rides paid for at reception or machines	

348 Holt

Baconsthorpe Castle

1–2 hrs   All year

Baconsthorpe Castle is a C15 part-moated, part-fortified house. The remains include the inner and outer gate house and curtain wall. The local post office sells guide books and postcards.

* English Heritage property

Location	Contact
Off A148 & B1149, ¾ mile N of Baconsthorpe village, off an unclassified road. 3 miles E of Holt	Baconsthorpe, Holt
	t 01223 582700
Opening	w english-heritage.org.uk
Daily: All reasonable times	
Admission	
Free	

349 Holt

Bishop's Boats Seal Trips

1 hr+   Apr–Oct

Take a boat trip to see the seals and birds on Blakeney Point. There are many species of birds to spot, and the grey and common seals form a colony of approximately 500.

* Optional landing trips
* Warm or waterproof clothing recommended

Location	Contact
Trips depart from Blakeney Point reached by A149	Blakeney Point, Blakeney, Holt
	t 0800 0740754/01263 740753
Opening	w bishopsboats.co.uk
Please phone for details as times vary depending on tides	e bishopsboats@bigfoot.com
Admission	
Adult £7, Child £4	

350 Hoveton

Wroxham Barns

2–3 hrs   All year

Wroxham Barns will keep all the family happy. Watch traditional and contemporary craftworkers at work, indulge in a spot of shopping, feed the friendly animals and have fun at the fair.

* Quality Assured Visitor Attraction
* Junior farm & country food shop

Location	Admission
Approximately 10 miles from Norwich. Follow A1151 towards Wroxham then follow brown tourist signs	*Admission & Car park* **Free**
	Junior Farm £2.85
Opening	Contact
Daily: 10am–5pm	Tunstead Road, Hoveton NR12 8QU
	t 01603 783762
	w wroxham-barns.co.uk
	e info@wroxham-barns.co.uk

351 Hunstanton

Hunstanton Sea Life Centre

1 hr+   All year

At this sanctuary you will see otters, penguins and more than 30 permanent displays all showcasing the diversity of life under the waves. The centre also provides a safe haven for sick, injured or orphaned seal pups that are cared for at the sanctuary.

* Penguin sanctuary, home to rare Humboldt penguins
* Marine Hospital

Location	Admission
Take A149 from King's Lynn to Hunstanton. Follow signs	Adult £9.50, Child £6.95, Concs £7.50
	Contact
Opening	Southern Promenade, Hunstanton PE36 5BH
Daily: 10am–4pm	
Times may vary during winter, please phone for details	t 01485 533576
	w sealsanctuary.co.uk
	e hunstantonsealifecentre@ merlinentertainments.biz

352 King's Lynn

Caithness Crystal Visitor Centre

2 hrs+   All year

Glassmaking is a magical craft that can transform sand into exquisite glassware using only the heat of a furnace and the skill of hand and eye. Witness it for yourself at the visitor centre in King's Lynn and marvel at a demonstration of the artistry involved.

* Quality Assured Visitor Attraction

Location
Off A149, A47 & A10. Follow brown tourist signs

Opening
Daily: Mon–Sat 9am–5pm, Sun 10.15am–4.15pm
Please phone for details of glassmaking demonstration times

Admission
Free

Contact
Paxman Road, Hardwick Industrial Estate, King's Lynn PE30 4NE

t 01553 765111
w caithnessglass.co.uk
e tchaytors@caithnessglass.co.uk

353 Norwich

Bank Boats

4 hrs+   All year

Hire all-weather dayboats and take a trip on the beautiful River Ant. Drift lazily past windmills and enjoy a leisurely picnic on the riverbank. Canoes are also available for hire.

* Electric dayboats

Location
On slip road off A149 between Stalham & Wroxham

Opening
Daily: 9am–5pm

Admission
From £25 for 2 hrs

Contact
Staithe Cottage, Wayford Bridge, Stalham, Norwich NR12 9LN

t 01692 582457

354 Norwich

Barton House Railway

2 hrs   Apr–Oct

Barton House has a miniature steam passenger railway and a steam and battery-electric railway. There are also full-size Midland and Great Northern accessories, including signals and signal boxes. Guaranteed fun for railway enthusiasts of all ages.

* Museum of railway

Location
On A1151 from Norwich

Opening
Apr–Oct 3rd Sun each month
2.30pm–5.30pm
Please phone for details

Admission
Adult £2, Child £1
By boat from Wroxham Bridge:
Adult £3, Child £1.50

Contact
Hartwell Road, The Avenue,
Wroxham, Norwich NR12 8TL

t 01603 782470

355 Norwich

Dinosaur Adventure Park

4 hrs+   Mar–Oct

Come face to face with life-size dinosaurs on the ultimate family adventure. The park includes a secret animal garden, adventure play areas, Climb-a-saurus, the Lost World Amazing Adventure and Jurassic Putt.

* New Adventurer's Guide
* Country Capers & Raptor Races

Location
9 miles from Norwich. Follow brown tourist signs from A47 or A1067 to Weston Park

Opening
Please phone or visit the website for details

Admission
Adult £7.95, Child & Concs £6.95

Contact
Weston Park, Lenwade,
Norwich NR9 5JW

t 01603 876310
w dinosaurpark.co.uk
e info@dinosaurpark.co.uk

356 Norwich

Fairhaven Woodland & Water Garden

2–4 hrs   All year

These delightful woodland and water-gardens have a fantastic combination of plants and flowers, and are ideal terrain for bird-watchers. There are also picturesque waterways spanned by small bridges and special events to enjoy on Sundays in summer.

* 120 acres of woodland
* Private broad

Location
Follow brown tourist signs off A47 at junction with B1140 through South Walsham

Opening
Nov–Apr daily 10am–5pm;
May–Aug Wed–Thu 10am–9pm

Admission
Adult £4.50, Child £2, Concs £4, Dogs 25p
Sanctuary £1.50 per person

Contact
School Road, South Walsham,
Norwich NR13 6DZ

t 01603 270449
w fairhavengarden.co.uk
e enquiries@fairhavengarden.co.uk

357 Norwich

Felbrigg Hall, Garden & Park

2 hrs+   Mar–Oct

One of the finest C17 houses in East Anglia, Felbrigg contains original C18 furniture, an outstanding library, and a beautifully restored walled garden with a working dovecote. The house is set in 500 acres of inviting parkland and woodland.

* Many woodland walks
* Changing programme of exhibitions

Location
In Felbrigg, 2 miles SW of Cromer, off B1346. Signed from A140 & A148

Opening
Mar–Oct Sat–Wed
Hall 1pm–5pm
Gardens 11am–5pm

Admission
Please phone for details

Contact
Felbrigg, Norwich NR11 8PR

t 01263 837444
w nationaltrust.org.uk
e felbrigg@nationaltrust.org.uk

©NTPL/Rupert Truman

358 Norwich

ILPH Hall Farm

1–2 hrs   All year

Visit this centre to learn about the work of the International League for the Protection of Horses. Meet some of the horses and ponies in care, many of whom have been rescued from cruelty and neglect.

* Visitor centre, stabling & indoor riding area

Location
Off A11, signed between Attleborough & Thetford

Opening
Wed–Sat, Sun & Bank Hols 11am–4pm

Admission
Free

Contact
Snetterton, Norwich NR16 2LR

t 01953 498898
w ilph.org
e info@ilph.org

359 Poringland

The Play Barn

2 hrs+   All year

A fun-packed centre with a host of activities for younger children. Play in the 'Haybarn' beach barn or the duck pond room. Venture outside for tractor rides, to feed the animals or try your hand at pond-dipping. You can even learn to ride a pony and go out on a hack.

* Illustrated talks & tours
* Seasonal special events

Location
10 min S of Norwich off B1332
Bungay Road

Opening
Mon–Fri 9.30am–3.30pm,
Sun 10am–5pm

Admission
Easter–Oct Adults £1.25, Child £4.75
Nov–Easter Adult £1, Child £4

Contact
West Green Farm, Shotesham Road,
Poringland NR14 7LP

t 01508 495526
w theplaybarn.co.uk
e barnclub@btopenworld.com

360 Sheringham

The Muckleburgh Collection

2 hrs   Feb–Oct

A collection of more than 120 military vehicles, tanks and guns, plus items from Operation Desert Storm, militaria from the C18 and scale models. Learn how to drive a tank, take a coastal ride on a US personnel Carrier, or visit by air, landing on the adjoining airstrip.

* Meteor on loan from Imperial War Museum
* Gama Goat Rides – in a US personnel carrier

Location
Signed from A149 W of Cromer,
3 miles W of Sheringham

Opening
12–19 Feb daily 10am–5pm;
26 Feb–26 Mar Sun 10am–5pm;
Apr–Oct daily 10am–5pm

Admission
Adult £5.50, Child £3, Concs £4.50

Contact
Weybourne Military Camp,
Holt NR25 7EG

t 01263 588210
w muckleburgh.co.uk
e info@muckleburgh.co.uk

361 Walsham

Elephant Playbarn

3 hrs   All year

A converted Norfolk flint barn filled with bouncy castles, ball pools and toys suitable for the under-eights. There is also a fully enclosed courtyard with an adventure play area and lots of pedal toys.

* Please phone in advance to ensure disabled access

Location
Off A149, S of Cromer, on B1145,
½ mile from Mundesley

Opening
Wed–Sun 10am–4pm; school hols
Tue–Sun

Admission
Adult Free, Child (1yr & under), £3.50
Child (2–7) £4

Contact
Mundesley Road, Knapton,
North Walsham NR28 0RY

t 01263 721080
w elephantplaybarn.co.uk

362 Walsham

Norfolk Motor Cycle Museum

3 hrs+   All year

Young motorcycle enthusiasts will be fascinated by the displays of more than 100 motorcycles and 100 bicycles, including a wide collection of two-wheelers from 1920 to 1960.

* Educational visits welcomed

Location
Near junction of B1150 Norwich road &
A149 Great Yarmouth–Cromer road
(town bypass)

Opening
Please phone for details

Admission
Adult £3, Child £1.50, Concs £2.50

Contact
Railway Yard,
North Walsham NR28 0DS

t 01692 406266

363 Brandon

High Lodge Forest Centre

8 hrs+   All year

Thetford Forest is Britain's largest lowland pine forest. High Lodge is located in the heart of the forest with walks, cycle hire, an adventure playground, deer safaris and much more.

* One of the largest mazes in Europe
* Bird walks & family fun walks

Location	Contact
Just off A11 on B1107 midway between Thetford & Brandon	Thetford Forest Park, Santon Downham, Brandon IP27 0TJ
Opening	t 01842 815434 (High Lodge Centre)
Daily: 9am–dusk	01842 810271 (Forestry Commission)
Please phone for details	w forestry.gov.uk
Admission	e e.anglia.fdo@forestry.gsi.gov.uk
£5 per car	

364 Bungay

Bungay Castle

1 hr   All year

The remains of this large Norman castle contain many interesting features. The massive gate house towers still stand, as do the bridge pit and curtain walls. A mine tunnel is exposed, along with the forebuilding with its latrine chamber (garderobe).

* Visitor centre
* Café & shop

Location	Contact
Off A143 & A144	6 Cross Street, Bungay NR35 1AU
Opening	t 01986 896756
Daily: 10am–4pm	w bungay-suffolk.co.uk
Admission	
Adult £1, Child & Concs 50p	

365 Bungay

Norfolk & Suffolk Aviation Museum

2 hrs+   All year

This unique museum has 40 aircraft on display, from the earliest experiments of flight and Luftwaffe crash planes right up to the machines of the present day. It houses the 446th (H) Bomb Group Museum, the RAF Bomber Command Museum and the Air Sea Rescue Museum.

* 40 aircraft within 7 hangars
* Aircraft from pre-WWI to the present day

Location	Contact
On B1062, off A143, 1 mile W of Bungay	The Street, Flixton NR35 1NZ
Opening	t 01986 896644
Apr–Oct Sun–Thu 10am–5pm;	w aviationmuseum.net
Nov–Mar Tue–Wed & Sun 10am–4pm;	e lcurtis@aviationmuseum.net
closed 15 Dec–15 Jan	
Admission	
Free, donations welcomed	

366 Bury St Edmunds

Bury St Edmunds Abbey Gardens

2 hrs   All year

Explore the remains of a Benedictine abbey, church and precinct with Norman tower, set in beautifully kept gardens. The two C14 gateways are the best-preserved buildings. There is also a visitor centre with interactive displays.

Location	Contact
Off A14, at E end of Bury St Edmunds	Bury St Edmunds
Opening	t 01284 764667
Daily: all reasonable times	w stedmundsbury.gov.uk
Please phone for details	
Admission	
Free	

367 Felixstowe

Manning's Amusement Park

3 hrs   Apr–Sep

This traditional children's amusement park has numerous rides and slides. There is also an amusement arcade, Sunday market, bowling green, nightclub, sports bar and indoor Adventure Golf-FX.

Location	Admission
Off A14 & A12 on seafront	*Rides:* Adult Free, Child £3 unlimited rides
Opening	*Golf:* £1.50–£2
Easter–Sep Sat–Sun & school hols	Contact
Please phone for details	Sea Road, Felixstowe IP11 2DN
	t 01394 282370

368 Ipswich

Ipswich Transport Museum

1 hr   Mar–Nov

The museum has the largest collection of transport items in Britain devoted to just one town. Everything was either made or used in and around Ipswich. The collection, started in 1965, consists of around 100 major exhibits, and numerous smaller transport-related items.

* Timetables, photographs, maps, tickets & uniforms
* Varied programme of events as advertised

Location	Contact
SE of Ipswich near junction 57 of A14	Old Trolleybus Depot, Cobham Road, Ipswich IP3 9JD
Opening	t 01473 715666
Mar–Nov Sun & Bank Hols 11am–4pm, school hols Mon–Fri 1pm–4pm	w ipswichtransportmuseum.co.uk
	e enquiries@ipswichtransportmuseum.co.uk
Admission	
Adult £3.50, Child £2.50, Concs £3	

369 Lowestoft

Lowestoft Maritime Museum

1 hr+   Easter–Oct

The museum records the history of the Lowestoft fishing fleet, with models of fishing and commercial ships, shipwrights' tools, fishing gear, a lifeboat display, an art gallery and a drifter's cabin with models of fishermen.

* Fine exhibition of evolution of lifeboats
* Collection of shipwrights' & coopers' tools

Location	Contact
Under Lighthouse on Whaplode Road in Sparrow's Nest Park	Whaplode Road, Lowestoft NR32 1XG
Opening	t 01502 561963
Daily: 6–15 Apr, 29 Apr–28 Oct 10am–5pm	
Admission	
Adult 75p, Child 25p, Concs 50p	

370 Lowestoft

Pleasurewood Hills Theme Park

6 hrs+   Easter–Sep

East Anglia's premier theme park has more than 50 acres of rides, attractions and shows for all the family. Roller coasters, water-rides, go-karts and many more thrills guaranteed. Fun for both younger members of the family and grandparents.

* Wizzy Dizzy, a spinning pendulum – not for the fainthearted
* Family tickets available

Location
Off A12 N of Lowestoft

Opening
Easter–Sep 10am–5pm
Please visit the website for details of days & dates

Admission
Please visit the website for details

Contact
Leisure Way, Corton,
Lowestoft, Suffolk NR32 5DZ

t 01502 586000
w pleasurewoodhills.com
e info@pleasurewoodhills.com

371 Newmarket

National Stud

1 hr+   Mar–Sep

Horse-crazy children will adore every minute of this stable tour, which takes in the superb stallion unit, along with the stallions in residence, nursery yards, and mares and foals in their paddocks.

* Quality Assured Visitor Attraction
* Booking recommended to guarantee places

Location
Take A11, A1304 & A1303. Stud
is 2 miles SW of Newmarket on A1304

Opening
Daily: Mar–Sep
Tours 11.15am, 2.30pm

Admission
Adult £5, Child £3.50, Concs £4

Contact
Newmarket CB8 0XE

t 01638 663464
Tours 01638 666789
w nationalstud.co.uk
e tours@nationalstud.co.uk

372 Southwold

Coastal Voyager

1 hr+   All year

Coastal Voyager, a 9m rigid inflatable, offers a variety of sea trips and river cruises. There is a half-hour high-speed blast trip and various wildlife cruises along the beautiful River Blyth, home to many important birds such as heron and osprey.

* Wrap-round seats, seatbelts & lifejackets
* Smooth, comfortable & safe rides

Location	Contact
Trips depart from Southwold Harbour	69 Pier Avenue, Southwold IP18 6BL
Opening	t 07887 525082
Please phone or visit website for details	w coastalvoyager.co.uk
Admission	e thrills@southwold.ws
½-hr high-speed blast	
Adult £17, Child (under 13) £9	
3hr wildlife cruise	
Adult £26, Child (under 13) £13	

373 Southwold

Southwold Pier

2–4 hrs   All year

Visit this seaside pier and amusement arcades for good old-fashioned fun. The new pier, completed in 2002 is the only one to be built since 1950. Browse in giftshops with beach accessories and have 623 feet of fun!

* Pier of the Year 2002
* Educational visits welcomed

Location	Contact
Off A12, follow signs for Southwold	North Parade, Southwold IP18 6BN
Opening	t 01502 722105
Daily: May–Oct 9am–10pm;	w southwoldpier.co.uk
Oct–Apr 10am–5pm	e admin@southwoldpier.co.uk
Admission	
Free	

374 Stowmarket

Mid-Suffolk Light Railway Museum

2 hrs   Apr–Sep

Dedicated to the Mid-Suffolk Light Railway, the museum illustrates the restoration of the station and trackwork, and displays artefacts and memorabilia.

* Visit website & check press for details of
  special events

Location	Admission
1 mile from A140 in Brockford-cum-Wetheringsett village	Adult £2.50, Child £1, Family £6
	Rates vary for special events
Opening	**Contact**
Good Fri–end Sep Sun & Bank Hols	Brockford Station, Wetheringsett,
11am–5pm; also Wed in Aug 2pm–5pm	Stowmarket IP14 5PW
	t 01449 766899
	w mslr.org.uk

375 Stowmarket

Suffolk Owl Sanctuary

2 hrs+   All year

The Suffolk Owl Sanctuary is home to a variety of owls and birds of prey from all over the world, and has spectacular flying displays daily. There is also a woodland walk with a songbird hide, and a red squirrel enclosure where you can observe these shy creatures.

* Children's play area
* Café & shop

Location	Contact
On A1120, 8 miles from Ipswich & Stowmarket	Stonham Barns, Pettaugh Road, Stonham Aspal, Stowmarket IP14 6AT
Opening	t 01449 711425
Daily: *summer* 10am–5pm	w suffolk-owl-sanctuary.org.uk
winter 10am–4pm	e info@owl-help.org.uk
Admission	
Free, donations appreciated	

376 Stowmarket

Redwings Rescue Centre

2 hrs   Apr–Oct

Redwings Rescue Centre aims to relieve the suffering of horses, ponies and donkeys by providing them with a caring home for the rest of their days. See the animals in their peaceful retirement and learn more about their care and upkeep.

* 20-acre site
* Horse care demonstrations

Location
Off A1120

Opening
Daily: Apr–Oct 10am–5pm

Admission
Free, donations welcomed

Contact
Stonham Barns, Pettaugh Road,
Stonham Aspal, Stowmarket

t 0870 040 0033
w redwings.co.uk
e info@redwings.co.uk

377 Stowmarket

Xcite Playworld

1 hr+   All year

An indoor play area for children under 10 years old, with ball ponds, scramble nets, slides, an aerial glide and a spooky room. There is also a toddlers' area.

* Large inflatable play area (May–Sep only)

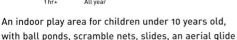

Location
Easy access from A14 into Stowmarket.
Signed to Leisure Centre from town
centre

Opening
Daily: Mon–Fri 9.30am–7pm, Sat–Sun
9am–6pm

Admission
Please phone for details

Contact
Mid-Suffolk Leisure Centre,
Gainsborough Road,
Stowmarket IP14 1LH

t 01449 674980

378 Sudbury

Clare Castle Country Park

3 hrs   All year

Spend a few hours exploring this 30-acre site fronting the River Stour. It combines the remains of a Norman motte and bailey castle and a Victorian railway station with natural history interest.

* History & nature trail
* Visitor centre

Location
Signed off A1092 in town centre

Opening
Park Daily: dawn–dusk
Visitor centre Daily: summer only,
10am–5pm

Admission
Free

Contact
Malting Lane, Clare,
Sudbury CO10 8NW

t 01787 277491
w suffolk.gov.uk/e-and-t/countryside
e john.laws@et.suffolkcc.gov.uk

379 West Stow

West Stow Country Park & Anglo-Saxon Village

1 hr+   All year

West Stow is a reconstructed Anglo-Saxon village, built on the site of an original settlement and set in a 125-acre country park. Finds from the site are displayed in an interpretation centre. This unique village is brought to life when authentic costume groups host special events.

* Nature trail & woodland walks
* New children's playground

Location
Off A1101, 6 miles NW of Bury
St Edmunds

Opening
Daily: *summer Country Park* 8am–8pm
Village 10am–5pm (last admission
4pm) *Café* 10am–4pm
winter Country Park 9am–5pm *Village*
10am–5pm (last admission 3.30pm)

Admission
Adult £5, Child & Concs £4, Family £15
Additional charges during events

Contact
Icklingham Road,
West Stow IP28 6HG

t 01284 728718
w stedmundsbury.gov.uk/weststow
e weststow@stedsbc.gov.uk

---

380 Woodbridge

Deben Cruises

2 hrs+   May–Sep

The MV *Jahan* cruises through 10 miles of lovely countryside, departing from the quay at Waldringfield Boatyard and returning to Waldringfield. The cruises last two to three hours, depending on tides. Visit the picturesque port of Woodbridge or travel to Felixstowe.

* Lunches & afternoon teas
* Group deals by appointment

Location
From A12 at Orwell Bridge signed to
Lowestoft. Follow sign at roundabout
to Waldringfield & road will take
you straight to village

Opening
Please phone for details

Admission
Adult £6, Child £4

Contact
Waldringfield Boatyard Ltd, The Quay,
Waldringfield, Woodbridge IP12 4QZ

t 01473 736260

---

381 Woodbridge

Sutton Hoo

2–3 hrs   All year

Excavations here in 1939 revealed a burial chamber containing a 90ft ship filled with treasures including a warrior's helmet, weapons, armour, ornaments, tableware and a purse with 37 gold coins from *c.*AD 620. The exhibition hall houses a full-size reconstruction of the chamber.

* Most important archaeological find in the UK
* Largest Anglo-Saxon ship ever discovered

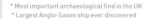

Location
On B1083 Melton-Bawdsey road.
Signed from A12 N of Woodbridge

Opening
Daily: 3 Jul–4 Sep 11am–5pm;
25 Mar–2 Apr, 19 Apr–2 Jul, 6 Sep–29
Oct Wed–Sun 11am–5pm. For all other
opening times please phone for details

Admission
Adult £5.50, Child £2.50

Contact
Tranmer House, Sutton Hoo,
Woodbridge IP12 3DJ

t 01394 389700
w nationaltrust.org.uk
e suttonhoo@nationaltrust.org.uk

athkill Dale, Derbyshire

East Midlands

Derbyshire Leicestershire Lincolnshire
Northamptonshire Nottinghamshire Rutland

LINCOLNSHIRE
Animal Attractions
Baytree Garden Centre & Owl Centre   154
The Butterfly & Wildlife Park   155
Hardy's Animal Farm   151
The Seal Sanctuary   153
Skegness Natureland Seal Sanctuary   154

Historic Sites
Tattershall Castle   155
Woolsthorpe Manor   151

Museums & Exhibitions
Cleethorpes Humber Estuary
 Discovery Centre   151
Lincoln Aviation Heritage Centre   155
Museum of Lincolnshire Life   152

Parks, Gardens & Nature
Gibraltar Point National Nature
 Reserve & Visitor Centre   154
Normanby Hall Country Park   153

Theme Parks & Adventure Playgrounds
Butlins (Skegness)   153
Magical World of Fantasy Island   152

NORTHAMPTONSHIRE
Historic Sites
Althorp House   156
Holdenby House, Gardens
 & Falconry Centre   157
Kirby Hall   156

Museums & Exhibitions
Abington Museum   157

Parks, Gardens & Nature
Brixworth Country Park   156
Irchester Country Park   158

Sport & Leisure
Billing Aquadrome   157

Theme Parks & Adventure Playgrounds
Wicksteed Park   157

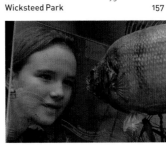

DERBYSHIRE
Animal Attractions
Chestnut Centre Otter Haven & Owl
Sanctuary   146

Historic Sites
Bolsover Castle   144
Haddon Hall   144
Peak Cavern   145

Museums & Exhibitions
Conkers   144
Denby Pottery Visitor Centre   145
Derby Museum of Industry & History   146
Donington Grand Prix Collection   145

Parks, Gardens & Nature
Heights of Abraham   147

Theme Parks & Adventure Playgrounds
The American Adventure   146
Gulliver's Kingdom   147

LEICESTERSHIRE
Animal Attractions
Tropical Birdland   148

Boat & Train Trips
Great Central Railway   149

Historic Sites
Ashby-de-la-Zouch Castle   147
Belvoir Castle   149
Rockingham Castle   150

Museums & Exhibitions
Foxton Canal Museum   150
National Space Centre   149
Snibston Discovery Park   148

Theme Parks & Adventure Playgrounds
Twinlakes Park   150

NOTTINGHAMSHIRE
Animal Attractions
White Post Farm Centre   158

Historic Sites
City of Caves   160
NCCL Galleries of Justice   160
Nottingham Castle   160

Museums & Exhibitions
Green's Mill & Science Centre   161
Making It! Discovery Centre   159
Newark Air Museum   159
Tales of Robin Hood   160
Wollaton Hall Museum   161

Parks, Gardens & Nature
Sherwood Forest Country Park &
 Visitor Centre   158

Theme Parks & Adventure Playgrounds
Go Ape!   159
Sundown Adventure Land   161

RUTLAND
Historic Sites
Lyddington Bede House   162

Museums & Exhibitions
Rutland County Museum   162

Sport & Leisure
Rutland Water   162

382 Ashby-de-la-Zouch

Conkers

4 hrs+   All year

Located in the heart of the national forest, Conkers offers a great mix of hands-on activities, from four indoor discovery zones for all ages to 23 outdoor activities, including lakeside walks, sculpture and nature trails, an assault course and train rides.

* Visitor Attraction of the Year finalist
* Summer shows in our covered amphitheatre

Location	Contact
5 miles from M42 junction 11	Rawden Road, Moira, nr Ashby-de-la-Zouch DE12 6GA
Opening	t 01283 216633
Daily: *summer* 10am–6pm	w visitconkers.com
winter 10am–5pm	e info@visitconkers.com
Admission	
Adult £6.50, Child £4.50, Concs £5.25	

383 Bakewell

Haddon Hall

2 hrs+   Apr–Oct

A perfect example of a Tudor hall with earlier and later elements, set in beautiful gardens. Guided tours are available and are adapted to suit different ages, abilities and interests. A costume room can be booked where the guide gives a talk illustrated with costumes.

* Location for the BBC drama *Jane Eyre*
* Film location for *Pride and Prejudice*

Location	Contact
2 miles S of Bakewell on A6	Bakewell DE45 1LA
Opening	t 01629 812855
Please phone or visit the website for details	w www.haddonhall.co.uk
	e info@haddonhall.co.uk
Admission	
Adult £7.75, Child £4, Concs £6.75	

384 Bolsover

Bolsover Castle

1 hr+   All year

An enchanting early C17 castle set on a hill, with restored walled gardens, a magnificent indoor riding house and outstanding craftsmanship everywhere. Visit the Discovery Centre and enjoy the interactive scale model of the castle and the audio tour.

* Regular living history events
* Visitor Attraction of the Year 2001

Location	Admission
In Bolsover, on A632, 6 miles E of Chesterfield	Adult £6.60, Child £3.30, Concs £5
Opening	Contact
Sep–Apr Thu–Fri & Sun–Mon 10am–5pm, Sat 10am–4pm; May–Aug Sun–Fri 10am–6pm, Sat 10am–4pm	Castle Street, Bolsover S44 6PR
	t 01246 822844
	w english-heritage.org.uk
	e bolsover.castle@english-heritage.org.uk

385 Castle Donington

Donington Grand Prix Collection

2–4 hrs   All year

Take a spin around the largest collection of Grand Prix cars in the world and journey through motor sport history. Exhibits include Schumacher's 1999 Williams, Coulthard's McLaren from 1997 and the car in which Senna won the 1993 European Grand Prix at Donington Park.

* Ferraris, Lotuses, Tyrells, Maseratis, Alfa Romeos
* Williams F1 cars from 1983 to 1999

Location
M1 junction 23a/24, access from NW via A50

Opening
Daily: 10am–5pm (last admission 4pm)

Admission
Adult £7, Child £2.50, Concs £5

Contact
Donington Park, Castle Donington DE74 2RP

t 01332 811027
w doningtoncollection.com
e enquiries@doningtoncollection.co.uk

386 Castleton

Peak Cavern

1 hr   All year

Set within a 250ft vertical cliff, and once home to a small village, there are various natural caverns within Peak Cavern, including the orchestra gallery, which has amazing acoustic properties, Roger Rain's House with a perpetual waterfall and the Devil's Cellar.

* Riverside walk past historic miners' cottages
* Guided tours & ropemaking demonstrations

Location
On A6187, between Hathersage & Whaley Bridge

Opening
Daily: 10am–5pm (last admission 4pm)

Admission
Adult £6.25, Child £4.25, Concs £5.25

Contact
Peak Cavern Road, Castleton, Hope Valley S33 8WS

t 01433 620285
w www.peakcavern.co.uk
e info@peakcavern.co.uk

387 Denby

Denby Pottery Visitor Centre

1 hr+   All year

Admire and compare examples of Denbyware, from early salt-glazed bottles and jars to the distinctive tableware of recent years. You can also see how Denbyware is made and have a go at painting a plate. There are extra activities for children during school holidays.

* Watch free cookery demonstrations
* New flagship store & tours of glass studio

Location
Next to Denby Pottery on B6179, off A38, 8 miles N of Derby

Opening
Daily: Mon–Sat 9.30am–5pm, Sun 10am–5pm

Admission
Factory tour Adult £5.25, Child & Concs £4.25

Contact
Derby Road, Denby, nr Ripley DE5 8NX

t 01773 74799
w denbyvisitorcentre.co.uk
e visitor.centre@denby.co.uk

388 Derby

Derby Museum of Industry & History

1 hr   All year

This museum introduces visitors to the history of Derby's industries. It has a major collection of Rolls-Royce aero engines, railway engineering and research galleries and a Power for Industry Gallery.

* On site of Derby's first silk mill
* History of Midland Railway

Location
Off A6, near Derby Cathedral

Opening
Daily: Mon 11am–5pm,
Tue–Sat 10am–5pm,
Sun & Bank Hols 1pm–4pm
Please phone to confirm
holiday opening times

Admission
Free

Contact
Silk Mill Lane, off Full Street,
Derby DE1 3AF
t 01332 255308
w derby.gov.uk/museums

389 High Peak

Chestnut Centre Otter Haven & Owl Sanctuary

2 hrs+   All year

Enjoy watching captive-bred otters and owls in their natural surroundings. Extensive nature trails weave through 50 acres of grounds. The sanctuary is a member of the Federation of Zoological Gardens of Great Britain.

* Also see Scottish wild cats & foxes
* Wildlife gift shop

Location
Off A625. Follow brown
tourist signs

Opening
Daily: 10.30am–5.30pm;
Jan–Feb Sat–Sun only

Admission
Adult £6, Child £4

Contact
Castleton Road,
Chapel-en-le-Frith,
High Peak SK23 0QR
t 01298 814099
w ottersandowls.co.uk
e info@chestnutcentre.co.uk

390 Ilkeston

The American Adventure

7 hrs   Mar–Oct

Visit The American Adventure and discover the epic story of the USA, from the Western Pioneers to the Pioneers of Space. With more than 100 attractions, live shows and rides, The American Adventure is an enjoyable family day out for everyone.

* Events held throughout the year
* Quality Assured Visitor Attraction

Location
Take junction 26 of M1 & follow
signs along A610 to A608 & then A6007

Opening
Daily: Mar–Oct 10.30am–5pm

Admission
Adult (13+) £16.50, Child £13.50

Contact
Derbyshire DE7 5SX
t 0845 330 2929
w www.americanadventure.co.uk
e sales@americanadventure.co.uk

391 Matlock Bath

Gulliver's Kingdom

6 hrs+   Apr–Sep

The park is designed for Lilliputians, but adults can have as much fun as the children. It is set on a wooded hillside and includes more than 40 attractions ranging from a log flume, roller coaster and chairlift to the Royal Mine Ride and family shows.

* Outdoor fantasy eating
* Disabled visitors are advised to phone before visiting

Location
Easily reached from M1 or M6.
Off A38 on A6 between Matlock &
Cromford

Opening
Please phone for details

Admission
Adult & Child £8.99, Child under 90cm
free, Concs £7.99

Contact
Temple Walk, Matlock Bath,
Derbyshire DE4 3PG

t 01925 444888
w gulliversfun.co.uk

392 Matlock Bath

Heights of Abraham

2 hrs+   Feb–Oct

Your journey begins with a spectacular scenic cablecar ride high above the gorge. From the summit station you can explore two caverns and learn what it was like to be a leadminer. You can even pick up some gems from our Rock-Shop.

* 2 adventure play areas
* Exhibition centre

Location
Off A6 in Matlock Bath

Opening
Feb half-term daily 10am–4.30pm;
Mar Sat–Sun 10am–4.30pm;
Apr–Oct daily 10am–5pm

Admission
Adult £9.50, Child £6.50, Concs £7

Contact
Matlock Bath, Derbyshire DE4 3PD

t 01629 582365
w heights-of-abraham.co.uk
e office@heights-of-abraham.co.uk

393 Ashby-de-la-Zouch

Ashby-de-la-Zouch Castle

1 hr+   All year

Ashby-de-la-Zouch Castle is a late medieval castle with impressive ruins that are dominated by the Hastings Tower. It offers panoramic views of the surrounding countryside and the chance to explore the secret tunnel used in the Siege of Ashby.

* Wonderful views across Leicestershire
* The setting for jousting scenes in the film *Ivanhoe*

Location
In Ashby-de-la-Zouch, 12 miles S of
Derby, on A511

Opening
Please phone for details

Admission
Adult £3.40, Child £1.70, Concs £2.60

Contact
South Street, Ashby-de-la-Zouch
LE65 1BR

t 01530 413343
w english-heritage.org.uk
e customers@english-heritage.org.uk

394 Coalville

Snibston Discovery Park

4–6 hrs   All year

A popular museum, Snibston is situated on the site of a former colliery. It displays a rich collection of historic objects telling the story of transport, mining and quarrying, engineering and the fashion industry. A visit includes a tour of the historic colliery buildings.

* Brand-new colliery-themed outdoor play area
* Train ride along the restored colliery railway

Location
On A511, on edge of Coalville town centre

Opening
Daily: 10am–5pm (Closed in early Jan)
Please phone for details

Admission
Adult £5.70, Child £3.60, Concs £3.90

Contact
Ashby Road, Coalville LE67 3LN

t 01530 278444
w leics.gov.uk/museums
e snibston@leics.gov.uk

395 Desford

Tropical Birdland

2 hrs+   All year

Come and see hundreds of beautiful and exotic birds, including macaws, parrots, parakeets, toucans and emus. Wander around the walk-through aviary, see where chicks are hatched, or sit with friendly free-to-fly birds in the café – some might even talk to you!

* Boarding service for pet birds when you go on holiday
* Hundreds of tropical birds from more than 70 species

Location
Just off junction 22 of M1

Opening
Daily: 10am–5pm

Admission
Adult £5, Child & Concs £3.50

Contact
Lindridge Lane, Desford,
Leicester LE9 9GN

t 01455 824603
w tropicalbirdland.co.uk
e info@tropicalbirdland.co.uk

396 Grantham

Belvoir Castle

3 hrs+   Apr–Sep

Belvoir Castle is still home to the Duke and Duchess of Rutland. This stunning building has a hilltop position, breathtaking views and glorious gardens. Events are staged every weekend throughout the season.

* Hidden spring garden
* Calendar of events

Location
Off A52, 7 miles from Grantham & 9 miles from Melton Mowbray

Opening
Easter–Sep Tue–Thu & Sat–Sun 11am–5pm

Admission
Adult £10, Child £5, Concs £9

Contact
Grantham NG32 1PE

t 01476 871002
w belvoircastle.com
e mary@belvoircastle.com

397 Leicester

National Space Centre

4–6 hrs   All year

This centre is dedicated to astronomy and space science. From its futuristic Rocket Tower find out about the personalities involved in the history of space exploration, about space technology past and present, and explore our understanding of space and how it affects our future.

* 6 themed galleries with hands-on activities
* Space theatre show

Location
Just off A6, 2 miles N of city centre

Opening
Tue–Sun 10am–5pm;
school hols daily 10am–5pm.
Please phone for details

Admission
Adult £11, Child & Concs £9

Contact
Exploration Drive, Leicester LE4 5NS

t 0870 607 7223
w spacecentre.co.uk
e info@spacecentre.co.uk

398 Loughborough

Great Central Railway

2 hrs+   All year

Mainline steam trains run every weekend throughout the year. Experience the famous expresses of the steam age. Relax in the comfort of classic corridor trains, which are steam-heated in winter. Buffet and griddle carriages are available on all trains.

* Steam through the glorious Leicestershire countryside
* Unique double-tracks network

Location
SE of town centre

Opening
Trains run at weekends all year
& midweek Jun–Aug.
Please phone for details

Admission
Adult £12, Child & Concs £8

Contact
Great Central Road,
Loughborough LE11 1RW

t 01509 230 726
w gcrailway.co.uk
e booking_office@gcrailway.co.uk

Foxton Canal Museum

3 hrs   All year

A canal museum featuring the story of the local canals and the rare boat lift, set in beautiful countryside with 10 locks and all supporting facilities. The museum contains models of the lift, interactive and social history displays and a canal playboat for younger visitors.

* Guided tour & walks
* Calendar of events

Location
Follow brown tourist signs from A6 Market Harborough–Leicester road or A4304 at Lubenham, or take M1 junction 20 to Market Harborough road

Opening
Daily: 10am–5pm (closed Thu–Fri in winter)

Admission
Adult £2.50, Child free, Concs £2

Contact
Middle Lock, Gumley Road, Foxton, Market Harborough LE16 7RA

t 0116 279 2657
w fipt.org.uk
e info@fipt.co.uk

Rockingham Castle

3 hrs   Easter–Sep

Built by William the Conqueror more than 900 years ago, the castle stands in beautiful grounds, with superb views across the Well and Valley. As well as being a stronghold, it was an important seat of government. It is now home to the Saunders Watson family.

* Best Small Visitor Centre in Excellence in England Award
* Regular events including kite & Viking days

Location
Off A6003, 1 mile N of Corby

Opening
Easter–May Sun & Bank Hol Mon 12noon–5pm; Jun–Sep Sun, Tue & Bank Hols 12noon–5pm

Admission
Adult £7.50, Child £4.50, Concs £6.50

Contact
Rockingham, Market Harborough, Leicestershire LE16 8TH

t 01536 770240
w rockinghamcastle.com
e estateoffice@rockinghamcastle.com

Twinlakes Park

7 hrs+   All year

A new family destination with a huge variety of activities for all ages, from climbing Black Knights Castle to shooting foam in the Master Blaster. Other fun attractions include a minicoaster and water play. Also sample our new ride, the Icarus Sky Flyers.

* Rowboats & pedalboats
* Falconry centre

Location
1 mile from Melton Mowbray & signed from A607 between Melton Mowbray & Grantham

Opening
Daily: 10am–5.30pm

Admission
Adult & Child £7.99, Under-3s free

Contact
Melton Spinney Road, Melton Mowbray LE14 4SB

t 01664 567777
w twinlakespark.co.uk
e fun@twinlakes.co.uk

402 Cleethorpes

Cleethorpes Humber Estuary Discovery Centre

1 hr   All year

Located on the boating lake surrounded by fantastic views and friendly wildlife, this family-friendly hands-on exhibition explores the Victorian seaside, history and nature of Cleethorpes. The second-floor observatory has outstanding views of the Humber Estuary.

* On the edge of an important wildlife habitat

Location	Admission
From A180 & A16 follow signs for lakeside	Adult £1.95, Child £1.30
	Contact
Opening	Lakeside, Kings Road, Cleethorpes
Daily: Jan–Jun & Sep–Oct 10am–5pm;	DN35 0AG
Jul–Aug 10am–6pm;	
Nov–Dec 10am–4pm	t 01472 323232
	w cleethorpesdiscoverycentre.co.uk
	e lynne.emeny@nelincs.gov.uk

403 Grantham

Woolsthorpe Manor

2 hrs   Mar–Oct

This C17 manor house was the birthplace and home of the scientist Sir Isaac Newton. Visitors can see his childhood scribblings on the walls. A gnarled old apple tree in the garden may be a descendant of the famous specimen that inspired Newton in his work.

* An interactive science discovery centre
* Replica of Newton's *Principia*

Location	Admission
From A1 take B676 at Colsterworth roundabout, turn right at 2nd crossroads & follow signs	Adult £4.50, Child £2.20
	Contact
Opening	23 Newton Way, Woolsthorpe-by-Colsterworth, nr Grantham NG33 5NR
3 Mar–25 Mar Sat–Sun 1pm–5pm;	
31 Mar–30 Sep Wed–Sun 1pm–5pm;	t 01476 860338
6 Oct–28 Oct Sat–Sun 1pm–5pm	w nationaltrust.org.uk
	e woolsthorpemanor@national trust.org.uk

404 Ingoldmells

Hardy's Animal Farm

3 hrs   Easter–Oct

Come to Hardy's Animal Farm to see commercial and rare breeds of cattle, sheep and goats. Visit the calf and pig units where you can see how the animals are cared for.

* Large adventure playground
* Horse & cart rides

Location	Admission
Take A52 N from Skegness to Ingoldmells. Go through Ingoldmells & take 1st right down Anchor Lane	Please phone for details
	Contact
Opening	Grays Farm, Anchor Lane, Ingoldmells, Skegness PE25 1LZ
Daily: Easter–Oct 10am–5pm	
	t 01754 872267

©NTPL/Tessa Musgrave

Magical World of Fantasy Island

3–5 hrs   Mar–Oct

This indoor theme park has rides and attractions to suit all ages, as well as live entertainment during the evenings throughout the main season. There are also outdoor rides to try and Europe's largest looping roller coaster, The Millennium Coaster.

* Movie-ride theatre
* Dazzling lightshows in the evenings

Location
Off A52, 4 miles N of Skegness

Opening
Daily: Easter–Oct from 10am
Closing times vary, please phone for details

Admission
Free. Tokens available for rides

Contact
Ingoldmells, Skegness PE25 1RH
t 01754 872030
w fantasyisland.co.uk
e info@fantasyisland.co.uk

Museum of Lincolnshire Life

2 hrs   All year

Experience the domestic, agricultural, industrial and social history of Lincolnshire through machinery built in the county. Also on show are Victorian room settings and a WWI tank. Special events are held throughout the year.

* Situated in Royal North Lincoln Military barracks
* Free parking available

Location
Take A46 in to Lincoln & follow signs

Opening
May–Sep daily 10am–5pm;
Oct–Apr Mon–Sat 10am–5pm
(last admission 4pm)

Admission
Please phone for details

Contact
Burton Road, Lincoln LN1 3LY
t 01522 528448
e lincolnshire.gov.uk/museumof lincolnshirelife
e lincolnshirelife_museum@ lincolnshire.gov.uk

402 Cleethorpes

Cleethorpes Humber Estuary Discovery Centre

1 hr   All year

Located on the boating lake surrounded by fantastic views and friendly wildlife, this family-friendly hands-on exhibition explores the Victorian seaside, history and nature of Cleethorpes. The second-floor observatory has outstanding views of the Humber Estuary.

* On the edge of an important wildlife habitat

Location
From A180 & A16 follow signs for lakeside

Opening
Daily: Jan–Jun & Sep–Oct 10am–5pm;
Jul–Aug 10am–6pm;
Nov–Dec 10am–4pm

Admission
Adult £1.95, Child £1.30

Contact
Lakeside, Kings Road, Cleethorpes
DN35 0AG

t 01472 323232
w cleethorpesdiscoverycentre.co.uk
e lynne.emeny@nelincs.gov.uk

404 Ingoldmells

Hardy's Animal Farm

3 hrs   Easter–Oct

Come to Hardy's Animal Farm to see commercial and rare breeds of cattle, sheep and goats. Visit the calf and pig units where you can see how the animals are cared for.

* Large adventure playground
* Horse & cart rides

Location
Take A52 N from Skegness to Ingoldmells. Go through Ingoldmells & take 1st right down Anchor Lane

Opening
Daily: Easter–Oct 10am–5pm

Admission
Please phone for details

Contact
Grays Farm, Anchor Lane,
Ingoldmells, Skegness PE25 1LZ

t 01754 872267

403 Grantham

Woolsthorpe Manor

2 hrs   Mar–Oct

This C17 manor house was the birthplace and home of the scientist Sir Isaac Newton. Visitors can see his childhood scribblings on the walls. A gnarled old apple tree in the garden may be a descendant of the famous specimen that inspired Newton in his work.

* An interactive science discovery centre
* Replica of Newton's *Principia*

Location
From A1 take B676 at Colsterworth roundabout, turn right at 2nd crossroads & follow signs

Opening
3 Mar–25 Mar Sat–Sun 1pm–5pm;
31 Mar–30 Sep Wed–Sun 1pm–5pm;
6 Oct–28 Oct Sat–Sun 1pm–5pm

Admission
Adult £4.50, Child £2.20

Contact
23 Newton Way, Woolsthorpe-by-
Colsterworth, nr Grantham NG33 5NR

t 01476 860338
w nationaltrust.org.uk
e woolsthorpemanor@national
trust.org.uk

405 Ingoldmells

Magical World of Fantasy Island

3–5 hrs   Mar–Oct

This indoor theme park has rides and attractions to suit all ages, as well as live entertainment during the evenings throughout the main season. There are also outdoor rides to try and Europe's largest looping roller coaster, The Millennium Coaster.

* Movie-ride theatre
* Dazzling lightshows in the evenings

Location
Off A52, 4 miles N of Skegness

Opening
Daily: Easter–Oct from 10am
Closing times vary, please phone for details

Admission
Free. Tokens available for rides

Contact
Ingoldmells, Skegness PE25 1RH
t 01754 872030
w fantasyisland.co.uk
e info@fantasyisland.co.uk

406 Lincoln

Museum of Lincolnshire Life

2 hrs   All year

Experience the domestic, agricultural, industrial and social history of Lincolnshire through machinery built in the county. Also on show are Victorian room settings and a WWI tank. Special events are held throughout the year.

* Situated in Royal North Lincoln Military barracks
* Free parking available

Location
Take A46 in to Lincoln & follow signs

Opening
May–Sep daily 10am–5pm;
Oct–Apr Mon–Sat 10am–5pm
(last admission 4pm)

Admission
Please phone for details

Contact
Burton Road, Lincoln LN1 3LY
t 01522 528448
e lincolnshire.gov.uk/museumof
lincolnshirelife
e lincolnshirelife_museum@
lincolnshire.gov.uk

407   Mablethorpe

The Seal Sanctuary

1 hr+   Easter–Sep

The Seal Trust is a registered charity with the twin aims of caring for local wild creatures in distress (especially seals) and encouraging visitors to help wildlife themselves. It acts as a sanctuary for seals, kestrels, as well as lynx, wildcats, snowy owls and harvest mice.

* Specially designed pools
* Educational natural history programmes

Location
Off A1031 via A1031, A104, A111 or A52

Opening
Daily: Easter–Sep from 10am
Please phone for details of winter opening times

Admission
Adult £5, Child £2.50, Senior £4

Contact
North End, Mablethorpe LN12 1QG

t 01507 473346

408   Scunthorpe

Normanby Hall Country Park

4 hrs   All year

Set in the heart of tranquil North Lincolnshire, 300 acres of country park provide the perfect day out for all the family. Learn about Lincolnshire's rich rural heritage in the fascinating Farm Museum or step back in time in the award-winning Victorian walled garden.

* Extensive woodland with a wealth of wildlife
* Adventure playground for younger children

Location
4 miles N of Scunthorpe on B1430

Opening
Hall & Museum Easter–Sep 1pm–5pm
Gardens All year 10.30am–4pm
Park All year 9am–dusk

Admission
Adult £4.40, Child £2.20, Concs £4

Contact
Normanby, Scunthorpe DN15 9HU

t 01724 720588
w northlincs.gov.uk/normanby
e normanby.hall@northlincs.gov.uk

409   Skegness

Butlins (Skegness)

6 hrs   Apr–Oct

Children can have great fun at Butlins. There's Splash, an indoor subtropical waterworld, with its exciting water rides, Hotshots, a terrific tenpin bowling centre, and the amazing Skyline Pavilion. Younger children can meet Bob the Builder in Bob's Yard.

* Quality Assured Visitor Attraction
* Live shows

Location
3 miles N of Skegness, on A52
Ingoldmells, Chapel St Leonards,
Sutton-on-Sea & Mablethorpe roads

Opening
Daily: Apr–Oct 10am–6pm
(last admission 4pm)

Admission
Please phone for details

Contact
Roman Bank, Ingoldmells,
Skegness PE25 1NJ

t 01754 765567 (day-visit hotline)
   01754 762311
w butlins.co.uk
   butlins.com/dayvisitor

410 Skegness

Gibraltar Point National Nature Reserve & Visitor Centre

2 hrs+   All year

This area of unspoilt coastline comprises sand dunes, saltmarshes and freshwater habitats which are a haven for rare plants, and animals including seals, water voles and pygmy shrews. Explore the five bird-watching hides, nature trail, interpretation centre, and various activities.

* Area of international scientific interest
* Home to many rare plants, insects & animals

Location
3 miles S of Skegness, signed from town centre

Opening
Daily: please phone for details

Admission
Free

Contact
Gilbraltar Road, Skegness PE24 4SU

t 01507 526667
w lincstrust.org.uk
e info@lincstrust.co.uk

411 Skegness

Skegness Natureland Seal Sanctuary

2 hrs   All year

Skegness Seal Sanctuary is well known for rescuing and rehabilitating orphaned and injured seal pups. It also has crocodiles, penguins, reptiles, insects and tropical birds. There is an aquarium as well, and from April to October you can view tropical butterflies.

* Baby seal & penguin pools
* Underwater viewing pool

Location
Signed from town centre

Opening
Daily: Jun–Sep 10am–5pm;
Oct–May 10am–4pm

Admission
Adult £5.50, Child £3.60, Concs £4.40

Contact
North Parade, Skegness PE25 1DB

t 01754 764345
w skegnessnatureland.co.uk
e natureland@fsbdial.co.uk

412 Spalding

Baytree Garden Centre & Owl Centre

2 hrs+   All year

Baytree Garden Centre has 72 owls from around the world, and is set in a beautiful landscaped area. There are tame owls to hold or just to enjoy watching in flying displays. It is home to more than 100 owls and birds of prey, including very rare Mexican striped owls.

* Discover Britain's No.1 grotto
* Visit tropical owls in the Hot House

Location
On main A151 at Weston, between Spalding & Holbeach

Opening
Please phone for details

Admission
Please phone for details

Contact
High Road, Weston, Spalding, Lincolnshire PE12 6JU

t Garden centre 01406 370242
Owl Centre 01406 372840
w baytree-gardencentre.com
e info@baytree-gardencentre.com

413 Spalding

The Butterfly & Wildlife Park

4 hrs · Mar–Oct

Set in the heart of the Fens, the park has a tropical house, a reptile area with crocodiles and snakes, a creepy-crawly house, and an ant room. Outdoor attractions include a birds of prey centre that runs twice-daily flying displays, an animal centre and an adventure playground.

* Quality Assured Visitor Attraction
* Lincolnshire Family Attraction of the Year 2003

Location
Signed off A17 at Long Sutton

Opening
Daily: end Mar–end Oct from 10am
Please phone for details

Admission
Please phone for details

Contact
Long Sutton, Spalding
PE12 9LE
t 01406 363833
w butterflyandwildlifepark.co.uk
e butterflypark@hotmail.com

414 Spilsby

Lincoln Aviation Heritage Centre

4 hrs · All year

The Heritage Centre is part of a wartime bomber airfield under restoration and includes a control tower, and displays depicting the history of flying in Lincolnshire. There is also an exhibition by the Royal Air Force Escaping Society.

* Avro Lancaster bomber NX611 Just Jane

Location
Off A16 North of Boston

Opening
Easter–Oct Mon–Sat 9.30am–5pm;
Nov–Easter Mon–Sat 9.30am–4pm

Admission
Adult £6.75, Child £2.50, Concs £5.75

Contact
East Kirkby Airfield, nr Spilsby
PE23 4DE
t 01790 763207
w lincsaviation.co.uk
e enquiries@lincsaviation.co.uk

415 Tattershall

Tattershall Castle

1 hr · Mar–Dec

Tattershall is a vast redbrick tower with a moat, built in medieval times for Ralph, Lord Cromwell, Chancellor of England. There are grand tapestries and four great chambers, each with spectacular views across the Fens.

* Tower is more than 100 ft high
* Special events throughout the year

Location
On S side of A153, 15 miles NE of
Sleaford, 10 miles SW of Horncastle

Opening
Apr–Oct Mon–Wed & Sat–Sun
11am–5pm; Mar & Nov–Dec Sat–Sun
12noon–4pm

Admission
Adult £4, Child £2

Contact
Tattershall, Lincoln LN4 4LR
t 01526 342543
w nationaltrust.org.uk
e tattershallcastle@nationaltrust.
org.uk

©NTPL/Andrew Butler

416 Althorp

Althorp House

4 hrs   Jul–Aug

The home of the Spencer family since 1508, the park came to world attention on 6 September 1997, when Diana, Princess of Wales was laid to rest here. See her final resting place on the island in the Round Oval, surrounded by her family's ancestral heritage.

* Magnificent Palladian stable block for 100 horses
* One of the world's finest collections of portraiture

Location
7 miles W of Northampton off A428.
Clearly signed from junction 16 of M1

Opening
Daily: Jul–Aug 11am–5pm

Admission
Adult £12, Child £6, Concs £10

Contact
The Stables, Althorp, Northampton
NN7 4HQ

t 01604 770107
w althorp.com
e mail@althorp.com

417 Brixworth

Brixworth Country Park

2 hrs+   All year

The park has many facilities including a café, cycle hire, play area, sensory garden and waymarked trails. It is now the main gateway to Pitsford Water and the 10km safe walking/cycling route called the Pitsford Water Trail. The park is also linked with the Brampton Valley Way.

* Take a walk along our sculpture trail
* Watch birds from our bird hide

Location
Close to Brixworth village & 7 miles N of Northampton on A508 Northampton –Market Harborough road

Opening
Daily: dawn–dusk

Admission
Free. Car park fees

Contact
Northampton Road, Brixworth
NN6 9DG

t 01604 883920
w northamptonshire.gov.uk/
  countryside
e brixworth@northamptonshire.gov.uk

418 Corby

Kirby Hall

1–2 hrs   All year

Featuring decorative carving and ornate gardens fit for a queen, Kirby Hall is one of the great Elizabethan houses, built in the hope of a royal visit. The great hall and state rooms have recently been refitted and redecorated to authentic C17 and C18 designs.

* Special events throughout the year

Location
On an unclassified road off A43,
4 miles NE of Corby

Opening
23 Mar–30 Jun Thur–Mon 10am–5pm;
1 Jul–31 Aug daily 10am–6pm;
1 Sep–31 Oct Thur–Mon 10am–5pm;
1 Nov–31 Mar Thur–Mon 10am–4pm

Admission
Adult £4.50, Child £2.30, Concs £3.40

Contact
Kirby Hall, Deene, nr Corby
NN17 1AA

t 01536 203230
w english-heritage.org.uk

419 Kettering

Wicksteed Park

6 hrs+   Mar–Oct

Wicksteed Park has a large playground and an adventure park with more than 30 different amusements including pirate ships, a water-chute, the Rockin' Tug and roller coasters. There are also shows throughout the year in the pavilion.

* UK's oldest theme park
* Regular calendar of events

Location
On A6, 1 mile S of Kettering town centre & 1½ miles from junction 10 of A14. Follow signs

Opening
Grounds All year
Rides Mar–Oct
Times vary, please phone for details

Admission
Please phone for details

Contact
Barton Road, Kettering, Northamptonshire NN15 6NJ

t 01536 512475
w wicksteedpark.co.uk
e information@wicksteedpark.co.uk

420 Northampton

Billing Aquadrome

3 hrs+   Mar–Nov

Billing Aquadrome is a leisure holiday park, set in 235 acres of parkland, woods and lakes. Facilities include an amusement centre, boating, coarse fishing and free children's play areas.

* Calendar of events & rallies

Location
Off A45, 3 miles from Northampton & 7 miles from junction 15 of M1

Opening
Daily: Mar–Nov until 8pm;
24-hr access for caravans & tents

Admission
Please phone for details

Contact
Crow Lane, Great Billing, Northampton NN3 9DA

t 01604 408181/784948
w billingaquadrome.com
e brochures@aquadrome.com

421 Northampton

Holdenby House, Gardens & Falconry Centre

2 hrs   Apr–Sep

Across the fields from Althorp lies Holdenby, a house whose royal connections go back more than 400 years. Its history is complemented by a regal collection of birds of prey which visitors can see soaring high in the sky over the grounds.

* Based on remaining kitchen wing of old palace
* Built in 1583 by Sir Christopher Hatton

Location
6 miles NW of Northampton, off A5199 or A428

Opening
Gardens & Falconry centre
Easter–Sep Sun & Bank Hols
1pm–5pm
House Easter Mon & Spring Bank Hol, pre-booked tours on other days

Admission
Gardens & Falconry centre
Adult £4.50, Child £3, Concs £4

Contact
Holdenby, Northampton NN6 8DJ

t 01604 770074
w holdenby.com
e enquiries@holdenby.com

422 Northampton South

Abington Museum

3 hrs+   All year

The museum combines social with military history. Displays illustrate Northamptonshire life and the history of the building, and that of Northamptonshire military at home and abroad. And the Victorian cabinet of curiosities and C19 costume gallery are not to be missed.

* C17 oak-panelled room
* Former home of Shakespeare's granddaughter

Location
Approximately 1½ miles E of town centre

Opening
March–Oct Sun–Tue 1pm–5pm;
Nov–Feb Sun–Tue 1pm–4pm;
Bank Hol Mon 1pm–5pm

Admission
Free

Contact
Abington Park, Park Avenue, South Northampton NN1 5LW

t 01604 838110
w northampton.gov.uk/museums

Irchester Country Park

4-6 hrs   All year

Explore a network of trails running across 83 hectares of mixed woodland and observe a wealth of wildlife, including woodpeckers and sparrowhawks. A Forestry Centre of Excellence, the park balances conservation with timber production and recreation.

* Park shop
* Accessible trails & orienteering trail

Location
2 miles S of Wellingborough, on B570, off A509, in Nene Valley

Opening
Park Daily: 24 hrs
Car park Daily: 24 hrs
Lower car park Daily: 9am-6pm

Admission
Free. Car park fees

Contact
Gypsy Lane, Little Irchester, Wellingborough NN29 7DL

t 01933 276866
w northamptonshire.gov.uk
e irchester@northamptonshire.gov.uk

Sherwood Forest Country Park & Visitor Centre

2 hrs   All year

Visit the hiding place of Robin Hood and see the major oak where he hid with his Merry Men, discover what life was like in the Middle Ages, learn about ecology in the Forests of the World exhibition or take a walk along one of many waymarked trails.

* Enjoy the trails & discover the forest
* National Nature Reserve

Location
In Edwinstowe, off B6034

Opening
Visitor centre Daily: summer
10am-5pm winter 10am-4.30pm
Park dawn-dusk

Admission
Free. Car park £3

Contact
Edwinstowe, nr Mansfield NG21 9HN

t 01623 823202
w nottinghamshire.gov.uk/country parks
e sherwood.forest@nottscc.gov.uk

White Post Farm Centre

5 hrs+   All year

With more than 3,000 animals ranging from the exotic to the domestic, there's plenty to see and do. Feed the goats, watch chicks and ducklings hatching, admire the snakes and reptiles or even catch a pantomime in the show barn.

* East Midlands Tourism Excellence in England Award 2005
* Birthday parties, indoor & outdoor play areas

Location
Take A617 signed Mansfield & Newark then A614 signed Nottingham

Opening
Daily: from 10am

Admission
Adults £7.30, Child & Concs £6.60

Contact
Farnsfield NG22 8HL

t 01623 882977
w whitepostfarmcentre.co.uk
e admin@whitepostfarmcentre.co.uk

Go Ape!

3 hrs+   All year

Go Ape! is a high-wire forest adventure course of bridges, tarzan swings and zip slides, up to 35ft above the forest floor. Ideal for friends and family, it provides hours of fun, laughter and adventure up in the trees as well as an exciting way to explore the forest.

* Children must be over 10 years old

Location
Off B6030 near Old Clipstone

Opening
Please phone for details or visit the website

Admission
Adult £20, Child (10–17) £15

Contact
Sherwood Pines Visitor Centre,
Sherwood Pines Forest Park,
Edwinstowe NG21 9JL

t 0870 444 5562
w goape.co.uk
e info@goape.co.uk

Making It! Discovery Centre

2 hrs+   Jul–Sep

Have a fun day out at this entertaining, educational and interactive hands-on centre. The galleries celebrate the inventiveness of a variety of industries including shoe manufacturing, brewing, engineering and electronics, printing, and the making of soft drinks and textiles.

* Nottinghamshire Visitor Attraction of the Year

Location
Close to town centre & Water Meadows leisure pool. Off A60 & A617

Opening
Daily: mid-Jul–Sep 10am–5pm

Admission
Adult £6.95, Child £6.25

Contact
Chadburn House, Weighbridge Road,
Littleworth, Mansfield,
Nottinghamshire NG18 1AH

t 01623 473297
w makingit.org.uk
e info@makingit.org.uk

Newark Air Museum

2 hrs   All year

An impressive collection of more than 60 aircraft and cockpit sections, including transport, training and reconnaissance aircraft, helicopters, jet fighters and bombers. Learn about the history of RAF Winthorpe, a WWII bomber-training base.

* Postwar air-to-air missile display

Location
Easily accessible from A1, A46, A17, A1133 & Newark-on-Trent bypass

Opening
Daily: Mar–Oct 10am–5pm;
Nov–Feb 10am–4pm

Admission
Please phone for details

Contact
Winthorpe Showground,
Newark-on-Trent NG24 2NY

t 01636 707170
w newarkairmuseum.co.uk
e newarkair@onetel.com

429 Nottingham

City of Caves

1 hr+   All year

Soak up the atmosphere of hundreds of years of local life in this ancient and mysterious labyrinth of sandstone caves deep beneath the city. Descend into the depths of these original Anglo-Saxon tunnels, meeting the cave dwellers from their dramatic hidden past.

* Visit our Rock Shop
* Special events throughout the year

WC

Location	Contact
In city centre. Inside Broadmarsh shopping centre on upper level	Drury Walk, Broadmarsh Centre, Nottingham NG1 7LS
Opening	t 0115 988 1955
Daily: 10.30am–4.30pm	w cityofcaves.com
	e info@cityofcaves.com
Admission	
Adult £4.95, Child & Concs £3.95 Combined ticket with NCCL Galleries available	

430 Nottingham

NCCL Galleries of Justice

2–3 hrs   All year

A tour through three centuries of crime, punishment and law. Located in the Shire Hall, the galleries include a Victorian street, C18 prison, exercise yard, courtrooms, cave cells, a women's prison with bath house and laundry, a medieval cave system and an Edwardian police station.

* Costumed interpreters bring the experience to life
* Narrow Marsh Victorian adventure for children

WC

Location	Contact
In central Nottingham, near Broadmarsh shopping centre	High Pavement, Lace Market, Nottingham NG1 1HN
Opening	t 0115 952 0555
Tue–Sun & Bank Hols 10am–5pm, daily during school hols. Please phone for details	w nccl.org.uk
	e info@nccl.org.uk
Admission	
Adult £7.95, Child & Concs £5.95	

431 Nottingham

Nottingham Castle

1–2 hrs   All year

Nottingham Castle is a C17 mansion housing a range of historical and contemporary art exhibitions. Interactive displays feature museum collections of silver, ceramics and Nottinghamshire treasures. Visitors can also explore the hidden passageways under the building.

* Network of caves & passageways beneath the castle
* Robin Hood statue

Location	Contact
In central Nottingham	Lenton Road, Nottingham NG1 6EL
Opening	t 0115 915 3700
Daily: Mar–Oct 10am–5pm; Nov–Feb 10am–4pm	w nottinghamcity.gov.uk/museums
	e helens@ncmg.demon.co.uk
Admission	
Adult £3, Child & Concs £1.50	

432 Nottingham

Tales of Robin Hood

1–2 hrs   All year

The swashbuckling adventures of Robin Hood have inspired storytellers for more than 700 years. Explore the world of this notorious and endearing outlaw and experience medieval life, legend and adventure by fleeing through the forest to escape the evil Sheriff.

* Regular Robin Hood events
* Medieval banquets held on Fri & Sat

WC

Location	Contact
In city centre, next to castle, signed from M1	30–38 Maid Marian Way, Nottingham NG1 6GF
Opening	t 0115 948 3284
Daily: 10am–5.30pm (last admission 4.30pm)	w robinhood.uk.com
	e robinhoodcentre@mail.com
Admission	
Adult £8.95, Child £6.95, Concs £7.95	

433 Nottingham

Wollaton Hall Museum

3 hrs+   All year

Set in more than 500 acres of deer park, Wollaton Hall is one of the finest Elizabethan houses in England and is now home to Nottingham's natural history collection and industrial museum.

* Steam-engine house
* Parts under restoration & closed until Easter 2007

Location	Admission
3 miles from city centre	Mon–Fri free, Sat–Sun each museum Adult £1.50, Child & Concs £1
Opening	
Natural History Museum, Industrial Museum & Yard Gallery	Contact
Daily: Oct–Mar 11am–4pm; Apr–Sep 11am–5pm	Wollaton Park, Nottingham NG8 2AE
	t 0115 915 3900
	w nottinghamcity.gov.uk
	e carolb@ncmg.demon.co.uk

434 Retford

Sundown Adventure Land

4 hrs+   Feb–Dec

This charming theme park aimed at younger children has a host of delightful rides and attractions. Meet your favourite nursery rhyme characters in the Story Book Village, get wet on the Boozy Barrel Boat Ride, or see magical things happen in the Witches' Kitchen.

* Special Christmas events
* New Robin Hood ride

Location	Admission
6 miles from A1 Markham Moor & signed 3 miles from Dunham on the A57	Adult £8, Child £8
	Contact
Opening	Treswell Road, Rampton, nr Retford DN22 0HX
Daily: May–Aug 10am–5pm; Feb–Apr & Sep–Dec 10am–4pm	t 01777 248274
	w sundownadventureland.co.uk
	e info@sundownadventureland.co.uk

435 Sneiton

Green's Mill & Science Centre

2 hrs   All year

One of the few working inner-city windmills in Britain, with interactive science exhibits, Green's Mill was once home to the C19 miller and mathematician George Green. Tour the mill and find out about the fascinating process of turning grain into flour.

* Included in Best 50 Small Museums
* Hands-on experiments exploring magnetism, electricity & light

Location	Contact
1 mile outside city centre	Windmill Lane, Sneinton, Nottingham NG2 4QB
Opening	
Wed–Sun & Bank Hols 10am–4pm	t 0115 915 6878
Admission	w greensmill.org.uk
Free	

Lyddington Bede House

1 hr   Apr–Oct

Lyddington Bede House was originally a wing of a medieval rural palace belonging to the bishops of Lincoln. In 1600 the building was converted into an alms house and it remained a home for pensioners until the 1930s.

* Great chamber features a beautiful ceiling cornice
* Bedesmen's rooms with tiny windows & fireplaces

Location
In Lyddington, 6 miles N of Corby, 1 mile E of A6003, next to church

Opening
Apr–Oct Thu–Mon 10am–5pm

Admission
Adult £3.30, Child £1.70, Concs £2.50
Prices for events vary

Contact
Bluecoat Lane, Lyddington LE15 9LZ

t 01572 822438
w english-heritage.org.uk

Rutland County Museum

1 hr+   All year

Learn about England's smallest county through the museum's displays of archaeology, architecture, agriculture and domestic life. See the tools and equipment used by tradesmen – the wheelwright, carpenter, blacksmith, farrier and cooper.

* Newly refurbished courtyard containing agricultural machinery
* Rare Saunderson tractor

Location
Off A603, near town centre

Opening
Daily: Mon–Sat 10.30am–5pm,
Sun 2pm–4pm

Admission
Free

Contact
Catmose Street, Oakham LE15 6HW

t 01572 758440
w rutnet.co.uk/rcc/rutlandmuseums
e museum@rutland.gov.uk

Rutland Water

2 hrs+   All year

The whole family can enjoy this award-winning attraction with a 3,100-acre lake set in beautiful countryside and more than 20 miles of off-road cycling or walking. Spend time at the butterfly and aquatic centre, then explore the nature reserve or have a go on the climbing wall.

* Bird-watching, windsurfing & canoeing
* Range of craft available for hire, or launch your own

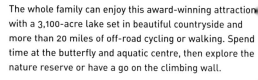

Location
Just off A606, signed from A1

Opening
Daily: 10am–5pm

Admission
Free. Car park fee

Contact
Tourist Information Centre, Sykes Lane, Empingham, Rutland LE 15 8PX

t 01572 653026
w anglianwaterleisure.co.uk
e tic@anglianwaterleisure.co.uk

West Midlands

Herefordshire Shropshire Staffordshire
Warwickshire West Midlands Worcestershire

HEREFORDSHIRE
Animal Attractions
Shortwood Family Farm 166
Small Breeds Farm Park &
  Owl Centre 166

Historic Sites
Berrington Hall 167
Eastnor Castle 167

Parks, Gardens & Nature
Brockhampton Estate 166

Sport & Leisure
Amazing Hedge Puzzle 167

SHROPSHIRE
Animal Attractions
Acton Scott 168
Hoo Farm 171
Park Hall Countryside Experience 170
Rays Farm Country Matters 168

Historic Sites
Stokesay Castle 169

Museums & Exhibitions
Ironbridge Gorge Museums 171
Mythstories, Museum of Myth
  & Fable 170
The RAF Museum – Cosford 169
Secret Hills – Shropshire Hills
  Discovery Centre 168
Wroxeter Roman City (Virconium) 171

Parks, Gardens & Nature
Hawkstone Park 170
Wonderland 171

STAFFORDSHIRE
Animal Attractions
Ash End House Children's Farm 175
Blackbrook Zoological Park 176
British Wildlife Rescue Centre 174

Historic Sites
Stafford Castle 174

Museums & Exhibitions
Coors Visitor Centre 173
Etruria Industrial Museum 174
Gladstone Pottery Museum 173
Sudbury Hall & Museum
  of Childhood 172

Parks, Gardens & Nature
The Snowdome 176

Theme Parks & Adventure Playgrounds
Alton Towers 172
Drayton Manor Theme Park 175
Waterworld 174

WARWICKSHIRE
Animal Attractions
Broomey Croft Children's Farm 177
Hatton Country World 177
Stratford Butterfly Farm 178
Twycross Zoo 176

Historic Sites
Shakespeare's Birthplace 178
Warwick Castle 179

Museums & Exhibitions
Bosworth Battlefield Visitor Centre
  & Country Park 178

Parks, Gardens & Nature
Brandon Marsh Nature Centre 176
Kingsbury Water Park 179
Organic Garden Ryton 177

WEST MIDLANDS
Animal Attractions
Dudley Zoological Gardens 182
National Sea Life Centre 180

Guided Tours
Tolkien's Birmingham 180

Museums & Exhibitions
Black Country Living Museum 182
Cadbury World 181
Dudley Canal Trust 182
Lapworth Museum of Geology 180
Midland Air Museum 179
National Motorcycle Museum 183
Red House Glass Cone 183
Selly Manor 181
ThinkTank 180

Parks, Gardens & Nature
Birmingham Botanical Gardens
  & Glasshouses 183

WORCESTERSHIRE
Animal Attractions
West Midland Safari & Leisure Park 184

Historic Sites
Worcester Cathedral 184

Museums & Exhibitions
The Hop Pocket Craft Centre 184
Upton Heritage Centre 184

439 Bromyard

Brockhampton Estate

1 hr   All year

This beautiful park with ancient woodland is a perfect habitat for wildlife including the dormouse, raven and buzzard. There are guided walks throughout the year and a C14 manor house with moat at the heart of the estate.

* Timber-framed gate house & ruined chapel
* Woodland is home to interesting range of wildlife

Location
2 miles E of Bromyard on A44

Opening
House Mar Sat–Sun 12noon–4pm;
Apr–Sep Wed–Sun 12noon–5pm;
Oct Wed–Sun 12noon–4pm
Estate All year. Daily: dawn–dusk

Admission
Adult £4, Child £2

Contact
Greenfields, Bringsty WR6 5TB

t 01885 488099/482077
w nationaltrust.org.uk
e brockhampton@nationaltrust.org.uk

---

440 Bromyard

Shortwood Family Farm

4 hrs+   Easter–Oct

Shortwood is an organic farm with a trail to walk and a pets' corner. Guided tours are run between 2pm and 4pm every afternoon. Visitors can collect eggs, feed the animals, milk a cow and watch a milking machine in action.

* Milk a cow by hand
* Play area & trailer rides

Location
Signed from A417 between Burley
Gate & Bodenham from Pencombe

Opening
Daily: Easter–Oct from 10am

Admission
Adult £5.50, Child £3.50

Contact
Pencombe,
Bromyard HR7 4RP

t 01885 400205
w shortwoodfarm.co.uk

441 Kington

Small Breeds Farm Park & Owl Centre

2 hrs+   All year

The main display field is home to Kune pigs, pygmy goats, Dexter cattle, Quessant and Soay sheep, and alpacas, many of which you can feed on your visit. Our owl garden provides a tranquil setting for our spectacular collection of owls. There's also a waterfowl enclosure and pet animal house.

* Herefordshire Family Attraction of the Year
* Owl garden collection probably the best in the UK

Location
On approaching Kington look out for
brown & white signs (Farm Park &
Owl Centre)

Opening
Daily: 10:30am–5:30pm

Admission
Adult £5.50, Child £3.50

Contact
Kington HR5 3HF

t 01544 231109
w owlcentre.com

442 Ledbury

Eastnor Castle

2–3 hrs | Easter–Oct

This fairytale castle in the dramatic setting of the Malvern Hills is surrounded by a beautiful deer park, arboretum and lake. Other attractions include the knight's maze, an assault course and pretty lakeside and woodland paths.

* Giant redwood grove
* Adventure playground

Location
2 miles from Ledbury on A438 Ledbury–Tewkesbury road. 5 miles from M50 junction 2 via Ledbury

Opening
Please phone for details

Admission
Castle & Grounds Adult £7, Child £4, Concs £6
Grounds £3, £2, £1

Contact
Eastnor, Ledbury HR8 1RL

t 01531 633160
w eastnorcastle.com

---

443 Leominster

Berrington Hall

2 hrs | Mar–Oct

Berrington Hall is an C18 mansion with a Georgian dairy, a Victorian laundry, a walled garden and a children's play area. Orienteering courses are available.

* Ugly bug safaris
* Quizzes organised

Location
3 miles N of Leominster

Opening
Times vary, please phone for details

Admission
Adult £5.30, Child £2.65

Contact
Leominster HR6 0DW

t 01568 615721
w nationaltrust.org.uk
e berrington@nationaltrust.org.uk

---

444 Symonds Yat

Amazing Hedge Puzzle

1 hr+ | All year

Have fun finding your way to the centre of the maze and try to avoid the 13 deadends. By making your own labyrinths you can follow in the footsteps of the heroes of Ancient Greece and India, Roman soldiers, Native Americans, medieval monks and English kings.

* Hands-on displays allow you to build your own maze
* Amazing Puzzle Shop – great fun!

Location
Follow signs on B4164, off A40 between Ross-on-Wye & Monmouth

Opening
Daily: Jan–Feb & Nov–Dec 11am–3pm; Apr–Sep & half-terms 11am–5pm; Mar & Oct 11am–4pm

Admission
Please phone for details

Contact
Jubilee Park, Symonds Yat West, Ross-on-Wye HR9 6DA

t 01600 890360
w mazes.co.uk
e info@mazes.co.uk

445 Bridgnorth

Rays Farm Country Matters

2 hrs   Mar-Oct

This attraction has many unusual animals and birds, including red fallow, Sika and Axis deer, and Bagot, pygmy, angora and other goats. Come and meet the owls, llamas, horses, ponies and donkeys, and follow the Sculpture Trail of Myth and Magic.

* Pull 'Excalibur' from its stone
* Many varieties of deer & goats

Location	Contact
Signed off B4363 near Billingsley between Bridgnorth & Cleobury Mortimer	Billingsley, Bridgnorth, Shropshire WV16 6PF
	t 01299 841255
Opening	w raysfarm.com
Daily: Mar-Oct 10am-5.30pm	
Admission	
Adult £5.50, Child £4, Concs £5	

446 Church Stretton

Acton Scott

3 hrs   Apr-Oct

Experience daily life on an upland farm at the turn of the C20. The waggoner and his team of heavy horses work the land with vintage farm machines. Every day you can see milking by hand and buttermaking in the dairy. You will also see the farrier and the blacksmith.

* Lambing, shearing, cidermaking, etc. in season
* Children's holiday activities

Location	Contact
Off A49, 17 miles S of Shrewsbury, 14 miles N of Ludlow	nr Church Stretton SY6 6QN
	t 01694 781306
Opening	w actonscottmuseum.co.uk
Apr-Oct Tue-Sun & Bank Hols 10am-5pm	e acton.scott.museum@shropshire-cc. gov.uk
Admission	
Adult £4.85, Child £2.50, Concs £4.25	

447 Craven Arms

Secret Hills – Shropshire Hills Discovery Centre

2 hrs+   All year

Learn about ecology, geology, culture and more at this new hands-on discovery centre, set in a grass-roofed building in the Shropshire Hills. Visitors can also take a simulated balloon flight. The centre provides a base for year-round entertainment and hands-on activities.

* Craft gallery & activities area
* Find out about earthquakes

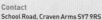

Location	Contact
Off A49, 7 miles N of Ludlow	School Road, Craven Arms SY7 9RS
Opening	t 01588 676000/676040
Daily: Apr-Oct 10am-5.30pm; Nov-Mar 10am-4.30pm	w shropshire-cc.gov.uk/discover.nsf
	e secrethills@shropshire-cc.gov.uk
Admission	
Adult £4.50, Child £3, Concs £4	

448 Ludlow

Stokesay Castle

1 hr   All year

Stokesay Castle is the finest and best-preserved C13 fortified manor house in England. It includes a medieval great hall, a timber-framed Jacobean gate house, the parish church and delightful cottage-style gardens.

* Magnificent great hall largely untouched & in excellent condition

Location
Off A49, 7 miles NW of Ludlow

Opening
Mar–Apr & Sep–Oct Thu–Mon
10am–5pm; May–Jun daily
10am–5pm; Jul–Aug daily 10am–6pm;
Nov–Feb Fri–Mon 10am–4pm

Admission
Adult £4.80, Child £2.40, Concs £3.60

Contact
Craven Arms SY7 9AH

t 01588 672544
w english-heritage.org.uk

449 Shifnal

The RAF Museum – Cosford

3 hrs+   All year

Follow the story of man's flight – the successes and failures – through one of the largest aviation collections in the UK. More than 70 historic aircraft are displayed in three wartime hangars on an active airfield. The museum also displays missiles, motor vehicles and aero-engines.

* National Cold War exhibition new in 2007
* State-of-the-art flight simulator

Location
On A41, less than 1 mile from M54
junction 3

Opening
Daily: 10am–6pm (last admission 4pm)

Admission
Free. Charges for special events
Under-16s must be accompanied
by an adult

Contact
Cosford, Shifnal TF11 8UP

t 01902 376200
w rafmuseum.org
e cosford@rafmuseum.com

450 Oswestry

Park Hall Countryside Experience

5 hrs+   **All year**

This farm is an all-weather visitor attraction. Popular with young and old alike, Park Hall puts on regular activities at which you can meet and feed the animals. This unique experience combines education, fun and adventure. An impressive 80 per cent of the activities are indoors.

* Children's 4x4 off-road course with replica Land Rovers
* Indoor & outdoor adventure areas

Location	Contact
In Oswestry, 30 min from Chester. Take A495 off Oswestry bypass (A483)	Park Hall, Oswestry SY11 4AS
Opening	t 01691 671123
Please phone or visit the website for details	w parkhallfarm.co.uk
	e rachel@parkhallfarm.co.uk
Admission	
Adult £5.50, Child & Concs £4.50, Family £23	

451 Shrewsbury

Hawkstone Park

3 hrs   **Jan–Oct**

Created in the C18, Hawkstone became one of the greatest historic parklands in Europe. The park is centred around the Red Castle and the awe-inspiring Grotto Hill, and features intricate pathways, ravines, arches and bridges, towering cliffs and follies.

* Woodland full of ancient oaks
* Has won numerous awards

Location	Contact
Off A49, between Shrewsbury & Whitchurch	Weston-under-Redcastle, Shrewsbury SY4 5UY
Opening	t 01939 200611
Please phone or visit the website for details	w hawkstone.co.uk
	e info@hawkstone.co.uk
Admission	
Adult £5.95, Child £3.95, Concs £4.95	

452 Shrewsbury

Mythstories, Museum of Myth & Fable

1 hr+   **Apr–Nov**

Enjoy colourful displays of traditional stories from Shropshire and around the world, with illustrations, photographs and artefacts. There are things to touch and play with, puzzles to do and live storytelling in the inglenook fireplace.

* Shropshire Family Attraction of the Year 2001
* Full programme of story walks

Location	Contact
On B5063 just off A49 near Whitchurch	The Morgan Library, Aston Street, Wem, Shrewsbury SY4 5AU
Opening	t 01939 235500
Apr–Aug Mon–Fri 2.30pm–6.30pm; Sep–Nov Sat–Sun 11am–4pm	w mythstories.com
	e info@mythstories.com
Admission	
Free	

453 Shrewsbury

Wroxeter Roman City (Virconium)

1 hr   All year

The largest excavated Roman city in Britain to have escaped development, Wroxeter was once home to 6,000 people. The impressive remains include C2 municipal baths. The site museum offers an insight into the lives of the people who lived here.

* Fourth-largest Roman settlement in Britain

Location	Admission
On B4380, 5 miles E of Shrewsbury	Adult £4, Child £2, Concs £3
Opening	**Contact**
Apr–Sep daily 10am–6pm;	Wroxeter, Shrewsbury SY5 6PH
Oct daily 10am–5pm;	t 01743 761330
Nov–Mar Thu–Mon 10am–4pm	w english-heritage.org.uk

454 Telford

Hoo Farm

4 hrs+   Easter–Dec

Come and see, pet and feed many of our animals. There are regular feeding sessions for the lambs, goats and deer; pet our friendly rabbits, mice and guinea pigs, and if you dare, take a peek at our snakes and reptiles. Other events include sheep, goat and ferret racing.

* Junior quad bikes, bouncy farm & pony rides
* Craft workshop

Location	Contact
M54 junction 6, signed to Hoo Farm	Preston-on-the-Weald Moors, Telford TF6 6DJ
Opening	
Mar–Sep daily 10am–6pm;	t 01952 677917
Oct–Nov Tue–Sun 10am–5pm;	w hoofarm.com
Dec please phone for details	e info@hoofarm.com
Admission	
Adult £5.25, Child £4.75, Concs £4.75	

455 Telford

Ironbridge Gorge Museums

1–6 hrs   All year

There are 10 award-winning museums spread along what is often called 'the valley that changed the world'. That valley, beside the River Severn, is still spanned by the world's first iron bridge. See the machines that set industry on its way and the products made by them.

* Blists Hill Victorian town, recreation of working community
* Enginuity – hands-on design & technology experiences

Location	Admission
5 miles S of Telford, signed from M54 junction 4	*Passport ticket to all 10 attractions* Adult £14, Child £9.50, Concs £12.50
Opening	**Contact**
Daily: 10am–5pm; reduced opening in winter	Ironbridge, Telford TF8 7DQ
	t 01952 884 391
	w ironbridge.org.uk
	e tic@ironbridge.org.uk

456 Telford

Wonderland

2 hrs+   All year

Set in a beautiful woodland setting, walks lead you through the world of fairytales where children can find their favourite characters around every corner. The characters come to life to sing songs and tell stories. Children can play on five outdoor rides and in the indoor softplay area.

* Crazy golf on the *Jolly Roger*
* Extensive hedge maze

Location	Admission
Follow signs for Telford Town Park & Wonderland off junctions 4 & 5 of M54	Please phone for details
Opening	**Contact**
Jan–Dec Sat & Sun & School Hols 10.30am–4pm; Easter–Sep daily 10am–4pm (open until 6pm at peak times)	Telford Town Park, Telford, Shropshire TF3 4AY
	t 01952 591633
	w wonderlandtelford.com
	e info@wonderlandtelford.com

457 Alton

Alton Towers

6 hrs+   Mar–Oct

A famous, extensive theme park with a mix of rides and attractions to suit every member of the family. It includes 200 acres of landscaped gardens, rides, live entertainment and the historic Towers building. Come along and enjoy a fun-packed family day out.

* Family spinning roller coaster
* 2 onsite hotels incorporating an indoor water-park

Location
Off B5030, near Uttoxeter (A50); take junction 15 or 16 from M6, or junction 23a or 28 from M1. Follow brown tourist signs

Opening
Daily: Mar–end Oct (gates open at 9am) 9.30am–5pm (later in summer) Please phone or visit the website before visiting

Admission
Please phone for details

Contact
Alton, Stoke-on-Trent ST10 4DB
t 0870 4444455
w altontowers.com

458 Ashbourne

Sudbury Hall & Museum of Childhood

3 hrs   Mar–Oct

This spectacular late C17 house has sumptuous interiors and a fine collection of portraits. The great staircase is one of the most elaborate of its kind in an English house. The C19 service wing is home to the Museum of Childhood with displays about children from the C18 onwards.

* Featured in BBC production of *Pride and Prejudice*
* Behind the Scenes tours

Location
6 miles E of Uttoxeter at junction of A50 Derby–Stoke road & A515 Ashbourne road

Opening
Hall & Museum Mar–Oct Wed–Sun 1pm–5pm
Grounds Mar–Oct Wed–Sun 11am–6pm; Open Bank Hols

Admission
Hall Adult £5.50, Child £2.50
Hall & Museum £10, £6
Garden £1, 50p

Contact
Sudbury, Ashbourne DE6 5HT
t 01283 585337/585305
w nationaltrust.org.uk
e sudburyhall@nationaltrust.org.uk

459 Burton upon Trent

Coors Visitor Centre

4 hrs   All year

Beer has been brewed in Burton upon Trent for centuries and the Museum of Brewing charts its history. It provides a blend of living heritage, historic galleries and family entertainment. The centre is home to two teams of shire horses and a vintage vehicle collection.

* See a working stationary steam engine
* Special events throughout the year

Location	Contact
A511 in centre of Burton upon Trent. Follow brown signs for visitor centre.	Horninglow Street, Burton upon Trent DE14 1YQ
Opening	t 0845 600 0598
Daily: 10am–5pm (last admission 4pm)	w coorsvisitorcentre.com
	e enquiries@coorsbrewers.com
Admission	
Adult £6, Child £3, Concs £4	

460 Longton

Gladstone Pottery Museum

2 hrs+   All year

A complete Victorian pottery factory where visitors can get to grips with the history and skills of the potteries. Throw your own pot or try your hand at a range of pottery crafts with the team of friendly expert presentation staff.

* Try your hand at pottery crafts
* Flushed with Pride exhibition, a gallery devoted to the WC

Location	Contact
From M6 follow A500, then take A50 to Longton	Uttoxeter Road, Longton, Stoke-on-Trent ST3 1PQ
Opening	t 01782 319232
Daily: 10am–5pm	w stoke.gov.uk/museums
	e gladstone@stoke.gov.uk
Admission	
Adult £4.95, Child £3.50, Concs £3.95	

461 Stafford

British Wildlife Rescue Centre

2 hrs   All year

The whole family will enjoy a visit to this refuge set up for the treatment of sick and injured British wildlife. Also on the farm are a play barn, steam railway, craft shops, a restaurant and a garden centre.

* Guided tours by appointment

Location
On A518 Stafford–Uttoxeter road,
1 mile from Weston

Opening
Daily: 10am–5pm

Admission
Adult £1.50, Child £1

Contact
Amerton Working Farm,
Stowe-by-Chartley,
Stafford ST18 0LA

t 01889 271308
w thebwrc.co.uk

462 Stafford

Stafford Castle

3 hrs+   All year

Built by William the Conqueror to subdue rebellious locals, Stafford Castle has dominated the landscape throughout 900 years. Visitors today will find a more peaceful setting – follow the castle trail, explore the castle ruins and take in the panoramic view.

* Try on armour & chainmail
* Host of archaeological finds

Location
Off A518, 1 mile SW of Stafford

Opening
Apr–Oct Tue–Sun & Bank Hols
10am–5pm; Nov–Mar Sat–Sun
10am–4pm

Admission
Free

Contact
Castle Bank, Newport Road,
Stafford ST16 1DJ

t 01785 257698
w staffordbc.gov.uk

463 Stoke-on-Trent

Etruria Industrial Museum

1 hr   All year

Etruria Industrial Museum is situated on the Caldon, Trent and Mersey canals and includes the Etruscan Bone and Flint Mill. It has a family-friendly interactive exhibition, a tearoom and a shop. It is also the last active steam-powered potter's mill in Britain.

* Family-friendly interactive exhibition & events programme
* Craft activities in school hols

Location
Signed from A500. Car park is off
Etruria Vale Road

Opening
Jan–Mar Mon–Wed 12noon–4.30pm;
Apr–Dec Sat–Wed 12noon–4.30pm

Admission
Adult £2.35, Child £1.20, Family £5.30

Contact
Lower Bedford Street, Etruria,
Stoke-on-Trent ST4 7AF

t 01782 233144
w stoke.gov.uk
e museums@stoke.gov.uk

464 Stoke-on-Trent

Waterworld

3–4 hrs   All year

Children will enjoy this wacky and wild water-park. It has 19 exciting rides and attractions including wave machines, flumes, rapids and slides. Very popular attractions include the Spacebowl, aqua assault course, Python, and Black Hole.

* Best Practice Accolade 2002

Location
Off junction 16 of M6. Follow A500 to
Stoke-on-Trent, then follow signs to
Festival Park

Opening
summer Mon–Thu & Sat–Sun
10am–6pm, Fri 10am–9pm
winter Wed–Thu 2pm–7pm, Fri
2pm–9pm, Sat–Sun 10am–6pm

Admission
Please phone for details

Contact
Etruria, Hanley,
Stoke-on-Trent ST1 5PU

t 01782 205747
w waterworld.co.uk

465 Tamworth

Ash End House Children's Farm

4 hrs   All year

This small family-owned farm has lots of friendly animals to feed and stroke. As well as outdoor activities and a play area, the farm offers many undercover attractions and is home to some fascinating rare breeds. There are activities during weekends and holidays, including Make a Memento.

* Tours for groups
* Birthday parties on the farm

Location
In Middleton, near Tamworth in Staffordshire. Signed off A4091 & on same road as Drayton Manor Park

Opening
Daily: *summer* 10am–5pm;
winter 10am–dusk;
closed Mon–Fri in Jan
Please phone for details

Admission
Adult £4.50, Child £4.90 (includes feed for animals & other activities)

Contact
Middleton Lane, Middleton,
nr Tamworth B78 2BL

t 0121 329 3240
w childrensfarm.co.uk
e **contact@**childrensfarm.co.uk

---

466 Tamworth

Drayton Manor Theme Park

6 hrs+   Mar–Oct

Everyone's favourite theme park, with more than 100 rides and attractions set in 280 acres of lakes and parkland. It boasts some of the biggest, wettest and scariest rides around – plus family and children's rides, a zoo, museums, shops and restaurants.

* Thrills & fun for everyone
* Live entertainment

Location
Near Tamworth on A4091. From M42 take junction 9 or 10

Opening
Daily: mid-Mar–31 Oct
Please phone or visit the website for details

Admission
Please phone or visit the website for details

Contact
Tamworth B78 3TW

t 08708 725252
w draytonmanor.co.uk
e info@draytonmanor.co.uk

467 Tamworth

The Snowdome

2 hrs   All year

The snowdome has a host of activities for all ages.
As well as skiing and snowboarding, try careering down
the slope on inflatable tubes, ice-skating or even driving
a snow-mobile. Younger children can make a snowman
or have a game of snowballs in the SnowPlay area.

*Live music events
*Bar and restaurant facilities

Location	Admission
5 min from junction 10 of M42. Only 1½ hours from N London, Bristol, Manchester & Leeds	Please phone for details
	Contact
Opening	Leisure Island, River Drive, Tamworth B79 7ND
Daily: 9am–11pm. Please phone for details of session times	t 08705 000011
	w snowdome.co.uk
	e info@snowdome.co.uk

469 Atherstone

Twycross Zoo

3–4 hrs   All year

Twycross is the leading primate zoo in the country, but
it also houses hundreds of other animals from around
the world, including elephants, big cats, birds, reptiles
and amphibians.

* Seal & penguin feeding times
* Pets' corner & rare breeds

Location	Admission
Just off M42 on A444 in Leicestershire, easily reached from all Midland counties	Adult £8.50, Child £5, Concs £6
	Contact
Opening	Burton Road, Atherstone CV9 3PX
Daily: *summer* 10am–5.30pm; *winter* (Nov–Mar) 10am–4pm	t 01827 880250
	w twycrosszoo.com

468 Winkhill

Blackbrook Zoological Park

2–4 hrs   All year

Set amid the Staffordshire Moorlands, this zoo contains
a large and varied collection of some of the most rare
and endangered species to be found in the world, from
swans and geese to vultures and flamingos, from
meerkats and marmots to piranhas and pythons.

* Pets, aquarium & educational building
* Largest collection of wildfowl in British Isles

Location	Admission
From Leek take A523 & 1st right, signed to park, then 1st right again	Adult £7.50, Child £5, Concs £5.95
	Contact
Opening	Winkhill, nr Leek ST13 7QR
Daily: 10.30am–5.30pm (earlier closing in winter)	t 01538 308293
Café summer only	w blackbrookzoologicalpark.co.uk
	e enquiries@blackbrookzoologicalpark.co.uk

470 Coventry

Brandon Marsh Nature Centre

1 hr+   All year

A visit to Brandon Marsh Nature Centre starts at the
visitor centre, opened by Sir David Attenborough in
1998. This contains displays, hands-on activities and
information about the nature reserve, which covers
220 acres and features many lakes and bird hides.

* Warwickshire Wildlife Trust Centre
* New tearoom & shop

Location	Contact
Off A45	Brandon Lane, Coventry CV3 3GW
	t 02476 308999
Opening	w warwickshire-wildlife-trust.org.uk
Daily: Mon–Sat 9am–4.30pm, Sun 10am–4pm	e enquiries@wkwt.org.uk
Admission	
Adult £2.50, Child & Concs £1.50	

471   Coventry

Organic Garden Ryton

4 hrs   All year

Organic Garden Ryton is the UK's national centre for organic gardening, set within 10 acres of glorious gardens. There is a fantastic new interactive visitor centre including The Vegetable Kingdom, an exciting addition especially for children.

* Children's garden
* Computer games

Location
Off A45 on Wolston road, 5 miles SE of Coventry

Opening
Daily: 9am–5pm

Admission
Adult £5, Child £2.50, Concs £4.50

Contact
Ryton-on-Dunsmore,
Coventry CV8 3LG

t 02476 303517
w gardenorganic.org.uk
e enquiry@hdra.org.uk

472   Hatton

Hatton Country World

3 hrs+   All year

Hatton Country World offers acres of fun for everyone, with a fun-packed schedule of events and activities, such as Farmyard Favourites and Adventure Land. Finish off your day with a relaxing browse around the unique shopping village or a trip to see the animals.

* Daft Duck trials, children's show & Birdobatics
* Soft play centre & Tristan the Runaway Tractor

Location
5 min from junction 15 of M40. Take A46 towards Coventry, turn on to A4177 & follow brown tourist signs

Opening
Daily: 10am–5pm

Admission
Please phone or visit the website for details

Contact
Dark Lane, Hatton CV35 8XA

t 01926 843411
w hattonworld.com
e hatton@hattonworld.com

473   Kingsbury

Broomey Croft Children's Farm

2 hrs+   All year

Set in the North Warwickshire countryside, Broomey Croft Children's Farm provides an opportunity for a family day of fun and relaxation. Children can meet and handfeed the farm animals, and see baby goats and chicks, sheep-shearing and a bee display.

* Free tractor & trailer rides
* Lambing & bottle-feeding lambs

Location
10 min from junction 9 of M42. Take A4091 towards Drayton Manor & follow brown tourist signs

Opening
Please phone or visit the website for details

Admission
Adult £4.40, Child £3.90

Contact
Bodymoor Heath Lane,
Bodymoor Heath,
Kingsbury B76 0EE

t 01827 873844
w broomeycroftfarm.co.uk
e info@broomeycroftfarm.co.uk

474 Nuneaton

Bosworth Battlefield Visitor Centre & Country Park

2 hrs+   Jan–Oct

This is the site of one of the most famous battles in English history, between Richard III and Henry Tudor. The result gave England a new king and marked the beginning of the Tudor dynasty. Discover what it was like to be a soldier at the time and follow the battle trail.

* Walk down a medieval street
* Annual re-enactment of the battle

Location
2 miles S of Market Bosworth near Sutton Cheney

Opening
Visitor centre Mar Sat–Sun 11am–5pm; Apr–Oct daily 11am–5pm
Country Park Jan–Oct daily 7am onwards (closing times vary)

Admission
Adult £3.25, Concs £2.25

Contact
Sutton Cheney, Nuneaton CV13 0AD

t 01455 290429
w leics.gov.uk
e bosworth@leics.gov.uk

475 Stratford-upon-Avon

Shakespeare's Birthplace

1 hr   All year

Home to the Shakespeare family and where William Shakespeare was born in 1564. The house contains both original artefacts and replicas depicting the house as Shakespeare would have known it as a child. An exhibition unfolds Shakespeare's life, work and times.

* Exhibitions tell the story of the house
* Exhibits of rare period items including *First Folio* (1623)

Location
Signed from town centre

Opening
Apr–May &Sep–Oct Mon–Sat 10am–5pm, Sun 10.30am–5pm; Jun–Aug Mon–Sat 9am–5pm, Sun 9.30am–5pm; Nov–Mar Mon–Sat 10am–4pm, Sun 10.30am–4pm

Admission
Adult £7, Child £2.75, Concs £6

Contact
Henley Street, Stratford-upon-Avon CV37 6QW

t 01789 201823
w shakespeare.org.uk
e info@shakespeare.org.uk

476 Stratford-upon-Avon

Stratford Butterfly Farm

1 hr+   All year

Wander through a tropical rainforest with a myriad of multicoloured butterflies, birds and fish. See fascinating animals in Insect City and view deadly spiders in perfect safety in Arachnoland.

* Expert staff
* Wildlife video shows

Location
On River Avon, opposite Royal Shakespeare Theatre. Easily accessible from town centre

Opening
Daily: *summer* 10am–6pm
winter 10am–dusk

Admission
Please phone for details

Contact
Traway Walk, Swan's Nest Lane, Stratford-upon-Avon CV37 7LS

t 01789 299288
w butterflyfarm.co.uk
e sales@butterflyfarm.co.uk

477 Sutton Coldfield

Kingsbury Water Park

2 hrs+   All year

Warwickshire's premier waterside attraction, Kingsbury Water Park has 15 lakes in more than 600 acres of country park. Stroll along the surfaced paths, explore hidden corners, spot birds and wildlife, hire a cycle, or join in on an event. There is also an adventure playground and a farm.

* Day-ticket fishing
* Miniature railway new in 2006

Location	Contact
Exit at junction 9 of M42 & follow A4097 towards Kingsbury	Bodymoor Heath, Sutton Coldfield B76 0DY
Opening	t 01827 872660
Please phone for details	w warwickshire.gov.uk/countryside
Admission	e parks@warwickshire.gov.uk
Car park £2.50	

479 Baginton

Midland Air Museum

2 hrs   All year

See a wide range of aircraft, both international and local. The collection includes WWII aircraft and memorabilia and outside are a number of rare aircraft, plus an anti-aircraft gun. A number of the aircraft have steps up to the cockpit area so you can look inside.

* Giant 1959 Armstrong Whitworth Argosy freighter
* Meteor, Vulcan, Hunter, Starfighter & Phantom

Location	Admission
Off A45, between roundabout & Baginton	Adult £4.50, Child £2.50, Concs £4
Opening	**Contact**
Daily: Apr–Oct Mon–Sat 10am–5pm, Sun & Bank Hols 10am–6pm; Nov–Mar 10.30am–5pm	Coventry Airport, Baginton, Coventry CV8 3AZ
	t 02476 301033
	w midlandairmuseum.org.uk
	e midlandairmuseum@aol.com

478 Warwick

Warwick Castle

  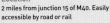

3 hrs+   All year

Britain's greatest medieval experience – discover 1,000 years of history at Warwick Castle. See the medieval preparation for battle in Kingmaker, join a Victorian Royal Weekend Party and enjoy special events throughout the year.

* Quality Assured Visitor Attraction
* Special events throughout the year, detailed on website

Location	Contact
2 miles from junction 15 of M40. Easily accessible by road or rail	Warwick CV34 4QU
Opening	t 0870 442 2000
Daily: Apr–Sep 10am–6pm; Oct–Mar 10am–5pm	w warwick-castle.co.uk
Admission	e info@warwick-castle.com
Please phone for details	

480 Birmingham

Lapworth Museum of Geology

1 hr   All year

For an educational few hours, bring the children to visit one of the oldest specialist geological museums in the UK. Dating back to 1880, Lapworth has an extensive and fascinating collection of fossils, minerals and rocks.

* More than 250, 000 specimens
* 420 million-year-old fossils

Location	
On A38 Bristol road into Birmingham	Admission
	Free
Opening	Contact
Daily: Mon–Fri 9am–5pm;	University of Birmingham, Edgbaston,
Sat–Sun 2pm–5pm. Other times by	Birmingham B15 2TT
appointment, please phone for details	t 0121 414 7294
	w lapworth.bham.ac.uk
	e lapworth@contacts.bham.ac.uk

481 Birmingham

National Sea Life Centre

3 hrs   All year

A unique insight into the lives of a myriad creatures – from shrimps to sharks. The unique, one-million-litre tropical ocean display has a Hawaiian volcanic theme, and the completely transparent 360° submarine tunnel provides a home for two giant green turtles.

* Programme of talks & feeding demonstrations
* Totally tropical centre

Location	Admission
Between National Indoor Arena & International Convention Centre	Adult £12.50, Child £8.50, Concs £9
Opening	Contact
summer daily 10am–5pm	The Waters Edge, Brindleyplace,
winter Mon–Fri 10am–4pm,	Birmingham B1 2HL
Sat–Sun 10am–5pm	t 0121 643 6777 / 633 4700
	w sealifeeurope.com
	e slcbirmingham@
	merlinentertainments.biz

482 Birmingham

ThinkTank

4 hrs   All year

ThinkTank is Birmingham's science museum. Visitors can explore everything from aircraft and steam engines to intestines and tastebuds! With prestigious events, exhibitions and tours, there really is something here for everyone, including ThinkTank's new Planetarium.

* Unravel the mysteries of the body
* Medical tour covers techniques & instruments

Location	Contact
Follow blue banners. 15 min walk from New Street railway station	Curzon Street, Birmingham B4 7XG
Opening	t 0121 202 2222
Daily: 10am–5pm	w thinktank.ac
	e findout@thinktank.ac
Admission	
Adult £6.95, Child £4.95, Concs £5	

483 Birmingham

Tolkien's Birmingham

2 hrs   Apr–Sep

Visit many of J R R Tolkien's childhood haunts and see the places that inspired him to write *The Hobbit* and *Lord of the Rings*. This is a fascinating guided tour, and a chance to encounter the young imagination of a C20 literary genius.

* Indepth knowledge from specialist tour guide, for groups only
* Please wear appropriate footwear

Location	Contact
Various areas of Birmingham	59 Springfield Road, Kings Heath,
Opening	Birmingham B14 7DU
Apr–Sep by appointment	
Please phone for details of guided tours	t 0121 444 4046
	w birminghamheritage.org.uk
Admission	e bobblackham@btinternet.com
Adult £5, Child £2.50	

Cadbury World

3 hrs   Feb–Dec

There is fun for all ages with the magical Cadabra journey and the Cadbury Fantasy Factory. Children can learn all about chocolate – where it came from and who first consumed this mysterious substance – and then visit the largest Cadbury shop in the world!

* Purple Planet – see yourself moulded in chocolate
* Essence – produce your own Cadbury product

Location	Contact
Signed from M42	Linden Road, Bournville, Birmingham B30 2LU
Opening	
Times vary, please phone for details	t 0845 4503599
	w cadburyworld.co.uk
Admission	e cadbury.world@csplc.com
Adult £12.50, Child £9.50, Concs £9.95	
Pre-booking recommended	

Selly Manor

2 hrs   All year

Learn about medieval life, the Tudors, old houses and furniture in this amazing medieval timber-framed house that was moved piece by piece by George Cadbury to the village of Bournville. Portable notes, torches and magnifying glasses are provided.

* In the unique village of Bournville near Cadbury World
* Events & activities throughout the year

Location	Admission
3 miles S of city centre on Maple Road next to Bournville village green	Adult £3, Child £1, Concs £2
	Contact
Opening	Bournville, Birmingham B30 1UB
Jan–Dec Tue–Fri 10am–5pm; Apr–Sep Tue–Fri 10am–5pm, Sat–Sun & Bank Hols 2pm–5pm	t 0121 472 0199
	w bvt.org.uk/sellymanor
	e sellymanor@bvt.org.uk

486 Dudley

Black Country Living Museum

3 hrs+   All year

Discover a fascinating world where an old-fashioned village has been created beside the canal. Wander around original shops and houses, ride on a tramcar or fairground swingboat, go down the mine or just soak up the atmosphere.

* Tramcars & trolleybuses transport visitors
* Costumed demonstrators & working craftsmen

Location	Contact
On A4037, 3 miles from M5 junction 2	Tipton Road, Dudley DY1 4SQ
Opening	t 0121 557 9643
Daily: Mar–Oct 10am–5pm;	w bclm.co.uk
Nov–Feb Wed–Sun 10am–4pm	e info@bclm.co.uk
Admission	
Adult £11, Child £6, Concs £9	

487 Dudley

Dudley Canal Trust

1 hr   Feb–Nov

Explore Dudley's subterranean world of limestone mines and canal systems. Visitors can admire the mining and engineering feats of the men of the C18 and modern tunnelling techniques of today. Computer displays show scenes from the past 200 years of mining.

* Learn about the geological history of the area
* Special events throughout the year

Location	Admission
Follow signs to Dudley past Black Country Living Museum to traffic lights, turn left & attraction is on the left	Adult £4.25, Child £3.55, Concs £3.90
	Contact
	The Ticket Office, Birmingham New Road, Dudley DY1 4SB
Opening	
Mar–Oct 10am–5pm;	t 01384 236275
Feb & Nov 10am–4pm	w dudleytunneltrust.org.uk
	e dcttrips@btclick.com

488 Dudley

Dudley Zoological Gardens

3 hrs+   All year

Dudley Zoo is a modern zoo set in the 40-acre wooded grounds of Dudley Castle. Visitors can enjoy a varied day combining zoology, history and geology, as the zoo is built on an important limestone escarpment.

* Breathtaking views over the Black Country
* Audio-visual display & visitor centre

Location	Contact
3 miles from M5 junction 2	2 The Broadway, Dudley DY1 4QB
Opening	
Daily: Mar–Oct 10am–4pm; Oct–Mar 10am–3pm	t 01384 215313
	w dudleyzoo.org.uk
Admission	
Adult £9.95, Child (4–15) £6.75	

489 Edgbaston

Birmingham Botanical Gardens & Glasshouses

2 hrs+   All year

In a series of giant glasshouses, each with different climatic conditions, you can visit a world of environments in just one day. There are four glasshouses (Tropical, Subtropical, Mediterranean and Arid) and a Study Centre running fun workshops aimed at children under 12.

* Designed by J C Loudon, a leading garden planner
* Sculpture trail, waterfowl & exotic birds

Location
Signed from Edgbaston

Opening
Apr–Sep Mon–Sat 9am–7pm,
Sun 10am–7pm; Oct–Mar Mon–Sat
9am–5pm, Sun 10am–5pm (or dusk)

Admission
Adult £6.10, Child & Concs £3.60

Contact
Westbourne Road, Edgbaston,
Birmingham B15 3TR
t 0121 454 1860
w birminghambotanicalgardens.
    org.uk
e admin@birminghambotanicalgardens.
    org.uk

490 Solihull

National Motorcycle Museum

3 hrs   All year

Internationally renowned, this is the largest motorcycle museum in the world. The exhibits cover 60 years of British motorcycling with more than 650 machines, all lovingly restored to the manufacturer's original specifications.

* Extensive book department
* Regular rallies & events

Location
Just off M42 junction 6

Opening
Daily: 10am– 6pm

Admission
Adult £6.95, Child & Concs £4.95

Contact
Coventry Road, Bickenhill,
Solihull B92 0EJ
t 01675 443311
w nationalmotorcyclemuseum.co.uk
e admin@nationalmotorcycle
    museum.co.uk

491 Stourbridge

Red House Glass Cone

2 hrs   All year

This fantastic museum spans 400 years of glassmaking history. Explore underground passages not previously open to the public and climb up a spiral staircase within the giant cone to a panoramic viewing platform. See craftsmen demonstrate the magical art of glassmaking.

* Demonstrations of glassmaking
* Stuart Crystal Gift Centre

Location
10 miles from M5 Junction 2 (Oldbury)
or junction 4 (Stourbridge). Situated
near Stourbridge town centre on A491
Stourbridge–Wolverhampton road

Opening
Daily: Apr–Oct Mon–Sat 10am–5pm,
Sun 10am–4pm; Nov–Mar 10am–4pm

Admission
Free
Audio guides £1.50

Contact
High Street, Wordsley,
Stourbridge DY8 4AZ
t 01384 812750
w dudley.gov.uk/redhousecone

492 Bewdley

West Midland Safari & Leisure Park

3 hrs+   Feb–Oct

A 4-mile drive-through safari covers an area of more than 150 acres and is home to a variety of exotic and unusual animals including rare and beautiful white tigers, elephants, rhinos, giraffes, lions, wallabies, emus, camels, zebras, bison, wolves and llamas.

* Safari bus tours
* Discovery trail

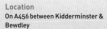

Location	Contact
On A456 between Kidderminster & Bewdley	Spring Grove, Bewdley DY12 1LF
Opening	t 01299 402114
Daily: Feb–Oct Mon–Fri 10am–4pm, Sat–Sun 10am–5pm	w wmsp.co.uk
	e info@wmsp.co.uk
Admission	
Please phone for details	

493 Worcester

The Hop Pocket Craft Centre

4 hrs   All year

The Hop Pocket Craft Centre is located in the beautiful Frome Valley. See displays of work by more than 300 different craftspeople, including pottery, glass engraving, jewellery, soft toys, paintings and woodturning – gifts to suit every pocket.

* Demonstrations by appointment
* New 11-shop shopping village

Location	Contact
On B4214 just off A4103 Worcester–Hereford road	New House Farm, Bishops Frome, Worcester WR6 5BT
Opening	t 01531 640323
Tue–Sun please phone for details	w thehoppocket.com
Admission	e john@thehoppocket.com
Free	

494 Worcester

Upton Heritage Centre

1 hr+   Apr–Sep

This restored bell tower, the Pepperpot, is the oldest surviving building in Upton-upon-Severn and is a local landmark. The centre tells the story of the Battle of Upton in 1651 during the Civil War. There are also exhibits on local history and the town's development.

* Battle of Upton display

Location	Admission
On B4211 from Great Malvern & A38 & A4104 from Worcester	Free
Opening	Contact
Daily: Apr–Sep 1.30pm–4.30pm; Open some mornings, please phone for details	Tourist Info Centre, 4 High Street, Worcester WR8 0HB
	t 01684 594200

495 Worcester

Worcester Cathedral

1 hr   All year

Worcester Cathedral has been a place of prayer and worship since AD680. The present building was begun in 1084. Its many attractions include King John's tomb, Prince Arthur's chantry, the early C12 Chapter House and St Wulstan's crypt.

* Tower open 10.30am–4.30pm Sat & summer hols
* Magnificent Victorian stained-glass windows

Location	Contact
In city centre, off College Street	10a College Green, Worcester WR1 2LH
Opening	t 01905 28854
Daily: 7.30am–6pm, services 3 times daily	w worcestercathedral.org.uk
Admission	e info@worcestercathedral.org.uk
Free, donations welcomed	

Dunraven Bay, Vale of Glamorgan

Wales

Mid Wales North Wales South Wales

MID WALES

Animal Attractions
Animalarium 188
Felinwynt Rainforest & Butterfly Centre 188
Gigrin Farm 190

Boat & Train Trips
Vale of Rheidol Railway 188

Museums & Exhibitions
Corris Craft Centre 190
Dolaucothi Gold Mines 190
King Arthur's Labyrinth 189
The National Cycle Collection 189

Parks, Gardens & Nature
Lake Vyrnwy Nature Reserve 190

Sport & Leisure
Llangorse Rope & Riding Centre 189

Historic Sites
Chirk Castle 193
Plas Newydd 191
Portmeirion 196

Museums & Exhibitions
Harlequin Puppet Theatre 194
Inigo Jones Slateworks 192

Parks, Gardens & Nature
The Fun Centre 192
Greenwood Forest Park 195
Henblas Country Park 191

Sport & Leisure
Plas Menai National Watersports
 Centre 192
Pony & Quad Treks 193
ProAdventure 196

SOUTH WALES

Animal Attractions
Cardigan Island Coastal Farm Park 199
Folly Farm 201

Guided Tours
Millennium Stadium Tours 198

Historic Sites
Caerphilly Castle 197
Caldicot Castle & Country Park 201
Cardiff Castle 197

Museums & Exhibitions
Big Pit National Mining Museum 197
Cardigan Heritage Centre 199
National Waterfront Museum 202
Pembrokeshire Motor Museum 200
St Fagans Natural History Museum 198
Techniquest 199
Welsh Chocolate Farm 201

Parks, Gardens & Nature
National Showcaves Centre for Wales 200

Sport & Leisure
Heatherton Country Sports Park 202
Welsh International Climbing
 & Activity Centre 202

Theme Parks & Adventure Playgrounds
Oakwood Theme Park 202

NORTH WALES

Animal Attractions
Anglesey Sea Zoo 191
The Welsh Mountain Zoo 194

Boat & Train Trips
The Ffestiniog Railway 196
Llangollen Wharf 195
Snowdon Mountain Railway 195
Welsh Highland Railway (Caernarfon) 192

496 Aberystwyth

Animalarium

3 hrs   All year

Meet a wide selection of exotic and domestic animals, birds and reptiles – including monkeys, marmosets, lemurs and wallabies. Pony rides run twice daily from Easter to September. There is an animal-petting area, a fruit bat cave and a daily snake-handling demonstration.

* Welsh Tourist Board seal of approval
* Crocodile-feeding twice a week

Location	Admission
At Borth, between Aberystwyth & Machynlleth	Please phone for details
Opening	Contact
Daily: summer 10am–6pm	Borth, Ceredigion SY25 6RA
winter 11am–4pm	t 01970 871224
	w animalarium.co.uk

497 Aberystwyth

Vale of Rheidol Railway

 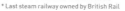

3 hrs+   Easter–Oct

Take a ride on a steam train for the 11 miles between Aberystwyth and Devil's Bridge. During the hour-long journey you'll have spectacular views of the wooded Rheidol Valley. From Devil's Bridge there are walks to Mynach Falls, Devil's Punchbowl and Jacob's Ladder.

* One of the Great Little Trains of Wales
* Last steam railway owned by British Rail

Location	Contact
Trains depart from Aberystwyth centre, beside main railway station	Park Avenue, Aberystwyth, Cardiganshire SY23 1PG
Opening	t 01970 625819
Please phone for details	w rheidolrailway.co.uk
Admission	e info@rheidolrailway.co.uk
Return fare Adult £12.50, Child from £3, Concs £11	

498 Cardigan

Felinwynt Rainforest & Butterfly Centre

1 hr+   .   Easter–Oct

This tropical rainforest in the heart of Wales is home to exotic and unusual plants, birds, insects and butterflies from all over the world. You'll see the scarlet swallowtail and the giant atlas moth free-flying in natural surroundings.

* Welsh Tourist Board Star Attraction
* Video room

Location	Contact
Off A487, 6 miles N of Cardigan. Follow brown tourist signs	Felinwynt, Cardigan, Ceredigion SA43 1RT
Opening	t 01239 810882/810250
Daily: Easter–Oct 10.30am–5pm	w butterflycentre.co.uk
Admission	e dandldevereux@btinternet.com
Adult £3.95, Child £1.95, Concs £3.75	

499 Corris

King Arthur's Labyrinth

2 hrs+   Apr–Nov

Glide in a boat through an underground waterfall and deep into the spectacular caverns under the mountains where tales of King Arthur are told with stunning sound and light effects. Back above ground, join the Bard's Quest to search for legends lost in the Maze of Time.

* Large fully operational craft centre
* Shop sells items on the Arthurian theme

Location
On A487 between Machynlleth
& Dolgellau

Opening
Daily: Apr–5 Nov 10am–5pm
(last tour 5pm)

Admission
Adult £5.50, Child £3.90, Concs £4.95

Contact
Corris, Machynlleth,
Powys SY20 9RF

t 01654 761584
w kingarthurslabyrinth.com
e king.arthurs.labyrinth@corris-wales.co.uk

500 Llandrindod Wells

The National Cycle Collection

1 hr+   All year

How big is a penny-farthing's wheel? And just how uncomfortable were those early cycles compared with today's high-tech versions? See more than 250 bicycles from 1819, such as the hobby-horse, boneshakers and penny-farthings, up to the most modern cycles of today.

* The Dunlop story
* Displays about past racing stars

Location
Just off Temple Street in town centre.
Llandrindod Wells is on A483

Opening
Mar–Oct daily 10am–4pm;
Nov–Feb Tue, Thu & Sun 10am–4pm

Admission
Adult £3, Child £1, Concs £2

Contact
The Automobile Palace, Temple Street,
Llandrindod Wells, Powys LD1 5DL

t 01597 825531
w cyclemuseum.org.uk
e cycle.museum@care4free.net

501 Llangorse

Llangorse Rope & Riding Centre

4 hrs+   All year

The centre offers a range of indoor and outdoor climbing and riding activities, from scaling rock surfaces and crossing rope bridges to trekking and hacking. There are qualified instructors on hand and onsite accommodation is available.

* Largest indoor climbing & riding centre in Wales
* WTB's Best New Business in Wales Award 2006

Location
On B4560, off A40
Brecon–Abergavenny road

Opening
Climb Mon–Sat 9am–10pm,
Sun 9am–5pm
Ride Daily: 10am–4.30pm

Admission
Please phone or visit the website for details

Contact
Gilfach Farm, Llangorse, Brecon
Beacons, Powys LD3 7UH

t 01874 658272
w activityuk.com
e info@activity.uk.com

502 Llanwrda

Dolaucothi Gold Mines

2 hrs+   Easter–Oct

Begun by the Romans, this site was worked again in the C19 and C20. Visitors are taken on fascinating guided tours of the Roman and more recent underground workings (the latter are not open to children under five).

* Historical tours
* Opportunity to pan for gold

Location
Between Lampeter & Llanwrda on A482

Opening
Daily: Easter–Oct 10am–5pm

Admission
Adult £3.40, Child £1.70

Contact
Pumsaint, Llanwrda SA19 8US
t 01558 650177
w nationaltrust.org.uk
e dolaucothi@nationaltrust.org.uk

503 Llanwyddyn

Lake Vyrnwy Nature Reserve

2 hrs+   All year

This man-made lake was completed in 1888. In dry weather, if the water level drops far enough, the ruins of the submerged village of Llanwyddyn reappear. With various hides, vantage points and nature trails, it is a spectacular place for bird-watching.

* Moorland, woodland & water habitats
* Craft shops & café

Location
10 miles W of Llanfyllin

Opening
Apr–Dec daily 10.30am–5.30pm;
Jan–Mar Sat–Sun 10.30am–4.30pm

Admission
Free

Contact
Brynawel, Llanwyddyn,
Powys SY10 0LZ
t 01691 870278
w rspb.org.uk
e vyrnwy@rspb.org.uk

504 Machynlleth

Corris Craft Centre

2 hrs+   Apr–Nov

Corris Craft Centre is home to 10 craft workshops in which visitors are invited to see the skills of the craftworkers and to buy from the displays of wooden toymaking, pottery, jewellery, leatherwork, handcarved candles, glassware, wood-turning and card-designing.

* Patchwork quilting & rustic furniture for sale

Location
On A487 between Machynlleth & Dolgellau

Opening
Daily: Apr–Nov 10am–5.30pm
Please phone for details of winter opening times

Admission
Free

Contact
Corris, Machynlleth,
Powys SY20 9RF
t 01654 761584
w kingarthurslabyrinth.com
e king.arthurs.labyrinth@corris-wales.
co.uk

505 Rhayader

Gigrin Farm

1 hr+   All year

A family-run upland sheep farm with wonderful views of the Wye and Elan valleys. It has breeding ewes along with ponies, assorted ducks and a number of pea fowl. In 1994 it became the Official Kite Country, Red Kite Feeding Station – a big draw for bird-watchers.

* Farm & nature trail, new wetland project
* Red kite feeding times 2pm summer & 3pm winter

Location
On A470, ½ mile S of Rhayader

Opening
Daily: 1pm–5pm

Admission
Adult £3, Child £1, Concs £2.50

Contact
South Street, Rhayader,
Powys LD6 5BL
t 01597 810243
w gigrin.co.uk
e redkites@gigrin.co.uk

499 Corris

King Arthur's Labyrinth

2 hrs+   Apr–Nov

Glide in a boat through an underground waterfall and deep into the spectacular caverns under the mountains where tales of King Arthur are told with stunning sound and light effects. Back above ground, join the Bard's Quest to search for legends lost in the Maze of Time.

* Large fully operational craft centre
* Shop sells items on the Arthurian theme

Location
On A487 between Machynlleth
& Dolgellau

Opening
Daily: Apr–5 Nov 10am–5pm
(last tour 5pm)

Admission
Adult £5.50, Child £3.90, Concs £4.95

Contact
Corris, Machynlleth,
Powys SY20 9RF

t 01654 761584
w kingarthurslabyrinth.com
e king.arthurs.labyrinth@corris-wales.
   co.uk

500 Llandrindod Wells

The National Cycle Collection

1 hr+   All year

How big is a penny-farthing's wheel? And just how uncomfortable were those early cycles compared with today's high-tech versions? See more than 250 bicycles from 1819, such as the hobby-horse, boneshakers and penny-farthings, up to the most modern cycles of today.

* The Dunlop story
* Displays about past racing stars

Location
Just off Temple Street in town centre.
Llandrindod Wells is on A483

Opening
Mar–Oct daily 10am–4pm;
Nov–Feb Tue, Thu & Sun 10am–4pm

Admission
Adult £3, Child £1, Concs £2

Contact
The Automobile Palace, Temple Street,
Llandrindod Wells, Powys LD1 5DL

t 01597 825531
w cyclemuseum.org.uk
e cycle.museum@care4free.net

501 Llangorse

Llangorse Rope & Riding Centre

4 hrs+   All year

The centre offers a range of indoor and outdoor climbing and riding activities, from scaling rock surfaces and crossing rope bridges to trekking and hacking. There are qualified instructors on hand and onsite accommodation is available.

* Largest indoor climbing & riding centre in Wales
*WTB's Best New Business in Wales Award 2006

Location
On B4560, off A40
Brecon–Abergavenny road

Opening
Climb Mon–Sat 9am–10pm,
Sun 9am–5pm
Ride Daily: 10am–4.30pm

Admission
Please phone or visit the website for
details

Contact
Gilfach Farm, Llangorse, Brecon
Beacons, Powys LD3 7UH

t 01874 658272
w activityuk.com
e info@activity.uk.com

502 Llanwrda

Dolaucothi Gold Mines

2 hrs+   Easter–Oct

Begun by the Romans, this site was worked again in the C19 and C20. Visitors are taken on fascinating guided tours of the Roman and more recent underground workings (the latter are not open to children under five).

* Historical tours
* Opportunity to pan for gold

Location
Between Lampeter & Llanwrda on A482

Opening
Daily: Easter–Oct 10am–5pm

Admission
Adult £3.40, Child £1.70

Contact
Pumsaint, Llanwrda SA19 8US

t 01558 650177
w nationaltrust.org.uk
e dolaucothi@nationaltrust.org.uk

503 Llanwyddyn

Lake Vyrnwy Nature Reserve

2 hrs+   All year

This man-made lake was completed in 1888. In dry weather, if the water level drops far enough, the ruins of the submerged village of Llanwyddyn reappear. With various hides, vantage points and nature trails, it is a spectacular place for bird-watching.

* Moorland, woodland & water habitats
* Craft shops & café

Location
10 miles W of Llanfyllin

Opening
Apr–Dec daily 10.30am–5.30pm;
Jan–Mar Sat–Sun 10.30am–4.30pm

Admission
Free

Contact
Brynawel, Llanwyddyn,
Powys SY10 0LZ

t 01691 870278
w rspb.org.uk
e vyrnwy@rspb.org.uk

504 Machynlleth

Corris Craft Centre

2 hrs+   Apr–Nov

Corris Craft Centre is home to 10 craft workshops in which visitors are invited to see the skills of the craftworkers and to buy from the displays of wooden toymaking, pottery, jewellery, leatherwork, handcarved candles, glassware, wood-turning and card-designing.

* Patchwork quilting & rustic furniture for sale

Location
On A487 between Machynlleth & Dolgellau

Opening
Daily: Apr–Nov 10am–5.30pm
Please phone for details of winter opening times

Admission
Free

Contact
Corris, Machynlleth,
Powys SY20 9RF

t 01654 761584
w kingarthurslabyrinth.com
e king.arthurs.labyrinth@corris-wales.co.uk

505 Rhayader

Gigrin Farm

1 hr+   All year

A family-run upland sheep farm with wonderful views of the Wye and Elan valleys. It has breeding ewes along with ponies, assorted ducks and a number of pea fowl. In 1994 it became the Official Kite Country, Red Kite Feeding Station – a big draw for bird-watchers.

* Farm & nature trail, new wetland project
* Red kite feeding times 2pm summer & 3pm winter

Location
On A470, ½ mile S of Rhayader

Opening
Daily: 1pm–5pm

Admission
Adult £3, Child £1, Concs £2.50

Contact
South Street, Rhayader,
Powys LD6 5BL

t 01597 810243
w gigrin.co.uk
e redkites@gigrin.co.uk

506 Anglesey

Anglesey Sea Zoo

2 hrs+   Feb–Oct

This is Wales's largest marine aquarium, nestling on the shores of the Menai Strait. With more than 50 displays, the Sea Zoo has recreated the habitats of the fauna and flora that can be found around Anglesey and the North Wales coastline.

* Major seahorse conservation project
* Lobster hatchery & gift & pearl shop

Location
On A55 cross Britannia Bridge on to Anglesey & follow brown lobster signs to Brynsiencyn. Nearest railway station is Bangor

Opening
Daily: Feb–Mar 11am–3pm;
Easter–Oct 10am–6pm

Admission
High season Adult £6.95, Child £5.95, Concs £6.50 *Low season* Adult £5.95, Child £4.95, Concs £5.50

Contact
Brynsiencyn, Isle of Anglesey LL61 6TQ

t 01248 430411
w angleseyseazoo.co.uk
e info@angleseyseazoo.co.uk

---

507 Anglesey

Plas Newydd

3 hrs   Apr–Oct

This C18 house built by James Wyatt is a fine mixture of classical and Gothic. Restyled in the 1930s, the house is famous for its association with Whistler, whose work is exhibited here.There is also a museum for the 1st Marquess of Anglesey who led the cavalry at the Battle of Waterloo.

* Halloween family fun day
* Children's quiz trails

Location
Junctions 7 & 8 off A55

Opening
Apr–Oct Sat–Wed
House 12noon–5pm
Gardens 11am–5.30pm

Admission
Adult £6, Child £3

Contact
Llanfairpwll, Anglesey LL61 6DQ

t 01248 715272/714795
w nationaltrust.org.uk
e plasnewydd@nationaltrust.org.uk

---

508 Bordorgan

Henblas Country Park

6 hrs+   Easter–Oct

There are 30 attractions in all on this site, including duck displays and sheep-shearing, plus indoor and outdoor adventure playgrounds. Visitors can also enjoy the crazy golf, face-painting, ball pool and bouncy castles.

* Tractor tours, pony & train rides
* Pets' corner & lamb-feeding

Location
Just off junction 6 of A55 & A5. Take B4422 from A5, 10 miles from Britannia Bridge

Opening
Easter–Oct Sun–Fri 10.30am–5pm; closed Sat except Bank Hol weekends

Admission
Adult £5, Child £4

Contact
Bordorgan, Anglesey LL62 5DL

t 01407 840440
w parc-henblas-park.co.uk

509 Caernarfon

The Fun Centre

1 hr+ | All year

With 14,000 sq ft of family fun including two 20ft-high drop slides the Fun Centre will keep even the most energetic child entertained for hours. There is even a driving track where you can take a number of different vehicles for a thrilling spin.

* Separate under-4s play area & birthday party hire
* Laser play area & small museum

Location
On A487 by main roundabout just outside Caernarfon town centre

Opening
School hols & Sat–Sun 10am–6pm
Please phone for details of other opening times

Admission
Please phone for details

Contact
Christchurch, Bangor Street, Caernarfon

t 01286 671911
w thefuncentre.co.uk
e info@thefuncentre.co.uk

510 Caernarfon

Inigo Jones Slateworks

1 hr | All year

See Welsh craftsmanship at first hand on a tour of the Inigo Jones Slateworks, and learn all about the unique development of the Welsh slate industry in the historical exhibition. The self-guided tour starts with a film on how slate is mined.

* Children's quiz with slate prize
* Engraving & calligraphy workshops

Location
On A487, 6 miles from Caernarfon

Opening
Daily: 9am–5pm

Admission
Free entry to showroom
Self-guided tour Adult £4, Child & Concs £3.50, Family £13.50

Contact
Groeslon, Caernarfon LL54 7UE

t 01286 830242
w inigojones.co.uk
e slate@inigojones.co.uk

511 Caernarfon

Plas Menai National Watersports Centre

6 hrs+ | All year

An unrivalled choice of watersports and adventure training and courses for all abilities. Courses include dinghy and yacht sailing, kayaking, canoeing, windsurfing, power sports and mountain biking. There are residential activity weeks during school holidays.

* Instructors are the most highly qualified in the UK
* Also great for mountain activities

Location
2 miles N of Caernarfon on A487

Opening
Daily

Admission
Prices vary per course. Please phone or visit the website for details

Contact
Llanfairisgaer, Caernarfon, Gwynedd LL55 1UE

t 01248 670964
w plasmenai.co.uk
e info@plasmenai.co.uk

512 Caernarfon

Welsh Highland Railway (Caernarfon)

3 hrs | All year

Take a 12-mile ride, from the coast to the slopes of Snowdon, on North Wales's newest railway. Enjoy the spectacular scenery of lakes, mountains and forest en route to the heart of Snowdonia itself.

* Charge of £2.50 for dogs

Location
Main railway station on St Helens Road in Caernarfon, signed from A487

Opening
Daily: Mar–Oct; limited winter service, please phone for details

Admission
Adult £16.50, Child £8.25, Concs £13.20
(Adult price includes 1 child)

Contact
Harbour Station, Porthmadog, Gwynedd LL49 9NF

t 01766 516000
w festrail.co.uk
e enquiries@festrail.co.uk

513 Chirk

Chirk Castle

2 hrs   Easter–Oct

Built in 1310, this National Trust property has a beautiful interior, medieval tower, dungeon and C18 servants' hall. Outside are a formal garden, shrub garden, rock garden and thatched hawk house. Events for children include haunted tours and picture trails.

* Renovated laundry room
* Terrace with stunning views & a classical pavilion

Location
1 mile off A5, 2 miles W of Chirk

Opening
Easter–Oct Wed–Sun 12noon–5pm

Admission
Adult £7, Child £3.50

Contact
Chirk, Wrexham LL14 5AF

t 01691 777701
w nationaltrust.org.uk
e chirkcastle@ nationaltrust.org.uk

©NTPL/Matthew Antrobus

514 Chirk

Pony & Quad Treks

1–4 hrs   Easter–Oct

Enjoy the beautiful Ceiriod Valley on horseback. Choose from a variety of treks, from one hour to a full day, on ponies and horses to suit all ages. For the more adventurous over-12s, there's off-road quad biking.

* Full safety equipment provided
* Full protective clothing available

Location
8 miles from Chirk on B4500

Opening
Daily: Easter–Oct from 10.30am

Admission
Pony trekking Day £55, 2 hrs £30,
1 hr £10
Quad trekking 1 hr £30

Contact
Pont-y-Meibion, Pandy,
Glyn Ceiriog, Chirk, Llangollen,
North Wales LL20 7HS

t 01691 718333/718413
w ponytreks.co.uk
e enquiry@ponytreks.co.uk

515 Colwyn Bay

Harlequin Puppet Theatre

2 hrs   Jul–Sep

This was the first permanent puppet theatre to be built in Britain, and opened on 7 July 1958. It was built as the headquarters for The Eric Bramall Marionettes, a touring company that had been founded in 1944 and presented a repertoire of opera, plays, musical comedies and fantasies.

* Theatre holds 120 people
* Beautiful Italianate interior

Location
From A55 Expressway take exit marked Rhos-on-Sea & follow signs

Opening
Jul–Sep & half-terms daily show at 3pm; Jul–Aug also show at 8pm on Wed

Admission
Adult £5, Child & Concs £4

Contact
Cayley Promenade, Rhos-on-Sea, Colwyn Bay LL28 4EP

t 01492 548166
w puppets.inuk.com
e seats@puppets.inuk.com

516 Colwyn Bay

The Welsh Mountain Zoo

4 hrs+   All year

The beautiful gardens which are home to this caring conservation zoo are set high above the breathtaking Colwyn Bay. Visit the New Sealions Rock! and watch the daily shows including Penguins' Playtime, Chimp Encounter, Sealion Feeding and Birds of Prey Display.

* Shows weather permitting, during summer
* Children's farm & Jungle Adventureland

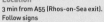

Location
3 min from A55 (Rhos-on-Sea exit). Follow signs

Opening
Daily: *summer* 9.30am–6pm
winter 9.30am–5pm

Admission
Adult £7.75, Child £5.50, Concs £6.60

Contact
Old Highway, Colwyn Bay, North Wales LL28 5UY

t 01492 532938
w welshmountainzoo.org

517 Gwynedd

Greenwood Forest Park

4 hrs+   Mar–Nov

Enjoy family adventure and fun at Greenwood Forest Park with its exciting Green Dragon family roller coaster. Ride the Great Green Run, the longest sledge slide in Wales. Have a Jungle Boat Adventure, shoot traditional longbows or build dens.

* World's only people-powered roller coaster
* Crocodile maze & treetop tower

Location
Take A4144, leading to B4366 between Bangor & Caernarfon, near Bethel off B4366

Opening
Daily: Mar–Sep 10am–5.30pm;
school summer hols 10am–6pm;
Oct–Nov 11am–5pm

Admission
Please phone or visit the website for details

Contact
Y Felinheli, Gwynedd,
North Wales LL56 4QN

t 01248 670076
w greenwoodforestpark.co.uk
e info@greenwoodforestpark.co.uk

518 Llanberis

Snowdon Mountain Railway

2 hrs+   Mar–Nov

Travel on the only public rack-and-pinion railway in Britain to the summit of Snowdon – the tallest mountain in England and Wales (3,560ft). It was built and opened in 1896. For those wishing to walk down, a single ticket to the summit station is available.

* Owing to renovations during 2007, trains will travel only as far as Clogwyn

Location
Llanberis railway station on A4086,
7½ miles from Caernarfon. 15 min drive from A55/A5 junction at Bangor.
Nearest railway station is Bangor

Opening
Daily: mid March–Nov
Please phone for details

Admission
Please phone for details

Contact
Llanberis, Gwynedd LL55 4TY

t 0870 4580033
w snowdonrailway.co.uk
e info@snowdonrailway.co.uk

519 Llangollen

Llangollen Wharf

1 hr+   Easter–Oct

You can embark on either a horse-drawn canal boat trip up to the spectacular Horseshoe Falls or a motorised cruise that takes you across Thomas Telford's famous aqueduct. There is also a self-steer day-hire boat available for groups of up to 10 people.

* Lunches & cream teas can be pre-ordered

Location
Off A5 Shrewsbury road & near A483 to Chester

Opening
Daily: Easter–Oct 10am–5pm

Admission
Horse-drawn boats Adult £4.50,
Child £2.50
Aqueduct cruise £9, £7

Contact
Welsh Canal Holiday Craft Ltd,
The Wharf, Llangollen LL20 8TA

t 01978 860702

520 Llangollen

ProAdventure

4 hrs+   All year

Try a wide variety of outdoor adventure activities from gentle open canoeing to adrenaline-filled white-water rafting. Other activities include gorge walking, kayaking, rock climbing, abseiling and mountain biking.

* Activity weekends & family days available
* Pre-booking essential

WC

Location
Situated in E of N Wales roughly 8 miles from Wrexham & 18 miles from Chester. Manchester, Liverpool & Birmingham are 1½ hours or less away

Opening
Please phone for details

Admission
Please phone for details

Contact
23 Castle Street,
Llangollen LL20 8NY

t 01978 861912
w proadventure.co.uk
e sales@proadventure.co.uk

521 Minffordd

Portmeirion

4 hrs+   All year

A private village created by Clough Williams-Ellis (1883–1978) on the coast of Snowdonia with woodland, gardens, shops, restaurants and hotels. Built in a fairytale style, it has grottos and cobbled squares. There is a sandy beach and playground for children.

* Used as a location for the cult TV series *The Prisoner*
* Cottages in the village let by Portmeirion Hotel

Location
Signed off A487 at Minffordd between Penrhyndeudraeth & Porthmadog

Opening
Daily: 9.30am–5.30pm

Admission
Adult £6.50, Child £3.50, Concs £5

Contact
Gwynedd LL48 6ET

t 01766 770000
w portmeirion-village.com
e info@portmeirion-village.com

522 Porthmadog

The Ffestiniog Railway

3 hrs+   All year

Climb aboard for a trip on a steam-hauled train with the world's oldest independent railway company. The track runs through 13 miles of spectacular scenery, from the sea right up to the mountains. Special events are held throughout the year.

* Regular special events
* Refurbished café/bar at Harbour railway station

Location
Next to harbour in Porthmadog on A487

Opening
Daily: Mar–Nov; limited winter service
Please phone for details

Admission
Adult £16.50, Child £8.25, Concs £13.20
(Adult price includes 1 child)

Contact
Harbour Station, Porthmadog,
Gwynedd LL49 9NF

t 01766 516000
w festrail.co.uk
e info@festrail.co.uk

© www.proadventure.co.uk, proadventure ltd

523 Blaenafon

Big Pit National Mining Museum

3 hrs+   Feb-Nov

This was a working coal mine until its closure in 1980. Now you can take an hour-long underground tour, led by ex-miners. Travel down in the pit cage and walk through underground roadways and engine houses. Above ground there's the colliery to explore.

* Enjoy simulated mining
* Winding engine house & blacksmith's workshop

Location	Admission
Leave M4 at junction 25a/26, then follow signs from A465	Free
Opening	**Contact**
Daily: Feb-Nov 9.30am–5pm	Blaenafon, Torfaen NP4 9XP
Underground tours run 10am–3.30pm	t 01495 790311
	w nmgw.ac.uk
	e bigpit@nmgw.ac.uk

524 Caerphilly

Caerphilly Castle

1 hr+   All year

One of the largest medieval fortresses in Britain, begun in 1268, the castle is famous for its leaning tower and its ringed stone and water defences. Enjoy the impressive great hall, two site exhibitions, an audio-visual display and replica medieval siege weapons.

* The Big Cheese weekend 27 Jul, nonstop entertainment
* Many summer demonstrations & events

Location	Admission
Exit M4 at junction 32, then take A470 or A469 for Caerphilly	Adult £3.50, Child & Concs £3
Opening	**Contact**
Daily: 31 Mar–31 May & 28 Sep–25 Oct 9.30am–5pm; 1 Jun–27 Sep 9.30am–6pm; 26 Oct–3. Mar Mon–Sat 9.30am–4.30pm, Sun 11am–4pm	Bridge Street, Caerphilly, Wales CF83 1JD
	t 02920 883143
	w cadw.wales.gov.uk
	e caerphilly.castle@cadw.co.uk

525 Cardiff

Cardiff Castle

2 hrs+   All year

Discover 2,000 years of history in the heart of the city. View the Roman wall, climb the Norman keep and take a guided tour of the fairytale apartments, created in the C19 for the 3rd Marquess of Bute.

* Guided tours of lavish & opulent interiors
* Set in beautiful grounds

Location	Contact
In Cardiff city centre	Castle Street, Cardiff CF10 3RB
Opening	t 02920 878100
Daily: Mar–Oct 9.30am–6pm; Nov–Feb 9.30am–5pm	w cardiffcastle.com
	e cardiffcastle@cardiff.gov.uk
Admission	
Adult £6.95, Child £4.30, Concs £5.40	

526 Cardiff

Millennium Stadium Tours

1 hr All year

Explore the changing rooms, training areas and medical rooms, imagine the pre-match tension, run down the players' tunnel, climb to the very top row of the highest tier in the stadium for breathtaking views, sit in the Royal Box, and have a trophy presented to you.

* World-class venue, home to 5 sporting bodies
* One of the proposed venues for the 2012 Olympics

Location
In Cardiff city centre

Opening
Daily: 9.30am–5.30pm

Admission
Adult £5.50, Child £3, Concs £3.50

Contact
Millennium Stadium Shop,
Gate 3, Westgate Street,
Cardiff CF10 1JE

t 02920 822040
w millenniumstadium.co.uk

527 Cardiff

St Fagans National History Museum

3 hrs+ All year

Set in 100 acres of beautiful parkland, this is one of Europe's biggest and most exciting open-air museums. 40 buildings have been transported and rebuilt here to recreate 500 years of Welsh history. Special events and craft demonstrations run throughout the year.

* Exhibitions of costume, daily life & farming tools

Location
4 miles W of Cardiff city centre.
Exit M4 at junction 33

Opening
Daily: 10am–5pm

Admission
Free. Car park £2.50

Contact
St Fagans, Cardiff CF5 6XB

t 02920 573500
w museumwales.ac.uk
e welshlife@museumwales.ac.uk

528 Cardiff

Techniquest

2 hrs+   All year

Try some of the 160 hands-on exhibits in this amazing science discovery centre, or experiment in the laboratory and discovery room. Fire a rocket, launch a hot-air balloon or play a giant piano. Don't miss the Science Theatre, either. Musiquest was new in autumn 2005.

* Explore the universe in the planetarium
* Enjoy a fascinating interactive Science Theatre show

Location
Exit M4 at junction 33 then follow signs on A4232

Opening
Daily: Mon–Fri 9.30am–4.30pm,
Sat–Sun & Bank Hols 10.30am–5pm

Admission
Adult £6.90, Child & Concs £4.80

Contact
Stuart Street, Cardiff CF10 5BW

t 02920 475475
w techniquest.org
e info@techniquest.org

529 Cardigan

Cardigan Heritage Centre

1 hr   Mar–Oct

The heritage centre, in a converted C18 warehouse, tells the story of Cardigan from just before Norman times to the present day. A child-friendly place, it provides arts activities for younger children and entertaining quizzes for older ones.

* Guided tours by appointment
* Static & interactive computer displays

Location
Take A487 to Cardigan. Centre is on bank of River Teifi, next to Cardigan Bridge

Opening
Mid Mar–Oct Sun–Fri 10am–5pm

Admission
Adult £2, Child £1, Concs £1.50

Contact
Teifi Wharf, Cardigan, Wales

t 01239 614404

530 Cardigan

Cardigan Island Coastal Farm Park

3 hrs+   Mar–Oct

There are a host of wild and domesticated animals for all the family to enjoy. On the cliffs below the park there is a colony of grey seals, and dolphins are seen frequently in the bay. On the farm there are pigs, sheep, ponies, a donkey and even some emus, wallabies and llamas.

* Outdoor adventure play area
* Tractor rides in summer

Location
Take M4 from Cardiff or Swansea to Camarthen. Then A484 to Cardigan. Follow B4548 signs to Gwbert. A487 from Aberystwyth. A478 from Tenby

Opening
Daily: Mar–Oct 10am–6pm

Admission
Adult 3.50, Child £2.50, Concs £3.20

Contact
Gwbert, Cardigan SA43 1PR

t 01239 612196
w cardiganisland.com

531 Dan-yr-Ogof

National Showcaves Centre for Wales

2 hrs+   Apr–Oct

Descend below ground to explore a wonderland of stalactites, waterfalls and natural cave formations extending over 10 kilometres. The tour of the showcaves is self-guided but commentaries play at selected points so you can enjoy a visit at your own speed.

* Top Wales visitor attraction
* One of 10 attractions on site

Location
On A4067 between Swansea & Brecon. Signed from junction 45 of M4

Opening
Daily: Apr–Oct 10am–5pm (last admission to caves 3pm)

Admission
Adult £10, Child £6

Contact
Dan-yr-Ogof, nr Abercraf, Upper Swansea Valley, Powys SA9 1GJ

t 01639 730801
w showcaves.co.uk
e james@showcaves.co.uk

532 Haverfordwest

Pembrokeshire Motor Museum

2 hrs+   Apr–Sep

More than 40 vehicles give a complete history of the motor car, ranging from a 1906 Rover to a more modern 1969 Jaguar E-type series II. In addition to the concourse display, there are a few exhibits in the workshop that are being meticulously restored.

* All cars occasionally used on rallies

Location
4 miles N of Haverfordwest on A487 to St David's

Opening
Apr–Sep Mon–Fri 10am–5pm, Sun 10am–4pm

Admission
Adult £3.50, Child £1.30, Concs £2.75

Contact
Keeston Hill, Keeston, Haverfordwest SA62 6EJ

t 01437 710950
w pembsmotormuseum.co.uk

533 Kilgetty

Folly Farm

4 hrs+   All year

Folly Farm is the big 4-in-1 family day out with farming fun, a spectacular zoo, indoor and outdoor adventure play and Europe's biggest indoor vintage funfair. Bottle-feed a goat, pet a rabbit, see a magical stage show and enjoy an amazing range of rare and exotic animals.

* Vintage fairground attractions
* Indoor play areas for children of all ages

Location
Take A477 Tenby road from A40 towards Kilgetty. Then take A478 for Narberth. Folly Farm is 1 mile on the left

Opening
Apr–Sep daily 10am–5.30pm;
Oct daily 10am–5pm;
Nov–Mar Sat–Sun 10am–4pm

Admission
Adult £6.25, Child & Concs £5.25

Contact
Begelly, Kilgetty,
Pembrokeshire SA68 0XA

t 01834 812731
w folly-farm.co.uk
e admin@folly-farm.co.uk

534 Llanboidy

Welsh Chocolate Farm

2 hrs   Apr–Oct

Engage all of your senses learning all about chocolate at this award-winning centre. Stroll through the model village and see the chocolate being crafted into a variety of delicious products. At the cinema learn about its history and cultivation.

* 2 chocolate shops & guided tours throughout the day
* Hands-on chocolate decorating

Location
Leave A40 at St Clares then follow signs

Opening
Apr–Oct Mon–Sat 10am–5pm

Admission
Adult 3.25, Child £2.85

Contact
Llanboidy SA34 0EX

t 01994 448800
w welshchocolatefarm.com
e chocolate.farm@btopenworld.com

535 Monmouth

Caldicot Castle & Country Park

2 hrs+   Apr–Sep

A fine medieval castle set in 55 acres of beautiful parkland with plenty on offer for children. At the activity station children can find out about castles, play giant chess and draughts, and try on historical hats.

* Audio tours for adults & children

Location
From M4 take junction 23 & B4245.
From M48 take junction 2 on to B4245. Signed from B4245

Opening
Daily: Apr–Sep 11am–5pm

Admission
Please phone for details

Contact
Church Road, Caldicot,
Monmouthshire NP26 4HU

t 01291 420241
w caldicotcastle.co.uk
e caldicot@monmouthshire.gov.uk

536 Narberth

Oakwood Theme Park

4 hrs+   Apr–Oct

One of Wales's largest tourist attractions, Oakwood has more than 400,000 visitors each year and boasts more than 30 rides and attractions. Test your nerves on our new ride – Speed: No Limits – the UK's first beyond-vertical drop. A great day out, with something to please everyone.

* Carousel, pirate ship, Megafobia roller-coaster & Hydro
* One of the UK's Top 10 theme parks

Location	Contact
Leave M4 at junction 49, take A48 to Carmarthen, then follow signs	Canaston Bridge, Narberth SA67 8DE
Opening	t 01834 861889
Please phone for details	w oakwoodthemepark.co.uk
	e info@oakwoodthemepark.co.uk
Admission	
Please phone for details	

537 Swansea

National Waterfront Museum

2 hrs+   All year

The museum explores the industrialisation of Wales in a series of interactive displays. Learn about people's lives and look at the factories, shops and houses where they worked and lived. See how industry has impacted on the landscape and environment both in the past and present.

* Regular events & special exhibitions throughout the year

Location	Contact
On Marina next to old Leisure Centre building opposite Princess Way	Oystermouth Road, Maritime Quarter, Swansea SA1 3RD
Opening	t 01792 638950
Daily: 10am–5pm	w waterfrontmuseum.co.uk
	e waterfront@museumwales.ac.uk
Admission	
Free	

538 Tenby

Heatherton Country Sports Park

4 hrs   All year

This leisure park offers a wide range of activities including clay-pigeon shooting, coarse fishing, archery, pitch and putt, indoor bowls, baseball, go-karting, paintball, adventure golf, horse-riding, bumper boats, a driving range and a maze.

* Play Robot Wars
* Suitable for groups & birthday parties

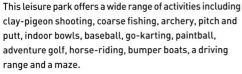

Location	Admission
2 miles outside Tenby on B4318 Tenby–Pembroke road	Free. Pay-as-you-go activities
Opening	Contact
Daily: Jun–Sep 10am–10pm; Oct–May 10am–6pm	St Florence, Tenby, Pembrokeshire SA69 9EE
	t 01646 651025
	w heatherton.co.uk

539 Trelewis

Welsh International Climbing & Activity Centre

4 hrs+   All year

In addition to climbing, the centre offers a wealth of indoor and outdoor activities for all abilities, including abseiling, caving, gorge walking, kayaking, mountain walking and expeditions. It also has a fitness suite and family and bunkhouse accommodation.

* One of the biggest indoor climbing walls in Europe
* High-ropes assault course

Location	Contact
From B4255 follow signs to Bedlinog, then ½ mile from Trelewis	Taff Bargoed Centre, Trelewis, Merthyr Tydfil CF46 6RD
Opening	t 01443 710749
Daily: Mon–Fri 9am–10pm, Sat–Sun 9am–7pm	w indoorclimbingwalls.co.uk
	e enquiries@indoorclimbingwalls.co.uk
Admission	
Prices vary according to activity	

owes Moor, Durham

Yorkshire

East Riding North Yorkshire
South Yorkshire West Yorkshire

EAST RIDING
Animal Attractions
Bempton Cliffs Nature Reserve 207
Cruckley Farm 208
The Deep 208
Park Rose Owl & Bird of Prey Centre 207

Historic Places
Fort Paull 209
Sewerby Hall & Gardens 208

Museums & Exhibitions
Bondville Model Village 207
Ferens Art Gallery 209
Hull & East Riding Museum 209
Streetlife Museum of Transport 210

Parks, Gardens & Nature
Burnby Hall Gardens 210

Sports & Leisure
Bridlington Leisure World 207
Hull Arena 209

NORTH YORKSHIRE
Animal Attractions
Betton Farm Visitor Centre
& Animal Farm 218
Big Sheep & Little Cow Farm 211
Monk Park Farm Visitor Centre 220
Pickering Trout Lake 216
Sea Life & Marine Sanctuary 219
Staintondale Shire Horse
Farm Visitor Centre 219

Boat & Train Trips
North Yorkshire Moors Railway 215

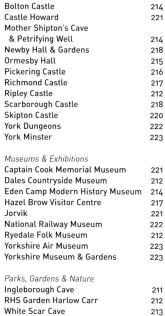

Historic Places
Bolton Abbey 220
Bolton Castle 214
Castle Howard 221
Mother Shipton's Cave
& Petrifying Well 214
Newby Hall & Gardens 218
Ormesby Hall 215
Pickering Castle 216
Richmond Castle 217
Ripley Castle 212
Scarborough Castle 218
Skipton Castle 220
York Dungeons 222
York Minster 223

Museums & Exhibitions
Captain Cook Memorial Museum 221
Dales Countryside Museum 212
Eden Camp Modern History Museum 214
Hazel Brow Visitor Centre 217
Jorvik 221
National Railway Museum 222
Ryedale Folk Museum 212
Yorkshire Air Museum 223
Yorkshire Museum & Gardens 223

Parks, Gardens & Nature
Ingleborough Cave 211
RHS Garden Harlow Carr 212
White Scar Cave 213

Sports & Leisure
Atlantis   218
Norwich Union Wheel of Yorkshire   222
The Quad Squad   211
Wykeham Lakes   219
York Maze   222

Theme Parks & Adventure Playgrounds
Flamingo Land Theme Park & Zoo   213
Lightwater Valley   217

SOUTH YORKSHIRE
Animal Attractions
Brockholes Farm Visitor Centre   224
Cannon Hall Farm   224
Tropical Butterfly House
  & Wildlife Centre   228

Historic Places
Conisbrough Castle   224

Museums & Exhibitions
Doncaster Aeroventure   225
Magna Science Adventure Centre   226
Millennium Galleries   227
Thorne Memorial Park
  Miniature Railway   225

Parks, Gardens & Nature
Renishaw Hall Gardens   227

Sports & Leisure
Barnsley Metrodome   224
Hatfield Water Park   225

Sheffield Cycle Speedway Club   228
Sheffield Ski Village   228
The Foundry Climbing Centre   226

WEST YORKSHIRE
Animal Attractions
St Leonard's Farm Park   234
Tropical World   233

Boat & Train Trips
Brontë Boats   231
Keighley & Worth Valley Railway   231

Historic Places
Harewood House & Bird Gardens   232
Sandal Castle   234
Shibden Hall   231
Temple Newsam House & Farm   232

Museums & Exhibitions
Bagshaw Museum   229
Bradford Industrial Museum
  & Horses at Work   229
Cliff Castle Museum   231
Colour Museum   230
Eureka! The Museum for Children   230
National Museum of Photography,
  Film & Television   230
Royal Armouries Museum   232
Thackray Museum   233

Parks, Gardens & Nature
Oakwell Hall Country Park   229
Yorkshire Sculpture Park   234

540 Bridlington

Bempton Cliffs Nature Reserve

2 hrs   All year

The best place in England to see seabirds – more than 200,000 nest on the cliffs. Rated one of Britain's most spectacular seabird colonies, it provides superb close-up views of breeding kittiwakes, fulmars, herring gulls, razorbills, guillemots, puffins and gannets.

* Gannets first colonised the cliffs in the 1920s
* Puffins can be seen in spring & summer

Location	Admission
On cliff road from Bempton, on B1229 from Flamborough to Filey	£3.50 car park fee for non-members
Opening	Contact
Visitor centre	11 Cliff Lane, Bempton, Bridlington YO15 1JD
Daily: Jan–Feb & Nov 9.30am–4pm; Mar–Oct 10am–5pm; Dec please phone for details	t 01262 851179
	w rspb.org.uk

541 Bridlington

Bondville Model Village

2 hrs   Easter–Sep

Town and countryside in miniature – Bondville is a masterpiece in landscape and gives lasting pleasure to young and old. It is complemented by hundreds of handmade model figures and buildings.

* One of the best model villages in the UK
* 1-acre site

Location	Contact
On A165	Sewerby Road, Sewerby, Bridlington YO15 1EL
Opening	
Daily: Apr–May & Sep 11am–4pm; Jun–Aug 10am–5pm	t 01262 401736
Admission	
Please phone for details	

542 Bridlington

Bridlington Leisure World

4 hrs+   All year

Attractions at this leisure centre include a wave pool with tropical rainstorm, and a water-slide. There are main and learner swimming pools, an expanded fitness suite, a refurbished sauna and solarium, a family entertainment centre and Kiddies' Kingdom.

* Small theatre
* One of the East Riding's premier leisure attractions

Location	Contact
Off A165 (off M62)	The Promenade, Bridlington, Yorkshire YO15 2QQ
Opening	
Please phone for details	t 01262 606715
Admission	w bridlingtonleisure.co.uk
Activities individually priced	e adam.mainprize@eastriding.gov.uk

543 Bridlington

Park Rose Owl & Bird of Prey Centre

3 hrs   Mar–Oct

The owl sanctuary is set in 3½ acres of woodland. There are 40 aviaries along a woodland walk, housing hundreds of owls and birds of prey, and flying displays to watch daily in the summer season. See our koi carp and aquatic plants, too.

* School visits & educational talks
* Guided information tours by arrangement

Location	Admission
On A165/A166, 2 miles S of Bridlington	Adult £2, Child & Concs £1.50
Opening	Contact
Daily: Mar–Oct 10am–5pm	Carnaby Covert Lane, Bridlington YO15 3QF
	t 01262 606800

544 Bridlington

Sewerby Hall & Gardens

3 hrs   Apr–Oct

Escape from your parents in the adventure playground, play a game of pitch and putt, hop on a train to the seaside, visit penguins, monkeys and wallabies in the zoo or take a woodland walk where you'll spot small animals, butterflies, birds and unusual plants.

* Display of Amy Johnson's awards & trophies
* Children's zoo includes monkeys & penguins

Location	Contact
From Bridlington follow signs for Flamborough & then Sewerby	Church Lane, Sewerby, Bridlington YO15 1EA
Opening	t 01262 673769
Hall Daily: Apr–Oct 10am–5pm	w sewerby-hall.co.uk
Gardens All year dawn–dusk	e sewerby.hall@eastriding.gov.uk
Admission	
Adult £3.50, Child £1.50, Concs £2.80	
Grounds Free	

545 Foston-on-the-Wold

Cruckley Farm

2 hrs+   Easter–Sep

Watch the daily routines of feeding animals and milking cows on a working farm, and meet a huge variety of rare breeds. You can also see the collection of vintage farm equipment that is regularly used by film companies. The farm keeps more than 50 different kinds of animal.

* Feed hand-reared animals in the paddock
* All 6 rare breeds of pig, plus minature donkey foals

Location	Contact
Just off B1249 between Driffield & Beeford	Foston-on-the-Wold, Driffield East YO25 8BS
Opening	t 01262 488337
Good Fri–Sep 10.30am–5.30pm	w cruckley.co.uk
	e cruckley@aol.com
Admission	
Adult £3.75, Child £3, Concs £3.25	

546 Hull

The Deep

2–3 hrs   All year

Discover the story of the world's oceans in this ship-shaped museum. See seven species of shark, plus conger eels, rays and hundreds of other stunning sea creatures. Travel in the world's only underwater lift and gaze up at sharks swimming overhead.

* 10m-deep tank containing 2.5 million litres of water
* Lots of hands-on & interactive activities

Location	Contact
Within walking distance of town centre on banks of Humber	Hull HU1 4DP
Opening	t 01482 381000
Daily: 10am–6pm	w thedeep.co.uk
	e info@thedeep.co.uk
Admission	
Adult £8, Child £6, Concs £6.50	

547 Hull

Ferens Art Gallery

1 hr+   All year

This award-winning gallery combines an internationally renowned permanent collection with exciting programmes of exhibitions and live art. The Children's Gallery runs a number of lively events that include educational tours, talks and art workshops.

* Innovative Children's Gallery new in autumn 2005
* Masterpieces by Canaletto, Spencer & Hockney

Location
In city centre

Opening
Daily: Mon–Sat 10am–5pm,
Sun 1.30pm–4.30pm

Admission
Free

Contact
Queen Victoria Square,
Kingston upon Hull HU1 3RA

t 01482 613902
w hullcc.gov.uk/museums/ferens
e museums@hull.gov.uk

---

548 Hull

Fort Paull

2 hrs+   Mar–Dec

Fort Paull has more than 1,000 years of history, dating back to the Viking landings. It has played a part in Britain's sea defences for almost 500 years – from its time as a fortress built by Henry VIII to the anti-aircraft defence visited by Sir Winston Churchill.

* The only surviving Blackburn Beverley aircraft
* Explore the underground labyrinths

Location
Village of Paull is S of Hull in direction
of Hedon

Opening
Daily: Apr–Oct 10am–6pm;
Nov–Dec & Mar 11am–4pm

Admission
Adults £4.50, Child &Concs £3

Contact
Battery Road, Paull,Hull HU12 8FP

t 01482 896236
w fortpaull.com
e fortpaull@aol.com

---

549 Hull

Hull Arena

2 hrs+   All year

An Olympic-size ice rink that is home to the Hull Stingrays, who play in the British National Ice Hockey Elite league. The rink is open to the public every day for a variety of family sessions and discos. Times for these vary so it is best to phone in advance.

* One of the North's leading music venues
* See ice hockey played at the highest level

Location
Just off A63 in centre of Kingston
upon Hull

Opening
Public skating
Mon–Fri 12.15pm–3.30pm,
Sat–Sun 10am–12noon &
2.15pm–4.15pm
Please phone to confirm disco sessions

Admission
All skating £3.20 + £1 skate hire
Evening disco £3.70

Contact
Kingston Street,
Kingston upon Hull HU1 2DZ

t 01482 325252
w hullcc.gov.uk/leisure
e hullarena@hullcc.gov.uk

---

550 Hull

Hull & East Riding Museum

1 hr+   All year

Exhibits range from displays of dinosaur bones, to treasures from eras as far apart as the Bronze and Middle Ages. There is also an Iron Age village and a Roman bath house to explore.

* Bronze Age warriors
* Treasures from the Middle Ages

Location
In city centre. Follow signs for the
Museum Quarter

Opening
Daily: Mon–Sat 10am–5pm,
Sun 1.30pm–4.30pm

Admission
Free

Contact
36 High Street, Hull HU1 1PS

t 01482 613902
e museums@hullcc.gov.uk

551 Hull

Streetlife Museum of Transport

2 hrs+   All year

Streetlife has some of the finest period displays in the country on railways, horse-drawn carriages, cycles, cars and trams. Come and meet the animated horses and experience a simulated carriage ride. Costumed figures and smells add to the visual experience.

* Motor car gallery
* Hands-on interactive exhibition area

Location	Contact
In high street near Wilberforce House	High Street, Hull HU1 1PS
Opening	t 01482 613902
Daily: Mon–Sat 10am–5pm,	w hullcc.gov.uk/museums/streetlife
Sun 1.30pm–4.30pm	e museums@hull.gov.uk
Admission	
Free	

552 Pocklington

Burnby Hall Gardens

3 hrs   Easter–Oct

Home to more waterlilies than anywhere else in Europe, Burnby Hall is also famous for its extensive range of ornamental trees, plants, shrubs and flowers. Enjoy feeding the birds, and numerous fish (including Koi carp). Fish food is available to buy.

* Winner of Yorkshire in Bloom 2004
* 2 large lakes in 10 acres of beautiful gardens

Location	Contact
20 min E of York off A1079	The Ball, Pocklington YO42 2QF
Opening	t 01759 307125
Daily: Easter–Oct 10am–6pm	w burnbyhallgardens.com
Admission	e brian@brianpetrie.plus.com
Adult £3.50, Child £1.60, Concs £2.75	
Gardens free in winter	

553 Bedale

Big Sheep & Little Cow Farm

2 hrs   Mar–Sep

This small family-run, friendly attraction is home to many farm animals. Under the supervision of a friendly guide, children can bottle-feed lambs and piglets, bath a pig, hold small animals, feed the cows and sheep, and talk to the donkey.

* Sand play area & new play barn
* Quad bikes

Location
11 miles S of Scotch Corner & 1 mile from A1 on A684 towards Bedale. Follow brown Farm Visitor Centre signs

Opening
Farm Daily: Mar–Sep 10.30am–5pm
Playbarn Daily: please phone for details

Admission
Adult £5, Child £6, Concs £4

Contact
nr Bedale DL8 1AW

t 01677 422125
w farmattraction.co.uk
e enquiries@farmattraction.co.uk

554 Clapham

Ingleborough Cave

2 hrs+   All year

Ingleborough Cave is a wonderland of sculpted passages and beautiful caves, part of the enormous 17km Gaping Gill cave system. An expert guide will lead you more than half a kilometre into the mountain to see the stunning calcite flows, stalagmites and stalactites.

* Nature trail near entrance
* Santa's Grotto at Christmas

Location
Just off B1249 between Driffield & Beeford

Opening
Mar–mid-Oct daily 10am–5pm;
mid-Oct–Feb Sat–Sun 10am–4pm

Admission
Adult £6, Child £3, Concs £4.50

Contact
Clapham LA2 8EE

t 015242 51242
w ingleboroughcave.co.uk
e info@ingleboroughcave.co.uk

555 Ebberston

The Quad Squad

1 hr+   All year

Enjoy the Quad Squad's trekking facility around the scenic Pheasant Hill Farm and parts of Dalby Forest. Children will be enthralled by this fun-packed and exhilarating adventure.

* Caters for everyone aged 6 to 65
* On a working farm

Location
On A170 W of Scarborough & E of Pickering

Opening
Daily: *summer* 9.30am–5.30pm
winter 9.30am–3pm

Admission
Adult £30 per hour, Child £25 per hour

Contact
Pheasant Hill Farm, Ebberston, Scarborough YO13 9TB

t 0771 575 7706
w quad-squad.biz

556 Harrogate

RHS Garden Harlow Carr

2 hrs   All year

One of Yorkshire's most relaxing yet inspiring locations. Highlights include the spectacular Gardens Through Time, streamside, alpine, scented and kitchen gardens, contemporary herbaceous borders, woodland and wildflower meadows.

* Double herbaceous borders
* All-year colour & interest

Location	Admission
Off B6162, 1½ miles from Harrogate town centre	Adult £6, Child £1.60 RHS members free
Opening	Contact
Daily: Mar–Oct 9.30am–6pm; Nov–Feb 9.30am–4pm (last admission 1 hr before close)	Crag Lane, Harrogate HG3 1QB
	t 01423 565418
	w rhs.org.uk/harlowcarr
	e admin-harlowcarr@rhs.org.uk

557 Harrogate

Ripley Castle

2 hrs+   All year

This 700-year-old castle is steeped in history. Learn how its inhabitants have survived wars, political and civil unrest, plague and pestilence and religious persecution. The story is fascinating and enthralling for all ages. Special tours for children are available.

* Guided tours leave the front door every hour
* Home to National Hyacinth Collection

Location	Admission
3 miles N of Harrogate on A61	Adult £7, Child £4.50, Concs £6
Opening	Contact
Daily: Jun–Sep 10.30am–3pm; Oct–Nov & Feb–May Tue, Thu, Sat–Sun & Bank Hols 10.30am–3pm; Dec–Jan Sat–Sun 10.30am–3pm	The Ripley Castle Estate, Harrogate HG3 3AY
	t 01423 770152
	w ripleycastle.co.uk
	e enquiries@ripleycastle.co.uk

558 Hawes

Dales Countryside Museum

   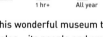

1 hr+   All year

This wonderful museum tells the story of the Yorkshire Dales – its people and environment from the Stone Age to Victorian times. Take a walk down a lead mine and see how the industry has changed over the years. There are also regular demonstrations of traditional crafts.

* Tourist Information & National Park Centre
* Guided tours for individuals

Location	Contact
Off A684 in Old Station Yard	Station Yard, Hawes DL8 3NT
Opening	t 01969 666210
Daily: 10am–5pm (last admission 4pm)	w dcmeyorkshiredales.org.uk
	e hawes@ytbtic.co.uk
Admission	
Adult £3, Child free, Concs £2	

559 Hutton-le-Hole

Ryedale Folk Museum

1 hr+   All year

Ryedale Folk Museum contains reconstructed local buildings, including long houses, an Elizabethan manor house and furnished cottages. See the oldest daylight photographic studio in the country, and archaeological displays from prehistory to the C10.

* Sanford Award for Education 2003

Location	Admission
Take A170 from Helmsley into Hutton-le-Hole	Please phone for details
Opening	Contact
Daily: mid-Mar–Oct 10am–5.30pm; Nov–22 Dec & 22 Jan–mid-Mar please phone for details (last admission 4.30pm)	Hutton-le-Hole YO62 6UA
	t 01751 417367
	w ryedalefolkmuseum.co.uk
	e enquiries@ryedalefolkmuseum. co.uk

560 Ingleton

White Scar Cave

1 hr+   All year

White Scar is the longest show cave in Britain. You can marvel at underground waterfalls, thousands of stalactites, and the massive 330ft Battlefield Cavern. Take the 80-minute guided tour, which covers more than a mile of underground adventure.

* Investigate a hidden world
* 200,000-year-old cavern

Location
In Yorkshire Dales National Park, 17 miles E of M6 junction 35, 1½ miles from Ingleton on B6255 to Hawes

Opening
Daily: Feb–Oct from 10am (weather permitting)
Nov–Jan weekends only

Admission
Adult £6.95, Child £3.95
Special rates for groups of 12 or more by phone only

Contact
Ingleton LA6 3AW

t 01524 241244
w whitescarcave.co.uk
e info@whitescarcave.co.uk

561 Kirby Misperton

Flamingo Land Theme Park & Zoo

6 hrs+   Apr–Nov

Flamingo Land offers something for all the family with a dozen white-knuckle thrillers, six great shows, kiddies' attractions and an extensive zoo which is home to many rare and exotic species including rhinos, hippos, giraffes and tigers.

* Lost Kingdom display
* New Kumsli roller coaster

Location
Off A64 Scarborough–York road on A169 Malton–Pickering road

Opening
Daily: Apr–Nov 10am–5pm or 6pm
Please phone for details

Admission
Please phone for details

Contact
Kirby Misperton, Malton YO17 6UX

t 01653 668287
w flamingoland.co.uk
e info@flamingoland.co.uk

562 Knaresborough

Mother Shipton's Cave & Petrifying Well

1 hr+   Mar–Oct

First opened in 1630, Mother Shipton's Cave and Petrifying Well are the oldest tourist attractions in Britain. As well as the cave and well, children will particularly enjoy the playground and 12 acres of riverside grounds.

* Learn about Mother Shipton in the museum
* Includes free all-day parking

Location
Signed from A1 on A59

Opening
Mar Sat–Sun 10am–5.30pm;
Apr–Oct daily 10am–5.30pm

Admission
Adult £5.50, Child £3.75, Concs £4.50
Family £15.95

Contact
Prophecy House,
Knaresborough HG5 8DD

t 01423 864600
w mothershipton.co.uk
e adrian@mothershipton.co.uk

563 Leyburn

Bolton Castle

1 hr+   All year

Bring the family along to this fascinating castle, one of the UK's best preserved, which has dominated its beautiful Yorkshire Dales setting since its completion in 1399. Mary, Queen of Scots was imprisoned here and it was besieged during the Civil War.

* Location for *Ivanhoe, Elizabeth & Heartbeat*

Location
6 miles W of Leyburn, just off A684.
Signed from Wensley

Opening
Daily: Mar–Nov 10am–5pm;
Dec–Feb 10am–4pm
Please phone for details

Admission
Adults £5, Child & Concs £3.50

Contact
Leyburn DL8 4ET

t 01969 623981
w boltoncastle.co.uk

564 Malton

Eden Camp Modern History Museum

4 hrs   All year

Eden Camp is the only history theme museum of its kind in the world. A visit here will transport you back to wartime Britain to experience the sights, the sounds and even the smells of those dramatic years.

* Covers complete C20 British military history
* Multiple award-winning attraction

Location
Just 100 yrds from A64
(York–Scarborough) & A169
(Malton–Pickering) interchange

Opening
Daily: 10am–5pm

Admission
Adult £4.50, Child & Concs £3.50

Contact
Malton YO17 6RT

t 01653 697777
w edencamp.co.uk
e admin@edencamp.co.uk

©NTPL/Dennis Gilbert

565 Ormesby

Ormesby Hall

2 hrs+   Apr–Oct

This C18 Palladian mansion is full of fascination for visitors of all ages. You can wander through the gardens and holly walk and enjoy the beautiful house and its famous stables. Visit the Victorian laundry and see the large model railway.

* Find out about 'wicked' Sir James Pennyman
* National Trust property

Location
3 miles SE of Middlesbrough.
Take A174 then A172 & follow signs

Opening
Apr–Oct Sat–Sun & Bank Hols
1.30pm–4.30pm

Admission
Adult £4, Child £2.50

Contact
Ormesby Hall,
Ormesby TS7 9AS

t 01642 324188
w nationaltrust.org.uk
e ormesbyhall@nationaltrust.org.uk

566 Pickering

North Yorkshire Moors Railway

3 hrs+   Mar–Nov

The North Yorkshire Moors Railway runs between the historic market town of Pickering, and Grosmont near Whitby, and is one of the world's oldest railway lines. Trains also call at the picturesque stations of Levisham and Goathland.

* Quality Assured Visitor Attraction

Location
Take A169 or A170 to Pickering

Opening
Daily: Mar–Nov; some winter opening dates. Times vary, please phone for details

Admission
Please phone for details

Contact
Pickering Station, Park Street,
Pickering YO18 7AJ

t 01751 472508
w northyorkshiremoorsrailway.com
e customerservices@nymr.fsnet.co.uk

567 Pickering

Pickering Castle

1 hr   Apr–Oct

Built shortly after the Norman Conquest, this splendid stone castle is very well preserved, with much of the original keep, towers and walls from Edward II's reign remaining. There is an exhibition on the history of the castle in the chapel.

* English Heritage property

Location
In Pickering, 15 miles SW of Scarborough

Opening
Daily: Apr–Sep 10am–6pm;
Oct Thu–Mon 10am–4pm

Admission
Adult £3, Child £1.50, Concs £2.30

Contact
Pickering YO18 7AX

t 01751 474989
w english-heritage.org.uk

568 Pickering

Pickering Trout Lake

4 hrs   Mar–Oct

Pickering Lake is stocked with rainbow trout so you can try fishing by float or fly methods. This is an ideal place for children to learn the art of angling – 99 per cent of visitors catch a fish!

* Guided tours for individuals
* Tackle available for hire or sale

Location
Signed Fun Fishing from Pickering, 400yrds past North Yorkshire Moors railway station

Opening
Daily: Mar–Oct 9.30am–5pm
(closes at dusk in summer)

Admission
Fun float fishing £5.50
Tackle hire £2.50

Contact
Newbridge Road, Pickering YO18 8JD

t 01751 474219

569 Richmond

Hazel Brow Visitor Centre

2 hrs+ Apr–Sep

Hazel Brow is an award-winning organic livestock farm in the heart of Swaledale. Farming is portrayed through displays, exhibitions and a video. Walk the riverside nature trail or take the paths through the hay meadows, herb-rich pastures and wild heather moorland.

* Lambing-time visits in April

Location
From Richmond take A6108 signed Leyburn for about 5 miles, branch off on to B6270 to Reeth, then continue for 9 miles to Low Row Village

Opening
Apr–Sep Sat–Sun & Tue–Thu 11am–4.30pm

Admission
Adult £4, Child (2–16) £3.75

Contact
Low Row Village, Richmond DL11 6NE

t 01748 886224
w hazelbrow.co.uk
e info@hazelbrow.co.uk

570 Richmond

Richmond Castle

1 hr+ All year

One of the most imposing Norman remains in England, Richmond Castle towers over the town of Richmond. The striking rectangular keep is 100 feet high and is one of the finest in the country.

* Exhibition centre
* Set in beautiful countryside

Location
In town centre, on A6108

Opening
Apr–Sep daily 10am–6pm;
Oct–Mar Thu–Mon 10am–4pm

Admission
Adult £3.60, Child £1.80, Concs £2.70

Contact
Richmond DL10 4QW

t 01748 822493
w english-heritage.org.uk

571 Ripon

Lightwater Valley

3 hrs+ Mar–Oct

A family theme park with rides to suit all ages. It boasts the longest roller coaster in Europe and thrilling rides including the Sewer Rat and the Black Widow's Web. There are also plenty of rides and attractions for younger or less daring members of the family.

* Boating lake & train ride around park
* Restaurants & picnic areas

Location
3 miles N of Ripon on A6108

Opening
Mar–Oct 10am–4.30pm in school hols & Sat–Sun. Please visit the website for specific dates

Admission
Over 1.2m £15.95, Under 1.2m £14.50
Family & season tickets available
Entry price includes all rides

Contact
North Stainley, Ripon HG4 3HT

t 0870 458 0040
w lightwatervalley.net
e leisure@lightwatervalley.co.uk

572 Ripon

Newby Hall & Gardens

4 hrs Easter–Sep

This beautiful late C17 house, built in the style of Sir Christopher Wren, has an Adam-designed interior. The extensive grounds include an adventure garden with swings, climbing frames, bridges, an aerial slide, pedalo boats and a miniature railway.

* 25 acres of award-winning gardens
* Miniature railway, woodland walk & special events

Location
Off B6265 between Boroughbridge & Ripon

Opening
Jul–Aug daily 11am–5.30pm;
Apr–Jun, Sep & Bank Hols Tue–Sun 11am–5.30pm

Admission
Adult £9.20, Child £6.40, Concs £8.20

Contact
Ripon HG4 5AE

t 0845 4504068
w newbyhall.com
e info@newbyhall.com

573 Scarborough

Atlantis

3 hrs+ May–Sep

Atlantis water-theme park has two of the world's largest water-slides, a river rapids run, a whirlpool bath and lots of other water-based activities!

* Ice-cream parlour
* Waveball

Location
Follow A64 into N Scarborough

Opening
Daily: May–Sep 10am–6pm
Please phone for details

Admission
Please phone for details

Contact
North Bay, Scarborough YO12 7TU

t 01723 372744
w www.yorkshirecoast.co.uk/
scarleisure/atlantis

574 Scarborough

Betton Farm Visitor Centre & Animal Farm

3 hrs All year

Betton Farm offers an animal farm, a pets' corner with a toy tractor area and a play area. There is also a honey-bee exhibition. Our gift shop sells aromatherapy oils, scented candles, pot pourri and many more natural products.

* Birds of prey centre
* Meet farmyard friends

Location
Just off A170, W of Scarborough, towards Pickering & Helmsley

Opening
Daily: 10am–5pm

Admission
Please phone for details

Contact
Racecourse Road, East Ayton, Scarborough YO13 9HT

t 01723 863143
w bettonfarm.co.uk

575 Scarborough

Scarborough Castle

1 hr All year

An Iron Age settlement was built on this great headland and in Roman times it was used as a look-out post. It was bombarded by German cruisers in 1914 and during WWII it was used as a listening station. There are viewing platforms with great views of the Yorkshire coastline.

* Vast C13 fortress

Location
In castle Road, E of town centre

Opening
Apr–Sep daily 10am–6pm;
Oct–Mar Thu–Mon 10am–4pm

Admission
Adult £3.50, Child £1.80, Concs £2.60

Contact
Castle Road, Scarborough

t 01723 372451
w english-heritage.org.uk/yorkshire

576 Scarborough

Sea Life & Marine Sanctuary

2 hrs+   All year

Meet creatures that live in the seas around the British Isles, ranging from starfish, turtles and crabs to rays, seals and otters. Marvel at the Penguin Sanctuary where seven endangered species including the Humboldt penguin are resident.

* Penguins, sharks & seahorses
* Feeding times

Location
Follow signs to North Bay Leisure Park on Whitby Road, beyond Atlantis & Kinderland. Look for white pyramids

Opening
Daily: *summer* 10am–6pm
winter 10am–5pm

Admission
Adult £10.50, Child (3–14) £8.95, Concs £9.95

Contact
Scalby Mills,
Scarborough YO12 6RP
t 01723 376125
w sealifeeurope.com

577 Scarborough

Staintondale Shire Horse Farm Visitor Centre

2 hrs+   May–Sep

Shire horse and Shetland pony lovers will love Staintondale. Live shows are a regular feature and include the shire horses and Shetland ponies in full Western roping rig. You can even learn how to spin a lariat, whatever the weather!

Location
Signed from A171

Opening
20 May–Sep Tue–Wed, Fri, Sun & Bank Hols 10.30am–4.30pm

Admission
Adult £5, Child (2–15) £3, Concs £4.50

Contact
Staintondale,
Scarborough YO13 0EY
t 01723 870458
w shirehorsefarm.co.uk

578 Scarborough

Wykeham Lakes

1 hr+   All year

The ideal place to enjoy a range of watersports, including sailing, windsurfing, boating, scuba-diving and canoeing. Tuition is available. If you prefer fishing, there are two trout lakes, three coarse-fishing lakes and pike-fishing all year round.

* A full range of ticket options, including day, part day, sporting & season tickets are available

Location
6 miles W of Scarborough off A170 between West Ayton & Wykeham

Opening
Boating & watersports lake Daily: 7am–dusk *Fishing* All year
Bird watching By arrangement with Wykeham Estate

Admission
Prices vary according to activity/duration, please phone for details

Contact
Charm Park, Wykeham,
Scarborough
t *Fishing* 07946 534001
Sailing 0845 4560164
w wykehamwatersports.co.uk

579 Skipton

Bolton Abbey

2 hrs+   All year

This estate covers 30,000 acres of beautiful countryside in the Yorkshire Dales. There are medieval buildings – C12 priory ruins – to explore and 80 miles of moorland, woodland and riverside footpaths. A guide book and walks leaflet are available. There is also a gift shop.

* Landscape was inspiration for Wordsworth & Turner
* Grounds include a 6-mile stretch of River Wharfe

Location
Between Harrogate & Skipton, off A59 on B6160

Opening
Daily: 9am–dusk

Admission
Vehicle pass £5 (occupants free), £3.50 for disabled badge holders

Contact
Skipton BD23 6EX

t 01756 718009
w boltonabbey.com
e tourism@boltonabbey.com

581 Thirsk

Monk Park Farm Visitor Centre

3 hrs+   Feb–Oct

This open farm in Hambleton Hills has indoor and outdoor viewing and feeding areas, a wildfowl lake and animal attractions. Meet wallabies, rheas, llamas, lambs, piglets, goats and ponies, and birds including ducks, geese, hens, swans and pheasants.

* Farm walks
* Picnic areas & gift shop

Location
In Bagby, just off A19 S of Thirsk

Opening
Daily: Feb–Oct 11am–5.30pm

Admission
Adult £4, Child & Concs £4

Contact
Monk Park Farm, Bagby, Thirsk YO7 2AG

t 01845 597730
w monkpark.co.uk

580 Skipton

Skipton Castle

1 hr+   All year

For more than 900 years Skipton Castle has stood at the gateway to the Yorkshire Dales, enduring wars and sieges. One of the best-preserved and most complete medieval castles in England, it can be explored in any season. See the dungeon, watch tower, chapel and Conduit Court.

* View the banqueting hall, kitchen & bedchambers
* Comprehensive tour sheets in 9 languages

Location
In town centre

Opening
Mar–Sep Mon–Sat 10am–6pm, Sun 12noon–6pm;
Oct–Feb 10am–4pm

Admission
Adult £5.40, Child £2.90, Concs £4.80

Contact
Skipton BD23 1AW

t 01756 792442
w skiptoncastle.co.uk
e info@skiptoncastle.co.uk

582 Whitby

Captain Cook Memorial Museum

1 hr+   Mar–Oct

This fascinating museum is in the harbourside house, with ship-timbered attic, where the young James Cook lodged as an apprentice. Learn all about his ships, his companions and his amazing explorations.

* Quality Assured Visitor Attraction

Location	**Admission**
Take A171 to Whitby (or A169 from Pickering & York). Museum is in town centre, 100 yrds from swing bridge	Adult £3.50, Child £2, Concs £2
Opening	**Contact**
Mar Sat–Sun only 11am–3pm; Apr–Oct daily 9.45am–5pm (last admission 4.30pm)	Grape Lane, Whitby YO22 4BA
	t 01947 601900
	w cookmuseumwhitby.co.uk
	e cookmuseum@tiscali.co.uk

---

583 York

Castle Howard

2 hrs+   Mar–Oct

Built in 1699, Castle Howard is the private home of the Howard family. Inside are art treasures and sculptures; outside are temples, statues and monuments. There is a whole range of summer activities for children.

* Adventure playground, boat trips & farm shop
* Outdoor guided tours & historical characters

Location	**Contact**
15 miles NE of York	Castle Howard, York YO60 7DA
Opening	t 01653 648333
Daily: Mar–Oct 10am–4pm	w castlehoward.co.uk
Admission	e house@castlehoward.co.uk
Adult £9.50, Child £6.50, Concs £8.50	

584 York

Jorvik

1 hr   All year

Discover what life was like in AD975 and meet Vikings face to face. See 800 items uncovered here, and journey through reconstructed Viking streets, complete with sounds and smells. Handle replica items and watch Viking craftsmen at work.

* Jorvik is the name given to York by Vikings in AD 975
* Wheelchair users please phone 01904 543402

Location	**Admission**
Take A64 to York & follow brown tourist signs	Adult £7.50, Child £5.50, Concs £6.60 Pre-booking recommended for individual tours
Opening	**Contact**
Daily: Apr–Oct 10am–5pm; Nov–Mar 10am–4pm	Jorvik, Coppergate, York YO1 9WT
	t 01904 543403/643211
	w vikingjorvik.com
	e jorvik@yorkarchaeology.co.uk

585 York

National Railway Museum

3 hrs+   All year

Marvel at more than 103 trains from 1813 to the present day, including a Japanese bullet train. Learn all about the engines from the *Rocket* to the *Eurostar*. Then ride on the miniature railway (weekends and school holidays) through the railway-themed children's play area.

* Home of *Flying Scotsman*
* Literally millions of photographs & artefacts

Location
200 yrds from railway station, signed from town centre

Opening
Daily: 10am–6pm

Admission
Free, except for special events

Contact
Leeman Road, York YO26 4XJ

t 01904 621261
w nrm.org.uk
e nrm@nmsi.ac.uk

586 York

Norwich Union Wheel of Yorkshire

4 hrs+   All year

The wheel, climbing 54 metres into the sky, has 42 enclosed air-conditioned pods each accommodating eight people. From your vantage point high above York enjoy panoramic views over the city's historic centre including the Minster and the River Ouse.

* Luxury VIP pod with leather interior
* Evening tickets available

Location
200 yrds from railway station, signed from town centre

Opening
Daily: 10am–6pm (last admission 5.15pm) please phone for details of evening tickets

Admission
Adult £6, Child £4

Contact
Leeman Road, York YO26 4XJ

t 01904 686282
w nrm.org.uk

587 York

York Dungeons

1 hr+   All year

Deep in the heart of historic York, buried beneath its paving stones, lies the North's most chilling horror attraction. The York Dungeons bring more than 2,000 years of gruesomely authentic history vividly back to life ... and death.

* See how torture was part of everyday life until the C19
* Judgement of Sinners new in 2005

Location
In city centre

Opening
Daily: Apr–Sep 10am–5pm;
Oct–Mar 10.30am–4.30pm

Admission
Adult £10.95, Child £7.95, Concs £8.95

Contact
The York Dungeons,
12 Clifford Street, York YO1 9RD

t 01904 632599
w thedungeons.com
e yorkdungeons@merlinentertainments.biz

588 York

York Maze

3 hrs   Jul–Sep

Created from more than 1.5 million maize plants and as big as 15 football pitches, York Maze is possibly the largest in the world. Explore the maze climbing towers and collect clues to try to win a prize. Other activities include go-karting, crazy golf and fun in the giant sandpit.

* Monster tractor rides
* Maze of illusions

Location
Located inside Grimston Bar park & ride site on A1079 Hull Road where it meets A64 York ring road

Opening
Daily: mid-Jul–mid-Sep 10am–6pm

Admission
Adult £5.50, Child £4.50, Concs £5, Family £18

Contact
Springfield, Heslington,
York YO10 5EQ

t 01904 415364
w yorkmaze.com
e info@yorkmaze.com

589 York

York Minster

1 hr+   All year

Built between the C12 and C15, York Minster is the largest Gothic cathedral in England. It is 524 feet long, 249 feet wide and more than 90 feet high. It was constructed on the site of a Norman cathedral, which was itself built on the foundations of a Roman fort.

* Largest Gothic cathedral in Northern Europe
* Visited by 2 million people every year

Location
In York city centre

Opening
Daily: Mon–Sat 9.30am–5pm,
Sun 12.30pm–3.45pm
Tower Please visit the website for details

Admission
Adult £5, Child free, Concs £4

Contact
Deangate, York YO1 7HH

t 01904 557216
w yorkminster.org
e visitors@yorkminster.org

590 York

Yorkshire Air Museum

3 hrs   All year

This award-winning museum is housed in the largest WWII Bomber Command station open to the public. Experience fascinating displays, such as the restored control tower, the Air Gunners Museum and the airborne forces display.

* See the only restored Halifax bomber
* Historical aircraft from the earliest days of flight

Location
Take B1228 off A63/A1079 roundabout

Opening
Daily: *summer* (Apr–Sep) 10am–5pm
winter (Oct–Mar) 10am–3.30pm

Admission
Adult £5, Child £3, Concs £4

Contact
Halifax Way, Elvington, York YO41 4AU

t 01904 608595
w yorkshireairmuseum.co.uk
e museum@yorkshireairmuseum.co.uk

591 York

Yorkshire Museum & Gardens

2 hrs   All year

The award-winning Yorkshire Museum is set in 10 acres of botanical gardens located in the historic centre of York. It displays some of the finest Roman, Anglo-Saxon, Viking and medieval treasures ever discovered in Britain.

* Ruins of St Mary's Abbey in grounds
* Events & exhibitions throughout the year

Location
5–10 min walk from railway station

Opening
Daily: 10am–5pm

Admission
Adult £4, Child £2.50, Concs £3

Contact
Museum Gardens, York YO1 7FR

t 01904 687687
w yorkshire.museum.org.uk
e yorkshire.museum@ymt.org.uk

592 Barnsley

Barnsley Metrodome

3 hrs+   All year

This super pool complex offers a total water experience. As well as lane swimming and diving boards, the Space Adventure, a fabulous water-theme park, has three white-knuckle water-rides – Space Bullet, the Terrorship 3000 and the Alien Mountain.

* Other activities include football, swimming & basketball
* Holiday activities including sports, games, arts & crafts

Location
Just off M1 junction 37. Follow signs for Metrodome

Opening
Daily: 9am–10pm
Pool opening times vary, please phone for details

Admission
Please phone for details

Contact
Queens Ground, Queens Road, Barnsley S71 1AN
t 01226 730060
w themetrodome.co.uk

593 Barnsley

Cannon Hall Farm

3 hrs   All year

This working farm is now open to visitors. Come and encounter cattle, pigs and sheep, as well as rabbits, ponies and horses. There are also exotic animals such as chinchillas, wallabies and llamas.

* National farm attractions network, Farm attraction of year 2005 & Gift shop

Location
Take A635 from Barnsley just after Cawthorne village. Signed on the right

Opening
Mon–Sat 10.30am–4.30pm,
Sun & Bank Hols 10.30am–5pm

Admission
Adult £3.25, Child & Concs £2.75

Contact
Barnsley S75 4AT
t 01226 790427
w cannonhallfarm.co.uk

594 Branton

Brockholes Farm Visitor Centre

3 hrs+   All year

This centre houses farm animals, including a pedigree herd of Limousin cattle, and exotic breeds, such as monkeys and wallabies. You can also see small animals, including rabbits, guinea pigs and hamsters. Children love the Octopus ride, train ride and free pony ride.

* Farm is 250 years old
* Woodland walks

Location
Take A638 from Doncaster towards Bawtry & turn on to B1396. Entrance off Warning Tongue Lane

Opening
Daily: 10.30am–5.30pm (last admission 4.30pm)

Admission
Adult £5, Child & Concs £4.50

Contact
Brockholes Lane,
Branton DN3 3NH
t 01302 535057
w brockholesfarm.co.uk

595 Conisbrough

Conisbrough Castle

2 hrs+   All year

This spectacular medieval castle was built in the 1180s by the 5th Earl of Surrey, Hamelin Plantagenet, half-brother of Henry II. It has been extensively restored with floodlighting and a visitor centre. Educational tours and children's parties are catered for.

* Inspiration for Sir Walter Scott's classic novel *Ivanhoe*
* Closed for private functions on some Sats during summer

 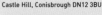

Location
NE of town centre on A630

Opening
Daily: Apr–Sep 10am–5pm;
Oct–Mar 10am–4pm

Admission
Adult £4, Child £2.15, Concs £2.75

Contact
Castle Hill, Conisbrough DN12 3BU
t 01709 863329
w conisbroughcastle.org.uk
e info@conisbroughcastle.org.uk

596 Doncaster

Doncaster Aeroventure

1 hr+   All year

A fascinating day out for any budding plane enthusiast. Come and see this collection of British jets and helicopters. Occupying the last remaining part of the former Doncaster airfield, the site also features other buildings of the WWII period.

* Collection includes a DH Vampire T11, DH Chipmunk T10, DH Dove Westland Scout & Whirlwind HAR 9

Location
Leave M18 at junction 3 & turn on to A6182. Also reached via A638 Doncaster–Bawtry road. Follow brown propeller signs

Opening
Wed–Sun including Bank Hols 10am–5pm (4pm in winter), Tue in school hols

Admission
Adult £4, Child £1.50, Concs £3

Contact
Dakota Way, Airborne Road, Doncaster Leisure Park, Doncaster DN4 7FD

t 01302 761616
w aeroventure.org.uk

597 Doncaster

Thorne Memorial Park Miniature Railway

1 hr+   Varies

Doncaster & District Model Engineering Society operates, builds and maintains this miniature railway, which has recently opened a new second track. There is steam operation at special events and visiting locomotives to see.

* Operated by volunteers of the Doncaster & District Model Engineering Society Ltd

Location
1 or 2 miles from M18, depending on whether you take junction 5 or 6. Next to Stainforth & Keadby Canal on A614 into town centre

Opening
Please phone or visit the website for details
Trains Easter–Sep Sun 12noon–4.30pm

Admission
Adult 30p, Child 30p, Under–3s free

Contact
76 Grange Avenue, Hatfield, Doncaster DN7 6RD

t 01302 842948
w thornerailway.org.uk

598 Doncaster South

Hatfield Water Park

2 hrs+   All year

This all-round watersports centre offers canoeing, kayaking, sailing, windsurfing and power-boating activities. The site also includes a three-star-rated caravan and camping site, and residential visitor centre.

* Adventure playground

Location
Off A18, just outside Hatfield village on road to Thorne

Opening
Daily: *summer* Mon–Fri 9am–4.30pm, Sat–Sun 9am–5.30pm
winter Mon–Fri 9am–4.30pm

Admission
Varies depending on activity
Please phone for details

Contact
Old Thorne Road, Doncaster DN7 6EQ

t 01302 841572
w doncaster.gov.uk/leisure
e hatfield.waterpark@doncaster.gov.uk

599 Rotherham

Magna Science Adventure Centre

3 hrs+   All year

A high-tech, hands-on centre, organised according to the elements, where you can walk into a wind tunnel, discover how fireworks work, squirt water on hot plates, find out how much water is in your body, make waves, or crawl through an underground tunnel.

* Feel the force of a tornado in the Air Pavilion
* Test your bravery as a virtual fireball races towards you

Location	Admission
Just off M1, 1 mile along A6178 from Meadowhall shopping centre	Adult £9.95, Child & Concs £7.95
Opening	**Contact**
Daily: 10am–5pm (closed some Mons in off-peak time, please phone for details)	Sheffield Road, Templeborough, Rotherham S60 1DX
	t 01709 720002
	w visitmagna.co.uk
	e info@magnatrust.co.uk

600 Sheffield

The Foundry Climbing Centre

2 hrs+   All year

The Foundry Climbing Centre provides indoor climbing experience for visitors aged seven upwards and of any ability – from novices to experts. Instruction is available on request and children's climbing clubs are run regularly. Booking is essential.

* Special events held regularly

Location	Admission
Near Sheffield Ski Village, ½ mile from city centre	Please phone for details
Opening	**Contact**
Daily: *summer* Mon–Fri 10am–10pm, Sat–Sun 10am–6pm	45 Mowbray Street, Sheffield S3 8EN
winter Mon–Fri 10am–10pm, Sat–Sun 10am–8pm	t 0114 279 6331
	w cragx.com/foundryclimbing
	e foundry@cragx.com

601   Sheffield

Millennium Galleries

2 hrs+   All year

This new museum has four galleries: Special Exhibitions, Metalwork, Craft & Design and the Ruskin Gallery. Many of the exhibitions have hands-on elements that will appeal to children, and exhibitions in other galleries change regularly, keeping the galleries up to date.

* Material regularly borrowed from the Tate & V&A

Location
In city centre near Winter Garden

Opening
Mon–Sat 10am–5pm,
Sun 11am–5pm

Admission
Free. Exhibitions may charge

Contact
Arundel Gate, Sheffield S1 2PP

t 0114 278 2600
w sheffieldgalleries.org.uk
e info@sheffieldgalleries.org.uk

602   Sheffield

Renishaw Hall Gardens

4 hrs+   Mar–Sep

Renishaw Hall's gardens, museum and galleries are set in 300 acres of parkland with nature trails, reserves and a sculpture park. Children's events are organised regularly and there is a children's play area.

* Hall open by special arrangement only
* Regular calendar of events

Location
Just 2 miles from junction 30 of M1,
between Ecrington & Renishaw
on A6135

Opening
Mar–Sep Thu–Sun & Bank Hol Mon
10.30am–4.30pm. Please phone for
details of special events

Admission
Adult £5, Child free, Concs £4.25

Contact
Renishaw Hall, nr Sheffield S21 3WB

t 01246 432310
w sitwell.co.uk
e info2@renishaw-hall.co.uk

Sheffield Cycle Speedway Club

2 hrs All year

Sheffield Cycle Speedway Club is a British Cycling 'Go-Ride' club. It provides cycling experience for children of all ages and abilities.

* Free loan of equipment
* Experienced qualified coach in attendance

Location
Bochum Parkway, Sheffield

Opening
Mar–Oct Mon or Wed 7.30–9.30pm;
Nov–Feb Sun fortnightly 2pm–4pm
Please phone before visiting

Admission
£2 per person

Contact
19 Stockley View, Bolsover,
Chesterfield S44 6HZ

t 01246 824220
w sheffieldstars.net
e martin_gamble@hotmail.com

Sheffield Ski Village

3 hrs+ All year

If you are looking for a totally unique and exhilarating day out, the Ski Village at Sheffield is the perfect destination for all the family. Here, at Europe's largest all-season ski resort, you can learn to ski and snowboard, or just chill out in the authentic Swiss atmosphere!

* More than 1 mile of piste
* Thunder Valley Toboggan Run

Location
5 min from city centre, off A61
Penistone Road

Opening
Daily: summer Mon–Fri 4pm–10pm,
Sat–Sun 10am–8pm, Bank Hols
10am–10pm winter Mon–Fri
10am–10pm, Sat–Sun, Bank Hols & 26
Dec–2 Jan 9am–10pm

Admission
Please phone for details

Contact
Vale Road, Sheffield S3 9SJ

t 0114 276 9459
w sheffieldskivillage.co.uk
e info@sheffieldskivillage.co.uk

Tropical Butterfly House & Wildlife Centre

3 hrs+ All year

Come and enjoy the host of exotic wildlife at this centre. Explore the tropical house in search of marmoset monkeys, beautiful butterflies, lizards and iguana. Hunt for snakes and tarantula in the reptile room and see amazing falcons and owls in the birds of prey centre.

* Tractor trailer rides
* Pets' corner

Location
Take junction 31 of M1, on to A57
to Worksop. At 2nd lights turn left to
Dinnington. Turn right before The
Cutler pub

Opening
Apr–Sep Mon–Fri 10am–4.30pm,
Sat–Sun 10am–5.30pm; Oct–Mar
Mon–Fri 11am–4.30pm, Sat–Sun
10am–5pm

Admission
Adult £5.99, Child £4.99, Concs £5.25

Contact
Hungerhill Farm, Woodsetts Road,
North Anston, nr Sheffield S25 4EQ

t 01909 569416
w butterflyhouse.co.uk
e info@butterflyhouse.co.uk

606 Batley

Bagshaw Museum

1 hr+   All year

Bagshaw Museum surrounds you with the sights and sounds of past times and faraway places. Journey through the vibrant colours of the Orient and tame the mythical beasts of four continents.

* Alpine mountain adventure themed play park
* Enchanted Forest

Location
Within easy access of A652, A62 & M62

Opening
Daily: Mon–Fri 11am–5pm, Sat–Sun 12noon–5pm (closed Good Fri)

Admission
Free

Contact
Wilton Park, Batley WF17 0AS

t 01924 326155
w kirkleesmc.gov.uk
e bagshaw.museum@kirkleesmc.gov.uk

607 Batley

Oakwell Hall Country Park

2 hrs   All year

History comes alive at Oakwell Hall. This beautiful Elizabethan manor house has delighted visitors for centuries. Stroll around the charming period garden or encounter the inhabitants of the wildlife access garden.

* Setting for Charlotte Brontë's novel *Shirley*
* 100 acres of estate to explore

Location
Take A652 Batley–Bradford road. Park is signed along this road. Take M62 exit at junction 26/27

Opening
Daily: Mon–Fri 11am–5pm, Sat–Sun 12noon–5pm

Admission
Adult £1.50, Child 60p

Contact
Nutter Lane, Birstall, Batley WF17 9LG

t 01924 326240
w oakwellhallcountrypark.co.uk
e oakwell.hall@kirklees.gov.uk

608 Bradford

Bradford Industrial Museum & Horses at Work

2 hrs   All year

The museum has an original C19 spinning mill complex, complete with mill owner's house, back-to-back cottages and job master's stables with working Shire and Clydesdale horses. There's spinning, weaving and demonstrations of horses at work, every day.

* Have a lesson in the Victorian school room
* Experience washday in Gaythorne Row

Location
Take A658 Harrogate road, then A6177 ring road

Opening
Tue–Sat 10am–5pm, Sun 12noon–5pm (closed Mon except Bank Hols)

Admission
Free

Contact
Moorside Mills, Moorside Road, Bradford BD2 3HP

t 01274 435900
w bradford.gov.uk

West Yorkshire

609 Bradford

Colour Museum

1 hr   All year

The Colour Museum is unique. Dedicated to the history of the use of colour, and the technology behind it, it is the only museum of its kind in Europe. A truly colourful experience for both kids and adults – it's fun, informative and well worth a visit.

* Situated in a former wool warehouse
* Workshops educational programme (please visit the website)

Location
In city centre, near Metro Interchange

Opening
Tue–Sat 10am–4pm

Admission
Adults £2, Child & Concs £1.50

Contact
PO Box 244, Perkin House, 1 Providence Street, Bradford BD1 2PW

t 01274 390955
w colour-experience.org.uk
e museum@sdc.org.uk

610 Bradford

National Museum of Photography, Film & Television

3 hrs   All year

Take a voyage of discovery at the National Museum of Photography, Film & Television. Explore the five floors of interactive galleries where you can ride on a magic carpet, read the news or look back at your TV favourites from the past.

* First moving pictures – 1888 film of Leeds Bridge
* IMAX© cinema

Location
In city centre off Little Horton Lane

Opening
Tue–Sun & Bank & Public Hols 10am–6pm

Admission
Free, except for cinemas

Contact
Bradford BD1 1NQ

t 0870 701 0200
w nmpft.org.uk
e talk.nmpft@nmsi.ac.uk

611 Halifax

Eureka!
The Museum for Children

3 hrs   All year

Eureka! is the UK's first and foremost interactive museum for children aged 12 and under, where they can deliver the post, mix their own music, play 'pinball digestion' and much more. There are fun events at weekends and during holidays – so you'll want to come back again!

* Interactive music gallery

Location
Next to railway station. From M62 junction 24 follow signs to Halifax & then brown tourist signs to Eureka!

Opening
Daily: 10am–5pm

Admission
Adult £6.95, Child (under 1) free, Child (1–2) £1.95, Child (over 3) £6.95

Contact
Discovery Road, Halifax HX1 2NE

t 01422 330069
w eureka.org.uk

612 Halifax

Shibden Hall

1 hr+   All year

This magnificent C15 hall, which was home to the Lister family for more than 300 years, is set in 90 acres of parkland, and offers a range of attractions including woodland walks, an orienteering course, children's rides, a miniature railway, pitch and putt, and a boating lake.

* See coopers, a Crispin inn & an old ale brewery
* Regular events & special children's projects

Location
Signed from Halifax & M62

Opening
Daily: Mar–Nov Mon–Sat 10am–5pm,
Sun 12noon–5pm;
Dec–Feb Mon–Sat 10am–4pm,
Sun 12noon–4pm
(last admission 30 min before close)

Admission
Adult £3.50, Child & Concs £2.50

Contact
Lister's Road, Halifax HX3 6XG
t 01422 352246
w calderdale.gov.uk/tourism
e shibden.hall@calderdale.gov.uk

613 Hebden Bridge

Brontë Boats

1 hr+   Feb–Dec

Enjoy the picturesque Rochdale Canal on our 58ft-long barge equipped with central heating, spacious dining tables and soft furnishing, and pass through locks and tunnels. Sunday carveries and evening meals are available.

* Boats also available for private hire
* Daily summer waterbus

Location
On A646 in middle of Hebden Bridge,
7 miles W of Halifax

Opening
Times vary, please phone for details
Advance booking recommended

Admission
Please phone for details

Contact
The Marina, New Road,
Hebden Bridge HX7 8AD
t 01422 845557
w bronteboats.co.uk
e info@bronteboats.co.uk

614 Keighley

Cliff Castle Museum

1 hr+   All year

Originally a millionaire's mansion, the castle opened as a museum in 1959. It houses old dolls and toys, the fossilised remains of a 300-million-year-old local giant newt, a working beehive of live honey-bees, and a natural history gallery with an interactive birdsong unit.

* Original 1880s reception rooms

Location
On A629 N of town centre

Opening
Tue–Sat & Bank Hols 10am–5pm,
Sun 12noon–5pm

Admission
Free

Contact
Spring Gardens Lane,
Keighley BD20 6LH
t 01535 618231
w bradford.gov.uk/tourism/museums

615 Keighley

Keighley & Worth Valley Railway

2 hrs+   All year

This fully operational, preserved railway branch line is 5 miles long and runs from Keighley to Oxenhope. Along the line are six award-winning stations. This is also the famous railway line featured in the 1970 film *The Railway Children*.

Location
Take A650 or A629 to Keighley,
or A6033 from Oxenhope

Opening
Sat–Sun 9am–6.30pm; Easter &
Christmas daily 11.30am–5pm;
Jul–Aug Mon–Fri 10am–5.30pm

Admission
Please phone for details

Contact
Haworth Station, Keighley BD22 8NJ
t 01535 645214
w kwvr.co.uk

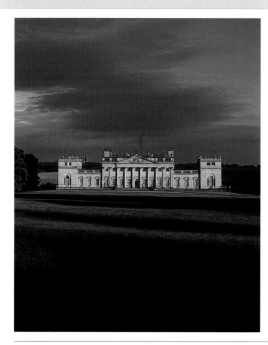

616 Leeds

Harewood House & Bird Gardens

3–4 hrs Mar–Nov

This fine Yorkshire home is situated in stunning grounds with lakeside and woodland walks and Capability Brown gardens. The avian collection has more than 100 rare and endangered species of birds.

* Boat trips across the lake & adventure playground
* Below Stairs exhibition

Location
On A61, 7 miles from Leeds & Harrogate

Opening
Daily: Mar–Nov 10am–5pm

Admission
All attractions Mon–Fri Adult £11.30, Child £8.50, Concs £10
Sat–Sun £13.50, £8.50, £12.20

Grounds Mon–Fri Adult £8.80, Child £5.90, Concs £7.95
Sat–Sun £10.90, £7.25, £10

Contact
Harewood House Estate Trust Ltd, Harewood, Leeds LS17 9LG

t 0113 218 1010
w harewood.org
e info@harewood.org

---

617 Leeds

Royal Armouries Museum

3 hrs+ All year

Learn about arms and armour from around the world in five themed galleries covering war, tournaments, self-defence, hunting and the Orient. During the summer months you can watch displays of jousting, falcony and horsemanship. You can even shoot a crossbow.

* See Henry VIII's tournament armour
* Live action events & interactive technology

Location
S of city centre, near junction 4 of M621

Opening
Daily: 10am–5pm

Admission
Free. Car park fee

Contact
Armouries Drive, Leeds LS10 1LT

t 08700 344344
w royalarmouries.org.uk
e enquiries@armouries.org.uk

---

618 Leeds

Temple Newsam House & Farm

2 hrs All year

In the grounds of this beautiful country house is a farm with rare breeds of sheep, pigs, cattle and poultry. On special days visitors can join in with the laundry maids washing at the dolly tub, watch the blacksmith hammer out shoes, and see logs cut at the saw mill.

* One of the largest rare breeds centres in the UK
* Grounds ideal for picnics

Location
On Temple Newsam Road, off Selby Road, 4 miles from city centre, off A63

Opening
Nov–Mar Tue–Sun 10.30am–4pm;
Apr–Oct Tue–Sun 10am–5pm
(last admission 45 min before close)

Admission
House & Farm Adult £5.50, Child £3.50
House or Farm £3.50, £2.50

Contact
Temple Newsam Road, Leeds LS15 0AE

t 0113 264 7321
w leeds.gov.uk/templenewsam
e temple.newsam@leeds.gov.uk

619 Leeds

Thackray Museum

  3 hrs All year

This award-winning interactive museum offers unusual family fun. Explore the slums of Victorian Leeds as one of the city 'characters', discover some of the weird medical treatments available at the time, and learn how people's lives have improved thanks to medical advances.

* Step inside the human body in the Life Zone
* Experience life as a Victorian character & decide their fate

Location
Follow signs for St James's Hospital. Museum is 100m past main entrance

Opening
Daily: 10am–5pm (last admission 3pm)

Admission
Adult £5.50, Child £4, Concs £4.50
Car park £1

Contact
Beckett Street, Leeds LS9 7LN

t 0113 244 4343
w thackraymuseum.org
e info@thackraymuseum.org

620 Leeds

Tropical World

  2 hrs   All year

Walk into a tropical atmosphere among exotic trees, waterfalls, and pools containing terrapins and carp. There are also meerkats, lemurs, reptiles, insects and butterflies, as well as a recreated South American rainforest, a desert house and a new tropical beach.

* Largest collection of tropical plants outside Kew
* Nocturnal & Insect zones

Location
Off A58 at Oakwood, 3 miles N of city centre

Opening
Daily: 10am–6pm (last admission 5.30pm)

Admission
Adult £3, Child (8–15) £2

Contact
Canal Gardens, Roundhay Park, Leeds LS8 2ER

t 0113 266 1850

621 Shipley

St Leonard's Farm Park

2 hrs   Feb–Oct

Meet Farmer James and his family on their award-winning farm. It has rare and modern breeds of animals (some of which you can feed), play areas, nature footpaths and listed barns and buildings.

* Junior ride-on electric tractors
* Tearoom in C16 barn

Location
Take A6038 from Otley/Ilkley, A6038 from Shipley/Bradford

Opening
Feb–Easter Sat–Sun 10am–4pm;
Easter–Sep Tue–Sun 10am–5pm;
Oct Sat–Sun 10am–5pm

Admission
Adult £3.75, Child & Concs £3.25

Contact
Station Road, Esholt,
Shipley BD17 7RB

t 01274 598795
w stleonardsfarm.com
e farmerjames1@aol.com

622 Wakefield

Sandal Castle

1 hr+   All year

Sandal Castle is an excavated medieval castle overlooking the site of the 1460 Battle of Wakefield, which was besieged in 1645 during the Civil War. It has beautiful views of the Calder Valley.

* Site of the exploits of 'The Grand Old Duke of York'
* Extensive fortifications

Location
On A61, 2 miles from city centre in direction of Barnsley

Opening
Castle Daily: dawn–dusk
Visitor centre Easter–Oct
half-term daily 11am–4.30pm,
otherwise Sat–Sun only
Please phone for details

Admission
Free

Contact
Manygates Lane, Sandal,
Wakefield WF2 7DG

t 01924 249779

623 Wakefield

Yorkshire Sculpture Park

2 hrs+   All year

An award-winning centre with changing outdoor sculpture exhibitions sited in 500 acres of landscaped grounds, gardens and parkland. Families are invited to touch and explore the artworks, which include monumental Henry Moore bronzes.

* 4 indoor galleries including underground gallery

Location
1 mile from M1 junction 38 on A637

Opening
Daily: *summer* 10am–6pm
winter 10am–5pm

Admission
Free. Car park £3

Contact
West Bretton, Wakefield WF4 4LG

t 01924 832631
w ysp.co.uk
e info@ysp.co.uk

oughrigg Tarn, Lake District

North West

Cheshire Cumbria Lancashire
Manchester Merseyside

Parks, Gardens & Nature
Lyme Park 245
Northwich Community Woodlands 243
Quarry Bank Mill & Styal Estate 247
Reddish Vale Country Park 246
Rivacre Valley Local Nature
 Reserve 245
Stapeley Water Gardens 242
Stretton Watermill 244

Sports & Leisure
Oulton Park Race Circuit 246

Theme Parks & Adventure Playgrounds
Gulliver's World 246

CHESHIRE
Animal Attractions
Alphabet Zoo/KK5 245
Blue Planet Aquarium 240
Chester Zoo 239
Cotebrook Shire Horse Centre
 & Countryside Park 240
Stockley Farm 244

Boat & Train Trips
Bithell Boats (Show Boats
 of Chester) 239
Brookside Miniature Railway 244

Historic Places
Air Raid Shelters 245
Beeston Castle 246
Capesthorne Hall 241
Hack Green Secret Nuclear Bunker 242

Museums & Exhibitions
Anderton Boat Lift 242
The Boat Museum 241
Catalyst Science Discovery Centre 247
Cheshire Military Museum 239
Chester Visitor Centre 239
Dewa Roman Experience 240
Jodrell Bank Science Centre
 & Arboretum 241
Lion Salt Works 243
Mouldsworth Motor Museum 240
Salt Museum 243
Walton Hall Gardens 247

CUMBRIA
Animal Attractions
Aquarium of the Lakes 256
Eden Ostrich World 257
Hawkshead Trout Farm 248
The Lake District Coast Aquarium 255
Lakeland Bird of Prey Centre 257
Lakeland Pony Trekking 261
Lakeland Wildlife Oasis 256
Low Sizergh Barn 253
South Lakes Wild Animal Park 251
Trotters World of Animals 255

Boat & Train Trips
Platty+ 249
Ravenglass & Eskdale Railway 258
South Tynedale Railway 248
Ullswater 'Steamers' 252
Windermere Lake Cruises 261

Historic Places
Carlisle Castle 250
Dalemain Historic House & Garden 257
Hill Top 248
Muncaster Castle 258
Sizergh Castle & Garden 259

Museums & Exhibitions
The Beacon 261
Beatrix Potter Gallery 252
Blackwell, The Arts & Crafts House 249
Border Regiment & King's Own
 Royal Border Regiment Museum 250
Cars of the Stars 254
Cumberland Pencil Museum 254
The Edward Haughey Solway
 Aviation Museum 251
Florence Mine Heritage Centre 251
Honister Slate Mine 249
Kendal Museum 253
Lakeland Miniature Village 252
Museum of Lakeland Life 253
Rheged – Enter into the Spirit
 of Cumbria 258
Sellafield Visitor Centre 259
Wetheriggs Pottery 258
The World of Beatrix Potter 249

Parks, Gardens & Nature
Bardsea Country Park 260
National Trust Fell Foot Park 260
Talkin Tarn Country Park 250
Whinlatter Forest Park 255

Sports & Leisure
Derwent Water Marina 254
Go Ape! 252
Keswick Climbing Wall 255
Laserquest 250

LANCASHIRE

Animal Attractions
Blackpool Sea Life Centre   263
Bolton Aquarium   265
Docker Park Farm Visitor Centre   266
Farmer Parr's Animal World   267
Sandcastle Tropical Waterworld   264

Boat & Train Trips
East Lancashire Railway   266

Guided Tours
Bolton Wanderers Football Club   265

Historic Places
Lancaster Castle   268
Leighton Hall   267
Rufford Old Hall   271

Museums & Exhibitions
Bolton Museum & Art Gallery   265
British in India Museum   269
Cedar Farm Galleries   270
National Football Museum   270
Pendle Heritage Centre   269
Worden Arts & Crafts Centre   269
Wyreside Ecology Centre   264

Parks, Gardens & Nature
Haigh Country Park   272
Hollingworth Lake Country Park   269
Pennington Flash Country Park   268
Williamson Park & Butterfly House   268

Sports & Leisure
Blackpool Illuminations   262
The Blackpool Piers   262
Burrs Activity Centre   265
Leisure Lakes   270
Oswaldtwistle Mills Shopping
  Village   262
Ski Rossendale   270
Whitworth Water Ski
  & Recreation Centre   271

Theme Parks & Adventure Playgrounds
Blackpool Pleasure Beach   263
Blackpool Tower & Circus   264
Camelot Theme Park   267
Rumble Tumble   272

MANCHESTER

Guided Tours
Airport Tour Centre   272
Old Trafford Museum & Tour   275

Historic Places
Ordsall Hall Museum   276

Museums & Exhibitions
Jewish Museum of Manchester   273
Manchester Art Gallery   273
Manchester Museum   274
Museum of Science & Industry in
  Manchester   274
Museum of Transport   274
People's History Museum   275

Parks, Gardens & Nature
Trafford Ecology Park   276
Wythenshawe Park   276

MERSEYSIDE
Animal Attractions
Knowsley Safari Park   281

Boat & Train Trips
Mersey Ferries River
  Explorer Cruise   282
Yellow Duckmarine   280

Guided Tours
Everton Football Club   278
Liverpool Football Club Museum
  & Tour Centre   278

Historic Places
Croxteth Hall & Country Park   277
Speke Hall, Garden & Estate   279
Williamson Tunnels   280

Museums & Exhibitions
Beatles Story   277
Liverpool Planetarium   278
Model Railway Village   282
National Wildflower Centre   277
Tate Liverpool   279
World of Glass   282

Parks, Gardens & Nature
Beacon Country Park   281
Formby   281

624 Chester

Bithell Boats (Show Boats of Chester)

5 hrs+   All year

Discover a delightful range of cruises on the River Dee. Take a 30-minute city cruise up past the suspension bridge following the long sweep of the meadows, or the two-hour cruise that continues up river past the Eccleston ferry and beautiful scenery of the Eaton Estate, to Ironbridge.

* Bus & boat trip tickets available
* Evening floodlight cruises & ghost tours

Location
All cruises depart from the Groves close to centre of Chester

Opening
Daily: 12noon–3.30pm

Admission
Adults £6, Child £2, Concs £4.50

Contact
River Cruise, Boating Station, Souters Lane, Chester CH3 6EA

t 01244 325394
w showboatsofchester.co.uk
e showboatschester@aol.com

625 Chester

Cheshire Military Museum

1 hr+   All year

Military-minded children will not want to leave this museum, which houses an interactive Soldiers of Cheshire exhibition, telling the story of the county's military history.

* Interactive computer displays
* Hands-on exhibits

Location
Close to city centre

Opening
Daily: 10am–5pm (last admission 4pm)

Admission
Adult £2, Child & Concs £1

Contact
The Castle, Chester CH1 2DN

t 01244 403933
w chester.ac.uk/militarymuseum
e museum@chester.ac.uk

626 Chester

Chester Visitor Centre

1 hr+   All year

The ideal starting point for exploring Chester. The Interpretation Centre has a wide variety of features that aim to inform and entertain people of all ages. Activities include guided walks.

* History of Chester displays
* 2 DVD shows & amphitheatre exhibition

Location
Accessible from A483, A56, A51, A41, A55 & M53. Follow signs for city centre

Opening
Daily: Mon–Sat 10am–5pm, Sun 10am–4pm

Admission
Free

Contact
Vicars Lane, Chester CH1 1QX

t 01244 402111
w chestertourism.com
e tis@chestercc.gov.uk

627 Chester

Chester Zoo

5 hrs+   All year

The UK's largest zoological gardens, Chester Zoo has more than 7,000 animals housed in spacious enclosures. The zoo is set in 100 acres of beautiful landscaped gardens and has many attractions specially designed to enthrall children.

* Elephant centre now open, secret world of the Okapi
* Internationally renowned for innovative enclosures

Location
Easily accessible from M53 & M56
Follow brown tourist signs

Opening
Daily: from 10am (closing times vary, please phone for details)

Admission
Prices vary, please phone or visit the website for details

Contact
Upton-by-Chester, Chester CH2 1LH

t 01244 380280
w chesterzoo.org
e reception@chesterzoo.co.uk

628 Chester

Dewa Roman Experience

1 hr +   All year

Spend an hour or two discovering what life was like in Roman Britain. Children can step aboard a Roman galley and stroll along reconstructions of Roman streets, experiencing the sights, sounds and smells of Roman Chester.

* Themed Roman games

Location
Accessible from all major road routes. Follow signs for Chester city centre

Opening
Daily: Feb–Nov 9am–5pm; Dec–Jan 10am–4pm

Admission
Adult £4.25, Child £2.50, Concs £3.75

Contact
Pierpoint Lane, Bridge Street, Chester CH1 1NL

t 01244 343407
w dewaromanexperience.co.uk

629 Chester

Mouldsworth Motor Museum

2 hrs   Feb–Nov

Mouldsworth Motor Museum was built in 1937. The Art Deco building is set in its own grounds in the heart of the Cheshire countryside. With more than 60 veteran and classic cars and motorcycles, the museum is also home to a 1920s replica garage, toys and pedal cars.

* Free quiz with prizes for children
* Experience the magic of Harry Potter's car

Location
On B5393 into Ashton & Mouldsworth. 6 miles E of Chester. Follow brown tourist signs

Opening
3 Feb–Nov Sun & Bank Hol Mon 12noon–5pm; Jul–Aug Wed & Sun 12noon–5pm

Admission
Adult £3, Child £1.50

Contact
Smithy Lane, Mouldsworth, Chester, Cheshire CH3 8AR

t 01928 731781
w mouldsworthmotormuseum.com

630 Cotebrook

Cotebrook Shire Horse Centre & Countryside Park

2 hrs+   All year

Meet our prize-winning collection of magnificent Shire stallions, mares and foals in a 50-acre centre set in the heart of the beautiful Cheshire countryside. In addition, we have miniature Shetland ponies, light horses and a wide collection of farmyard animals to stroke and feed.

* Stroll around our nature trail
* Gift shop

Location
Located on A49 two miles N of Tarporley, in Cheshire

Opening
Daily: 10am–5pm

Admission
Adult £5.45, Child £3.45, Concs £4.45

Contact
Cotebrook, Tarporley, Cheshire CW6 9DS

t 01829 760506
w cotebrookshirehorses.co.uk

631 Ellesmere Port

Blue Planet Aquarium

2 hrs   All year

One of Britain's largest aquariums, Blue Planet has two floors of interactive displays and exhibits. Take a voyage through the waters of the world, and see one of the largest collections of sharks in Europe.

* Shark-inhabited Caribbean reef
* Touchpools with anemones & rays & an octopus play park

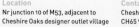

Location
Nr junction 10 of M53, adjacent to Cheshire Oaks designer outlet village

Opening
Daily: from 10am (closing times vary, please phone for details)

Admission
Adult £9.95, Child & Concs £7.50

Contact
Cheshire Oaks, Ellesmere Port CH65 9LF

t 0151 357 8800
w blueplanetaquarium.com
e info@blueplanetaquarium.com

632 Ellesmere Port

The Boat Museum

2 hrs   All year

This unique award–winning canal museum has more than 5,000 artefacts ranging from large boats to canal company buttons. It covers more than 7 acres of the historic canal port. Don't miss the new interactive exhibition.

* Programme of events throughout the year
* World's largest collection of traditional canal craft

Location
Junction 9 of M53 and follow signs

Opening
Apr–Oct daily 10am–5pm;
Nov–Mar Sat–Wed 11am–4pm

Admission
Adult £7.10, Child £5.25, Concs £5.80,
Family ticket £20.65

Contact
South Pier Road,
Ellesmere Port CH65 4FW

t 0151 355 5017
w boatmuseum.org.uk
e bookings@thewaterwaystrust.org

---

633 Macclesfield

Capesthorne Hall

2-4 hrs   Apr–Oct

Capesthorne Hall is where the Bromley-Davenports and their ancestors have lived since Domesday times. It contains a variety of treasures including fine paintings, furniture, marbles and Greek vases. It lies in gardens and parkland extending over 100 acres.

* Special events including craft fairs
* Car & motorcycle events throughout the year

Location
Off A34 between Manchester & Stoke-
on-Trent, 3 miles S of Alderly Edge,
junction 6 of M56

Opening
Apr–Oct Sun, Mon & Bank Hols
12noon–5pm

Admission
Adult £6.50, Child £3, Concs £5.50
£10 per car for 4 people

Contact
Siddington, Macclesfield SK11 9JY

t 01625 861221
w capesthorne.com
e info@capesthorne.com

---

634 Macclesfield

Jodrell Bank Science Centre & Arboretum

2 hrs+   Mar–Oct

Travel aboard the spacecraft *Elysium 7* en route to Mars for an amazing 3D flight over Martian volcanoes and canyons. Special events include meeting astronomers and guided walks in the arboretum for children. There are themed activity trails and hands-on exhibits.

* 35-acre arboretum is a tree lover's paradise
* Environmental discovery centre

Location
Between Holmes Chapel & Chelford,
on A535, 8 miles W of Macclesfield

Opening
Daily: Mar–Oct 10.30am–5.30pm

Admission
Adult £1.50, Child £1

Contact
Lower Withington,
Macclesfield SK11 9DL

t 01477 571339
w jb.man.ac.uk/scicen
e visitorcentre@jb.man.ac.uk

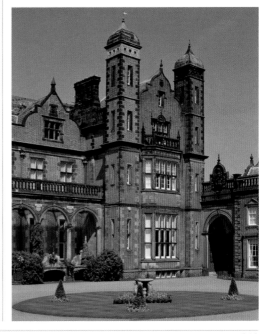

635 Nantwich

Hack Green Secret Nuclear Bunker

1 hr+   Jan–Nov

A real government nuclear war headquarters, Hack Green was a secret for more than 50 years. It contains decontamination facilities, a minister of state's office, life-support systems and much more. There are two cinemas and hands-on activities for all age groups.

* Soviet Spy Mouse Trail for children
* WWII radar station

Location	Admission
Off A530 Whitchurch road, outside Nantwich, 30 min from Chester	Adult £6.30, Child £4, Concs £5.90 Family ticket £19
Opening	**Contact**
Mar–Oct 10.30am–5.30pm; Jan–Feb & Nov Sat–Sun 11am–4.30pm	PO Box 127, Nantwich CW5 8AQ
	t 01270 623353
	w hackgreen.co.uk
	e coldwar@hackgreen.co.uk

636 Nantwich

Stapeley Water Gardens

3 hrs+   All year

A garden centre specialising in water gardening with display pools, a pet centre and an angling superstore. The Palms Tropical Oasis is a huge glass pavilion housing exotic plants, fish, birds and animals including sharks and toucans.

* Pet centre
* Meet Santa in his grotto at Christmas

Location	Admission
1 mile S of Nantwich on A51, signed from M6 junction 16	Adult £4.45, Child £2.60, Concs £3.95
Opening	**Contact**
Stapely Water Gardens Daily: Mar–Sep Mon–Sat 9am–6pm (8pm on Wed), Sun 10am–4pm; Oct–Feb Mon–Sat 9am–5pm, Sun 10am–4pm	London Road, Stapeley, Nantwich CW5 7LH
Palms Tropical Oasis Daily: opens 10am	t 01270 623868
	w stapeleywg.com
	e info@stapeleywg.com

637 Northwich

Anderton Boat Lift

1 hr+   Mar–Oct

Reopened in 2002 after a £7 million restoration, the Anderton Boat Lift is one of the greatest monuments to Britain's last canal age and is known as the 'Cathedral of the Canals'. Built in 1875, it was the world's first, and is currently England's only, boat lift.

* New Operations Centre open
* Quality Assured Visitor Attraction

Location	Admission
Follow A556 & then A559 to Northwich town centre, then follow signs	Please phone or visit website for details
Opening	**Contact**
Daily: Mar–Oct 10am–5pm Please phone or visit the website for boat & lift times	Lift Lane, Anderton, Northwich CW9 6FW
	t 01606 786777
	w andertonboatlift.co.uk
	e info@andertonboatlift.co.uk

Northwich

Lion Salt Works

1 hr   All year

The Lion Salt Works is a unique survival of the traditional inland salt works that once produced this essential commodity. The site illustrates the whole process of salt production and dates from the late C19 and C20. It is the only such surviving site in Cheshire.

* Cheshire once produced 86% of the nation's salt
* Building renovation in progress

Location
Take A556 from Junction 19 of M6, or
A559 from Junction 10 of M56

Opening
Sun–Thu 1.30pm–4.30pm

Admission
Adult £1, Child 50p

Contact
Ollershaw Lane, Marston,
Northwich CW9 6ES

t 01606 41823
w lionsaltworkstrust.co.uk
e afielding@lionsalt.demon.co.uk

Northwich

Northwich Community Woodlands

1 hr+   All year

Set in 1,000 acres of woodland, this park has a large lake and self-guided trails and is a great location for orienteering. It is also ideal for walkers, horse-riders, cyclists and picnickers.

* Children's play area
* Lakeside walks

Location
Leave M56 at junction 10, then take
A523 & A559

Opening
Daily: Apr–Sep 9am–8pm;
Oct–Mar 9am–5pm

Admission
Free. Car park fee

Contact
Comberbach,
Northwich CW9 6AT

t 01606 77741
w northwichcommunitywoodlands.
   org.uk
e marbury@cheshire.gov.uk

Northwich

Salt Museum

1 hr   All year

The museum tells the fascinating history of mid-Cheshire and the industry that shaped the landscape and life of the area. Through temporary exhibitions and special activities, find out why salt is vital in so many ways.

* New galleries

Location
Take A533 N to Northwich & follow
signs for Salt Museum

Opening
Tue–Fri 10am–5pm,
Sat–Sun 2pm–5pm; Aug Mon
10am–5pm; Bank Hol Mon 10am–5pm

Admission
Adult £2.50, Child £1.20, Concs £2

Contact
162 London Road,
Northwich CW9 8AB

t 01606 41331
w saltmuseum.org.uk
e cheshiremuseums@cheshire.gov.uk

641 Northwich

Stockley Farm

2 hrs+   Mar–Oct

Stockley Farm is a modern working organic dairy farm. It comprises 700 acres on the Arley Estate in the glorious Cheshire countryside. Visitors can watch a herd of 150 British Friesians being milked in one of the most modern computerised milking parlours in the country.

* Bird of prey display, bottle-feed lambs & goats
* Tractor & trailer rides, play area & pottery painting

Location
Leave M56 at junction 7, 9 or 10, or M6 at junction 19/20 & follow signs

Opening
End Mar–early Oct Sat–Sun 11am–5pm, Wed 1pm–5pm; school summer hols please phone for details

Admission
Adult £5, Child & Concs £4

Contact
Arley, Northwich CW9 6LZ

t 01565 777323
w stockleyfarm.co.uk
e enquiries@stockleyfarm.co.uk

---

642 Northwich

Stretton Watermill

1 hr+   Apr–Sep

Visit this small working watermill set in beautiful Cheshire countryside and discover the traditional skills of flour milling.

* Displays on wildlife

Location
Near Farndon, 10 miles from Chester, signed from A534

Opening
May–Aug Tue–Sun 1pm–5pm; Apr & Sep Sat–Sun 1pm–5pm; open Bank Hols

Admission
Adult £2, Child 75p

Contact
c/o Cheshire Museums, 162 London Road, Northwich CW9 8AB

t 01606 41331
w strettonwatermill.org.uk

---

643 Poynton

Brookside Miniature Railway

1 hr+   All year

An extensive miniature railway layout that runs through the grounds of a large garden centre. There are lots of features of interest on the journey such as river bridges a pond filled with koi carp and a craft centre.

* Steam & diesel locomotives
* Halloween special, santa specials at Christmas.

Location
On A523 midway between Hazel Grove & Poynton. Follow brown tourist signs

Opening
Apr–Sep Sat–Sun & Wed 11am–4pm; mid-Jul–mid-Aug, Bank Hols & school hols daily 11am–4pm. Please phone for details of all other dates

Admission
£1 (10 rides £8)

Contact
Macclesfield Road, Poynton

t 01625 872919
w brookside-miniature-railway.co.uk

644 South Wirral

Rivacre Valley Local Nature Reserve

1 hr+   All year

A natural area that has been thoughtfully landscaped with an orienteering trail and guided walks. It is a great place for kids to let off steam, and for adults simply to enjoy the surroundings.

* Guided tours
* Occasional events

Location
Leave M53 at junction 7, follow signs for Overpool, take 1st right at Rivacre Road, then 3rd right

Opening
Daily: 24 hrs

Admission
Free

Contact
Rivacre Road, Ellesmere Port, South Wirral CH64 2UQ

t 0151 357 1991
w cheshire.gov.uk/countryside
e rivacre@cheshire.gov.uk

645 Stockport

Air Raid Shelters

1 hr+   All year

These wartime shelters, now a visitor attraction, were carved into the cliffs in the town centre. Children can experience the sights and sounds of the Blitz and life in general in 1940s Britain.

* Guided tours by arrangement
* Monthly explorer tour

Location
In town centre. Leave M60 at junction 1. Shelters are in town centre

Opening
Daily: 1pm–5pm

Admission
Adult £3.95, Child & Concs £2.95

Contact
61 Chestergate, Stockport SK1 1NE

t 0161 474 1940

646 Stockport

Alphabet Zoo/KK5

1 hr+   All year

KK5 is a fun-packed children's play centre that helps to develop body and mind through play. Umpteen activities such as ball ponds keep your child amused all day. There is a café and a separate toddler play area.

* Unlimited play for toddlers until 3pm Mon–Fri
* Children's birthday parties

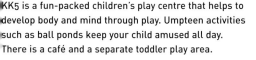

Location
Easily reached from M60 junction 1. On corner of King Street West & Chestergate

Opening
Daily: 10am–7pm

Admission
Mon–Fri Child £3 (over 4)
Child (under 4) £2.50
Sat–Sun £3.50, £3.50

Contact
Mentor House, King Street West, Stockport SK3 0DY

t 0161 4 772225

647 Stockport

Lyme Park

2 hrs+   Mar–Oct

This Tudor house offers beautiful interiors plus extensive gardens and a medieval deer park of moorland, woodland and parkland. Visitors will recognise the place as the setting for Pemberley in the last BBC adaptation of *Pride and Prejudice*.

* Children's guide to the house
* Children's quiz & trail

Location
On A6, 12 miles S of city centre. Follow signs

Opening
Daily: late Mar–Oct
House, Park & Gardens Please phone for details

Admission
House Adult £5, Child £2.50
Gardens £3.50, £2
House & Gardens £6.50, £3.30

Contact
Disley, Stockport SK12 2NX

t 01663 762023/766492
w nationaltrust.org.uk
e lymepark@nationaltrust.org.uk

648 Stockport

Reddish Vale Country Park

2 hrs · All year

A beautiful country park offering a variety of walks through woodlands, river valleys and meadows. It also features displays on the area's heritage, wildlife and future. Fishing is available on two large mill ponds.

* Cycle trail
* Butterfly park & community organic garden

Location	Admission
Take B6167 Reddish road from Stockport	Free
	Contact
Opening	Mill Lane, Reddish,
Park Daily	Stockport SK5 7HE
Visitor centre Please phone for details	t 0161 4775637

649 Tarporley

Beeston Castle

1 hr+ · All year

Standing majestically on sheer, rocky crags, Beeston has stunning views. Its history stretches back more than 4,000 years, to when it was a Bronze Age hill fort. The castle was built in 1226 and soon became a royal stronghold, only falling four centuries later in the English Civil War.

* Exhibition outlines the history of this strategic site
* Panoramic views of the Cheshire Plain

Location	Admission
11 miles SE of Chester on a minor road off A49	Adult £4, Child £2, Concs £3
	Contact
Opening	Tarporley CW6 9TX
Daily: Apr–Sep 10am–6pm; Oct–Mar Thu–Mon 10am–4pm	t 01829 260464
	w english-heritage.org.uk

650 Tarporley

Oulton Park Race Circuit

All day · Apr–Oct

Watch spectacular car and motorcycle racing with British superbikes, Formula 3s and British touring cars. One-to-one instruction with the Racing and Rally Experiences is available and safe training is available with young-drive activities.

* Full racing programme
* Driving experiences throughout the year.

Location	Admission
Take junction 18 of M6 & follow A54 to Chester for 12 miles. Turn left on to A49 to Whitchurch & follow signs	Please phone for details
	Contact
Opening	Motorsport Vision, Little Budworth,
Please phone for details	Tarporley, Cheshire CW6 9BW
	t 01829 760301
	w oultonpark.co.uk

651 Warrington

Gulliver's World

7 hrs · Apr–Nov

A theme park for families set in beautiful woodlands around a lake. It is aimed at children from 2 to 13 years old and has more than 50 rides, attractions and shows to amuse them. A fun day out for all.

* Lost World Dino area
* Special events

Location	Admission
Via M6 junction 21a & M62 junction 8 or 9, then follow signs	Please phone for details
	Contact
Opening	Warrington,
Apr–5 Nov	Cheshire WA5 9YZ
Please phone for details	t 01925 230088
	w gulliversfun.co.uk

652 Warrington

Walton Hall Gardens

2 hrs+   All year

An ideal place for a family day out with attractions including ornamental gardens and woodland trails. Families can try our crazy pitch and putt and bowling, and children can play in our special play area.

* Children's zoo
* Park ranger service & heritage centre

Location
Leave M56 at junction 11 & follow A56.
2 miles from town centre on A56

Opening
Daily: May–Sep 10.30am–5pm;
Oct–Apr Sat–Sun, Bank Hol Mon
& school hols 10.30am–4.30pm
Park All year 8am–dusk

Admission
Free. Car park fee

Contact
Walton Lea Road, Higher Walton,
Warrington WA4 6SN

t 01925 601617
w warrington.gov.uk/waltongardens
e waltonhall@warrington.gov.uk

653 Widnes

Catalyst Science Discovery Centre

3 hrs   All year

Science and technology come alive through a host of interactive exhibits and hands-on displays. Children and adults can tug, tease and test more than 100 different exhibits in four interactive action-packed galleries.

* Only science centre devoted to chemistry
* Virtual-reality theatre & discovery lab

Location
Junction 12 of M56 & junction 7 of M62

Opening
Tue–Fri & Bank Hols 10am–5pm,
Sat–Sun 11am–5pm

Admission
Adult £4.95, Child & Concs £3.95,
Family ticket £15.90

Contact
Mersey Road, Widnes WA8 0DF

t 0151 420 1121
w catalyst.org.uk
e info@catalyst.org.uk

654 Wilmslow

Quarry Bank Mill & Styal Estate

2 hrs+   All year

A country park with a Georgian water-powered cotton mill, plus the Apprentice House, where visitors can see where pauper children stayed and the conditions in which they lived. Marvel at the most powerful working waterwheel in Europe.

* Woodland & riverside walks
* Turbine in mill

Location
1½ miles N of Wilmslow off B5166, 2½
miles from M57 junction 5

Opening
Please phone for details

Admission
Please phone for details

Contact
Styal, Wilmslow, Cheshire SK9 4LA

t 01625 527468
w nationaltrust.org.uk
e quarrybankmill@nationaltrust.
org.uk

655 Alston

South Tynedale Railway

2 hrs   Easter–Oct

Visit England's highest narrow-gauge railway and take a trip by diesel or steam from Alston to Kirkhaugh. The 2-mile journey passes through the South Tyne Valley and through an Area of Outstanding Natural Beauty.

* Railway shop & picnic area
* Special events

Location
Alston is on A686, A689 & B6277 16 miles NE of Penrith. Follow signs to railway from village centre

Opening
Easter–Oct, please phone for details

Admission
Please phone for details

Contact
Alston CA9 3JB

t 01434 382828 (timetable)
01434 381696
w strps.org.uk
e strps@hotmail.com

656 Ambleside

Hawkshead Trout Farm

1 hr+   All year

A well-stocked lake where you can fish by boat or from the shore. It is suitable for inexperienced, intermediate and expert anglers. Tuition is available and children can feed and catch their own fish.

* Shop selling tackle, bait & local produce
* Purpose-built children's fishing area

Location
1½ miles S of Hawkshead, on road to Newby Bridge

Opening
Daily: 9am–6pm

Admission
Fishing Adult £22, Child £6, Concs £19

Contact
Ambleside LA22 0QF

t 01539 436541
w hawksheadtrout.com
e trout@hawkshead.demon.co.uk

657 Ambleside

Hill Top

1 hr   Apr–Oct

This delightful C17 house was home to Beatrix Potter when she wrote many of her stories. It remains as she left it and every room contains something that appears in her books. The pretty cottage garden contains a mix of flowers and vegetables, just as Beatrix would have had it.

* Timed entry to avoid overcrowding
* Shop specialising in Beatrix Potter gifts

Location
2 miles S of Hawkshead, near Sawrey, 3 miles from Bowness via ferry

Opening
Apr–May & Sep–Oct Sat–Wed 10.30am–4.30pm; Jun–Aug Sat–Thu 10.30am–4.30pm
Garden Apr–Oct daily 10.30am–5pm

Admission
Adult £5.40, Child £2.70

Contact
Nr Sawrey, Hawkshead, Ambleside LA22 0LF

t 015394 36269
w nationaltrust.org.uk
e hilltop@nationaltrust.org.uk

658 Borrowdale

Honister Slate Mine

1hr+   All year

An opportunity to see ancient craftsmanship and to learn the history of bygone years as you take an underground tour of this working mine. Deep inside the mountain you can explore some caverns hacked out by Victorian miners with hand tools by candlelight.

* Quality Assured Visitor Attraction
* All tours are guided

Location
From Keswick take B5289 through Borrowdale & Rosthwaite for 9 miles. From Cockermouth follow B5292 & B5289 for 14 miles

Opening
Daily: 9am–5pm, Sat–Sun & Bank Hols 10am–5pm

Admission
Visitor centre Free
Mine tour Adult £9.50, Child £4.50

Contact
Honister Pass, Borrowdale, Keswick CA12 5XN

t 01768 777230
w honister.com
e info@honister.com

---

659 Borrowdale

Platty+

1hr+   Mar–Oct

A family-based centre where visitors can enjoy canoeing, kayaking, dinghy sailing, dragonboating, rowing and a Viking longship! Children and adults with special needs are particularly welcomed.

* RYA (Royal Yachting Association) training centre
* British Canoe Union approved

Location
From Keswick take B5289 Borrowdale road for about 3 miles. Park in Lodore Falls Hotel car park & walk down to boat landing. Please see porter at hotel for parking permit

Opening
Daily: Mar–Oct 10am–6pm
Otherwise open by prior arrangement

Admission
Activities priced individually

Contact
Lodore Boat Landings, Derwentwater, Borrowdale, Keswick CA12 5UX

t 01768 777282
w plattyplus.co.uk
e jplatt@plattyplus.co.uk

---

660 Bowness-on-Windermere

Blackwell, The Arts & Crafts House

1 hr   Feb–Dec

Inspired by lakeland wild flowers, trees, berries and birds, Baillie Scott designed every last detail of this house. Outside, from the garden terraces, there are wonderful views of Windermere. Children can have a go at the Blackwell quiz.

* Royal Institute of British Architects Award for excellence

Location
Follow A5074 from Bowness (Lyth Valley road). 1 mile from Bowness

Opening
Daily: Feb–Dec 10.30am–5pm (4pm Feb–Mar & Nov–Dec)

Admission
Please phone for details

Contact
Bowness-on-Windermere LA23 3JT

t 01539 446139
w blackwell.org.uk
e info@blackwell.org.uk

---

661 Bowness-on-Windermere

The World of Beatrix Potter

2 hrs   All year

See all of Beatrix Potter's tales brought to life in this enchanting model attraction. Step through the garden to enjoy Peter's adventures or look for your favourite character in Mr Macgregor's greenhouse. Meet Jemima Puddle-Duck, Jeremy Fisher and many more.

* Tailor of Gloucester tearoom
* Shop with merchandise from around the globe

Location
In centre of Bowness-on-Windermere, in heart of Lake District

Opening
Summer 10am–5.30pm
Winter 10am–4.30pm

Admission
Adult £6, Child £3

Contact
The Old Laundry, Bowness-on-Windermere, Lake District, Cumbria LA23 3BX

t 01539 488444
w hop-skip-jump.com
e information@hop-skip-jump.com

662 Brampton

Talkin Tarn Country Park

3 hrs | All year

Get active when you visit this park with a 65-acre lake set amid 120 acres of farmland and woodland. A permanent orienteering course is laid out around the park, and there are wooden rowing boats for hire plus woods to explore.

* Sailing, boating, canoeing & windsurfing
* Coarse fishing available on a day-ticket basis

Location
On B6413, 9 miles E of Carlisle & 2 miles S of Brampton

Opening
Park Daily: dawn–dusk. Please phone for details of other facilities

Admission
Free

Contact
Brampton CA8 1HN

t 01697 741050
 Park warden 07976 062153
w visitcumbria.com

663 Carlisle

Border Regiment & King's Own Royal Border Regiment Museum

1 hr | All year

This museum has a large collection of uniforms, weapons, medals, trophies, models, silver and pictures. Displays on two floors depict the 300-year history of the regiment. The museum is in the medieval castle, the regiment's home since 1873.

* Field & anti-tank guns

Location
On N side of city centre, accessible from M6 junction 43 or 44

Opening
Daily: Apr–Sep 9.30am–6pm; Oct–Mar 10am–4pm

Admission
Adult £4, Child £2, Concs £3

Contact
Queen Mary's Tower, The Castle, Carlisle CA3 8UR

t 01228 532774
w armymuseums.org.uk
e korbrmuseum@aol.com

664 Carlisle

Carlisle Castle

1 hr+ | All year

This is a formidable border fortress with a rich and colourful history spanning more than 900 years. Once commanding the western end of the Anglo-Scottish border, Carlisle Castle has endured countless sieges over the centuries.

* Admission includes entrance to Roman exhibition
* See the legendary 'licking stones'

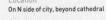

Location
On N side of city, beyond cathedral

Opening
Daily: Apr–Sep 9.30am–5pm; Oct–Mar 10am–4pm

Admission
Adult £4.10, Child £2.10, Concs £3.10

Contact
Carlisle CA3 8UR

t 01228 591922
w english-heritage.org.uk
e northwest@english-heritage.org.uk

665 Carlisle

Laserquest

1 hr | All year

Unleash a volley of laser fire in the battle zone – the ultimate sci-fi action adventure for children over seven. Each thrilling game lasts for 20 minutes.

* Simple or complex games
* Play solo or in a team

Location
In city centre

Opening
Daily: Mon–Fri 11am–9pm, Sat 10am–9pm, Sun 10am–7pm

Admission
£3.50 for 1 game, £6 for 2, £7.50 for 3

Contact
Bush Brow, Victoria Viaduct CA3 8AN

t 01228 511155
w lquk.com
e info@lquk.com

666 Crosby-on-Eden

The Edward Haughey Solway Aviation Museum

2 hrs+   Apr–Oct

Young people interested in civil and military aviation history will be fascinated by this museum. Among the items on display are aircraft from the 1950s and 1960s and the Blue Streak Rocket Programme. Visitors can sit in the pilot's seat of the Canberra bomber.

* Mock-up control tower
* Vulcan B2, Canberra T4 & Sikorsky 5-55a among aircraft

Location
10 min drive from junction 44 of M6 & Carlisle city centre

Opening
Apr–Oct Sat–Sun & Bank Hols 10.30am–5pm; also Fri during school hols

Admission
Adult £3.50, Child £1.75, Concs £2.25

Contact
Aviation House, Carlisle Airport, Crosby-on-Eden CA6 4NW
t 01228 573823
w solway-aviation-museum.co.uk
e info@solway-aviation-museum.co.uk

667 Dalton-in-Furness

South Lakes Wild Animal Park

3 hrs+   All year

One of Europe's leading conservation zoos, this rolling 17-acre park is home to some of the rarest animals on earth. Many, such as lemurs, parrots, kangaroos and wallabies, have complete freedom to wander at will.

* Rhinos, giraffes, tigers as close as you can safely get
* Hand feed lemurs, kangaroos & giraffes

Location
Follow signs from junction 36 of M6

Opening
summer 10am–5pm
winter 10am–4.30pm

Admission
Adult £10.50, Child & Concs £7

Contact
South Lakes Wild Animal Park, Dalton-in-Furness LA15 8JR
t 01229 466086
w wildanimalpark.co.uk
e office@wildanimalpark.co.uk

668 Egremont

Florence Mine Heritage Centre

3 hrs   All year

Based at the last deep iron-ore mine in western Europe, this heritage centre offers a mining museum, a geology and mineral room and an authentic reconstruction of an underground mine.

* Guided underground tours

Location
On outskirts of Egremont, just off A595 on the Haile/Wilton turn off

Opening
Mon–Fri 9.30am–3.30pm; also Sat–Sun 10am–4pm in summer Please phone in the morning to book tours

Admission
Museum Adult £2, Child £1
Underground £6.50, £4.50

Contact
Egremont CA22 2NR
t 01946 825830
w florencemine.co.uk

669 Glenridding

Ullswater 'Steamers'

2 hrs+   All year

Cruises between Glenridding, Howtown and Pooley Bridge run daily, weather permitting. There is access to a variety of walks including Howtown to Glenridding and spectacular picnic spots in unspoilt scenery.

* Best Large Visitor Attraction 2004
* Japanese feature completed in 2006

Location
Accessible from M6 junction 40 or over Kirkstone Pass from Windermere & Ambleside

Opening
Daily: Sailing times vary, please phone or visit the website for details

Admission
Please phone for details

Contact
Pier House, Glenridding CA11 0US

t 01768 482229
w ullswater-steamers.co.uk
e office@ullswater-steamers.co.uk

670 Grange-over-Sands

Lakeland Miniature Village

1 hr   All year

Visit Lakeland in a day at Cumbria's only miniature village. It has more than 100 buildings made from local Coniston slate, including houses, farms, barns and tiny wishing wells. A new Japanese tea house was completed in 2005.

* See Beatrix Potter's house in miniature
* Play area for children

Location
From Grange-over-Sands take B5277 to Flookburgh, follow signs for Ravenstown & turn left after post office

Opening
Daily: 10.30am–dusk

Admission
Adult £3.50, Child £1.50, Concs £3

Contact
Winder Lane, Flookburgh, Grange-over-Sands LA11 7LE

t 01539 558500
w lakelandminiaturevillage.com

671 Grizedale Forest Park

Go Ape!

2 hrs+   Feb–Nov

Discover the thrill of the high wire with an assault course of rope bridges, Tarzan swings and zip slides. Scramble up rope nets and swing through the trees at this award-winning attraction.

* For children over 10 and adults only
* Pre-booking essential

Location
Off Hawkshead–Satterthwaite road. Follow brown tourist signs to Grizedale Forest Park

Opening
Apr–Oct & Feb half-term daily; Mar & Nov open Sat–Sun
Please phone for details

Admission
Adult £20, Child £14

Contact
Grizedale Forest Visitor Centre, Ambleside LA22 0QJ

t 0870 444 5562
w goape.co.uk
e info@goape.co.uk

672 Hawkshead

Beatrix Potter Gallery

1 hr   Apr–Oct

Housed in what was once Beatrix Potter's husband's office, the gallery has an annually changing exhibition of illustrations from her famous children's books, including *The Tale of Benjamin Bunny*, *The Tale of Jemima Puddle-Duck* and *The Tale of Squirrel Nutkin*.

* Interior remains substantially unaltered
* 2007 exhibit The Tale of Tom Kitten

Location
In town centre

Opening
Apr–Oct Sat–Wed 10.30am–4pm

Admission
Adult £3.60, Child £1.80
Family ticket £9

Contact
Main Street, Hawkshead LA22 0NS

t 01539 436355
w nationaltrust.org.uk
e beatrixpottergallery@nationaltrust.org.uk

673 Kendal

Kendal Museum

1 hr+   Feb–Dec

This museum houses displays of the archaeology and natural history of the Lake District, alongside a world wildlife exhibition. There are free quizzes, worksheets and activities for children, and events throughout the year.

* Wildlife garden simulates local habitats
* Changing programme of temporary exhibitions

Location	Contact
10 min from junction 36 of M6	Station Road, Kendal LA9 6BT
Opening	t 01539 721374
Apr–Oct Mon–Sat 10.30am–5pm;	w kendalmuseum.org.uk
Feb–Mar & Nov–Dec Mon–Sat	e info@kendalmuseum.org.uk
10.30am–4pm	
Admission	
Adult £2.70, Child free, Concs £2.10	

674 Kendal

Low Sizergh Barn

2 hrs   All year

Walk along the farm trail and enjoy the beautiful countryside around this organic dairy farm. See the cows and hens, and watch out for wildlife and birds in the fields, pond and woods.

* Watch cows being milked at 3.45pm daily

Location	Admission
On A591, 4 miles S of Kendal. From M6 junction 36 take A591 & follow signs	Free
Opening	**Contact**
Daily: 9am–5.30pm	Sizergh, Kendal LA8 8AE
(closes 5pm Jan–Easter)	t 01539 560426
	w lowsizerghbarn.co.uk
	e apark@low-sizergh-barn.co.uk

675 Kendal

Museum of Lakeland Life

1 hr+   All year

The Museum of Lakeland Life shows how the Cumbrian people worked, lived and entertained themselves in the changing social climate of the past 200 years. Exhibits include a street scene, reconstructed workshops and a Victorian bedroom and parlour.

* Captain Flint children's room
* Arthur Ransome's study

Location	Admission
Next to Abbots Hall Gallery, junction 36 of M6	Adult £3.75, Child £2.75
Opening	**Contact**
Apr–Oct Mon–Sat 10.30am–5pm;	Kendal LA9 5AL
20 Jan–Mar & Nov–Dec	t 01539 722464
Mon–Sat 10.30am–4pm	w lakelandmuseum.org.uk
	e info@lakelandmuseum.org.uk

676 Keswick

Cars of the Stars

1 hr+   Easter–Dec

An opportunity to see some of the most famous cars from film and TV. This incredible collection includes Batmobiles, Bond cars and 'character' cars such as Chitty Chitty Bang Bang, Knightrider, Herbie and Harry Potter's Ford Anglia. Recently added was a Starsky and Hutch Ford Torino.

* Exhibition varies, so please phone for details of cars
currently on show to avoid potential disappointment

Location
Well signed from Keswick town centre

Opening
Easter–Nov: daily 10am–5pm;
Dec–Christmas Sat–Sun only
10am–5pm

Admission
Adult £4, Child £3

Contact
Standish Street, Keswick,
Cumbria CA12 5LS

t 01768 773757 (museum)
  01768 772090 (office)
w carsofthestars.com
e cotsmm@aol.com

677 Keswick

Cumberland Pencil Museum

1 hr   All year

The Cumberland Pencil Museum traces the history of pencilmaking from the discovery of graphite to present-day methods of pencil manufacture. Also on show is the world's largest pencil.

* Brass-rubbing
* Children's drawing area

Location
Follow A66 to Keswick. Located 300 yrds W of town centre

Opening
Daily: 9.30am–4pm

Admission
Adult £3, Child & Concs £1.50

Contact
Southey Works,
Keswick CA12 5NG

t 01768 773626
w pencils.co.uk

678 Keswick

Derwent Water Marina

1 hr+   All year

If you want to go sailing, windsurfing or canoeing, this marina offers lots of RYA watersports courses, with canoe, kayak and dinghy hire available. Other activities include ghyll scrambling, abseiling, climbing and walking. A great experience for families, friends and groups.

* Self-catering apartments available
* Boats for sale

  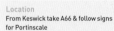

Location
From Keswick take A66 & follow signs for Portinscale

Opening
Daily: 9am–5.30pm
(closed 20 Dec–12 Jan)

Admission
Activities priced individually. Please phone or visit the website for details

Contact
Portinscale, Keswick,
Cumbria CA12 5RF

t 01768 772912
w derwentwatermarina.co.uk
e info@derwentwatermarina.co.uk

Keswick Climbing Wall

1 hr+   All year

Come and enjoy an adventurous day out at our centre. Try your hand at abseiling from our 12m tower, or climbing and bouldering on more than 400 metres of wall, or enjoy a multi-activity day where you can try ghyll scrambling, mountain biking, canoeing and raft building.

* New bungey trampoline
* Full range of courses for all abilities

Location
Leave M6 at junction 40 (Penrith) & follow A66 W towards Keswick. Take the 1st exit left at roundabout on to Crosthwaite Road then turn left at T-junction. Take the 1st left turn & follow brown & white tourist signs

Opening
Please phone for details

Admission
Please phone for details

Contact
Southey Hill, Keswick CA12 5NR

t 01768 772000
w keswickclimbingwall.co.uk
e info@keswickclimbingwall.co.uk

Trotters World of Animals

2–4 hrs   Feb–Dec

At Trotters you will meet animals from all over the world, as well as many zoo favourites. Handling of the animals is encouraged during audience participation sessions, plus there's a large soft play centre, picnic areas and special events.

* Pony & tractor trailer rides (weekends & holidays)
* Bird of prey centre

Location
Follow brown tourist signs from A591 & A66

Opening
Daily: Feb–Nov 10am–5.30pm (last admission 5pm)
Christmas hols 11am–4pm (last admission 3.30pm)

Admission
Adult £5.50, Child £4.25

Contact
Coalbeck Farm, Bassenthwaite, Keswick CA12 4RD

t 01768 776551
w trottersworld.com
e info@trottersworld.com

Whinlatter Forest Park

2 hrs+   All year

Nestling in England's only mountain forest, this park offers a wide variety of activities, from way-marked walks to orienteering courses, for all abilities and ages.

* Adventure playground
* Live TV pictures of nesting ospreys in season

Location
Follow signs on A66 from Keswick

Opening
Daily: Oct–Easter 10am–4pm;
Easter–summer school hols 10am–5.30pm;
(closed Christmas Eve–mid-Jan)

Admission
Free. Car park fee

Contact
Braithwaite, Keswick CA12 5TW

t 01768 778469
w forestry.gov.uk/whinlatter
e whinlatter@forestry.gsi.gov.uk

The Lake District Coast Aquarium

1 hr+   All year

This independently owned aquarium has a comprehensive collection of native marine species. Exciting displays recreate natural habitats, including the 'walk-over' ray pool and 'hands-in' rock pool. There is also a miniature golf attraction.

Location
Take junction 40 of M6 & A66 to Maryport, or junction 44 & A595 S to connect with A596 coastal route

Opening
Daily: 10am–5pm

Admission
Adult £5, Child £3.25, Concs £4.50

Contact
South Quay, Maryport CA15 8AB

t 01900 817760
w lakedistrict-coastaquarium.co.uk
e info@ld-coastaquarium.co.uk

683 Milnthorpe

Lakeland Wildlife Oasis

1hr+   All year

Enjoy a fascinating journey through the animal kingdom – encountering everything from microbes to monkeys – in this unique, award-winning wildlife exhibition, with live animals and hands-on displays.

* Cumbria Winner, *Good Britain Guide*
* Animal-handling sessions

Location
On A6, 2½ miles S of Milnthorpe, near junction 35 of M6

Opening
Daily: 10am–5pm
(last admission 4pm)

Admission
Adult £6, Child £4, Concs £5

Contact
Milnthorpe LA7 7BW
t 01539 563027
w wildlifeoasis.co.uk

684 Newby Bridge

Aquarium of the Lakes

1 hr   All year

Explore a range of naturally themed Lake District habitats featuring the UK's largest collection of freshwater fish. See otters, British sharks and a variety of British mammals. Discover our underwater tunnel featuring giant carp and diving ducks.

* Midnight at the Water's Edge
* Large number of nocturnal creatures

Location
15 min from junction 36 of M6. Take A590 to Newby Bridge & follow signs

Opening
Daily: Apr–Oct 9am–6pm;
Nov–Mar 9am–5pm
(last admission 1 hr before close)

Admission
Adult £7, Child £4.50, Concs £6

Contact
Lakeside, Newby Bridge LA12 8AS
t 01539 530153
w aquariumofthelakes.co.uk
e aquariumofthelakes@reallive.co.uk

685 Penrith

Dalemain Historic House & Garden

2 hrs   Easter–Oct

Dalemain is a beautiful Tudor and Georgian house with fascinating interiors, set among fine gardens, parkland with red squirrels and fallow deer and the Lakeland Fells. Children love the nursery, Mrs Mouse's House on the back stairs and the hiding hole in the housekeeper's room.

* Children's garden
* Cruises available on nearby Ullswater

Location	Contact
On A592 Penrith–Ullswater road	Penrith CA11 0HB
Opening	t 01768 486450
House Sun–Thu 11am–4pm	w dalemain.com
Gardens & Tearoom 10.30am–5pm	e admin@dalemain.com
Please phone for details	
Admission	
Adult £6.50, Child free	

686 Penrith

Eden Ostrich World

2 hrs+   All year

Come face to face with African black ostriches, rare breeds of cattle, donkeys, shire horses, pigs, goats, red deer, ducks and geese.

* Soft play centre & hayloft gallery
* Tractor & trailer rides

Location	Admission
In Eden Valley, 5 miles from M6 junction 40. Follow A686 towards Alston	Adult £4.95, Child £3.95, Concs £4.50
	Contact
Opening	Langwathby Hall Farm, Langwathby, Penrith CA10 1LW
Mar–Oct daily 10am–5pm; Nov–Feb Wed–Mon 10am–5pm	t 01768 881771
	w ostrich-world.com

687 Penrith

Lakeland Bird of Prey Centre

 2 hrs+   Apr–Oct

Situated in the walled garden of Lowther Castle and enclosed by parkland, this centre gives visitors the chance to observe fascinating birds of prey at close quarters.

* Daily flying demonstrations

Location	Admission
From the N take A6, 5 miles S of Penrith. From the S leave M6 at junction 39 on to A6 through Shap, about 15 miles N of Kendal	Adult £6, Child £3, Concs £5
	Contact
	Old Walled Garden, Lowther, Penrith CA10 2HH
Opening	t 01931 712746
Daily: Apr–Oct 11am–5pm	e info@lbpc.co.uk

688 Penrith

Rheged – Enter into the Spirit of Cumbria

2 hrs+   All year

This essential Lake District experience boasts a giant cinema screen showing up to five spectacular films daily, the National Mountaineering Exhibition, a children's indoor play area and a Tourist Information Centre. It is Europe's largest grass-covered building.

* International award-winning attraction, 12 speciality shops
* Taste Food Hall, toy shop & 2 exhibition halls

Location	Admission
2 min from M6 junction 40 at Penrith, on A66 towards Keswick	Free parking & admission. Charge per activity or event
Opening	Contact
Daily: 10am–5.30pm	Redhills, Penrith CA11 0DQ
	t 01768 868000
	w rheged.com
	e enquiries@rheged.com

689 Penrith

Wetheriggs Pottery

2 hrs   All year

Come and see potters at work in the country's only remaining steam-powered pottery. Explore the old workings and restored steam engine, and have a go at throwing your own pots or painting models. Additionally, there's a collection of rare pigs and a children's play area.

* Pottery & craft shops
* Tearoom

Location	Admission
Only 4 miles S of Penrith. Follow brown signs from M6 junction 40 or A6 roundabouts	Free
	Contact
Opening	Clifton Dykes, Penrith, Cumbria CA10 2DH
Easter–Oct 10am–5.30pm; Nov–Easter 10am–4.30pm	t 01768 892733
	w wetheriggs-pottery.co.uk
	e info@wetheriggs-pottery.co.uk

690 Ravenglass

Muncaster Castle

4 hrs+   All year

A historic castle and headquarters of the World Owl Centre, Muncaster has 70 acres of gardens, a meadow vole maze and children's play area. It's also rumoured to be haunted …

* Cumbria & North West excellence awards
* Darkest Muncaster – a winter evening of magic

Location	Admission
On A595, 1 mile S of Ravenglass. Take junction 40 of M6 S & junction 36 of M6 N	Gardens, Owl Centre & Maze Adult £6.50, Child £4.50
	Castle upgrade £2.50, £1.50
Opening	Contact
Castle Sun–Fri 12noon–5pm	Ravenglass CA18 1RQ
Gardens, Owl Centre & Maze Daily: 10.30am–6pm. Please phone for details of winter opening times	t 01229 717614
	w muncaster.co.uk
	e info@muncaster.co.uk

691 Ravenglass

Ravenglass & Eskdale Railway

2 hrs+   All year

Take a gentle steam train ride from the coast at Ravenglass to the foot of England's highest mountain at Eskdale, through the beautiful Lake District landscape. Depending on the weather, visitors can travel in open carriages or cosy covered ones.

* New station & visitor centre at Eskdale

Location	Admission
On A595 Whitehaven–Barrow road	All-day return ticket Adult £9, Child £4.50
Opening	Contact
Daily: mid-Mar–early Nov 9am–5pm; winter open Sat–Sun, Feb half-term & Christmas–New Year Please phone for details	Ravenglass CA18 1SW
	t 01229 717171
	w ravenglass-railway.co.uk
	e steam@ravenglass-railway.co.uk

692 Seascale

Sellafield Visitor Centre

2 hrs+   All year

With interactive exhibits, exciting science workshops and plenty of hands-on fun, Sellafield Visitor Centre is an educational and entertaining family day out. Join in the great energy debate. Plug in to an attraction that's free, fascinating and fun.

» Recharge your batteries in our bright dairy coffee shop

Location
11 miles S of Whitehaven on A595

Opening
Daily: Apr–Oct 10am–5pm;
Nov–Mar 10am–4pm

Admission
Free

Contact
Sellafield, Seascale CA20 1PG

t 01946727027
w sellafield.com

---

693 Sizergh

Sizergh Castle & Garden

2 hrs+   Apr–Oct

This small medieval castle includes a C14 tower and oak-panelled Elizabethan interiors. There are gardens, woodland, pasture and a rock garden with waterfalls and pools to explore.

» Identify butterflies in the ancient woods
» Children's quiz daily in the castle

Location
Follow signs from A590, 3½ miles S of Kendal

Opening
House Apr–Oct Sun–Thu
1.30pm–5.30pm *Gardens* Apr–Oct
Sun–Thu 12.30pm–5.30pm
Café & Shop Apr–Oct Sun–Thu
12noon–5pm

Admission
House & Gardens Adult 6.20,
Child £3.10

Contact
Sizergh, nr Kendal LA8 8AE

t 01539 560951
w nationaltrust.org.uk
e sizergh@nationaltrust.org.uk

694 Ulverston

Bardsea Country Park

2 hrs+   All year

A beautiful wild location on the north side of Morecambe Bay, its large woodland area reaching down almost to the sea. It is ideal for walking and spotting flora and fauna. Seawood, a Site of Special Scientific Interest, is next to the park and is managed by the Woodland Trust.

* Seashore & woodland walks

Location
S of Ulverston. Take A5087
Ulverston–Barrow coastal road

Opening
Daily: All reasonable times

Admission
Free

Contact
Ulverston Tourist Information Centre,
Coronation Hall, County Square,
Ulverston LA12 7LZ

t 01229 587120
e ulverstontic@southlakeland.gov.uk

695 Ulverston

National Trust Fell Foot Park

4 hrs+   All year

An 18-acre Victorian park, restored to its prior splendour providing access to the lakeshore of Windermere and its watery activities. Picnic areas and rowing-boat hire, and wonderful spring and summer displays of flowers, are set off by breathtaking views of the Lakeland Fells.

* Children's quiz & trail
* Hands-on family activities

Location
At extreme S end of Lake
Windermere, on E shore. Entrance
from A592

Opening
Park Daily: 9am–5pm or dusk if earlier
Shop & Tearoom Daily: Easter–Oct
11am–5pm

Admission
Free, donations welcomed
Car park fee

Contact
Newby Bridge,
Ulverston LA12 8NN

t 01539 531273
w nationaltrust.org.uk
e fellfootpark@nationaltrust.org.uk

696 Ulverston

Windermere Lake Cruises

1hr+   All year

Steamers and launches sail daily throughout the year from Ambleside, Bowness and Lakeside with connections for the Lake District Visitor Centre (Brockdale), the World of Beatrix Potter, the Aquarium of the Lakes and the Lakeside & Haverthwaite Railway.

* Cumbria Large Visitor Attraction of the Year 2003
* Rowing boats available for hire

Location
Take junction 36 of M6. Follow brown tourist signs along A590 to Lakeside or A591 to Windermere for Bowness & Ambleside

Opening
Daily: *summer* open during daylight hours *winter* 9.45am–4.30pm

Admission
Adult from £5.50, Child from £2.75

Contact
Lakeside, Newby Bridge, Ulverston LA12 8AS

t 01539 531188
w windermere-lakecruises.co.uk
e mail@windermere-lakecruises.co.uk

697 Whitehaven

The Beacon

1hr+   All year

Discover the fascinating history of Whitehaven, West Cumbria's Georgian port. Situated on the harbourside, the beacon tells the story of the town's maritime, social and industrial heritage through audio-visual, graphic and interactive presentations.

* Quality Assured Visitor Attraction

Location
Follow A595 to Whitehaven & then town centre signs to S harbour

Opening
Tue–Sun 10am–5.30pm (4.30pm in winter)
Please phone for details

Admission
Adult £4.50, Child £2.90, Concs £3.60

Contact
West Strand,
Whitehaven CA28 7LY

t 01946 592302
w thebeacon-whitehaven.co.uk
e thebeacon@copelandbc.gov.uk

698 Windermere

Lakeland Pony Trekking

1hr+   Mar–Nov

Lakeland Pony Trekking offers horse-riding for all ages and abilities including short, hill, farm and trail rides. All are undertaken with qualified staff and on suitable mounts for each rider, ranging from ex-competition horses to native breeds.

* Treks from ½ hour to 1 day

Location
On A592, 2½ miles from Windermere

Opening
Daily: 1 Mar–1 Nov 10am–4pm, booking essential

Admission
From £15, please phone for details

Contact
Limefitt Park, Trout Beck,
Windermere LA23 1PD

t 01539 431999
w lakelandequestrian.co.uk

699 Accrington

Oswaldtwistle Mills Shopping Village

2 hrs+   All year

A friendly family attraction, set within a working mill and its grounds, Oswaldtwistle Mills offers an interesting range of facilities as well as shopping. Retail therapy with a twist.

* Sweet factory
* Indoor children's play area

Location
Accessible from M65 junction 7, M62, A58 & M6 junction 29

Opening
Daily: Mon–Sat 9.30am–5.30pm (8pm Thu), Sun 11am–5pm; 11 Nov–19 Dec Mon–Thu 9.30–10pm

Admission
Free

Contact
Moscow Mill, Colliers Street, Oswaldtwistle, Accrington BB5 3DE
t 01254 871025
w o-mills.co.uk

700 Blackpool

Blackpool Illuminations

2 hrs   Aug –Nov

Britain's biggest and brightest light show shines brilliantly for 66 nights from September to November each year. It stretches for 6 miles and lights up the sky for many miles around. Displays include alien space ships, pirates, jelly monsters and Tiffany lamps.

* View the giant clifftop tableaux
* Festival of Light throughout the town

Location
Promenades

Opening
Nightly: 31 Aug–4 Nov

Admission
Free

Contact
Blackpool Tourism, 1 Clifton Street FY1 1LY
t 01253 478222
w visitblackpool.com
e tourism@blackpool.gov.uk

701 Blackpool

The Blackpool Piers

4 hrs+   Easter–Nov

Blackpool's Piers are fantastic entertainment for all the family. Great rides for older children are Adrenaline Zone and the Crazy Mouse roller coaster. Ride the famous big wheel, dodgems, waltzers, carousel, pepita and Noah's Ark.

* Children's entertainer (all piers)
* Fairground rides (South & Central Piers)

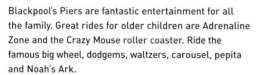

Location
North Pier on North Promenade, South Pier on South Promenade, Central Pier on Central Promenade

Opening
Daily: Easter–Nov from 10am (subject to weather conditions)

Admission
Free, except North Pier (50p toll)
Charges for individual rides

Contact
6 Piers Ltd, Saga House, Ecclestone, Churley, Lancs PR7 5PH
t 01253 292029
w blackpoollive.com

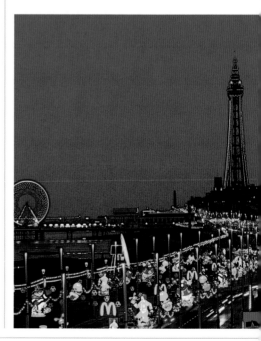

696 Ulverston

Windermere Lake Cruises

1 hr+   All year

Steamers and launches sail daily throughout the year from Ambleside, Bowness and Lakeside with connections for the Lake District Visitor Centre (Brockdale), the World of Beatrix Potter, the Aquarium of the Lakes and the Lakeside & Haverthwaite Railway.

* Cumbria Large Visitor Attraction of the Year 2003
* Rowing boats available for hire

Location
Take junction 36 of M6. Follow brown tourist signs along A590 to Lakeside or A591 to Windermere for Bowness & Ambleside

Opening
Daily: *summer* open during daylight hours *winter* 9.45am–4.30pm

Admission
Adult from £5.50, Child from £2.75

Contact
Lakeside, Newby Bridge, Ulverston LA12 8AS

t 01539 531188
w windermere-lakecruises.co.uk
e mail@windermere-lakecruises.co.uk

---

697 Whitehaven

The Beacon

1 hr+   All year

Discover the fascinating history of Whitehaven, West Cumbria's Georgian port. Situated on the harbourside, the beacon tells the story of the town's maritime, social and industrial heritage through audio-visual, graphic and interactive presentations.

* Quality Assured Visitor Attraction

Location
Follow A595 to Whitehaven & then town centre signs to S harbour

Opening
Tue–Sun 10am–5.30pm (4.30pm in winter)
Please phone for details

Admission
Adult £4.50, Child £2.90, Concs £3.60

Contact
West Strand, Whitehaven CA28 7LY

t 01946 592302
w thebeacon-whitehaven.co.uk
e thebeacon@copelandbc.gov.uk

---

698 Windermere

Lakeland Pony Trekking

1 hr+   Mar–Nov

Lakeland Pony Trekking offers horse-riding for all ages and abilities including short, hill, farm and trail rides. All are undertaken with qualified staff and on suitable mounts for each rider, ranging from ex-competition horses to native breeds.

* Treks from ½ hour to 1 day

Location
On A592, 2½ miles from Windermere

Opening
Daily: 1 Mar–1 Nov 10am–4pm, booking essential

Admission
From £15, please phone for details

Contact
Limefitt Park, Trout Beck, Windermere LA23 1PD

t 01539 431999
w lakelandequestrian.co.uk

699 Accrington

Oswaldtwistle Mills Shopping Village

2 hrs+   All year

A friendly family attraction, set within a working mill and its grounds, Oswaldtwistle Mills offers an interesting range of facilities as well as shopping. Retail therapy with a twist.

* Sweet factory
* Indoor children's play area

Location	Admission
Accessible from M65 junction 7, M62, A58 & M6 junction 29	Free
Opening	Contact
Daily: Mon–Sat 9.30am–5.30pm (8pm Thu), Sun 11am–5pm; 11 Nov–19 Dec Mon–Thu 9.30–10pm	Moscow Mill, Colliers Street, Oswaldtwistle, Accrington BB5 3DE
	t 01254 871025
	w o-mills.co.uk

700 Blackpool

Blackpool Illuminations

2 hrs   Aug –Nov

Britain's biggest and brightest light show shines brilliantly for 66 nights from September to November each year. It stretches for 6 miles and lights up the sky for many miles around. Displays include alien space ships, pirates, jelly monsters and Tiffany lamps.

* View the giant clifftop tableaux
* Festival of Light throughout the town

Location	Contact
Promenades	Blackpool Tourism, 1 Clifton Street FY1 1LY
Opening	
Nightly: 31 Aug–4 Nov	t 01253 478222
Admission	w visitblackpool.com
Free	e tourism@blackpool.gov.uk

701 Blackpool

The Blackpool Piers

4 hrs+   Easter–Nov

Blackpool's Piers are fantastic entertainment for all the family. Great rides for older children are Adrenaline Zone and the Crazy Mouse roller coaster. Ride the famous big wheel, dodgems, waltzers, carousel, pepita and Noah's Ark.

* Children's entertainer (all piers)
* Fairground rides (South & Central Piers)

Location	Admission
North Pier on North Promenade, South Pier on South Promenade, Central Pier on Central Promenade	Free, except North Pier (50p toll) Charges for individual rides
Opening	Contact
Daily: Easter–Nov from 10am (subject to weather conditions)	6 Piers Ltd, Saga House, Ecclestone, Churley, Lancs PR7 5PH
	t 01253 292029
	w blackpoollive.com

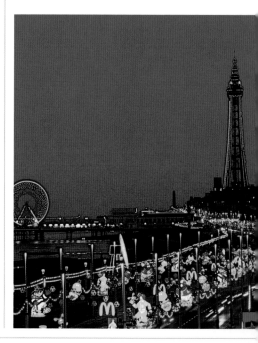

702 Blackpool

Blackpool Pleasure Beach

4 hrs+   Mar–Nov

Visit the entertainment adventure capital, with more roller coasters than any other amusement park in the UK, including the Pepsi Max Big One and the new Spin Doctor. There's also the Beaver Creek Theme Park for younger children, and award-winning shows.

* Ride Pepsi Max Big One tallest & fastest roller coaster in Europe at 235feet t high & turning at speeds of up to 87mph

Location
From M6 junction 32 follow brown tourist signs to Blackpool S Shore, then to Pleasure Beach

Opening
Mar–Nov, please phone for details

Admission
A range of tickets are available, please phone for details

Contact
Ocean Boulevard,
Blackpool FY4 1EZ

t 0870 444 5566
w blackpoolpleasurebeach.com

703 Blackpool

Blackpool Sea Life Centre

2 hrs   All year

The Sea Life Centre houses one of Europe's largest marine collections. It has more than 50 fascinating displays, making for exciting close-up encounters with marine life, including sharks, rays, seahorses and piranhas.

* Fascinating display of jellyfish

Location
On Blackpool's Golden Mile between Central Pier & the Tower. Leave M55 at junction 4

Opening
Daily: from 10am

Admission
Adult £10.95, Child £7.50, Concs £9.95, Family ticket £33

Contact
The Promenade,
Blackpool FY1 5AA

t 01253 622445
w sealife.co.uk
e slcblackpool@leisureparks.com

704 Blackpool

Blackpool Tower & Circus

5 hrs+   Easter–Nov

Visit Blackpool's answer to the Eiffel Tower to enjoy the aquarium, dinosaur ride, indoor adventure play area and family entertainment at the Hornpipe Gallery, then be delighted by the award-winning circus.

* Please phone for details of evening entertainment
* Take the Walk of Faith 380 feet above the promenade

Location
Take M55 for Blackpool & follow signs

Opening
Daily: Easter–May 10am–6pm;
Jun–Nov 10am–11pm

Admission
Tower Adult £12.95, Child £8.95,
Concs £7.95

Contact
Leisure Park Ltd, 97 Church Street,
Blackpool FY1 4BJ

t 01253 622242 / 01253 292029
w blackpooltower.co.uk
e website@leisure-parcs.co.uk

705 Blackpool

Sandcastle Tropical Waterworld

4 hrs+   All year

A water-based leisure complex with four pools, it offers a variety of thrills including water-slides, a children's pool, a wave pool, white-knuckle water chutes and a new interactive water play area.

* Quality Assured Visitor Attraction

Location
On South Promenade

Opening
Please phone for details

Admission
Please phone for details

Contact
South Promenade,
Blackpool FY4 1BB

t 01253 343602
w sandcastle-waterworld.co.uk

706 Blackpool

Wyreside Ecology Centre

2 hrs   All year

A visitor centre set in the heart of the Wyre Estuary Country Park, the Wyreside Ecology Centre provides an excellent base for nature trails and riverside walks.

* Riverside path suitable for blind visitors
* Cycles available for hire for disabled visitors

Location
Follow M55, then A585 & B5268

Opening
Daily: Apr–Oct 10.30am–4.30pm;
Nov–Mar 11am–3pm

Admission
Free

Contact
Wyre Estuary Country Park,
River Road, Thornton–Cleveleys,
Blackpool FY5 5LR

t 01253 857890
w wyrebc.gov.uk
e wyresidetic@wyrebc.gov.uk

702 Blackpool

Blackpool Pleasure Beach

4 hrs+   Mar–Nov

Visit the entertainment adventure capital, with more roller coasters than any other amusement park in the UK, including the Pepsi Max Big One and the new Spin Doctor. There's also the Beaver Creek Theme Park for younger children, and award-winning shows.

* Ride Pepsi Max Big One tallest & fastest roller coaster in Europe at 235feet t high & turning at speeds of up to 87mph

Location
From M6 junction 32 follow brown tourist signs to Blackpool S Shore, then to Pleasure Beach

Opening
Mar–Nov, please phone for details

Admission
A range of tickets are available, please phone for details

Contact
Ocean Boulevard,
Blackpool FY4 1EZ

t 0870 444 5566
w blackpoolpleasurebeach.com

703 Blackpool

Blackpool Sea Life Centre

2 hrs   All year

The Sea Life Centre houses one of Europe's largest marine collections. It has more than 50 fascinating displays, making for exciting close-up encounters with marine life, including sharks, rays, seahorses and piranhas.

* Fascinating display of jellyfish

Location
On Blackpool's Golden Mile between Central Pier & the Tower. Leave M55 at junction 4

Opening
Daily: from 10am

Admission
Adult £10.95, Child £7.50, Concs £9.95, Family ticket £33

Contact
The Promenade,
Blackpool FY1 5AA

t 01253 622445
w sealife.co.uk
e slcblackpool@leisureparks.com

704 Blackpool

Blackpool Tower & Circus

5 hrs+   Easter–Nov

Visit Blackpool's answer to the Eiffel Tower to enjoy the aquarium, dinosaur ride, indoor adventure play area and family entertainment at the Hornpipe Gallery, then be delighted by the award-winning circus.

* Please phone for details of evening entertainment
* Take the Walk of Faith 380 feet above the promenade

Location	Contact
Take M55 for Blackpool & follow signs	Leisure Park Ltd, 97 Church Street, Blackpool FY1 4BJ
Opening	
Daily: Easter–May 10am–6pm; Jun–Nov 10am–11pm	t 01253 622242 / 01253 292029
	w blackpooltower.co.uk
Admission	e website@leisure-parcs.co.uk
Tower Adult £12.95, Child £8.95, Concs £7.95	

705 Blackpool

Sandcastle Tropical Waterworld

4 hrs+   All year

A water-based leisure complex with four pools, it offers a variety of thrills including water-slides, a children's pool, a wave pool, white-knuckle water chutes and a new interactive water play area.

* Quality Assured Visitor Attraction

Location	Contact
On South Promenade	South Promenade, Blackpool FY4 1BB
Opening	
Please phone for details	t 01253 343602
	w sandcastle-waterworld.co.uk
Admission	
Please phone for details	

706 Blackpool

Wyreside Ecology Centre

2 hrs   All year

A visitor centre set in the heart of the Wyre Estuary Country Park, the Wyreside Ecology Centre provides an excellent base for nature trails and riverside walks.

* Riverside path suitable for blind visitors
* Cycles available for hire for disabled visitors

Location	Contact
Follow M55, then A585 & B5268	Wyre Estuary Country Park, River Road, Thornton–Cleveleys, Blackpool FY5 5LR
Opening	
Daily: Apr–Oct 10.30am–4.30pm; Nov–Mar 11am–3pm	t 01253 857890
	w wyrebc.gov.uk
Admission	e wyresidetic@wyrebc.gov.uk
Free	

707 Bolton

Bolton Aquarium

2 hrs   All year

If you are curious about catfish, partial to piranhas or want to be knowledgeable about knifefish, visit Bolton's unique aquarium. Fish from around the world can be seen in an environment designed to offer an insight into their hidden lives.

* One of the oldest aquariums in the UK
* Predatory giant green knifefish from Venezuela

Location
In town centre

Opening
Mon–Sat 9am–5pm
(closed Bank Hols)

Admission
Free

Contact
Le Mans Crescent, Bolton BL1 1SE

t 01204 332200
w boltonmuseums.org.uk
e aquarium@bolton.gov.uk

708 Bolton

Bolton Museum & Art Gallery

2 hrs   All year

Bolton Museum and Art Gallery has something for the whole family. Visit galleries on the themes of Ancient Egypt, Costume, Local History and the Story of Bolton, Natural History and Wildlife on Your Doorstep, as well as a temporary gallery with up to six exciting exhibitions.

* Varied programme of events & exhibitions
* Educational play area & organised workshops

Location
In town centre

Opening
Mon–Sat 9am–5pm
(closed Bank Hols)

Admission
Free

Contact
Le Mans Crescent, Bolton BL1 1SE

t 01204 332211
w boltonmuseums.org.uk
e museums@bolton.gov.uk

709 Bolton

Bolton Wanderers Football Club

2 hrs   All year

Look behind the scenes at the Reebok Stadium, home of Bolton Wanderers. Begin at the interactive museum where the history of the club is brought to life. Visit the players' dressing and warm-up rooms, the officials' changing rooms and the manager's dugout.

* All stadium tours must be pre-booked

Location
Junction 6 of M61

Opening
Daily: Mon–Fri 9.30am–5pm,
Sat 9am–5pm, Sun 11am–5pm

Admission
Adult £2.50, Child & Concs £1.50

Contact
Reebok Stadium, Burnden Way,
Bolton BL6 6JW

t 01204 673650
w bwfc.premiumtv.co.uk
e sparker@bwfc.co.uk

710 Bury

Burrs Activity Centre

1 hr+   All year

Children will have lots of fun at this outdoor activity centre, where they can try canoeing, climbing, orienteering, hiking, kayaking, abseiling and archery.

* Function room – accommodation in a bunkhouse

Location
Leave M66 at junction 2, follow A58 to
Bolton, then take B6214

Opening
Daily: Please phone for details

Admission
Free. Charges for activities

Contact
Woodhill Road, Bury BL8 1DA

t 0161 764 9649
w burrs.org.uk
e burrs@btconnect.com

East Lancashire Railway

3 hrs+   All year

This mainly steam-hauled service runs between
Hayward, Bury, Ramsbottom and Rawtenstall every
weekend. Visitors can break their journey at any
station to visit the shops in quaint Ramsbottom and
the stalls at Bury Market.

Location
In town centre. Accessible from A56,
A58 & M66

Opening
Sat–Sun 9am–5pm;
May–Sep also Wed–Fri
10am–4.30pm

Admission
Adult £9.50, Child & Concs £6.50

Contact
Bolton Street Station,
Bury BL9 0EY

t 0161 764 7790
w east-lancs-rly.co.uk
e admin@east-lancs-rly.co.uk

Docker Park Farm Visitor Centre

4 hrs+   All year

Get up close to the animals at this working livestock
farm with horses, pigs, sheep, goats and poultry. Visitors
can hold some of the animals, including rabbits and
chickens, and enjoy pony rides and bottle-feeding.

* Collect eggs & feed poultry
* Tractor rides during school holidays

Location
Exit M6 at junction 35 on to B6254

Opening
Mar–Oct daily 10.30am–5pm;
Nov–Feb Sat–Sun 10.30am–4pm

Admission
Adult £4.75, Child £3.75

Contact
Arkholme, Carnforth LA6 1AR

t 01524 221331
w dockerparkfarm.co.uk

713 Carnforth

Leighton Hall

2 hrs   May–Sep

Explore the past of an old Lancashire family and, wander through the extensive grounds and pretty gardens of this interesting historic building. There is a maze to explore, woodland walks and displays by trained birds of prey.

* C19 walled garden, landscaped parkland & woodland
* Entertaining guides reveal the family's history

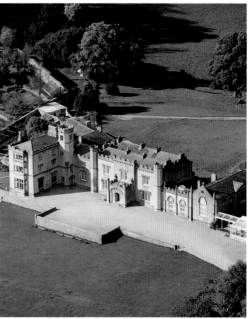

Location
Take junction 35A of M6 to North Carnforth & follow brown tourist signs

Opening
May–July & Sep Tue–Fri & Sun 2pm–5pm, Bank Hols 2pm–5pm; Aug Tue–Fri & Sun 12noon–5pm, Aug Bank Hol 12.30pm–5pm

Admission
Adult £5.50, Child £4, Concs £5

Contact
Carnforth LA5 9ST
t 01524 734474
w leightonhall.co.uk
e info@leightonhall.co.uk

714 Chorley

Camelot Theme Park

4 hrs+   Apr–Oct

There is fun for all the family here, with breathtaking rides and nailbiting medieval jousting tournaments. The Whirlwind, a spinning roller coaster, will keep even the most courageous thrill-seekers happy.

* Park Hall hotel on site

Location
Leave M6 at junction 27/28 & M61 at junction 8

Opening
Daily: Apr–Oct 10am–5pm. Please phone for details

Admission
Adult & Child £16.50, Concs £12.50

Contact
Park Hall Road, Charnock Richard, Chorley PR7 5LP
t 01257 452100
w camelotthemepark.co.uk
e kingarthur@camelotthemepark.co.uk

715 Fleetwood

Farmer Parr's Animal World

3 hrs+   All year

Explore more than 20 acres of farmland, with a collection of more than 200 farm animals and rare breeds, including poultry and pets. There are both outdoor and indoor areas so you'll have fun whatever the weather.

* Autism Initiatives pottery shop
* Pony & tractor rides

Location
Follow M55 to Fleetwood, then take A585 (Fleetwood Road & Amounderness Way). Opposite Cala Gran Caravan Park

Opening
Daily: 10am–5pm

Admission
Adult £4.25, Child £3, Concs £3.50, Family ticket (2 Adult & 2 Child) £12

Contact
Wyrefield Farm, Rossall Lane, Fleetwood FY7 8JP
t 01253 874389/770484
w farmerparrs.com

716 Lancaster

Lancaster Castle

1 hr+   All year

One of the best-preserved and hardest-working castles in the country, still used today as a court and prison. Visitors can see where the Lancashire Witches were tried and condemned to death, the Hanging Corner where prisoners were hanged, the dungeons and the Drop Room.

* Display of heraldic shields in the Shire Hall
* Beautiful Gillow furniture in grand jury room

Location
Off Meetinghouse Lane, turn right into Castle Hill

Opening
Daily: 10am–5pm
Admission by guided tour only

Admission
Adult £5, Child & Concs £4

Contact
Castle Parade, Lancaster LA1 1YJ
t 01524 64998
w lancastercastle.com
e christine.goodier@mus.lancscc.gov.uk

717 Lancaster

Williamson Park & Butterfly House

1 hr+   All year

Bring the family to Williamson Park to visit the Ashton Memorial, a Victorian folly, a conservation garden and a tropical butterfly house. There is also a new children's playground.

* Mini beasts & animal centre
* Small mammal enclosure

Location
Follow Lancaster signs from A6/M6 junction 33 or 34. Follow brown tourist signs from city

Opening
Daily: Apr–Sep 10am–5pm;
Oct–Mar 10am–4pm

Admission
Adult £4, Child £2.50, Concs £3.50

Contact
Williamson Park, Quernmore Road, Lancaster LA1 1UX
t 01524 33318
w williamsonpark.com

718 Leigh

Pennington Flash Country Park

4 hrs+   All year

Roam nearly 500 acres of country park, surrounding a 172-acre lake. World-renowned as a bird-watcher's paradise, this is a popular beauty spot, lake and nature reserve. More than 230 bird species have been recorded here.

* 9-hole pay & play golf course
* 7 viewing hides

Location
Take A572 from town centre & A580 from Manchester & Liverpool

Opening
Daily: Ranger on site 8.30am–dusk

Admission
Free. Car park fee

Contact
Helens Road, Leigh WN7 3PA
t 01942 605253
w wlct.org
e pfcp@wlct.org

719 Leyland

Worden Arts & Crafts Centre

2 hrs+   Apr–Sep

Set in 157 acres of parkland, this arts and crafts centre has a fully-equipped theatre, six craft workshops and an exhibition display room.

* Maze
* Garden for the blind

Location
Leave M6 at junction 28 & follow signs for Worden Arts Centre

Opening
Park Daily: 8.30am–8.30pm
Arts & Crafts centre Please phone for details

Admission
Free

Contact
Worden Park, Worden Lane, Leyland PR25 1DJ

t 01772 455908
w worden-arts.co.uk

720 Littleborough

Hollingworth Lake Country Park

4 hrs+   All year

A country park consisting of a lake and surrounding countryside, with boating, a nature reserve, trails, events, guided walks, a visitor centre, play areas and picnic sites.

* Refurbished visitor centre with exciting exhibits

Location
Leave M62 at junction 21 & take B6225. Follow brown tourist signs

Opening
Daily: Apr–Sep 10.30am–6pm;
Oct–Mar 11am–4pm

Admission
Free. Car park fee

Contact
Rakewood Road,
Littleborough OL15 0AQ

t 01706 373421
w rochdale.gov.uk

721 Nelson

British in India Museum

1 hr   All year

An absorbing museum full of artefacts relating to the British in India. On display are Indian regimental ties, paintings, photographs of military and civilian subjects, model soldiers, medals, coins, picture postcards, postage stamps, toys and examples of Indian dress.

* Learn about the people behind the Raj

Location
Take A56–A6068 between Burnley & Keighley

Opening
Mon–Fri 10am–4pm

Admission
Adult £3.50, Child 50p

Contact
Hendon Mill, Hallam Road, Nelson, Lancs DV9 8AD

t 01282 613129

722 Nelson

Pendle Heritage Centre

2 hrs+   All year

Set in the beautiful Pendle landscape, the Heritage Centre is the perfect starting point for a variety of local walks. Stroll through the C18 walled garden or take the woodland walk, stopping at the medieval cruck barn to visit the farmyard animals.

* Cruck-frame barn
* Pendle Witches exhibition

Location
Leave M65 at junction 13 & take A682 on to B6247

Opening
Daily: 10am–5pm

Admission
Please phone for details

Contact
Park Hill, Barrowford,
Nelson BB9 6JQ

t 01282 661701
e heritage.centre@pendle.gov.uk

Ormskirk

Cedar Farm Galleries

4 hrs+   All year

There are contemporary crafts, farm animals and a funky playground at these galleries, which include nine working craft retail studios, where craftspeople can be seen at work and commissions are taken. The new Wickerfish Art Studio offers watercolour painting classes.

* Art & yoga workshops
* Pots of Fun pottery painting studio

Location
From M6 junction 27 follow brown tourist signs. At crossroads in Mawdesley village turn into Gorsey Lane & then into Back Lane

Opening
Tue–Sun & Bank Hol Mon 10am–5pm

Admission
Free

Contact
Back Lane, Mawdesley,
Ormskirk L40 3SY

t 01704 822038
w cedarfarm.net
e cedarfarm@hotmail.co.uk

Preston

Leisure Lakes

4 hrs+   All year

The 30 acres of lakes with sandy beaches provide the perfect base for a wide range of water pursuits, from windsurfing and canoeing to sailing and jet-skiing. A 20-bay driving range offers professional golf tuition for adults and children.

* Mountain bike centre

Location
Off A565, 6 miles from Southport
& 10 miles from Preston

Opening
Daily: 9am–7pm

Admission
Adult £2.50, Child £2 or £5 per car
Additional charges for some activities

Contact
Mere Brow, Tarleton,
Preston PR4 6JX

t 01772 813446
e gab@leisurelakes.co.uk

Preston

National Football Museum

2 hrs   All year

Embark on a journey through football's history. Learn how the game was invented, how it has developed over the past 150 years, and what the future may hold for players and supporters. Learn about the individuals and teams who have helped to shape the game we know today.

* Football Hall of Fame
* Enjoy our penalty shoot-out game

Location
2 miles from junction 31, 31A or 32 on M6. Follow signs

Opening
Tue–Sat 10am–5pm, Sun 11am–5pm

Admission
Free

Contact
Sir Tom Finney Way, Deepdale,
Preston PR1 6RU

t 01772 908403/442
w nationalfootballmuseum.com
e enquiries@nationalfootballmuseum.
   com

Rawtenstall

Ski Rossendale

2 hrs+   All year

Ski Rossendale is the North's premier ski centre. Open all year round, it is ideal for beginners and expert skiers alike. Set amid trees and parkland, it commands a superb view over the Rossendale Valley.

* Intermediate slope is 80 yards long
* Novices, please phone before visiting

Location
Follow M66 to Rawtenstall.
Centre is on town outskirts

Opening
Daily: Mon–Fri 1pm–9pm,
Sat 1pm–5pm, Sun 9am–5pm

Admission
Adult £16, Child £10

Contact
Haslingden Old Road,
Rawtenstall BB4 8RR

t 01706 226457
w rltmst.co.uk
e info@ski-rossendale.co.uk

©National Trust Photographic Library/Andreas von Einsiedel

727 Rochdale

Whitworth Water Ski & Recreation Centre

4 hrs+ Apr–Oct

The aim of the centre, run in conjunction with an able-bodied ski club, is to teach people with a range of disabilities how to water-ski and to help them integrate with able-bodied members. Full instruction and equipment are provided.

* Banana & Ringo rides
* Bikes for disabled visitors

Location
Take A671 from Rochdale

Opening
Apr–Oct Mon–Fri 9.30am–dusk,
Sat–Sun 8am–dusk

Admission
Free. All activities individually priced,
please phone for details

Contact
Cowm Reservoir, Tong Lane,
Whitworth, Rochdale OL12 8BE

t 01706 852534
w whitworth-waterski.co.uk
e andynflo@whitworthwaterski.co.uk

728 Rufford

Rufford Old Hall

2 hrs+ Mar–Oct

Rufford is one of Lancashire's finest C16 buildings, famed for its spectacular great hall, where Shakespeare is believed to have once performed. There's lots to entertain children here, with quizzes and trails through the house and garden.

* Fine collections of C16–C17 oak furniture
* Arms, armour & tapestries

Location
7 miles N of Ormskirk in Rufford
village on E side of A59

Opening
17 Mar–Oct Sat–Wed 1pm–5pm

Admission
House & Gardens Adult £4.90, Child £2.50
Gardens £2.80, £1.30

Contact
Rufford, Ormskirk L40 1SG

t 01704 821254
w nationaltrust.org.uk
e ruffordoldhall@nationaltrust.org.uk

729 Wigan

Haigh Country Park

5 hrs+   All year

Explore every corner of this extensive country park that offers woodland trails and a wide variety of events and activities including archery, rock climbing and abseiling. The model village has a railway, helipad, pub and castle.

* Miniature railway, crazy golf & children's play area
* 9–18-hole golf complex

Location	Contact
Near B5238 & B5239	Haigh, Wigan WN2 1PE
Opening	t 01942 832895
Park Daily: dawn–dusk	w haighhall.net
Visitor centre Daily: times vary, please	e hhgen@wlct.org
phone for details	
Admission	
Free	

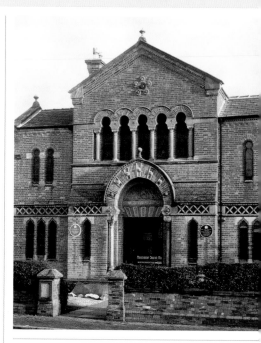

730 Wigan

Rumble Tumble

1½ hrs   All year

Children can have fun and be challenged in this giant indoor play zone, which includes a supervised free-fall slide (for children over five only), ball pools for both toddlers and older children, a bouncy castle and even more for the most energetic of children.

* Birthday party groups accommodated by prior arrangement

Location	Contact
Off A49, in Wallgate	10 Tower Enterprise Park,
Opening	Great George Street,
Daily: 10am–7pm	Wigan WN3 4DP
Admission	t 01942 494922
Mon–Fri 10am–3pm in school term	
£1.55 for 1 hr. £2.30 unlimited play.	
After 3pm £3.30 for 1½ hrs. Sat–Sun	
& school hols £3.50 for 1½ hrs	

731 Manchester

Airport Tour Centre

2 hrs+   All year

Children interested in aeroplanes will love this tour of the airport. Trained guides explain in detail the inner workings of the airport's various busy departments. Pre-booking is essential.

Location	Contact
Leave M56 at junction 5	Terminal 1,
Opening	Manchester Airport,
Daily: 9am–9pm	Manchester M90 1QX
Admission	
Adult £6, Child £5	t 0161 489 2442
	w webmaster.tasmanchester.com
	e tourcentre@tasmanchester.com

732 Manchester

Jewish Museum of Manchester

2 hrs   All year

Manchester's Jewish Museum is unique, as it is housed in a former Spanish and Portuguese synagogue. The former Ladies Gallery tells the history of Manchester Jewry using pictures, documents, room settings and handsets with testimonies from people of the past.

* Lavish Moorish decor & stained glass
* Events & exhibitions throughout the year

Location	Contact
On A665, 1 mile from city centre	190 Cheetham Hill Road, Manchester M8 8LW
Opening	
Mon–Thu 10.30am–4pm, Sun 10.30am–5pm (closed Sat & Jewish hols)	t 0161 834 9879
	w manchesterjewishmuseum.com
	e info@manchester jewishmuseum.com
Admission	
Adult £3.95, Child & Concs £2.95	

733 Manchester

Manchester Art Gallery

4 hrs+   All year

Enjoy some family fun in the Clore Interactive Gallery and take part in a wide range of events. Highlights include outstanding Pre-Raphaelite paintings, craft and design and C20 British art. An exciting exhibitions programme offers the best in visual art and design.

* Collection spans 6 centuries of fine & decorative art
* Exceptional collection of C19 British paintings

Location	Contact
In city centre	Mosley Street, Manchester M2 3JL
Opening	
Tue–Sun 10am–5pm (closed Mon except Bank Hols)	t 0161 235 8888
	w manchestergalleries.org
Admission	
Free	

© Len Grant

734 Manchester

Manchester Museum

1 hr   All year

The museum's collections include fossils, minerals, natural history specimens, archaeological finds and a unique collection from Ancient Egypt. Visit the Prehistoric Life Gallery featuring 'Stan', a full-size T. Rex, and the Zoology Gallery containing mammals and birds.

* Ethnology collections from South America
* Vivarium, housing live reptiles & amphibians

Location	Contact
In Oxford Road to S of city centre	University of Manchester, Oxford Road, Manchester M13 9PL
Opening	
Daily: Tue–Sat 10am–5pm, Sun–Mon & Bank Hols 11am–4pm	t 0161 275 2634
	w museum.manchester.ac.uk
Admission	e michael.rooney@manchester.ac.uk
Free. Special events may charge	

735 Manchester

Museum of Science & Industry in Manchester

4 hrs+   All year

The museum comprises five buildings over a 7½-acre site and tells the story of Manchester, the world's first industrial city, its industry and the science behind it. Stimulate the senses in Xperiment, an interactive science gallery.

* Steam engines & locomotives
* Morphis simulator rides

Location	Contact
On Liverpool Road in Castlefield, signed from city centre	Liverpool Road, Castlefield, Manchester M3 4FP
Opening	
Daily: 10am–5pm	t 0161 832 2244
	w msim.org.uk
Admission	e marketing@msim.org.uk
Free. Exhibitions may charge	

736 Manchester

Museum of Transport

2 hrs   All year

Housed in a former bus depot, this wonderfully quirky museum is packed with vintage vehicles, including buses, fire engines and lorries – some 100 years old. There are vehicles from horse-drawn through to the earliest models of the Metrolink trams.

* Biggest collection of vintage buses in the UK

Location	Admission
1 mile N of city centre at N end of Boyle Street, next to Queen's Road bus garage	Adult £4, Child & Concs £2
	Contact
Opening	Boyle Street, Cheetham, Manchester M8 8UW
Mar–Oct Wed, Sat–Sun & Bank Hols 10am–5pm; Nov–Feb 10am–4pm	t 0161 205 2122
	w gmts.co.uk
	e busmuseum@btconnect.com

737 Manchester

Old Trafford Museum & Tour

2 hrs · All year

See the Manchester United trophy room, kits through the ages, and memorabilia of the 'greats', from Charlton to Cantona, Best to Beckham. A stadium tour takes you to the players' tunnel, the dressing room, the dugout and more.

Record your own commentary on United games
Multi-award winner

Location
From Chester Road (A56) turn into Sir Matt Busby Way, or use Old Trafford Metrolink station

Opening
Museum Daily: 9.30am–5pm
Tour Daily: 9.40am–4.30pm
Pre-booking is recommended

Admission
Museum & Tour Adult £9.50, Child & Concs £6.50

Contact
Sir Matt Busby Way, Old Trafford, Manchester M16 0RA

t 0870 442 1994
w manutd.com
e tours@manutd.co.uk

738 Manchester

People's History Museum

2 hrs · All year

Discover the extraordinary story of ordinary people, with interactive exhibits looking at their lives at work, at home and at leisure over the past 200 years.

* From mill workers to the first professional footballers
* Housed in an Edwardian pumping station

Location
Via A6, M602, M62, A56. Follow signs to Castlefield

Opening
Tue–Sun & Bank Hols 11am–4.30pm; (closed Good Fri)

Admission
Free

Contact
The Pump House, Bridge Street, Manchester M3 3ER

t 0161 839 6061
w phm.org.uk
e info@phm.org.uk

Trafford Ecology Park

1 hr   All year

Once an industrial wasteland, Trafford Ecology Park has been transformed into a thriving activity centre and haven for wildlife. Visitors can see the displays, take part in the events, or simply discover the wealth of wild flowers, trees, birds and animals that flourish here.

* Surrounds a reclaimed boating lake
* Based in what was Europe's largest industrial estate

Location
From M602 take A576. From M60 junction 9 take A5081

Opening
Mon–Fri 9am–5pm
(closed Sat–Sun & Bank Hols)

Admission
Free

Contact
Lake Road, Trafford Park, Manchester M17 1TU

t 0161 873 7182
w trafford.gov.uk
e ecology.reception@groundworks.
   org.uk

Wythenshawe Park

4 hrs+   All year

This C16 hall is set in 275 acres of parkland, offering a range of leisure facilities. Beautifully maintained, it has numerous sporting attractions including several football pitches, tennis courts, bowling greens and children's play areas.

* Museum, gallery & glasshouses
* Farm centre

Location
Just off M56, 4 miles from Manchester Airport

Opening
Park Daily: dawn–dusk
Please phone for details of opening times of other facilities

Admission
Please phone for details

Contact
Wythenshawe Road, Northenden, Manchester M23 0AB

t 0161 998 2117
e s.west@manchester.gov.uk

Ordsall Hall Museum

2 hrs   All year

Ordsall Hall is a haunted Tudor manor house in the surroundings of inner city Salford. Visitors can admire the impressive great hall, Star Chamber and Tudor kitchen.

* Family events
* Exhibitions programme

Location
Signed from A57 & A5063

Opening
Mon–Fri 10am–4pm, Sun 1pm–4pm
(closed Good Fri, Easter Sun & Christmas)

Admission
Free

Contact
Ordsall Lane, Salford, Manchester M5 3AN

t 0161 872 0251
w salford.gov.uk/ordshallmuseum
e ordsall.hall@salford.gov.uk

National Wildflower Centre

2 hrs   Apr–Sep

A family-friendly visitor attraction that promotes the creation of new places for wild flowers and illustrates their importance to the environment. Enjoy the demonstration gardens, a plant nursery and a rooftop walkway.

Children's play area
Wall with climbing handles

Location
In Knowsley's Court Hey Park, off
junction 5 of M62

Opening
Daily: Apr–Sep 10am–5pm

Admission
Adult £3, Child free, Concs £1.50

Contact
Court Hey Park, Knowsley L16 3NA

t 0151 738 1913/722 8292
w nwc.org.uk
e info@nwc.org.uk

Beatles Story

2 hrs   All year

The award-winning Beatles Story is the ultimate tribute to Liverpool's most famous sons – John, Paul, George and Ringo. The magical history tour takes the visitor on a trip from the Cavern Club, through the years of Beatlemania and Flower Power to the eventual break-up of the group.

* New living history audio tour
* Personal insights from those who really knew the Fab Four

Location
Follow signposts to Albert Dock

Opening
Daily: 10am–6pm (last admission 5pm)

Admission
Adult £8.99, Child £4.99, Concs £5.99

Contact
Albert Dock, Britannia Vaults,
Liverpool L3 4AD

t 0151 709 1963
w beatlesstory.com
e info@beatlesstory.com

Croxteth Hall & Country Park

2 hrs+   Apr–Sep

Enjoy a great day out at Croxteth! Historic Croxteth Hall comes to life with character figures, conversations to eavesdrop on and even smells in the rooms. Everyone will have fun meeting the animals on Home Farm, while the walled garden is a haven of peace and tranquillity.

Kids can let off steam in the adventure playground
Explore 500 acres of heritage countryside

Location
Leave M57 at junction 4 & take
A580 towards Liverpool

Opening
Daily: Easter–Sep 10.30am–5pm

Admission
Adult £4.20, Child & Concs £2.10

Contact
Croxteth Hall Lane,
Liverpool L12 0HB

t 0151 228 5311
w croxteth.co.uk
e croxtethcountrypark@liverpool.
gov.uk

745 Liverpool

Everton Football Club

1 hr+   All year

Discover at first hand what goes on behind the scenes at Goodison Park. Walk down the tunnel to the roar of 40,000 fans, visit the dressing room where the players get changed and see where they relax and celebrate or commiserate after a game.

WC

Location	**Contact**
3 miles N of city centre	Goodison Park, Liverpool L4 4EL
Opening	t 0870 442 1878
Tours Mon, Wed, Fri & Sun 11am & 1pm	w evertonfc.com
	e stadiumtours@evertonfc.com
Admission	
Adult £8.50, Child & Concs £5	
Pre-booking essential	

746 Liverpool

Liverpool Football Club Museum & Tour Centre

1 hr   All year

A must for any Liverpool fan, young or old. The museum includes a display of the club's trophies and films on the history of the club. Visit the dressing room, walk down the tunnel to the sound of 45,000 cheering fans, touch the famous 'This is Anfield' sign, and sit in the team dugout.

* Film takes visitors through the life of the club
* Hillsborough memorial tribute to 96 fans who died at Hillsborough

WC

Location	**Admission**
3 miles from city centre, 4 miles from M62, 7 miles from end of M57 & M58	Adult £9, Child & Concs £5.50
Opening	**Contact**
Daily: 10am–5pm	Anfield Road, Liverpool L4 0TH
(last admissions 4pm;	t 0151 260 6677
closes 1 hr before kick-off)	w liverpoolfc.tv
	e events@liverpoolfc.tv

747 Liverpool

Liverpool Planetarium

1 hr   All year

Enjoy an exciting visual experience of space in a domed auditorium at this planetarium. The support programme *A Tale of Two Planets* takes a look at the night sky.

* 30-minute performance
* Wonders of the Solar System show

WC

Location	**Contact**
In city centre. Follow signs from M62	William Brown Street, Liverpool L3 8EN
Opening	t 0151 478 4283
Daily: Mon–Fri with shows at 2.30pm, 3.15pm & 4.05pm, Sat–Sun at 1.15pm, 2.15pm, 3.15pm & 4.05pm	w liverpoolmuseums.org.uk
	e jennifer.mchale@liverpoolmuseums.
Admission	org.uk
Free	

748 Liverpool

Speke Hall, Garden & Estate

2 hrs   Mar–Dec

One of the most famous half-timbered houses in the country, dating from 1530. A fully-equipped Victorian kitchen and servants' hall enable visitors to see behind the scenes. The nearby Home Farm is a restored model Victorian farm building with orchard.

Fine Jacobean plasterwork & carved furniture

Location
8 miles SE of central Liverpool, next to Liverpool Airport, signed

Opening
Mar–Oct Wed–Sun 1pm–5.30pm; Nov–Dec Sat–Sun 1pm–4.30pm

Admission
Adult £6.50, Child £3.50

Contact
The Walk, Speke, Liverpool L24 1XD

t 0151 427 7231
w nationaltrust.org.uk
e mendips@nationaltrust.org.uk

749 Liverpool

Tate Liverpool

2 hrs   All year

Bring the children along for a cultural day out at Tate Liverpool, the home of the National Collection of modern art in the North of England. Part of the historic Albert Dock, it has four floors of art to appreciate, free daily talks, a shop and a café.

* Photography, printmaking, painting & sculpture
* Video, performance art & installations

Location
Walking distance from Liverpool Lime Street railway station, signed from city centre

Opening
Jan–May & Sep–Dec Tue–Sun 10am–5.50pm; Jun–Aug daily 10am–5.50pm

Admission
Tate Liverpool Free
Exhibition Adult £4, Child free, Concs £3

Contact
Tate Liverpool, Albert Dock, Liverpool L3 4BB

t 0151 702 7400
w tate.org.uk/liverpool
e visitliverpool@tate.org.uk

750 Liverpool

Williamson Tunnels

1 hr   All year

When you enter Williamson Tunnels, you enter a strange underground kingdom that has lain beneath the city of Liverpool since the early C19. Visitors can see and touch the brick and sandstone workings of this key section of the tunnels.

* Entertaining commentary from an expert guide

Location
From city centre head towards Edgehill

Opening
summer Tue-Sun 10am–5pm;
winter Thu–Sun 10am–4pm,
Tue & Wed open by arrangement;
Feb & Oct half-terms open daily

Admission
Adult £3.50, Child £2, Concs £3

Contact
The Old Stableyard, Smithdown Lane,
Liverpool L7 3EE

t 0151 709 6868
w willliamsontunnels.co.uk
e enquiries@willliamsontunnels.co.uk

751 Liverpool

Yellow Duckmarine

1 hr   All year

This unique amphibious city tour takes you through the historic city, docks and waterfront. On dry land, visit the Pier Head, St George's Hall, both cathedrals, Chinatown and the Philharmonic Hall, before you 'splash down' into the Salthouse Dock.

Location
Follow brown tourist signs from M62
or city centre to Albert Dock

Opening
Daily: 11am–4pm

Admission
Adult £9.95, Child £7.95, Concs £8.95,
Family ticket £29

Contact
32 Anchor Courtyard,
Britannia Pavilion, Albert Dock,
Liverpool L3 4AS

t 0151 708 7799
w theyellowduckmarine.co.uk

752 Prescot

Knowsley Safari Park

3 hrs+ All year

During the 5-mile-long drive, visitors can see a wide range of wild animals, including camels, buffalo, white rhinos, emus, wallabies and lions. A separate reptile house is home to snakes, iguanas, lizards, scorpions and stick insects.

* 500 acres of rolling countryside
* Elephants, giraffes, otters & meerkats in walkaround attraction

Location
Leave M62 at junction 6 then M57 at junction 2, & follow signs

Opening
Daily: Mar–Oct 10am–4pm;
Nov–Feb 10.30am–3pm

Admission
Adult £10, Child & Concs £7,
Family ticket (2 Adult & 2 Child) £30

Contact
Prescot, Merseyside L34 4AN

t 0151 430 9009
w knowsley.com
e safari.park@knowsley.com

753 Skelmersdale

Beacon Country Park

All day All year

There is space to walk, run, ride horses or cycles, fly kites, or just get away from it all and relax at Beacon Country Park. The park consists of more than 300 acres of rolling countryside with a combination of rolling meadows and woodlands.

* 18-hole golf course & driving range
* Heritage trail & orienteering course

Location
Leave M6 at junction 26 then M58 at junction 5

Opening
Daily: 7am–10pm

Admission
Free

Contact
Beacon Lane, Upholland,
Skelmersdale WN8 7RU

t 01695 622794
w westlancsdc.gov.uk
e beacon.park@westlancsdc.gov.uk

754 Southport

Formby

2 hrs All year

This nature reserve is home to one of Britain's last thriving colonies of red squirrels. These can be seen in the pine trees, while the shoreline attracts waders such as oystercatchers and sanderlings. As well as the beautiful beach, there are miles of walks across the sand dunes.

* Programme of events throughout the year
* Country walks

Location
15 miles N of Liverpool, 2 miles W of Formby, 2 miles off A565 & 6 miles S of Southport

Opening
Daily: dawn–dusk

Admission
Free. Car park £3.30

Contact
Blundell Avenue, Formby L37 1PH

t 01704 878591
w nationaltrust.org.uk
e formby@nationaltrust.org.uk

755 Southport

Model Railway Village

2 hrs   Mar–Oct

Set within sheltered gardens, this beautiful miniature village has more than 200 1:18 scale models including watermills, churches, shops and houses. There is also a garden gauge railway.

Location
In town centre. Opposite Royal Clifton Hotel on the promenade, next to marine lake footbridge

Opening
Daily: Mar–Oct 10am–5pm (6pm in Jul–Aug); last admission 1 hr before closing

Admission
Adult £2.95, Child £2.50, Concs £2.50

Contact
Lower Promenade, Kings Gardens, Southport PR8 1RB
t 01704 214266
w southportmodelrailwayvillage.co.uk

756 St Helens

World of Glass

2 hrs   All year

Make a journey of discovery into one of the most common substances on earth. Watch live demonstrations of glassblowing by resident artists and wander through a maze of tunnels that are the remains of the oldest glassmaking tank furnace in the world.

* Gift shop & cafeteria
* Fun zone with distorting mirrors & kaleidoscopes

Location
Leave M62 at junction 7 & M6 at junction 24, then head into town centre

Opening
Tue–Sun & Bank Hols 10am–5pm

Admission
Adult £5.30, Child & Concs £3.80

Contact
Chalon Way East, St Helens WA10 1BX
t 08700 114466
w worldofglass.com
e info@worldofglass.com

757 Wallasey

Mersey Ferries River Explorer Cruise

1 hr+   All year

This cruise along the River Mersey takes 50 minutes and has a recorded commentary. A stop-off at the Wirral Terminal allows for a visit to an aquarium, children's play area, shop and café.

* Space-themed children's play area at Seacombe
* New space port

Location
Pier Head Liverpool is signed from Albert Dock. Follow signs on M53 for Seacombe & Woodside-on-Wirral

Opening
Daily: Mon–Fri 10am–3pm, Sat–Sun & Bank Hols 10am–6pm

Admission
Adult £4.95, Child £2.75, Concs £3.60, Family ticket £13.20

Contact
Victoria Place, Seacombe, Wallasey CH44 6QY
t 0151 330 1444
w merseyferries.co.uk
e info@merseyferries.co.uk

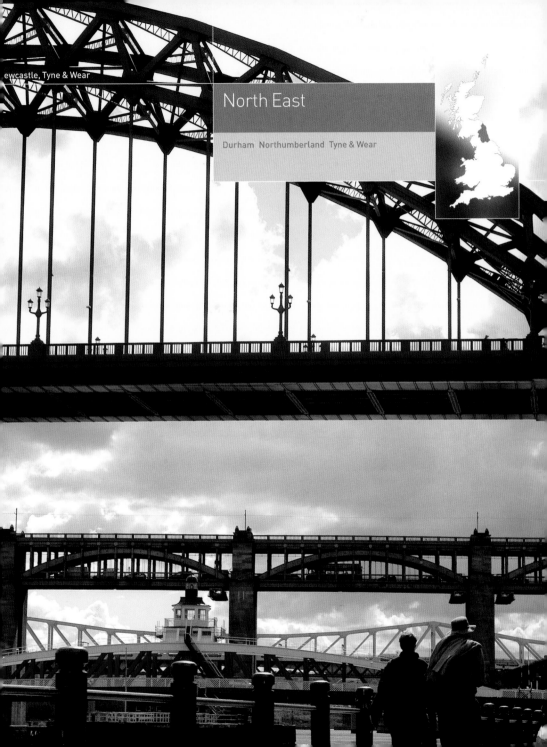

North East

Durham Northumberland Tyne & Wear

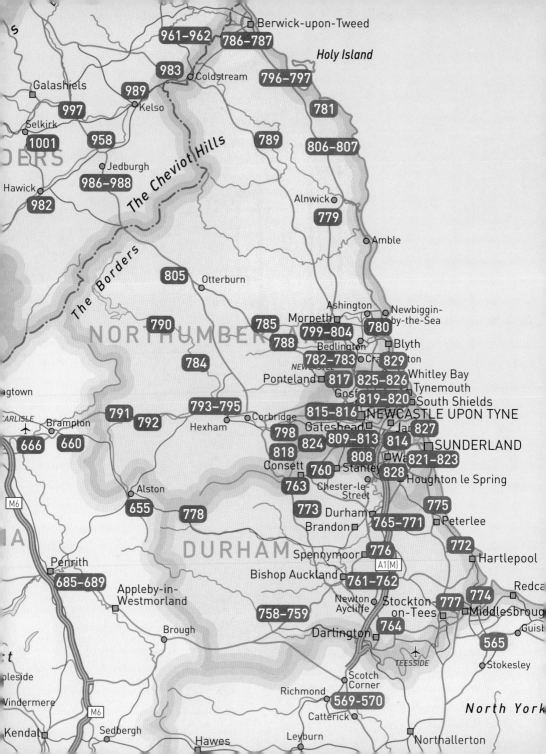

North East

Durham Northumberland Tyne & Wear

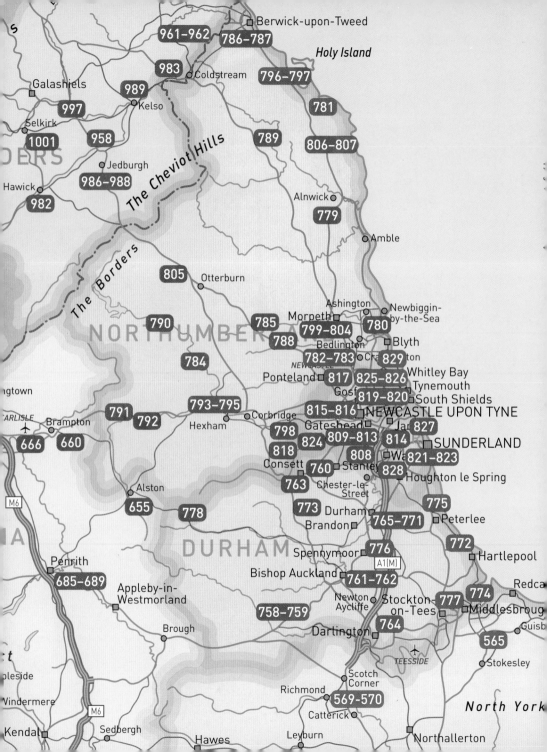

North East

Durham Northumberland Tyne & Wear

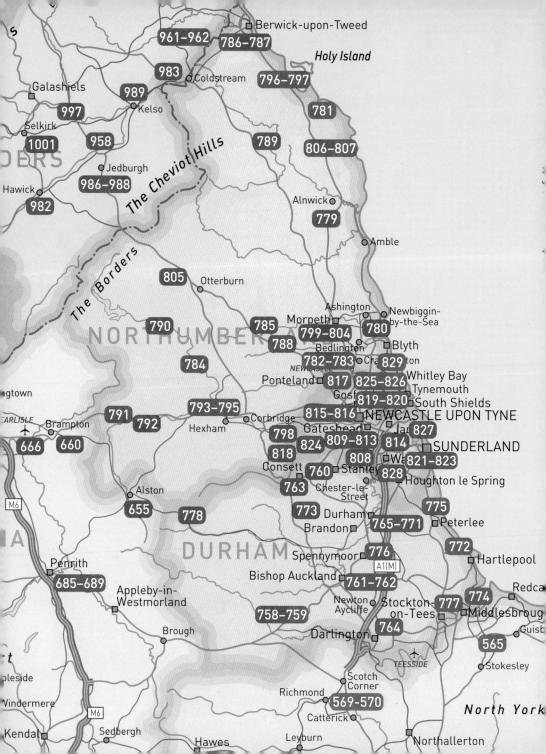

DURHAM

Animal Attractions
Hall Hill Farm   290

Boat & Train Trips
Prince Bishop River Cruiser   289

Historic Places
Barnard Castle   286
Durham Castle   289
Harperley POW Camp   287
Raby Castle   288

Museums & Exhibitions
Beamish, The North of England
 Open-Air Museum   286
Bowes Museum   286
The DLI Museum   288
Dorman Museum   291
Hartlepool's Maritime Experience   290
Killhope Lead Mining Museum   292
Old Fulling Museum of Archaeology   289

Parks, Gardens & Nature
Castle Eden Dene Nature Reserve   291
Crook Hall Gardens   288
Hamsterley Forest   287
Whitworth Hall Country Park   291

Sports & Leisure
Four Seasons White Water Rafting   291
Top Gear Indoor Karting   290

Theme Parks & Adventure Playgrounds
Diggerland   288
Mister Twisters, Consett   287

NORTHUMBERLAND

Historic Places
Alnwick Castle   292
Bamburgh Castle   293
Belsay Hall, Castle & Gardens   298
Carlisle Park   298
Cherryburn   296
Chillingham Castle   295
Cragside Estate   298
Housesteads Roman Fort,
 Hadrian's Wall   296
Lindisfarne Castle   297
Lindisfarne Priory   297
Vindolanda   297
Wallington Estate   295

Museums & Exhibitions
Berwick Barracks Museum
 & Art Gallery   294
Brigantium   300
Heritage Centre, Bellingham   293
Roman Army Museum   295
Seahouses Heritage Centre   300

Parks, Gardens & Nature
Bedlington Country Park   293
Bolam Lake Country Park   294
Cresswell Dunes   299
Druridge Bay Country Park   299
Farne Islands   300
Kielder Water Leaplish
 Waterside Park   295
Plessey Woods Country Park   293
Scotch Gill Woods Local Nature
 Reserve   299
South Tyne Trail   296
Tyne Riverside Country Park   298
Wansbeck Riverside Park   292

Sports & Leisure
Pot-a-Doodle-Do   294

TYNE & WEAR

Animal Attractions
Bill Quay Farm   301
Blue Reef Aquarium   307

Boat & Train Trips
Tanfield Railway   306

Historic Places
Arbeia Roman Fort   304
Segedunum Roman Fort, Baths
 & Museum   308
Souter Lighthouse   305
Tynemouth Priory & Castle   307

Museums & Exhibitions
BALTIC   301
Bede's World & St Paul's Church   302
Centre for Life   303
Discovery Museum   303
National Glass Centre   305
Shipley Art Gallery   302
Stephenson Railway Museum   303
Sunderland Museum
 & Winter Gardens   306

Parks, Gardens & Nature
Gibside   304
Saltwell Park   302
Wildfowl & Wetlands Trust
 Washington   308

Sports & Leisure
Whickham Thorns Outdoor
 Activity Centre   301
Whitley Bay Ice Rink   308

Theme Parks & Adventure Playgrounds
The New Metroland   301
Pier Amusements Centre   305

758 Barnard Castle

Barnard Castle

1 hr+   All year

Towering high above the River Tees, this C12 stone castle was once one of the largest in northern England, the principal residence of the Baliol family, and a major power base in the many conflicts between England and Scotland.

* Beautiful views of River Tees
* Home to Richard III & Henry VII

Location
In Barnard Castle town, off Galgate on A688

Opening
Daily: Apr–Sep 10am–6pm; Oct 10am–4pm; Nov–Mar Thu–Mon 10am–4pm

Admission
Adult £3.40, Child £1.70, Concs £2.60

Contact
Barnard Castle, County Durham DL12 8PR

t 01833 638212
w english-heritage.org.uk

759 Barnard Castle

Bowes Museum

3 hrs   All year

A French-style château housing one of Britain's finest museums. Collections in the museum include paintings, textiles, furniture and ceramics. There are beautiful gardens for visitors to wander through and fascinating exhibitions throughout the year.

* Set in 23 acres of parkland, with parterre garden
* Outstanding temporary art exhibition programme

Location
Just off A66, 20 min from Scotch Corner (A1)

Opening
Daily: 11am–5pm

Admission
Adult £7, Child free, Concs £6

Contact
Barnard Castle DL12 8NP

t 01833 690606
w thebowesmuseum.org.uk
e info@thebowesmuseum.org.uk

760 Beamish

Beamish, The North of England Open-Air Museum

4 hrs+   All year

Beamish is an extraordinary day out for the whole family. Touch, taste and experience the past at this living open-air museum, which vividly illustrates life in the Great North in the early C19 and early C20.

* Costumed guides explain each attraction
* Former European Museum of the Year

Location
Follow signs from junction 63 of A1(M)

Opening
Apr–Oct daily 10am–5pm; Nov–Mar Tue–Thu & Sat–Sun 10am–4pm

Admission
Adult £16, Child £10, Concs £12.50
Nov–Mar £6 per person

Contact
Beamish DH9 0RG

t 0191 370 4000
w beamish.org.uk
e museum@beamish.org.uk

761 Bishop Auckland

Hamsterley Forest

2–4 hrs   All year

Covering some 2,000 hectares, Hamsterley Forest has something for everyone – play and picnic areas, several walks, and cycle routes ranging from a 1½-mile easy-access footpath to a 7-mile black cycle route and downhill descent course for the more adventurous.

* Largest forest in County Durham

Location
From A68 at Witton-le-Wear follow brown tourist signs

Opening
Forest Daily: 7.30am–sunset
Visitor centre Apr–Oct Mon–Fri
10am–4pm, Sat–Sun 11am–5pm
Please phone for details of Nov–Mar

Admission
Free. Toll for forest drive & car park fee (£2 per car)

Contact
Redford, Bishop Auckland DL13 3NL

t 01388 488312
w forestry.gov.uk

762 Bishop Auckland

Harperley POW Camp

2 hrs+   All year

Harperley was one of the few purpose-built POW camps in Britain. It housed low-risk prisoners, first from Italy and then from Germany; at its height it held 1,500. In addition to the museum, there is a garden centre and a farm shop.

* Children's outdoor play area & 1940s house
* Featured in BBC programme *Restoration*

Location
Approximately 250m from junction of A68 & A689 near village of Crook

Opening
Daily: 10am–5pm

Admission
Free

Contact
Firtree, Crook,
County Durham DL15 8DX

t 01388 767098
w powcamp.com
e info@powcamp.com

763 Consett

Mister Twisters, Consett

1 hr+   All year

This exciting indoor play and party centre includes a multi-level soft play climbing frame, inflatable temple and spooky tomb. There is a separate under-fives play village with a baby crawling pit and activity room. There are also centres in Gateshead and Hartlepool.

* Large Visitor Attraction of the Year finalist in 2003

Location
From A1(M) take A691 to Consett. From Gateshead take A692 to Consett

Opening
Daily: Sun–Thu 9am–7pm,
Fri–Sat 9am–8pm

Admission
School hols Mon–Fri Child (1–3) £3.50,
Child (4–12) £4.45

Bank Hols & Sat–Sun £3.50, £3.95
(Additional adult 50p)

Contact
Unit 40, No. 1 Industrial Estate,
Medomsley Road,
Consett DH8 6TW

t 01207 500007
w mistertwisters.co.uk

764 Darlington

Raby Castle

3 hrs+   Easter–Sep

Raby Castle is a magnificent example of a medieval castle in Teesdale. It provides a wonderful day out for all the family, with stunning rooms to wonder at, walled gardens, a deer park and a children's adventure playground.

* Great kitchen little altered in 600 years
* Paintings by Reynolds & other Old Masters

Location
1 mile N of Staindrop on A688

Opening
Castle, Park & Gardens May–June & Sep 1pm–5pm; Jul–Aug Sun–Fri 1pm–5pm; Easter weekend & all other Bank Hols Sat–Mon 1pm–5pm; *Park & Garden* May–Sep & Bank Hols Sun–Fri 11am–5.30pm

Admission
Castle, Park & Gardens Adult £9, Child £4, Concs £8; *Park & Gardens* £4, £2.50, £3.50

Contact
PO Box 50, Staindrop, Darlington DL2 3AH

t 01833 660202
w rabycastle.com
e admin@rabycastle.com

765 Durham

Crook Hall Gardens

1 hr+   Easter–Sep

Crook Hall is a Grade I-listed medieval manor house. If you are scared of spooks, avoid the haunted Jacobean room, home to the ghost of the White Lady. Outside you can visit the moat pool, wildflower meadow and orchard or find your way out of the maze.

* Fruit trees wreathed in rambling roses
* 'A tapestry of colourful blooms', according to Alan Titchmarsh

Location
Short walk from Durham's Millburngate shopping centre, opposite Gala Theatre

Opening
Easter weekend 11am–5pm; May Sun & Bank Hol Mon 11am–5pm; 26 May–8 Sep Wed–Sun 11am–5pm; Halloween weekend 3pm–dusk; Dec please phone for details

Admission
Adult £4.50, Concs £4

Contact
Frankland Lane, Sidegate, Durham DH1 5SZ

t 0191 384 8028
w crookhallgardens.co.uk
e info@kbacrookhall.co.uk

766 Durham

Diggerland

4 hrs   Feb–Nov

Based on the world of construction machinery, this is a unique adventure park where children and adults can experience the thrill of riding and driving real JCBs and dumpers in safety.

* Educational day out with a difference

Location
Exit A1(M) at junction 62. Head W, signed to Consett. After 6 miles turn left at roundabout, signed to Langley Park, then turn right into Riverside Industrial Estate

Opening
Feb–Nov weekends, Bank Hols & school hols 10am–5pm

Admission
Adult/Child £12.50 all inclusive, under-3s Free

Contact
Langley Park DA7 9TT

t 08700 344437
w diggerland.com

767 Durham

The DLI Museum

2 hrs+   All year

Enter the world of County Durham Light Infantry soldiers and their families. Dramatic and interactive displays and a set walk let you see for yourself what their lives were like. Our art gallery runs a programme of exhibitions related to all aspects of visual art.

* Dress up as a soldier
* Hands-on experience of exhibits

Location
½ mile NW of Durham city centre, off A691, near railway station

Opening
Daily: Apr–Oct 10am–5pm; Nov–Mar 10am–4pm

Admission
Adult £3, Child £1.25, Concs £2

Contact
Aykley Heads, Durham DH1 5TU

t 0191 384 2214
w durham.gov.uk/dli
e dli@durham.gov.uk

Durham Castle

1 hr   Mar–Sep

Built by William the Conqueror in 1072 as a fortress, the castle has been in constant use for more than 900 years and is one of the largest Norman castles in England. It was also once a bishop's palace and today it is a residential college for the University of Durham.

* World Heritage Site
* Entrance by guided tour only

WC

Location
In city centre. Uphill walk or No. 40 bus to Palace Green

Opening
Daily: mid-Mar–mid-Apr & Jul–Sep 10am–12.30pm & 2pm–4.30pm. Other times usually Mon, Wed, Sat–Sun afternoons but please phone to confirm

Admission
Adult £5, Child & Concs £3.50

Contact
Durham DH1 3RW

t 0191 334 3800
w durhamcastle.com
e university-college.www@durham.ac.uk

Old Fulling Museum of Archaeology

1 hr   All year

This old mill has become one of the most photographed buildings in the North East. It now houses the Museum of Archaeology, among whose striking exhibits is a major collection of Roman inscriptions from the north of England and an outstanding collection of Samianware.

* Artefacts from ancient Greece & Rome
* Medieval finds from Durham city centre

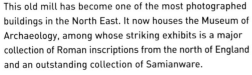

Location
Between Cathedral and Castle in city centre

Opening
Apr–Oct 11am–4pm;
Nov–Mar Fri–Mon 11.30am–3.30pm

Admission
Adult £1, Child & Concs 50p

Contact
The Banks, Durham DH1 3EB

t 0191 334 1823
e fulling.mill@dur.ac.uk
w dur.ac.uk/fulling.mill

Prince Bishop River Cruiser

1 hr   All year

The *Prince Bishop* river cruiser sails on the River Wear. It offers the best views of Durham Cathedral, Durham Castle and the bridges. The trip includes a commentary that will suit children of all ages. There is wheelchair access to the upper deck and saloons.

* Sun deck & onboard barbecue
* 1-hour Santa cruises in Dec

Location
Cruiser is found below Prince Bishop shopping centre in Durham

Opening
Please phone for details

Admission
Adult £4.50, Child £2, Concs £4

Contact
The Boathouse, Elvet Bridge, Durham DH1 3AH

t 0191 386 9525

771 Durham

Top Gear Indoor Karting

2 hrs+   All year

Top Gear is a go-karting leisure centre. It provides indoor go-karting fun for everyone from 8 to 88 (minimum height requirement 1.4 metres) and is a great place for family birthdays.

* New go-karts recently arrived
* Regular race meetings

Location	Admission
From A1(M) take A690 towards Durham & follow brown tourist signs	£20 per person for 30 laps
	£25 per person for 40 laps
Opening	Contact
Daily: Mon–Fri 12noon–9pm	13 Renny's Lane,
Sat–Sun 9am–7pm	Gilesgate Moor DH1 2RS
	t 0191 386 0999
	w durhamkarting.co.uk
	e durhamkarting@lineone.net

772 Hartlepool

Hartlepool's Maritime Experience

2–4 hrs   All year

Built in Bombay in 1816–17 for the princely sum of £23,000, HMS *Trincomalee* is the oldest ship afloat in the UK. Today you can experience what life was like on board. Visit the captain's cabin, the bread room, the sleeping quarters, the quarter deck, and even the toilets.

* Excellent disabled access to most decks
* Experience a sea battle with our powder monkey Jim Henshaw

Location	Contact
Follow signs for Hartlepool Historic Quay	Hartlepool's Maritime Experience, Jackson Dock, Hartlepool TS24 0XZ
Opening	t 01429 860077
Daily: 10am–5pm	w hartlepoolmaritimeexperience.com
Admission	e info@hartlepoolmaritimeexperience.com
Adult £7, Child £4.25, Concs £5.50	

773 Lanchester

Hall Hill Farm

2 hrs   Mar–Dec

There is a wide range of friendly animals to meet face to face including fluffy chicks, baby lambs, pigs, donkeys, ponies and rabbits. Then there are more unusual animals such as llamas, wallabies and Highland cattle. Tractor rides take you around this working farm.

* Fantastic views of Durham countryside
* Children's playground & gift shop

Location	Admission
10 miles W of Durham off B6296, S of Lanchester	Adult £4.40, Child £3.30, Concs £3.90
Opening	Contact
Mar–Aug daily 10.30am–5pm;	Lanchester, Durham DH7 0TA
Sep–Oct Sat–Sun 10.30am–5pm;	t 01388 731333
Dec Sat–Sun 10.30am–5pm	w hallhillfarm.co.uk
	e info@hallhillfarm.co.uk

774 Middlesbrough

Dorman Museum

1 hr   All year

After a three-year programme of major alterations, the Dorman Museum re-opened in 2003 with a diverse range of galleries and exhibitions. The museum, first opened in 1904, now houses hands-on science sections such as H_2O and Earth in Space as well as local history displays.

* Learn the story of Linthorpe Pottery
* Constantly changing art exhibitions

Location
In centre of Middlesbrough, at junction of Ayresome Street & Linthorpe Road

Opening
Apr–Oct Tue–Sun 10am–5.30pm;
Nov–Mar Tue–Sun 9am–4.30pm

Admission
Free

Contact
Linthorpe Road, Middlesbrough
TS5 6LA

t 01642 813781
w dormanmuseum.co.uk
e dormanmuseum@middlesbrough.gov.uk

775 Peterlee

Castle Eden Dene Nature Reserve

1 hr+   All year

This wooded ravine, cut deep into limestone, is the largest area of semi-natural woodland in north-east England, renowned for its yew trees. The tangled landscape is home to many different birds and red squirrels may also be seen. Access is by marked paths only.

* 12 miles of footpaths within its 500 acres
* More than 450 species of plants recorded in wood

Location
On A19, follow signs

Opening
Daily: dawn–dusk

Admission
Free

Contact
Oakerside Dene Lodge,
Stanhope Chase, Peterlee,
County Durham SR8 1NJ

t 0191 586 0004
w englishnature.org.uk

776 Spennymoor

Whitworth Hall Country Park

3 hrs   All year

Feed the red and fallow deer in this 73-acre historic parkland. There is an ornamental lake, a Victorian walled garden, a woodland garden and indoor and outdoor play facilities for children. Special events are arranged throughout the year.

* Feed the ducks
* Charity fun days & car shows

Location
7 miles W of Durham & A1.
At A1 junction 61 join A688 signed for Spennymoor. Continue following signs for Whitworth Hall Hotel

Opening
Daily: 12noon–dusk

Admission
Free

Contact
nr Spennymoor DL16 7QX

t 01388 811772
w whitworthhall.co.uk

777 Stockton-on-Tees

Four Seasons White Water Rafting

2 hrs   All year

A nationally recognised centre for canoeing, kayaking and white-water rafting. The tidal River Tees guarantees white water all year, with fast-flowing rapids carrying you down the course on an exhilarating and adrenaline-fuelled trip. Equipment can be hired.

* Customisable difficulty for beginners & experts
* Training for all levels

Location
On N bank of River Tees near Tees Barrage Bridge, Stockton-on-Tees

Opening
All year – booking advised
Please phone for details

Admission
From £15 according to activities

Contact
Tees Barrage, Stockton-on-Tees
TS18 2QW

t 01642 678000
w 4seasons.co.uk
e kanu@4seasons.co.uk

778 Upper Weardale

Killhope Lead Mining Museum

4 hrs   Easter–Oct

Wearing hard hat, cap-lamp and wellies, you are guided down the original tunnel of a lead mine to find out about the lives of the miners who toiled here. There is a woodland walk, too.

* Warm clothes required even during summer
* Winner of Family Friendly Museum Award 2004

Location
Off A689 between Stanhope & Alston

Opening
Daily: Easter–Oct 10.30am–5pm

Admission
Adult £6, Child £3, Concs £5.50
No under-4s allowed in mine

Contact
The North of England Lead Mining Museum, nr Cowshill, Upper Weardale DL13 1AR

t 01388 537505
w durham.gov.uk/killhope
e killhope@durham.gov.uk

779 Alnwick

Alnwick Castle

3 hrs+   Apr–Oct

This foreboding medieval castle, known as the Windsor of the North, has stunning state rooms, a glorious garden, fine furniture and paintings by Canaletto, Van Dyck and Titian. Home to the Percy family for 700 years, it has even been a *Harry Potter* film location.

* Knight school & superb gift shop
* Museum of Royal Northumberland Fusiliers

Location
Alnwick, 35 miles N of Newcastle upon Tyne, 1 mile from A1

Opening
Daily: Apr–Oct 10am–6pm

Admission
Adult £8.50, Child £3.50, Concs £7.50
Family ticket (2 Adult & up to 4 Child)
£22

Contact
Alnwick NE66 1NQ

t 01665 510777
w alnwickcastle.com
e enquiries@alnwickcastle.com

780 Ashington

Wansbeck Riverside Park

2–5 hrs   All year

An award-winning country park with a delightful camping and caravan site, plus a wide range of activities on hand, many of which are on the water. There is a play area, a paddle pool and an island nature reserve.

* Caravan park & cafeteria
* 4-mile riverside walk

Location
Take A1068. Park is located between Ashington & Bedlington

Opening
Daily: 8am–dusk

Admission
Free

Contact
Green Lane,
Ashington NE63 8TX

t 01670 843444
w wansbeck.gov.uk
e i.graham@wansbeck.gov.uk

781 Bamburgh

amburgh Castle

2 hrs   Mar–Oct

his magnificent coastal castle contains collections of urniture, paintings, arms and armour. The rocky outcrop ecame a royal centre in AD547. The present fortress has museum room, grand King's Hall, Cross Hall, armoury nd a Victorian scullery for children to explore.

Still home to the Armstrong family
Exhibits include fine furniture & tapestries

Location
20 miles S of Berwick-upon-Tweed by B1342

Opening
Daily: mid-Mar–Oct 11am–4.30pm

Admission
Adult £6, Child £2.50, Concs £5

Contact
Bamburgh NE69 7DF

t 01668 214515
w bamburghcastle.com
e bamburghcastle@aol.com

782 Bedlington

Bedlington Country Park

3 hrs   All year

This country park covers 5 miles of horse and nature trails and woodland walks on the banks of the River Blythe. It is teeming with wildlife such as otters, kingfishers, woodpeckers and red squirrels, as well as native trees, shrubs and rare flora.

* Unique wild orchid only found growing here

Location
Between A189 & A1068, S of Bedlington

Opening
Daily: dawn–dusk

Admission
Free

Contact
Wansbeck District Council, Council Offices, Front Street, Bedlington NE22 5TU

t 01670 843444
w wansbeck.gov.uk
e i.graham@wansbeck.gov.uk

783 Bedlington

Plessey Woods Country Park

2 hrs+   All year

his country park is set in 100 acres of woodland, meadow and riverside, with a good network of paths nd bridleways linking with the surrounding area.

Children's play area
Visitor centre with displays

Location
On A192, just off A1068 & close to A1

Opening
Parkland Daily: All reasonable times
Car park Daily: dawn–dusk

Admission
Car park £1.20, All day £2.40

Contact
nr Bedlington NE22 6AN

t 01670 824793
w northumberland.gov.uk
e plesseywoods@northumberland.gov.uk

784 Bellingham

Heritage Centre, Bellingham

2 hrs   Apr–Oct

This small folk museum situated in the old railway station yard houses photographs, artefacts and memorabilia recording the life and times of the people of the North Tyne Valley and Redewater Valley.

* The Border Counties Railway
* Special attractions for children

Location
Follow B6320 from Hexham to Bellingham (17 miles). Heritage Centre is in Woodburn Road, in Station Yard opposite Hillside Estate

Opening
Easter–Oct Fri–Mon 10.30am–4.30pm
Please phone for details

Admission
Adult £2, Child (5–16) & Concs £1

Contact
Station Yard, Woodburn Road, Bellingham, Hexham NE48 2DF

t 01434 220050
w bellingham-heritage.org.uk
e info@bellingham-heritage.org.uk

785 Belsay

Bolam Lake Country Park

2–4 hrs   All year

Bolam Lake Country Park has everything for a fun family day out in the countryside. There is a lake surrounded by beautiful woodland and meadows with paths and picnic areas. It is ideal for bird-watching.

* Lakeside walk made by local architect John Dobson

Location	Admission
Signed from A696 at Belsay & B6524 at Whalton	Free. Car park up to 1 hr £1.20, over 1 hr £2.40
Opening	**Contact**
Park Daily: All reasonable times	nr Belsay NE20 0HE
Car park Daily: dawn–dusk	t 01661 881234
Café Weekends, Bank Hols & school hols	
Please phone for details	

786 Berwick-upon-Tweed

Berwick Barracks Museum & Art Gallery

1hr+   All year

The barracks are home to a number of attractions, including 'By Beat of Drum', showing what life was like for British infantry soldiers until Queen Victoria's reign. The regimental museum tells the history of the King's Own Scottish Borderers.

* One of the first purpose-built barracks
* Walk on ramparts affords great views of River Tweed

Location	Contact
Off Church Street in town centre	The Parade, Berwick-upon-Tweed PD15 1DF
Opening	
Daily: Easter–Sep 10am–5pm;	t 01289 304493
Oct 10am–4pm;	w english-heritage.org.uk
Nov–Mar please phone for details	
Admission	
Adult £3.30, Child £1.70, Concs £2.50	

787 Berwick-upon-Tweed

Pot-a-Doodle-Do

2 hrs   Feb–Dec

An oasis of creativity for all – there is a wide range of art and craft activities to try, as well as a large children's play area, quad-bike trekking, fishing and country walks. Friendly staff are on hand to help make sure your day is the best it can be.

* Wooden wigwam village accommodation
* Mosaicmaking – part of national curriculum in history

Location	Contact
On A1, S of Berwick-upon-Tweed	Borewell Farm, Scremerston, Berwick-upon-Tweed TD15 2RJ
Opening	
Daily: Easter–Oct 10am–5pm;	t 01289 307107
31 Oct–Easter Wed–Sun 10am–4pm	w potadoodledo.com
(closed Jan)	e info@potadoodledo.com
Admission	
Free. Pay-as-you-go activities	

788 Cambo

Wallington Estate

2–4 hrs   All year

The impressive grounds surrounding the historic house of Wallington have plenty of walks, covering formal gardens, woodland and high moorland, plus an adventure playground.

* Redecorated & refurbished in 2004
* Fine collection of doll's houses

Location
12 miles W of Morpeth & 6 miles NW of Belsay

Opening
House 1 Apr–5 Sep Wed–Mon 1pm–5.30pm; Oct 1pm–4.30pm
Grounds Daily: Apr–Sep 10am–7pm; Oct 10am–6pm; Nov–Mar 10am–4pm

Admission
House & Grounds Adult £8, Child £4, Family ticket £20
Grounds only £6.80, £2.75

Contact
Cambo, Morpeth NE61 4AR
t 01670 773600
w nationaltrust.org.uk
e wallington@nationaltrust.org.uk

789 Chillingham

Chillingham Castle

1 hr+   May–Sep

This medieval fortress has Tudor additions, a torture chamber and dungeon, and a woodland walk. It also glories in beautifully furnished rooms and an Italian topiary garden with herbaceous borders.

* Beautiful grounds with commanding views
* Formal gardens & woodland walks open to public

Location
Signed from A1 & A697

Opening
May–Sep Sun–Fri 12noon–5pm;
Oct–Apr by appointment

Admission
Adult £6.75, Child (under 5) £1, Child (over 5) £3, Concs £5.50

Contact
Chillingham NE66 5NJ
t 01668 215359
w chillingham-castle.com
e enquiries@chillingham-castle.com

790 Falstone

Kielder Water Leaplish Waterside Park

6 hrs+   All year

Situated in the North Tyne Valley, this waterside park is surrounded by breathtaking scenery and has a 27-mile shoreline. There are facilities and activities to suit all ages.

* Luxury Scandinavian-style holiday lodges
* Adventure playground

Location
8 miles from Scottish border, 12 miles N of Bellingham at middle of Kielder Reservoir; 45 min N of Hexham

Opening
Daily: some facilities are seasonal
Please phone for details

Admission
Activities priced individually

Contact
Leaplish Waterside Park, Falstone, Hexham NE48 1BT
t 0870 2403549
w nwl.co.uk/kielder
e kielder.holidays@nwl

791 Greenhead

Roman Army Museum

2 hrs   Feb–Nov

Ever wanted to be a Roman soldier? Here you can watch the recruiting film, fill in the join-up sheet and join the Roman army for a day. Learn about weapons, uniforms, pay, training and what soldiers did in their free time.

* Superb eagle's-eye film & virtual tour of Hadrian's Wall
* Fascinating display of Roman military objects

Location
Off B6318, nr Greenhead, 3 miles from Haltwhistle. Follow heritage signs for Hadrian's Wall & Roman Museum

Opening
Daily: Feb–Mar 10am–5pm; Apr–Sep 10am–6pm; Oct–Nov 10am–5pm

Admission
Adult £3.95, Child £2.50, Concs £3.50

Contact
Greenhead CA8 7JB
t 01697 747485
w vindolanda.com
e info@vindolanda.com

792 Haltwhistle

South Tyne Trail

3 hrs+   All year

This former railway line is open to walkers of all ages, and for much of its length to cyclists and horse-riders. The trail has excellent views of the South Tyne Valley and it includes the spectacular Lambley Viaduct.

* Interpretation displays near Coanwood
* Self-guided trail

Location	**Admission**
Runs for 13 miles between Haltwhistle	Free
& Alston parallel to A689. Best access	
from Haltwhistle, Alston & car parks	**Contact**
at Featherstone Park & Coanwood (for	The Railway Station, Station Road,
Lambley Viaduct)	Haltwhistle NE49 0AH
Opening	t 01434 322002
Daily: All reasonable times	

794 Hexham

Housesteads Roman Fort, Hadrian's Wall

1 hr+   All year

Children will be fascinated to encounter life as it was on Rome's northernmost frontier at Housesteads – a jewel in the crown of Hadrian's Wall and the most complete Roman fort still standing in Britain. There is also an indoor museum to explore.

* Best-preserved of 16 forts along the Wall
* Dramatic countryside

Location	**Contact**
Take B6318, 2¾ miles NE of	Hexham NE47 6NN
Bardon Mill	
	t 01434 344363
Opening	w nationaltrust.org.uk
Daily: Apr–Sep 10am–6pm;	english-heritage.org.uk
Oct–Mar 10am–4pm	e housesteads@english-heritage.
	org.uk
Admission	
Adult £3.80, Child (5–16) £1.90,	
Concs £2.90, Family ticket £9.50	

793 Hexham

Cherryburn

1 hr   Mar–Oct

This delightful cottage, with farmyard, garden and play lawn, was once home to the artist, engraver and naturalist Thomas Bewick. Visitors can enjoy an exhibition of his work and see demonstrations of wood engraving and handprinting from woodblocks.

* Occasional demonstrations of printing
* 'Folk in the Farmyard' every Sun afternoon

Location	**Contact**
Take A695 to Mickley Square & follow	Station Bank, Mickley,
signs, 11 miles from Hexham	nr Stocksfield NE43 7DD
Opening	t 01661 843276
18 Mar–29 Oct Thu–Tue 11am–5pm	w nationaltrust.org.uk
(last admission 4.30pm)	e cherryburn@nationaltrust.org.uk
Admission	
Adult £3.75, Child £1.75	

795 Hexham

Vindolanda

2½ hrs   Feb–Nov

A fascinating Roman fort and settlement lying just to the south of Hadrian's Wall. On the site itself stands a full-size replica of a section of Hadrian's Wall in both stone and timber, giving the visitor a true idea of the impressive might of the monument.

* Ongoing excavations Apr–Aug 2007
* Rare & fascinating personal documents to be read

Location
Take A69 & B6318 near Bardon Mill, then follow signs

Opening
Apr–Sep 10am–6pm;
Feb–Mar & Oct–Nov 10am–5pm

Admission
Adult £4.95, Child £3, Concs £4.10

Contact
Chesterholm Museum, Bardon Mill, Hexham, Northumberland NE47 7JN

t 01434 344277
w vindolanda.com
e info@vindolanda.com

796 Holy Island–Lindisfarne

Lindisfarne Castle

½ hr   Feb–Oct

Imposing atop a rocky crag and accessible only across a causeway at low tide, Lindisfarne Castle, originally a Tudor fort, was converted into a private house in 1903 by the young Edwin Lutyens. The small rooms are full of intimate decoration and design.

* Charming walled garden planned by Gertrude Jekyll
* Check crossing times before making a long journey

Location
Holy Island, 6 miles E of A1, across causeway

Opening
Daily: mid-Feb–end Feb (please phone for details); mid-Mar–Oct Tue–Sun
Times vary depending on tides, usually 10.30am–3pm or 12noon–4pm

Admission
Adult £5.20, Child £2.60, Family ticket £13

Contact
Holy Island, Berwick-upon-Tweed TD15 2SH

t 01289 389244
w nationaltrust.org.uk
e lindisfarne@nationaltrust.org.uk

797 Holy Island–Lindisfarne

Lindisfarne Priory

1 hr+   All year

Lindisfarne was founded in the C7 by St Aidan, razed by the Vikings in AD 793, rebuilt in the C12 and destroyed again in the C16 by Henry VIII, who used the stones to build Lindisfarne Castle. The priory is reached by a causeway accessible only at low tide so check tide times.

* Anglo-Saxon carvings in museum
* Refurbished museum

Location
Holy Island, 6 miles E of A1, across causeway

Opening
Daily: Apr–Sep 9.30am–5pm; Oct 9.30am–4pm; Nov–Jan Sat–Mon 10am–2pm; Feb–Mar 10am–4pm
Times vary depending on tides

Admission
Adult £3.70, Child £1.90, Concs £2.80

Contact
Holy Island, Berwick-upon-Tweed TD15 2RX

t 01289 389200
w english-heritage.org.uk

798 Low Prudhoe

Tyne Riverside Country Park

2–4 hrs   All year

This delightful country park includes a riverside walk that links through to Newcastle upon Tyne. It can also offer canoeing access to the river, and there are orienteering courses and several prime picnic locations.

* Off-road cycle route
* Children's play area

Location
On A695, just off A69

Opening
Daily: All reasonable times (car park dawn–dusk)

Admission
Free. Car park fee

Contact
Station Road,
Low Prudhoe NE42 6NP

t 01661 834135
w northumberland.gov.uk
e tyneriverside@northumberland.
  gov.uk

799 Morpeth

Belsay Hall, Castle & Gardens

3 hrs   All year

This wonderful estate has a C14 castle, C17 manor house and C19 neoclassical hall set in 30 acres of landscaped gardens and grounds. Explore the quarry gardens with a microclimate where rhododendrons are found in bloom even in the middle of winter.

* 2 acres of rhododendrons at their best May–Jun
* Formal terraces & winter garden, original planting

Location
In Belsay, 14 miles NW of Newcastle upon Tyne on A696

Opening
Apr–Oct daily 10am–5pm;
Nov–Mar Thu–Mon 10am–4pm

Admission
Adult £5.50, Child £2.80, Concs £4.10

Contact
Belsay NE20 0DX

t 01661 881636
w english-heritage.org.uk

800 Morpeth

Carlisle Park

1–3 hrs   All year

Situated on the riverside in Morpeth, Carlisle Park's attractions include woodland and riverside walks, a castle, the William Turner Herb Garden, an aviary, tennis courts, bowling greens, a play area, an ancient woodland walk, a C12 castle and an C11 motte.

* Green Flag award & Quality Assured Visitor Attraction
* Tennis, paddling pool, picnic areas & beautiful gardens

Location
Follow signs to Morpeth town centre.
Carlisle Park is within walking distance of many car parks, as well as bus station & railway station

Opening
Daily: All reasonable times
Turner Garden Daily: 7.30am–dusk
Sporting facilities Apr–Oct 10am–9pm

Admission
Free

Contact
Castle Morpeth Borough Council,
Coopies Lane Depot, Coopies Lane
Industrial Estate, Morpeth NE61 6JT

t 01670 500777
w castlemorpeth.gov.uk
e firstcall@castlemorpeth.gov.uk

801 Morpeth

Cragside Estate

3 hrs+   Apr–Dec

Described as the palace of a modern magician, Cragside was at the cutting edge of technology when built in the 1880s. It had hot and cold running water, central heating, telephones, a passenger lift, a Turkish bath suite and was lit by hydroelectricity.

* Famous handmade rock garden
* Tallest Douglas fir in England

Location
1 mile N of Rothbury on B6341

Opening
Estate Apr–Oct Tue–Sun & Bank Hol
Mon 10.30am–7pm (last admission
5pm); Nov–16 Dec 11am–4pm (last
admission 3pm)

Admission
Please phone for details

Contact
Rothbury, Morpeth NE65 7PX

t 01669 620333
w nationaltrust.org.uk
e cragside@nationaltrust.org.uk

302 Morpeth

Cresswell Dunes

1 hr+   All year

This site is in the southern section of Druridge Bay, a 5-mile sandy beach with nationally important wildlife and beautiful dunes. Close by are the delights of Cresswell village and the bird-watching hide at Cresswell Pond.

Go rockpooling
Expert guides available

Location
Follow signs to Cresswell from A1068 Ashington–Amble road, then take unnamed road leading N out of Cresswell

Opening
Daily: All reasonable times

Admission
Free

Contact
Castle Morpeth Borough Council, Coopies Lane, Morpeth NE61 6JT

t 01670 535000
e sam.talbot@castlemorpeth.gov.uk

---

803 Morpeth

Druridge Bay Country Park

2–4 hrs   All year

At Druridge Bay you can enjoy lakeside walks and 5 miles of beautiful beach. Visitors can also windsurf and use non-motorised boats (by permit, available from the information centre or ticket machine).

* Different events throughout the year
* Annual kite festival

Location
Off A1068

Opening
Park Daily: All reasonable times (car park dawn–dusk)
Café & visitor centre Sat–Sun, Bank Hols & local school hols
Please phone for details

Admission
Free. Car park up to 2 hrs £1.20, all day £2.40

Contact
Hadston, Morpeth NE61 5BQ

t 01670 760968
w northumberland.gov.uk

---

804 Morpeth

Scotch Gill Woods
Local Nature Reserve

1–3 hrs   All year

Otters and dippers can be seen in the River Wansbeck, which runs along Scotch Gill Woods. Red squirrels are present here, as well as at the adjacent nature reserves of Bracken Bank and Davies Wood (accessible from the same car park).

* Always wear appropriate clothing & footwear

Location
Follow B6343 from Morpeth for ½ mile, then turn right into car park at 1st bridge over river

Opening
Daily: All reasonable times

Admission
Free

Contact
Castle Morpeth Borough Council, Coopies Lane, Morpeth NE61 6JT

t 01670 535319
w castlemorpeth.gov.uk
e sam.talbot@castlemorpeth.gov.uk

805 Rochester

Brigantium

1 hr   Easter–Oct

This archaeological reconstruction centre has plenty to stimulate the young historian. Wander round the Roman British farm, round house, willow maze, Mesolithic hunting camp, Roman defences and road, and marvel at the Bronze Age burial site and stone circle.

* Display & video room
* Dowsing displays

Location
On A68 from Jedburgh or Corbridge or A696 from Newcastle upon Tyne

Opening
Daily: Easter–Oct 10.30am–4.30pm
Special visits & guided tours can be booked in advance

Admission
Adult £2.50, Child & Concs £1.50

Contact
Rochester Café,
Rochester NE19 1RH

t 01830 520801

806 Seahouses

Farne Islands

2¹/₂ hrs   Varies

Take the family on a boat trip to the Farne Islands. They house a bird reserve hosting around 70,000 pairs of breeding birds, from 21 species. Puffins can be seen in season, and the islands are also home to a large colony of grey seals throughout the year.

* Most famous seabird sanctuary in Britain
* Views of Bamburgh Castle

WC

Location
Islands are 2–3 miles off N Northumberland coast. Take B1340, then a boat from Seahouses harbour

Opening
Please phone for details

Admission
May–Jul Adult £5.20, Child £2.60
All other times £4.20, £2.10

Contact
The Sheiling, 8 St Adams,
Seahouses NE68 7SR

t 01665 721099
w nationaltrust.org.uk

807 Seahouses

Seahouses Heritage Centre

2–3 hrs   Feb–Oct

The museum and aquarium include a touch pool for crabs and other sealife and an exhibition with audio-visual conversations between fishing families. Visitors can also enjoy virtual-reality displays in our cinema.

* 50,000-litre trout pond
* Reconstructed fisherman's house

Location
Off B1340 on the coast

Opening
Daily: 28 Feb–31 Oct 10.30am–5pm

Admission
Adult £3, Child £2.50

Contact
8–10 Main Street,
Seahouses NE68 7RG

t 01665 721257
w marinelifecentre.co.uk

808 Dunston

Whickham Thorns Outdoor Activity Centre

  1 hr+ All year

This activity centre offers plenty of excitement, including an assault course, a climbing wall, cycle hire, a ski slope, archery and orienteering. There is also a snowboarding club.

* High-ropes aerial assault course
* First boulder park in the North East

Location
Off A1 on opposite side of motorway from MetroCentre

Opening
Apr–Sep daily: Mon–Fri 9am–8pm, Sat 11am–6pm, Sun 12noon–3pm;
Oct–Mar please phone for details
Closed Bank Hols

Admission
Free. Please phone for activity prices

Contact
Market Lane, Dunston,
Gateshead NE11 9NX

t 0191 433 5767
w gateshead.gov.uk

809 Gateshead

BALTIC

  1 hr+ All year

Housed in a 1950s grain warehouse, this contemporary art centre has five galleries, artists' studios, a cinema/lecture space, a media lab, a library, an archive for the study of contemporary art and a tempting shop.

* Constantly changing programme of exhibitions
* Displays of work by artists in residence

Location
Gateshead Quayside, 10 min walk from town centre

Opening
Times vary, please phone or visit the website for details

Admission
Free

Contact
Gateshead Quays, South Shore Road,
Gateshead NE8 3BA

t 0191 478 1810
w balticmill.com
e info@balticmill.com

810 Gateshead

Bill Quay Farm

  2 hrs All year

Bring your children to this lovely urban farm to enjoy spectacular views of the River Tyne and to meet farmyard breeds, both traditional and unusual. The farm includes a green retreat for wildlife.

* Family picnic area

Location
Take A185 from Heworth interchange, turn left down Station Road (1¼ miles from Heworth) & take 1st left at crossroads

Opening
Daily: 12noon–5pm
Some buildings have restricted access, please phone for details

Admission
Free

Contact
Hainingwood Terrace,
Bill Quay,
Gateshead NE10 0UE

t 0191 433 5780
e billquayfarm@gateshead.gov.uk

811 Gateshead

The New Metroland

 3 hrs+ All year

Among the many children's attractions here are a roller-coaster, a pirate ship, swinging chairs, dodgem cars, a children's railway, a ferris wheel, aeroplanes, helicopters, slides and climbing nets.

* Europe's largest indoor funfair
* Mr B's Amusement Arcade

Location
Take A1(M) to Gateshead MetroCentre

Opening
Term time Mon–Fri from 12noon–8pm,
Sat 10am–8pm, Sun 11am–6pm;
in school hols Mon–Sat 10am–8pm,
Sun 11am–6pm

Admission
Please phone for details

Contact
39 Garden Walk, MetroCentre,
Gateshead NE11 9XY

t 0191 493 2048
w metroland.uk.com

812 Gateshead

Saltwell Park

1-3 hrs   All year

At Saltwell Park you can enjoy bedding displays, a rose garden, a wooded den, a children's play area and a boating lake. There are brass bands at the bandstand and bowls during the summer.

* Original & Victorian public garden
* Saltwell Tower – a Gothic mansion

Location
Off A184 or A692 S of Newcastle upon Tyne

Opening
Daily: 7.30am–dusk

Admission
Free

Contact
East Park Road,
Gateshead NE8 5AX

t 0191 433 5900
w gateshead.gov.uk
e saltwellpark@gateshead.gov.uk

813 Gateshead

Shipley Art Gallery

2 hrs   All year

Shipley Art Gallery is home to a collection of more than 700 pieces by the country's leading craftspeople. It includes studio ceramics, glass, metalwork, jewellery, textiles and furniture. The exhibition Made in Gateshead tells the fascinating history of the town.

* Art Kart with materials, puzzles, jigsaws & activity
sheets for all ages

Location
Off A167. Nearest Metro station is Gateshead. Limited free street parking outside gallery

Opening
Daily: Mon–Sat 10am–5pm, Sun 2pm–5pm;

Admission
Free

Contact
Prince Consort Road,
Gateshead NE8 4JB

t 0191 477 1495
w twmuseums.org.uk/shipley

814 Jarrow

Bede's World & St Paul's Church

3 hrs   All year

Discover what life was like for St Bede, who established a monastery and church here in the C7. During the summer enjoy a range of children's activities, including tours of an Anglo-Saxon demonstration farm, storytelling, tilemaking, archery and breadmaking.

* Herb garden based on Anglo-Saxon & medieval plants
* Anglo-Saxon demo farm, complete with animals

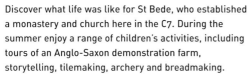

Location
Near S end of Tyne Tunnel, off A185

Opening
Apr–Oct Mon–Sat 10am–5.30pm,
Sun 12noon–5.30pm;
Nov–Mar Mon–Sat 10am–4.30pm,
Sun 12noon–4.30pm;
Church closed during services

Admission
Adult £4.50, Child & Concs £3

Contact
Church Bank NE32 3DY

t 0191 489 2106
w bedesworld.co.uk
e visitorinfo@bedesworld.co.uk

815 Newcastle upon Tyne

Centre for Life

3 hrs+   All year

There's always something new at the Life Science Centre. Meet your 4-billion-year-old family, explore what makes us all different, test your brainpower and enjoy the thrill of the Crazy Motion ride.

* Mars Quest space exhibition
* Open-air ice rink in winter (separate charge)

Location
Near Newcastle Central station

Opening
Daily: Mon–Sat 10am–6pm,
Sun 11am–6pm

Admission
Adult £6.95, Child £4.50, Concs £5.50

Contact
Times Square,
Newcastle upon Tyne NE1 4EP

t 0191 243 8210
w life.org.uk
e info@life.org.uk

816 Newcastle upon Tyne

Discovery Museum

3 hrs   All year

Explore Newcastle's past, from Roman times to the present day. See Tyneside inventions that changed the world and take a walk through changing fashions. The Discovery Museum offers a fun approach to science and a great day out for all the family.

* See Roman, Norman & medieval Newcastle upon Tyne
* Find out about life along the River Tyne

Location
Short walk from Newcastle Central station

Opening
Daily: Mon–Sat 10am–5pm,
Sun 2pm–5pm

Admission
Free

Contact
Blandford Square,
Newcastle upon Tyne NE1 4JA

t 0191 232 6789
w twmuseums.org.uk/discovery
e discovery@twmuseums.org.uk

817 North Shields

Stephenson Railway Museum

1 hr   May–Oct

Relive the glorious days of the steam railway at the Stephenson Railway Museum. Take a ride on a steam train and discover the impact of coal and electricity on the lives of ordinary people.

* Many activities throughtout the year
* Gift shop selling souvenirs, etc

Location
Well signed from junction of A19/A1058

Opening
May–Oct Sat–Sun 11am–4pm
School hols daily 11am–4pm

Admission
Free

Contact
Middle Engine Lane,
North Shields NE29 8DX

t 0191 200 7146
w twmuseums.org.uk/stephenson
e stephenson@twmuseums.org.uk

818 Rowlands Gill

Gibside

3 hrs All year

Gibside is one of the North's finest landscapes, embracing many miles of riverside and forest walks. The park is very child-friendly with woods to explore, streams to paddle in and wildlife to look out for – including deer, kingfishers, herons, red kites and badgers.

* Former home of Queen Mother's family
* Greenhouse & stables

Location
6 miles SW of Gateshead on B6314

Opening
Daily: *summer* 10am–6pm
(last admission 4.30pm)
winter 10am–4pm
(last admission 3.30pm)

Admission
Adult £5, Child £3

Contact
nr Rowlands Gill,
Burnopfield NE16 6BG

t 01207 541820
w nationaltrust.org.uk
e gibside@nationaltrust.org.uk

819 South Shields

Arbeia Roman Fort

2 hrs All year

Arbeia was once an essential part of a mighty frontier system. Built in approximately AD160, it guarded the entrance to the River Tyne. See excavated remains, stunning reconstructions of original buildings and displays of finds discovered at the site.

* 3 reconstructed buildings on their original sites
* Time Quest archaeological dig

Location
10 min walk from South Shields
Metro & bus station; signed from
Ocean Road

Opening
Easter–Sep Mon–Sat 10am–5.30pm,
Sun 1pm–5pm; Oct–Easter Mon–Sat
10am–3.30pm

Admission
Free

Contact
Baring Street,
South Shields NE33 2BB

t 0191 456 1369
w twmuseums.org.uk
e info@twmuseums.org.uk

820 South Shields

Pier Amusements Centre

2 hrs   All year

At the Pier Amusements Centre you can play Quasar, a futuristic game in which each player is armed with a laser gun and shoots the opposition to win points.

* Bowling lanes
* New café

Location
On pier front at South Shields.
Reached via A183, A1018 or A185

Opening
Daily: 10am–10pm

Admission
Please phone for details

Contact
Pier Parade, South Shields NE33 2JS

t 0191 455 3885

821 Sunderland

National Glass Centre

2 hrs   All year

Discover how glass has been used since it was invented in 5000 BC. See it magnify a bee's knee and a fly's tongue 100 times, listen to a glass orchestra, have fun with crazy mirrors, and hear how glass is used to protect astronauts when they re-enter the earth's atmosphere.

* Home of International Institute for research in glass

Location
Signed from all major roads

Opening
Daily: 10am–5pm

Admission
Adult £3, Child £1.50

Contact
Liberty Way,
Sunderland SR6 0GL

t 0191 515 5555
w nationalglasscentre.com
e info@nationalglasscentre.com

822 Sunderland

Souter Lighthouse

1 hr+   Apr–Oct

Built in 1871, Souter boasted the most advanced lighthouse technology of its day. The lighthouse is full of interest for children. They can see the engine and rooms, the Victorian keeper's cottage and the light tower itself.

* When operational, light could be seen for 26 miles
* See engine room & cramped living quarters

Location
2½ miles S of South Shields on A183

Opening
31 Mar–Oct Sat–Thu 11am–5pm
(last admission 4.30pm)

Admission
Adult £4, Child £2.50

Contact
Coast Road, Whitburn,
Sunderland SR6 7NH

t 0191 529 3161
w nationaltrust.org.uk
e souter@nationaltrust.org.uk

823 Sunderland

Sunderland Museum & Winter Gardens

3 hrs   All year

This museum tells the story of Sunderland. It includes paintings by L S Lowry and exciting hands-on exhibits and interactive displays. The stunning Winter Gardens will stimulate the senses with more than 1,500 flowers and plants – a showcase of the world's natural beauty.

* Good facilities for disabled visitors
* Many educational exhibits & audio guides in Winter Gardens

Location
In city centre on Burdon Road

Opening
Daily: Mon–Sat 10am–5pm,
Sun 2pm–5pm

Admission
Free

Contact
Burdon Road,
Sunderland SR1 1PP

t 0191 553 2323
w twmuseums.org.uk/sunderland
e sunderland@twmuseums.org.uk

824 Sunniside

Tanfield Railway

2 hrs+   All year

Tanfield is a 3-mile steam railway and the oldest existing railway in the world. See the 1727 Causey Arch bridge, the centrepiece of the scenic Causey Woods, and walk the deep valley with display boards giving the area's C18 railway history.

* Large collection of locally built locomotives
* Oldest working engine shed in Britain

Location
On A6076 Stanley–Gateshead road

Opening
Daily: Viewing only
Please phone or visit the website
for details

Admission
Train ride Adult £6, Child (5–14) £3,

Concs £4, Family ticket (2 Adult &
2 Child) £4

Contact
Old Marley Hill, Sunniside,
Gateshead NE16 5ET

t 0191 388 7545
w tanfield-railway.co.uk
e tanfield@ingsoc.demon.co.uk

Blue Reef Aquarium

1 hr+   All year

The ultimate under-the-sea safari, Blue Reef brings the magic of the underwater world alive. Explore the drama of the North Sea and the dazzling beauty of a spectacular coral reef. This giant tropical ocean tank has its own underwater tunnel and more than 30 living displays.

* See Asian short-clawed otters
* Giant Pacific octopus

Location
From A19 take A1058 to town centre & follow brown tourist signs

Opening
Daily: Mar–Oct 10am–5pm;
Nov–Feb 10am–4pm

Admission
Adult £5.99, Child £3.99, Concs £4.99

Family ticket (2 Adults & 2 Child) £17.50

Contact
Grand Parade,
Tynemouth NE30 4JF

t 0191 258 1031
w bluereefaquarium.co.uk
e tynemouth@bluereefaquarium.co.uk

Tynemouth Priory & Castle

1 hr   All year

A burial place of saints and kings, this commanding castle has provided defence against the Vikings, medieval Scots, Napoleon and C20 Germany. The Benedictine priory was founded in 1090 on the site of an ancient Anglian monastery.

* Restored magazines of a coastal defence gun battery on view at weekends

Location
In Tynemouth, near North Pier

Opening
Apr–Sep daily 10am–5pm; Oct–Mar
Thu–Mon 10am–4pm

Admission
Adult £3.40, Child £1.70, Concs £2.60

Contact
Tynemouth NE30 4BZ

t 0191 257 1090
w english-heritage.org.uk

827 Wallsend

Segedunum Roman Fort, Baths & Museum

2 hrs+   All year

The last outpost of Hadrian's Wall, Segedunum has stood on the banks of the River Tyne since AD122. It was built to protect the coast from barbarians in the north, and was once home to 600 Roman soldiers. There are hands-on displays of life in Roman Britain.

* The most extensively excavated site in Britain
* 100ft-high viewing tower plus audio guide

Location
1 min walk from Wallsend Metro & bus station

Opening
Daily: Apr–Oct 10am–5pm;
Nov–Mar 10am–3pm

Admission
Adult £3.95, Child free, Concs £2.25

Contact
Buddle Street, Wallsend NE28 6HR

t 0191 236 9347
w twmuseums.org.uk

828 Washington

Wildfowl & Wetlands Trust Washington

3 hrs   All year

The Trust is home to more than 500 ducks, geese, swans and flamingos. Many birds will take food from your hand. The annual highlight is the series of downy duckling days (May to July) when visitors can see young birds take their first wobbly steps in the nursery.

* Nuthatch sighted in 2003 for the first time in 10 years
* See waders, kingfishers, snipe, shovelers & flamingos

Location
E of Washington, 4 miles from A1(M)

Opening
Daily: *summer* 9.30am–5.30pm;
winter 9.30am–4pm

Admission
Adult £5.95, Child £3.95, Concs £4.95
Family ticket £15.50

Contact
Pattinson, Washington NE38 8LE

t 0191 416 5454
w wwt.org.uk
e info.washington@wwt.org.uk

829 Whitley Bay

Whitley Bay Ice Rink

2 hrs   All year

Whitley Bay Ice Rink offers something for everyone. Come and enjoy a morning of tenpin bowling. Family skate and disco sessions are available as well.

* Fantastic fun on the ice
* Snacks & drinks available

Location
From S take A1 through Tyne Tunnel, then A1058. From Newcastle upon Tyne take A1058

Opening
Daily: please phone for details

Admission
Adult £4.50, Child £4 (£1.50 skate hire)

Contact
Hillheads Road,
Whitley Bay NE25 8HP

t 0191 291 1000
e icerink@ukonline.co.uk

ld Man of Storr, Isle of Skye

Scotland

Central Scotland Grampian
Highlands and Islands Southern Scotland

Outer Hebrides

Ronay

Pabbay
Berneray

Fuidheigh Madadh
(Lochmaddy)

Taransay

Hushinish
Point

Gallan
Head

Harris

Scalpay

Isle of Lewis

WESTERN ISLES

939
Steornabhagh
(Stornoway)

938

Rudha Rhobhanais
(Butt of Lewis)

Port Nis
(Port of Ness)

Shiant
Islands

Cellar Head

Eye Peninsula

Rudha
Reidh

Greenstone
Point

Dunvegan

Portree

Uig

Rona

Raasay

Luachrascro

Gairloch

Kinlochewe

Torridon

Ullapool

Garrison

Achnasheen

Garve

H i g h l a n d s

Lochinver

Cape Wrath

Durness

Whiten
Head

Dingwall

Inverness
935-936

927

953

Nairn

Forres

Beauly

Muir of Ord

Alness

Dingwall

Evanton

Conon Bridge

Tain

951

Bonar Bridge

Dornoch

928

Lairg

Tarbat
Ness

Helmsdale

Altnaharra

Kinbrace

Bettyhill

Tongue

Strathy
Point

Melvich

Dunnet
Head

Scrabster

Thurso

Castletown

John O'Groats

Duncansby
Head

Mainland

924

926

Kirkwall

948-949

952

955

957

Orkney Islands

Island of Stroma

Latheron

Lybster

Wick

Noss
Head

930

931

913

Elgin

Buckie

Cullen

MORAY

Aberlour

Dufftown

Keith

Lossiemouth

916

Banff

Macduff

Huntly

Turriff

911

914

917

Peterhead

Fraserburgh

©MAPS IN MINUTES™ 2006. ©Crown Copyright, Ordnance Survey 2006.

CENTRAL SCOTLAND
Animal Attractions
Auchingarrich Wildlife Centre 314
Blair Drummond Safari
& Adventure Park 335
Deep Sea World 332
Edinburgh Butterfly & Insect World 318
Edinburgh Zoo 319
Highland Adventure Safaris 314
Lamont City Farm 327
Peel Farm 331
Scottish Deer Centre 324
Scottish Seabird Centre 322
St Andrews Aquarium 325

Historic Places
Barrie's Birthplace 331
Brechin Castle Centre 314
Discovery Point 316
Dunfermline Abbey & Palace 316
Edinburgh Castle 318
Glamis Castle 325
Kellie Castle & Garden 334
Linlithgow Palace 331
New Lanark World Heritage Site 332
The Royal Yacht *Britannia* 321
Scotland's Secret Bunker 334
Stirling Castle 336
Tall Ship in Glasgow Harbour 329

Museums & Exhibitions
Almond Valley Heritage Centre 317
Atholl Country Life Museum 315
Bannockburn Heritage Centre 335
British Golf Museum 334
The Cadies & Witchery Tours 318

Callendar House Museum 323
Clydebuilt Scottish Maritime Museum 326
Craigencalt Ecology Centre 330
Edinburgh Crystal Visitor Centre 319
Edinburgh Dungeon 319
The Falkirk Wheel 323
The Famous Grouse Experience at
Glenturret Distillery 315
Glasgow Police Museum 326
Glasgow Science Centre 326
Inverkeithing Museum 324
Killiecrankie Visitor Centre 333
The MacRobert Centre 336
Motoring Heritage Centre 327
Museum of Flight 317
Museum of Scotland 320
Museum of Scottish Country Life 328
Museum of Transport 328
National Portrait Gallery 320
Our Dynamic Earth 320
People's Palace 328
The Piping Centre 328
Royal Museum of Scotland 321
Scottish Crannog Centre 330
Scottish Fisheries Museum 324
Scottish Football Museum 329
Scottish Railway Exhibition 322
Scottish Vintage Bus Museum 325
Sensation: Dundee 316
The Spirit of the Tattoo 323

Parks, Gardens & Nature
Calderglen Country Park 325
Falls of Clyde Visitor Centre
& Wildlife Reserve 326
Plean Country Park 334
Polkemmet Country Park 320
Royal Botanic Garden Edinburgh 321

Sports & Leisure
Bedlam Paintball, Edinburgh 317
Dewar's Centre 332
Forest Hills Watersports 314
Glasgow Ski & Snowboarding Centre 327
Knockhill Racing Circuit 316
Loch Rannoch Watersports & Quads 330
Megazone 323
Scotkart 329
Xscape – Braehead 330

Theme Parks & Adventure Playgrounds
M&D's Theme Park 333
Noah's Ark 333

GRAMPIAN
Animal Attractions
Macduff Marine Aquarium 34

Historic Places
Balmoral Castle & Estate 33
Drum Castle, Garden & Estate 34
Leith Hall 34

Museums & Exhibitions
Aberdeen Maritime Museum 33
Aberdeenshire Farming Museum 34
Archaeolink 33
Findhorn Heritage Icehouse 34
Gordon Highlanders Museum 338
The Museum of Scottish Lighthouses 34
The Old Royal Station, Ballater 34
Peterhead Maritime Heritage 342
Satrosphere 339

Sports & Leisure
Beach Leisure Centre 33
Codona's Pleasure Fair 338

HIGHLANDS & ISLANDS
Animal Attractions
Cairngorm Reindeer Centre 342
Highland Wildlife Park 350
Scottish Sealife & Marine Sanctuary 353
WDCS Wildlife Centre 346
Working Sheepdogs 350

Boat & Train Trips
Bella Jane Boat Trips 349
Family's Pride II Glassbottom
  Boat Trips 350
Inverness Dolphin Cruises 347
Seaprobe Atlantis 351
Strathspey Steam Railway 343
Whale Watching Trips 349

Guided Tours
Inverness Terror Tour 347

Historic Places
Balfour Castle 353
Ballindalloch Castle 343
Cawdor Castle 353
Culloden Battlefield 345
Elgin Cathedral 345
Kisimul Castle 347

Museums & Exhibitions
The Black House Museum 348
The Bright Water Visitor Centre 349
Corrigall Farm Museum 344
Glencoe Visitor Centre 346
Highland Folk Museum, Newtonmore 350
Historylinks Museum 345
Inveraray Jail 347
Kirbuster Museum 344
Loch Ness Monster Exhibition Centre 345
The Orkney Museum 351
Scapa Flow Visitor Centre & Museum 351
Tomb of the Eagles 352
Westray Heritage Centre 354

Parks, Gardens & Nature
Ferrycroft Countryside Visitor Centre 352
Loch Lomond National Nature
  Reserve 343

Sports & Leisure
The Fun House 342
Lewis Karting Centre 348
Monster Activities 354
Raasay Outdoor Centre 349
Vertical Descents 346

Theme Parks & Adventure Playgrounds
Landmark Forest Theme Park 344

SOUTHERN SCOTLAND
Animal Attractions
Galloway Red Deer Range 368
Galloway Wildlife Conservation Park 367
Jedforest Deer & Farm Park 364

Historic Places
Brodick Castle, Garden
  & Country Park 364
Caerlaverock Castle 358
Drumlanrig's Tower 362
Dundonald Castle 361
Floors Castle 365
Jedburgh Castle Jail & Museum 364
Kelburn Castle & Country Centre 361
Paxton House & Country Park 355
Robert Burns House 360
Robert the Bruce's Cave 367
Three Hills Roman Centre & Fort 367

Museums & Exhibitions
Creetown Heritage Museum 357
Dalbeattie Museum 357
Dalgarven Mill Museum 366
Devil's Porridge Exhibition 354
Dumfries Museum & Camera Obscura 358
Eyemouth Museum 361
Gretna Green World Famous
  Blacksmith's Shop & Centre 362
Halliwell's House Museum 369
Harestanes Countryside Visitor Centre 354
Mary Queen of Scots Visitor Centre 365
North Ayrshire Museum 368
Old Bridge House Museum 359

Robert Burns Centre 359
Robert Smail's Printing Works 363
Sanquhar Tolbooth Museum 369
Scottish Maritime Museum 366
Shambellie House Museum of
  Costume 360
Tam O'Shanter Experience 355
The Viking Experience 367

Parks, Gardens & Nature
Coldstream 363
Cream O'Galloway 356
St Abb's Head Nature Reserve 357
Threave Garden, House & Estate 357
WWT Caerlaverock Wetlands Centre 356

Sports & Leisure
Fishwick Mains Amazing Maize Maze 355
Galleon Centre 365
The Garage 366
Rowallan Activity Centre 361

Theme Parks & Adventure Playgrounds
Loudoun Castle Family Theme Park 362
Neverland Adventure Play Centre 358

830 Aberfeldy

Highland Adventure Safaris

  2 hrs All year

An exciting way to experience the exhilaration and freedom of this beautiful part of the Highlands. Visitors can immerse themselves in the great outdoors a little closer by trying out Land Rovers on Ecotours, wildlife-watching trips or an exciting off-road driving experience.

* 4-star Visitor Attraction with shop, café & deer park
* Skills courses available (also try gold-panning)

Location
From A827 at Aberfeldy follow B846 for 2 miles past Castle Menzies until you see the signs

Opening
Daily: *summer* 9am–5pm
winter please phone for details

Admission
Prices vary, please phone for details

Contact
Drumdewan, Aberfeldy, Perthshire PH15 2JQ

t 01887 820071
w highlandadventuresafaris.co.uk
e info@highlandadventuresafaris.co.uk

831 Aberfoyle

Forest Hills Watersports

 3 hrs+ All year

The centre offers a range of 'wet' and 'dry' activities that can be enjoyed individually or combined. Watersports of all descriptions are available in addition to quad biking, mountain biking and 4×4 drives.

* Equipment available for hire
* Courses taught by qualified instructors

Location
Off junction 10 of M9 & junction 16 of M8. Follow signs for Aberfoyle, then to Forest Hills Watersports, 4 miles along B829

Opening
Daily: *summer* 9.30am–7pm
winter 10.30am–5pm

Admission
Activities priced individually

Contact
Kinlochard, Aberfoyle, Stirlingshire FK8 3TL

t 01877 387775
w goforth.co.uk
e info@goforth.co.uk

832 Brechin

Brechin Castle Centre

  2 hrs+   All year

Brechin Castle is a country park with a working model farm covering 65 acres and a children's activity area with an adventure castle. Take a ride on the miniature railway or enjoy a stroll along the nature trail.

* Scottish Tourist Board 4-star Visitor Attraction
* Santa at Christmas

Location
Between Aberdeen & Dundee, off A90; on A935 to Brechin turn-off, well signed from there

Opening
Daily: Mon–Sat 9am–6pm, Sun 10am–6pm

Admission
Adult £2, Child £1

Contact
Haughmui, by Brechin, Angus DD9 6RL

t 01356 626813
w brechincastlecentre.co.uk
e enquiries@brechincastlecentre.co.uk

833 Crieff

Auchingarrich Wildlife Centre

  2 hrs+ All year

Set in 100 acres of Perthshire countryside, the centre has animals and birds from all over the world. Attractions include falconry displays, indoor and outdoor play areas, animal and chick handling, a unique bird hatchery and the Highland Castle Centre.

* More than 150 species of animals & birds
* Hatchings every day Easter–Oct

Location
On B827, 2 miles N of Comrie

Opening
Daily: 10am–5pm

Admission
Adult £5.50, Child & Concs £4

Contact
Glascorrie Road, Crieff, Perthshire PH6 2JS

t 01764 679469
w auchingarrich.co.uk
e gillianscarter@tiscali.co.uk

834 Crieff

The Famous Grouse Experience at Glenturret Distillery

1 hr+   All year

Scotland's only five-star, Bafta award-winning interactive whisky attraction is fun for young and old alike. Crack some ice, splash in the water and do a jigsaw puzzle with your feet or 'fly' over the wondrous beauty of Scotland on the back of a grouse.

* Audio-visual presentation
* Award-winning famous restaurant

Location
Off A85, 1 mile from Crieff

Opening
Daily: 10am–6pm (last tour 4.30pm)

Admission
1-hour tour Adult £7.50, Child (over 10) & Concs £5, Child (under 10) free
½-hour tour please phone for details

Contact
Glenturret Distillery, The Hosh, Crieff, Perthshire PH7 4HA

t 01764 656565
w famousgrouse.com
e enquiries@famousgrouse.com

---

835 Dundee

Atholl Country Life Museum

1 hr   May–Sep

This lively museum explores the reality of country life and the social history of the Atholl people. It uses detailed facts, 100 historical photographs, and stories set in a wide range of imaginative displays to entertain visitors.

* Gamekeeper's corner
* Display of stuffed wild animals

Location
Turn off A9 for Blair Atholl, 7 miles N of Pitlochry

Opening
Daily: Easter & May–Sep 1.30pm–5pm; Jul–Aug Mon–Fri from 10am

Admission
Adult £3, Child £1, Concs £2.50

Contact
Blair Atholl, Pitlochry, Perthshire PH18 5SP

t 01796 481232
w blairatholl.org.uk
e john.museum@virgin.net

836 Dundee

Discovery Point

1 hrs +   All year

Discovery Point is home to Captain Scott's ship *Discovery*, which was built in Dundee for his expedition to the Antarctic, and the Verdant Works, winner of the European Industrial Museum of the Year Award. It has original working machinery, and computer and hands-on displays.

* State-of-the-art multimedia exhibitions
* Scottish Family Attraction of the Year 2004

Location	Admission
In city centre, opposite railway station	Adult £6.45, Child £3.85, Concs £4.90
Opening	**Contact**
Daily: Apr–Oct Mon–Sat 10am–6pm, Sun 11am–6pm; Nov–Mar Mon–Sat 10am–5pm, Sun 11am–5pm	Discovery Quay, Dundee DD1 4XA
	t 01382 201245
	w rrsdiscovery.com
	e info@dundeeheritage.co.uk

837 Dundee

Sensation: Dundee

2 hrs+   All year

If you thought science was boring, this centre may change your mind. The hands-on experiments, live workshops and investigations bring science to life. Discover how we use our five senses to interact with the world around us, in 12 specially designed exhibits.

* Scottish Family Attraction of the Year 2003
* £1.4million Roborealm

Location	Contact
In city centre, 5 min walk from Dundee railway station. Follow brown tourist signs	Greenmarket, Dundee DD1 4QB
	t 01382 228800
Opening	w sensation.org.uk
Daily: 10am–6pm (5pm in winter)	e staff@sensation.org.uk
Admission	
Adult £6.50, Child & Concs £4.50	

838 Dunfermline

Dunfermline Abbey & Palace

1 hr   All year

The elegant ruins of Dunfermline Abbey are what is left of a great Benedictine abbey founded by Queen Margaret in the C11. Robert the Bruce was buried in the choir and the royal palace next door, also partially ruined, was the birthplace of Charles I.

* Substantial parts of the abbey nave remain
* Next to the ruin of the royal palace

Location	Admission
Off M90, in town centre	Adult £3, Child £1.30, Concs £2.30
Opening	**Contact**
Apr–Sep daily 9.30am–6.30pm; Oct–Mar Mon–Wed & Sat 9.30am–4.30pm, Sun 2pm–4.30pm (last admission ¹/₂ hr before close)	St Margaret Street, Dunfermline, Fife KY12 7PE
	t 01383 739026
	w historic-scotland.gov.uk

839 Dunfermline

Knockhill Racing Circuit

3 hrs   All year

Get behind the wheel of a Formula 1 single-seater racing car or rally car, go off-road in a 4×4 or be driven round the racing circuit by a professional. Alternatively, sit back and enjoy the races. Choose from British touring cars, superbikes, stock cars and Formula Woman.

* Hands -on driving experiences
* Relaxing hospitality at race events

Location	Contact
Signed from M90 junction 4	Dunfermline, Fife KY12 9TF
Opening	t 01383 723337
Daily: 9am–6pm	w knockhill.co.uk
Admission	e enquiries@knockhill.co.uk
Prices vary depending on event, please phone for details	

East Fortune

Museum of Flight

2 hrs+   All year

Man's fascination with flight is celebrated at this protected WWI and WWII airfield. Experience the highs and lows of the supersonic Concorde, and explore more than 40 other aircraft, from earliest designs to the supersonic fighter.

* See a Britten-Norman Islander, an aircraft described as the most versatile in the world

Location
Off A1, 20 miles E of Edinburgh

Opening
Apr–Jun & Sep–Oct daily 10am–5pm;
Jul–Aug daily 10am–6pm; Nov–Mar
Sat–Sun 10am–4pm

Admission
Museum Adult £5, Child free,
Concs £4

Concorde booking pass extra:
Adults £3, Child & Concs £2.
Must be booked in advance.
Booking line 0870 421 4299

Contact
East Fortune Airfield,
East Lothian EH39 5LF

t 01620 897240
w nms.ac.uk
e info@nms.ac.uk

---

841 Edinburgh

Almond Valley Heritage Centre

3 hrs   All year

This is an innovative museum exploring the history and environment of West Lothian with award-winning children's activities and interactive displays. The centuries-old farm buildings are home to a variety of friendly animals that the children can see and pet.

* Demonstrations & seasonal activities
* Gift shop

Location
Signed from M8 junction 3,
2 miles from motorway

Opening
Daily: 10am–5pm

Admission
Adult £3, Child £2

Contact
Millfield, Livingston,
West Lothian EH54 7AR

t 01506 414957
w almondvalley.co.uk
e info@almondvalley.co.uk

---

842 Edinburgh

Bedlam Paintball, Edinburgh

3 hrs+   All year

Get the ultimate adrenaline rush at Bedlam Paintball. Be prepared to utilise tactics, teamwork and quick thinking as you experience all the multiple game scenarios available here.

* Other venues at Glasgow & Edzell
* For children aged 12 yrs+

Location
If travelling from Edinburgh, Fife,
Falkirk, Stirling, Livingston &
surrounding areas, Bedlam is off
A8000

Opening
Daily: from 10am

Admission
From £35 per person, please phone
for details

Contact
Milton Wood, Dundas Estate,
South Queensferry, Edinburgh

t 07000 233526
w bedlam.co.uk
e info@bedlam.co.uk

843 Edinburgh

The Cadies & Witchery Tours

1 hr+   All year

Witchery Tours take a light-hearted look at tales of witchcraft, plague and torture. Explore the eerie alleyways and creepy courtyards of the Old Town with your ghostly guide, who will blend history with humour and fact with fable.

* 'Jump-ooters' make ghastly appearances
* Re-enactments & live performances

Location	Contact
In city centre, off Royal Mile	84 West Bow (Victoria Street), Edinburgh EH1 2HH
Opening	
Daily: tours operate 7pm–10pm, please phone to check times & availability	t 0131 225 6745
	w witcherytours.com
	e lyal@witcherytours.demon.co.uk
Admission	
Adult £7.50, Child (over 5) £5, Child (under 5) free	

844 Edinburgh

Edinburgh Butterfly & Insect World

3 hrs+   All year

Walk through an indoor tropical rainforest inhabited by thousands of the world's most beautiful butterflies. Don't forget to visit the unique Scottish honey-bee zone.

* Bugs & Beasties section
* Meet the Beasties handling sessions

Location	Contact
3 miles S of city centre on A702. Just off the bypass, A720 at Gilmerton exit	Dobbies Garden World, Lasswade, Edinburgh EH18 1AZ
Opening	t 0131 663 4932
Daily: *summer* 9.30am–5.30pm *winter* 10am–5pm	e edinburgh-butterfly-world.co.uk
	w info@edinburgh-butterfly-world.co.uk
Admission	
Adults £5, Child & Concs £3.85	

845 Edinburgh

Edinburgh Castle

1 hr+   All year

A majestic landmark that dominates the city's skyline, Edinburgh Castle is the most visited of Scotland's historic buildings. Perched on an extinct volcano and offering stunning views, this fortress is a powerful national symbol, and part of Edinburgh's World Heritage Site.

* Guided & audio tours
* Scottish Crown Jewels & Stone of Destiny

Location	Contact
In city centre, at top of Royal Mile	Castle Hill, Edinburgh EH1 2NG
Opening	t 0131 225 9846
Daily: Apr–Sep 9.30am–6pm; Oct–Mar 9.30am–5pm	w historic-scotland.gov.uk
Admission	
Adult £10.30, Child £4.50, Concs £8.50	

846 Edinburgh

Edinburgh Crystal Visitor Centre

1 hr   All year

Edinburgh Crystal Visitor Centre displays the entire Edinburgh Crystal range as well as unique pieces created by our cutters and engravers. See the craftsmen at work engraving and cutting glass, and watch all the processes involved in glassmaking on TV.

Location
30 min S of city centre. From city bypass take A701 S for 4 miles, following signs for Penicuik

Opening
Daily: Mon–Sat 10am–5pm, Sun 11am–5pm

Admission
Free

Contact
Penicuik, Midlothian EH26 8HB

t 01968 675128
w edinburgh-crystal.com
e visitorcentre@edinburgh-crystal.co.uk

847 Edinburgh

Edinburgh Dungeon

1 hr   All year

Are you brave enough to delve into the darkest chapters of history? Enjoy a unique feast of fun with history's horrible bits. Real history, horror and humour bring gruesome goings-on to life. Live actors, special effects and boat rides transport you back in time.

* Horror rides & actors re-enacting the past
* Great Fire of Edinburgh 'Inferno', new attraction

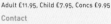

Location
In city centre

Opening
Daily: 10 Mar–29 Jun 10am–5pm;
30 Jun–29 Jul 10am–6pm;
30 Jul–3 Sep 10am–7pm;
4 Sep–31 Oct 10am–5pm;
1 Nov–9 Mar Fri–Mon 11am–4pm,
Sat–Sun 10am–4pm

Admission
Adult £11.95, Child £7.95, Concs £9.95

Contact
31 Market Street, Edinburgh EH1 1QB

t 0131 240 1000
w thedungeons.com
e edinburghdungeon@merlinentertainments.biz

848 Edinburgh

Edinburgh Zoo

4 hrs   All year

This is Scotland's most popular wildlife attraction, with more than 1,000 animals, including meerkats, koala bears, tigers, lions and blue poison arrow frogs. Set in beautiful parkland, the zoo has the world's biggest penguin pool.

* African Plains Experience & Magic Forest
* Hilltop safari, tour & maze & animal handling

Location
10 min from city centre

Opening
Daily: Mar & Oct 9am–5pm;
Apr–Sep 9am–6pm;
Nov–Feb 9am–4.30pm

Admission
Adult £10, Child* £7, Concs £7.50

Contact
134 Corstorphine Road, Edinburgh EH12 6TS

t 0131 334 9171
w edinburghzoo.org.uk
e info@edinburghzoo.org.uk

*Adult (over 17) must accompany children under 14 at all times

849 Edinburgh

Museum of Scotland

2 hrs+   All year

This magnificent museum tells the story of Scotland – its land, people and culture – through the rich national collections. Stunning themed galleries cover landscape and wildlife, early people, the kingdom of the Scots, industry and empire, Scotland transformed and the C20.

* More than 10,000 artefacts
* Same site as Royal Museum

Location
Off A7 South Bridge, in city centre

Opening
Daily: 10am–5pm

Admission
Free

Contact
Chambers Street, Edinburgh EH1 1JF

t 0131 247 4422
w nms.ac.uk
e info@nms.ac.uk

850 Edinburgh

National Portrait Gallery

2 hrs   All year

The gallery provides a visual history of Scotland, told through the portraits of those who shaped it: royals and rebels, poets and philosophers, heroes and villains. Mary, Queen of Scots, Robert Burns, Sir Walter Scott and Sir Sean Connery are all here.

* Works by Gainsborough, Copley & Rodin
* Unparalleled collection of Scottish portraits

Location
At E end of Queen Street, in city centre

Opening
Daily: 10am–5pm, Thu 10am–7pm;
1 Jan 12noon–5pm

Admission
Free

Contact
1 Queen Street, Edinburgh EH2 1JD

t 0131 624 6200
w nationalgalleries.org
e enquiries@nationalgalleries.org

851 Edinburgh

Our Dynamic Earth

2 hrs   All year

Explore our planet's past, present and future. You'll be shaken by volcanoes, fly over glaciers, feel the chill of polar ice, and get caught in a tropical rainstorm. New! Journey to the Earth's Core. New! Take your crew seat in the FutureDome and consider our planet's future.

* Live 4,500 million years in a day

Location
At foot of Arthur's Seat, adjacent to new Scottish Parliament

Opening
Please phone or visit the website for details

Admission
Adult £8.95, Child & Concs £5.45

Contact
112 Holyrood Road,
Edinburgh EH8 8AS

t 0131 550 7800
w dynamicearth.co.uk
e enquiries@dynamicearth.co.uk

852 Edinburgh

Polkemmet Country Park

2 hrs+   All year

Polkemmet Country Park is a very attractive area of mixed mature woodlands and grassy open spaces along the upper reaches of the River Almond. Facilities include a public bowling green, a 15-bay floodlit golf range and barbecue areas for all.

* Fantasy Forest
* 9-hole golf course

Location
Between junctions 4 & 5 of M8, mid way between Edinburgh & Glasgow. Entry is from B7066, on outskirts of Whitburn

Opening
Daily: 7am–9pm

Admission
Free

Contact
Whitburn, West Lothian EH47 0AD

t 01501 743905
w beecraigs.com
e mail@beecraigs.com

846 Edinburgh

Edinburgh Crystal Visitor Centre

1 hr   All year

Edinburgh Crystal Visitor Centre displays the entire Edinburgh Crystal range as well as unique pieces created by our cutters and engravers. See the craftsmen at work engraving and cutting glass, and watch all the processes involved in glassmaking on TV.

Location
30 min S of city centre. From city bypass take A701 S for 4 miles, following signs for Penicuik

Opening
Daily: Mon–Sat 10am–5pm, Sun 11am–5pm

Admission
Free

Contact
Penicuik, Midlothian EH26 8HB

t 01968 675128
w edinburgh-crystal.com
e visitorcentre@edinburgh-crystal.co.uk

847 Edinburgh

Edinburgh Dungeon

1 hr   All year

Are you brave enough to delve into the darkest chapters of history? Enjoy a unique feast of fun with history's horrible bits. Real history, horror and humour bring gruesome goings-on to life. Live actors, special effects and boat rides transport you back in time.

* Horror rides & actors re-enacting the past
* Great Fire of Edinburgh 'Inferno', new attraction

Location
In city centre

Opening
Daily: 10 Mar–29 Jun 10am–5pm;
30 Jun–29 Jul 10am–6pm;
30 Jul–3 Sep 10am–7pm;
4 Sep–31 Oct 10am–5pm;
1 Nov–9 Mar Fri–Mon 11am–4pm,
Sat–Sun 10am–4pm

Admission
Adult £11.95, Child £7.95, Concs £9.95

Contact
31 Market Street, Edinburgh EH1 1QB

t 0131 240 1000
w thedungeons.com
e edinburghdungeon@merlinentertainments.biz

848 Edinburgh

Edinburgh Zoo

4 hrs   All year

This is Scotland's most popular wildlife attraction, with more than 1,000 animals, including meerkats, koala bears, tigers, lions and blue poison arrow frogs. Set in beautiful parkland, the zoo has the world's biggest penguin pool.

* African Plains Experience & Magic Forest
* Hilltop safari, tour & maze & animal handling

Location
10 min from city centre

Opening
Daily: Mar & Oct 9am–5pm;
Apr–Sep 9am–6pm;
Nov–Feb 9am–4.30pm

Admission
Adult £10, Child* £7, Concs £7.50

Contact
134 Corstorphine Road, Edinburgh EH12 6TS

t 0131 334 9171
w edinburghzoo.org.uk
e info@edinburghzoo.org.uk

*Adult (over 17) must accompany children under 14 at all times

849 Edinburgh

Museum of Scotland

2 hrs+   All year

This magnificent museum tells the story of Scotland – its land, people and culture – through the rich national collections. Stunning themed galleries cover landscape and wildlife, early people, the kingdom of the Scots, industry and empire, Scotland transformed and the C20.

* More than 10,000 artefacts
* Same site as Royal Museum

Location	Contact
Off A7 South Bridge, in city centre	Chambers Street, Edinburgh EH1 1JF
Opening	t 0131 247 4422
Daily: 10am–5pm	w nms.ac.uk
	e info@nms.ac.uk
Admission	
Free	

850 Edinburgh

National Portrait Gallery

2 hrs   All year

The gallery provides a visual history of Scotland, told through the portraits of those who shaped it: royals and rebels, poets and philosophers, heroes and villains. Mary, Queen of Scots, Robert Burns, Sir Walter Scott and Sir Sean Connery are all here.

* Works by Gainsborough, Copley & Rodin
* Unparalleled collection of Scottish portraits

Location	Contact
At E end of Queen Street, in city centre	1 Queen Street, Edinburgh EH2 1JD
Opening	t 0131 624 6200
Daily: 10am–5pm, Thu 10am–7pm; 1 Jan 12noon–5pm	w nationalgalleries.org
	e enquiries@nationalgalleries.org
Admission	
Free	

851 Edinburgh

Our Dynamic Earth

2 hrs   All year

Explore our planet's past, present and future. You'll be shaken by volcanoes, fly over glaciers, feel the chill of polar ice, and get caught in a tropical rainstorm. New! Journey to the Earth's Core. New! Take your crew seat in the FutureDome and consider our planet's future.

* Live 4,500 million years in a day

Location	Contact
At foot of Arthur's Seat, adjacent to new Scottish Parliament	112 Holyrood Road, Edinburgh EH8 8AS
Opening	t 0131 550 7800
Please phone or visit the website for details	w dynamicearth.co.uk
	e enquiries@dynamicearth.co.uk
Admission	
Adult £8.95, Child & Concs £5.45	

852 Edinburgh

Polkemmet Country Park

2 hrs+   All year

Polkemmet Country Park is a very attractive area of mixed mature woodlands and grassy open spaces along the upper reaches of the River Almond. Facilities include a public bowling green, a 15-bay floodlit golf range and barbecue areas for all.

* Fantasy Forest
* 9-hole golf course

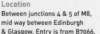

Location	Admission
Between junctions 4 & 5 of M8, mid way between Edinburgh & Glasgow. Entry is from B7066, on outskirts of Whitburn	Free
	Contact
	Whitburn, West Lothian EH47 0AD
Opening	t 01501 743905
Daily: 7am–9pm	w beecraigs.com
	e mail@beecraigs.com

853 Edinburgh

Royal Botanic Garden Edinburgh

2 hrs   All year

Founded in the C17 as a 'physic garden', growing medicinal plants, the Royal Botanic Garden is now acknowledged to be one of the finest in the world, where unusual and beautiful plants can be found. It's a place to rest and relax away from the city's hustle and bustle.

Guided & themed tours, refurbished Victorian palm house
Queen Mother's memorial garden, opened by the Queen July 2006

Location
Off A902, 1 mile N of city centre

Opening
Daily: Mar & Oct 10am–6pm;
Apr–Sep 10am–7pm;
Nov–Feb 10am–4pm

Admission
Free. Charges apply to glasshouses

Contact
20a Inverleith Row,
Edinburgh EH3 5LR

t 0131 552 7171
w rbge.org.uk
e info@rbge.org.uk

854 Edinburgh

Royal Museum of Scotland

2 hrs+   All year

Explore galleries of exhibits covering decorative art, the natural world, science and industry. See steamships and sculptures, black holes and brown bears. Check out the Connect Gallery filled with exciting objects and interactives.

* More than 10,000 artefacts
* Same site as Museum of Scotland

Location
Off A7 South Bridge, in city centre

Opening
Daily: Mon–Sun 10am–5pm

Admission
Free

Contact
Chambers Street, Edinburgh EH1 1JF

t 0131 247 4422
w nms.ac.uk
e info@nms.ac.uk

855 Edinburgh

The Royal Yacht *Britannia*

1 hr+   All year

The *Britannia* experience starts in the visitor centre where you can discover her fascinating story. Then step aboard for a self-led audio tour of five decks, giving a unique insight into what life was like on board.

* See royal apartments & the crew's quarters
* Children's audio tour

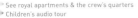

Location
At Leith Docks, signed from
city outskirts

Opening
Daily: Apr–Sep 9.30am–4.30pm;
Oct–Mar 10am–3.30pm
Pre-booking advised in Aug

Admission
Adult £9.25, Child £5.25, Concs £7.25

Contact
Ocean Terminal, Leith,
Edinburgh EH6 6JJ

t 0131 555 5566
w royalyachtbritannia.co.uk
e enquiries@tryb.co.uk

856 Edinburgh

Scottish Railway Exhibition

2 hrs   Apr–Oct

The Scottish Railway Exhibition tells the story of the railways in Scotland. Carriages, locomotives and wagons are on display, including *Glen Douglas* and a royal saloon coach. The Bo'ness and Kinneil railway offers a 7-mile round trip by steam train.

* Demonstrations workshop
* 100 years of railways

Location
Access by footbridge from Bo'ness Station, West Lothian, 8 miles W of Forth bridges. Access via junction 3 or 5 of M9

Opening
Apr–Jun & Sep–Oct Sat–Sun 11am–4.30pm; Jul–Aug daily 11am–4.30pm

Admission
Train ride Adult £5, Child £2.50, Concs £4
Exhibition Adult £1, Child free

Contact
Bo'ness Station, Union Street, Bo'ness, West Lothian EH51 9AQ
t 01506 822298
w srps.org.uk

857 Edinburgh

Scottish Seabird Centre

1 hr+   All year

Set on a dramatic promontory at North Berwick, the centre enables visitors to explore the fascinating world of seabirds, including puffins, via remote cameras on the nearby islands of Fidra, May and Bass Rock.

* 5-star Visitor Attraction
* Queen's Award for Enterprise

Location
North Berwick Harbour, 25 miles from Edinburgh (regular train & bus services from city)

Opening
Please phone for details

Admission
Adult £6.95, Child & Concs £4.50

Contact
Scottish Seabird Centre, The Harbour, North Berwick, East Lothian EH39 4SS
t 01620 890202
w seabird.org.uk

858 Edinburgh

The Spirit of the Tattoo

1 hr   All year

Many visitors to Edinburgh may never have the opportunity to see the Tattoo in August, so this year-round attraction, which presents the Tattoo's colourful story, provides them with a comprehensive review of Scotland's matchless spectacle of music, dance and display.

Interactive exhibition & film theatre
Rooftop café

Location
In city centre, on Royal Mile just below castle

Opening
Daily: Mon–Sat 10am–5pm,
Sun 11am–5pm.
winter opening times shorter,
please phone for details.

Admission
Free

Contact
555 Castlehill, The Royal Mile,
Edinburgh EH1 2ND

t 0131 225 9661
w edinburgh-tattoo.co.uk
e administration@edintattoo.co.uk

859 Falkirk

Callendar House Museum

2 hrs   All year

Callendar House is an imposing mansion, with a 600-year history, where you can go back in time to experience life in the 1820s. There is also extensive parkland with many activities to enjoy.

* Costumed interpreters
* Changing exhibitions

Location
From Callendar Road (A803) enter Estate Avenue. Located ½ mile E of town centre

Opening
Mon–Sat 10am–5pm; Apr–Sep also Sun 2pm–5pm

Admission
Please phone for details

Contact
Callendar Park, Falkirk FK1 1YR

t 01324 503770
w falkirkmuseum.gov.uk
e monica.mcfeat@falkirk.gov.uk

860 Falkirk

The Falkirk Wheel

1 hr   All year

For a truly uplifting experience, visit the world's first and only rotating boat lift, linking two canals. There is a fascinating visitor centre with interactive exhibits and a viewing gallery.

* Boat trips available (please phone for details)
* Fun Factory for kids

Location
Signed from M9

Opening
Daily: 9.30am–6pm. Times may vary, please phone for details.

Admission
Visitor centre **Free**

Contact
Lime Road, Tamfourhill,
Falkirk FK1 4RS

t 08700 500208
w thefalkirkwheel.co.uk
e info@thefalkirkwheel.co.uk

861 Falkirk

Megazone

1 hr+   All year

Megazone laser adventure is a futuristic wasteland filled with smoke, sounds, flashing lights – and enemies. Stalk your opponents with the latest technology. Use stealth and cunning, strategy and skill to score points.

* Regular family nights
* Fantastic shop

Location
5 min walk from Grahamston railway station & Central Retail Park

Opening
Daily: Mon 4pm–10pm, Tue–Fri 12noon–10pm, Sat–Sun 10am–10pm

Admission
1 game £3.75
2 games £6.50

Contact
104 Grahams Road,
Falkirk FK2 7BZ

t 01324 634828

862 Fife

Inverkeithing Museum

1 hr+   All year

Housed in the hospitium of the old Friary, this local history museum tells the story of Inverkeithing and nearby Rosyth. It contains artefacts belonging to Admiral Sir Samuel Greig, a son of Inverkeithing and the father of the modern Russian Navy.

* Please note: very steep external staircase

Location	Admission
Located in Inverkeithing. Take 1st exit over Forth Road Bridge from Edinburgh, junction 1 of M90	Free
	Contact
Opening	The Friary, Queen Street, Inverkeithing KY11 1LS
Thu–Sun 11am–12.30pm & 1pm–4pm; open Bank Hols	t 01383 313838
	w fifedirect.org.uk/museums
	e dunfermline.museum@fife.gov.uk

863 Fife

Scottish Deer Centre

2 hrs +   All year

You'll never forget your visit to this beautiful countryside centre, where a large herd of deer roam free. Under the guidance of expert rangers you are able to meet these majestic animals and even enjoy a nose-to-nose encounter with a stag.

* Falconry displays
* Wolf wood now includes 2 European wolves

Location	Contact
On outskirts of Cupar, 12 miles from St Andrews on A91	Bow-of-Fife, Cupar, Fife KY15 4NQ
	t 01337 810391
Opening	w tsdc.co.uk
Daily: May–Sep 10am–6pm; Oct–Apr 10am–5pm	e info@tsdc.co.uk
Admission	
Adult £5.50, Child (over 3) £3.95, Concs £4.55, Child (under 3) free	

864 Fife

Scottish Fisheries Museum

1 hr+   All year

The Scottish Fisheries Museum tells the story of Scottish fishing and its people from the earliest times to the present. There are many fine paintings and photographs on display as well as a variety of real and model boats, fishing gear and other accoutrements.

* Overlooks a beautiful harbour
* Regular calendar of events and exhibitions

Location	Admission
Leave M90 at junction 3, then follow A92 to Anstruther	Adult £4.50, Child free, Concs £3.50
	Contact
Opening	St Ayles, Harbourhead, Anstruther, Fife KY10 3AB
Daily: Apr–Sep Mon–Sat 10am–5.30pm, Sun 11am–5pm; Oct–Mar Mon–Sat 10am–4.30pm, Sun 12noon–4.30pm	t 01333 310628
	w scotfishmuseum.org
	e info@scotfishmuseum.org

865 Fife

Scottish Vintage Bus Museum

2 hrs   Apr–Oct

Possibly Britain's largest collection of historic buses dating from the 1920s to the 1980s. There are beautifully restored buses to see in the main exhibition hall, as well as buses under restoration in the large workshops.

Regular bus rallies
Fire engines

Location
On B915, near Dunfermline.
Follow signs to museum from
M90 junction 4

Opening
Easter–early Oct Sun only
12.30pm–5pm

Admission
Adult £3, Concs £1.50

Contact
Commerce Park, Lathalmond,
nr Dunfermline,
Fife KY12 0SJ

t 01383 623380
w busweb.co.uk/svbm

---

866 Fife

St Andrews Aquarium

1 hr+   All year

Enjoy a sense of discovery and enjoyment at St Andrews Aquarium, which welcomes you to the wonderful world of the sea and its inhabitants – from shrimps to sharks, octopuses to eels, rays to seals.

* More than 30 exhibition tanks
* Touch some of the fish

Location
At Bruce Embankment near Royal
& Ancient Golf Club

Opening
Daily: Easter–end Oct Mon–Fri
10am–5pm, Sat–Sun 10am–6pm.
Please phone for winter timetable

Admission
Adult £6.20, Child £4.40, Concs £5.20

Contact
The Scores, St Andrews,
Fife KY16 9AS

t 01334 474786
w standrewsaquarium.co.uk
e info@standrewsaquarium.co.uk

---

867 Glamis by Forfar

Glamis Castle

2 hrs+   Mar–Dec

This is a place of legends and fairy tales. It has been a royal residence since 1372 and was the childhood home of HM Queen Elizabeth The Queen Mother, birthplace of HRH The Princess Margaret and the legendary setting for Shakespeare's famous play *Macbeth*.

Rich variety of furnishings, tapestries & art
Extensive estate & formal gardens

Location
On A94, between Aberdeen & Perth

Opening
Daily: Mar–Oct 10am–6pm;
Nov–23 Dec 11am–3pm

Admission
Adult £7.30, Child £4.10, Concs £6.10,
Family ticket £21

Contact
The Castle Administrator,
Estates Office, Glamis by Forfar,
Angus DD8 1RJ

t 01307 840393
w glamis-castle.co.uk
e enquiries@glamis-castle.co.uk

---

868 Glasgow

Calderglen Country Park

2 hrs   All year

This is a large country park with a myriad of activities. The visitor centre has a good range of displays and a Hidden Worlds wildlife experience. There is also a children's zoo, conservatory, adventure playground and miles of fascinating trails to follow.

* 4-star Visitor Attraction

Location
In Calderglen Country Park in East
Kilbride on Strathaven Road, just out
of town

Opening
Park Daily: All reasonable times
Visitor centre Daily: *summer*
10.30am–5pm *winter* 11.30am–4pm

Conservatory & Zoo summer **daily**
10.30am–8.30pm

Admission
Free

Contact
East Kilbride G75 0QZ

t 01355 236644
w southlanarkshire.gov.uk

869 Glasgow

Clydebuilt Scottish Maritime Museum

2 hrs   All year

Clydebuilt charts the development of Glasgow and the River Clyde from 1700 to the present day. It tells the story of Glasgow's rivers, its ships and its people, through award-winning audio-visuals, computer interpretation, hands-on displays and video.

* 5-star Museum Attraction
* Take control of a real steam engine

Location	Contact
Turn off at junctions 25 & 26 on Glasgow's M8	Braehead Shopping Centre, Kings Inch Road, Glasgow G51 4BN
Opening	t 0141 886 1013
Mon–Sat 10am–5.30pm, Sun 11am–5.30pm	w scottishmaritimemuseum.org
Admission	e clydebuilt@scotmaritime.org.uk
Adult £4.25, Child £2.50, Concs £3	

870 Glasgow

Falls of Clyde Visitor Centre & Wildlife Reserve

2 hrs+   All year

The Falls of Clyde Wildlife Reserve includes ancient gorge woodland along both sides of the River Clyde, with its famous and spectacular waterfalls. The visitor centre has an exhibition and offers a programme of educational events and guided walks in the reserve.

* Watch nesting peregrine falcons (Mar–Jun)
* Badger-watching

Location	Admission
Visitor centre is in New Lanark, which is signed from all major routes and lies 1 mile S of Lanark	*Visitor centre* Adult £3, Child free, Concs £2 *Reserve* Free
Opening	**Contact**
Reserve: Daily: *summer* 8am–8pm *winter* during daylight hours	Falls of Clyde Reserve, New Lanark, Lanarkshire ML11 9DB
	t 01555 665262
	w swt.org.uk
	e fallsofclyde@swt.org.uk

871 Glasgow

Glasgow Police Museum

1 hr+   All year

Visit the museum of Britain's first police force to gain historical insight into the people and the events that contributed to the founding, development and progress of the force. See how this pioneering force helped shape law enforcement throughout the world.

* International police exhibition
* More than 5,000 exhibits

Location	Admission
From London Road, via James Morrison Street, or Saltmarket via St Andrew's Street, or Greendyke Street via Turnball Street	Free
	Contact
	68 St. Andrew's Square, Glasgow G1 5PR
Opening	t 0141 552 1818
Daily: Apr–Oct 10am–4.30pm (opens 12noon Sun); Nov–end Mar Tue 10am–4.30pm, Sun 12noon–4.30pm	w policemuseum.org.uk
	e curator@policemuseum.org.uk

872 Glasgow

Glasgow Science Centre

3 hrs+   All year

Shake hands with yourself, make a 3D image of your face and see how you will look in years to come. Enjoy more than 300 hands-on and interactive exhibits, take in a live science show, see the latest IMAX® film, visit the Scottishpower planetarium and observe the stars.

* IMAX® cinema
* Several new exhibitions for 2007

Location	Contact
Opposite Scottish Exhibition & Crowne Plaza Hotel on River Clyde	50 Pacific Quay, Glasgow G51 1EA
	t 0871 540 1000
Opening	w glasgowsciencecentre.org
Apr–Oct daily 10am–6pm; Nov–Mar Tue–Sun 10am–6pm	e admin@glasgowsciencecentre.org.uk
Admission	
Adult £6.95, Child & Concs £4.95	

Glasgow

Glasgow Ski & Snowboarding Centre

1 hr+   All year

An artificial ski and snowboarding centre with three slopes that caters for children and adults of all levels, and offers lessons in group or private sessions. Floodlit slopes mean that visitors can enjoy the facilities well into the evening.

* Race training & freeride clubs
* Kids' toboggan (5 yrs+) & tubing (10 yrs+) parties

Location
In Bellahouston Park off junction 23 of M8

Opening
Daily: *summer* Mon–Fri 10am–10pm, Sat–Sun 10am–7pm
winter Mon–Fri 10am–11pm, Sat–Sun 10am–9pm

Admission
Activities individually priced
Please phone for details

Contact
16 Dumbreck Road,
Glasgow G41 5BW

t 0141 427 4991
w ski-glasgow.co.uk
e info@ski-glasgow.co.uk

Glasgow

Lamont City Farm

2 hrs   All year

Come and meet all sorts of animals, including sheep, goats, horses, ponies, pigs, rabbits, chinchillas, chipmunks, guinea pigs, hens, ducks, geese and Highland cows.

* Under-5s play area
* Snack bar

Location
On M8 travel to St James roundabout & then take Erskine cut-off. At 3rd roundabout turn left then 1st right into Barhill Road

Opening
Daily: 10.30am–4.30pm (3.30pm in winter)

Admission
Families free, donations welcomed
Groups please phone for details

Contact
Barhill Road, Erskine,
Renfrewshire PA8 6BX

t 0141 812 5335
w farmgarden.org.uk

Glasgow

Motoring Heritage Centre

1 hr   All year

The centre's display tells the story of Scotland's motoring history with fine cars and unique archive film. Guided tours are available. The Motoring Heritage Centre is housed in the building that was once occupied by Europe's largest car manufacturer.

* 2-star Visitor Attraction

Location
In Alexandria within walking distance of Balloch by Loch Lomond. Follow A82 to Balloch

Opening
Mon, Fri & Sat 10am–5.30pm,
Sun 11am–5pm
(closed Tue–Thu)

Admission
Adult £1.50, Child 75p, Concs £1

Contact
Loch Lomond Outlets,
Main Street, Alexandria,
West Dunbartonshire G83 0UG

t 01389 607862
w motoringheritage.co.uk

876 Glasgow

Museum of Scottish Country Life

3 hrs   All year

Set in 170 acres of farmland, with a Georgian Farm house and steadings, this museum gives an excellent insight into the working lives of the people of Scotland over the centuries.

* Exhibition building
* Historic farm & demonstrations

Location
Just off A749 or A726 S of Glasgow & W of East Kilbride

Opening
Daily: 10am–5pm

Admission
Adult £4.50, Child (under 12) free, Concs £3

Contact
West Kittochside, East Kilbride G76 9HR

t 0131 247 4377
w nms.ac.uk
w info@nms.ac.uk

877 Glasgow

Museum of Transport

2 hrs   All year

The museum uses its collections of vehicles and models to demonstrate the story of transport by land and sea, with a unique Glasgow flavour. Here you will find the oldest surviving pedal cycle and the finest collection in the world of Scottish-built cars.

* World-famous makes such as Argyll & Albion

Location
In city's West End, opposite Kelvingrove Art Gallery & Museum

Opening
Daily: Mon–Thu & Sat 10am–5pm, Fri & Sun 11am–5pm

Admission
Free

Contact
Kelvin Hall, 1 Bunhouse Road, Glasgow G3 8DP

t 0141 287 2720
w glasgowmuseums.com

878 Glasgow

People's Palace

2 hrs+   All year

The People's Palace is a social history museum offering the opportunity to discover the story of Glasgow and its people, from 1760 to the present. You can see paintings, prints and photographs displayed alongside a wealth of historic artefacts, films and computer interactives.

* Discover how a family lived in a typical single-end Glasgow tenement

Location
Short walk from city centre

Opening
Daily: Mon–Thu & Sat 10am–5pm, Fri & Sun 11am–5pm

Admission
Free

Contact
Glasgow Green, Glasgow G40 1AT

t 0141 271 2951
w glasgowmuseums.com

879 Glasgow

The Piping Centre

2 hrs   All year

The Piping Centre houses the National Museum of Scotland's fine collection of bagpipes, making it the most authoritative display of its kind. The priceless collection is presented in a lively audio-visual format that is as entertaining as it is enlightening.

* 4-star Museum Attraction

Location
In Glasgow, off junction 16 of M8 & along A804 towards the E

Opening
Daily: Mon–Sat 9am–9pm, Sun 9am–5pm Closed Sun in winter

Admission
Adult £3, Child & Concs £2

Contact
30–34 McPhater Street, Glasgow G4 0HW

t 0141 353 0220
w thepipingcentre.co.uk
e reception@thepipingcentre.co.uk

380 Glasgow

Scotkart

1 hr+   All year

Experience the thrill, the speed and the buzz of Scotland's largest and fastest indoor go-karting centre. The exciting circuit features 200cc race go-karts, and all the equipment, instruction and computer timings are included in the price.

Track includes a flyover & tunnel

Location
Follow Clydebank signs along express-way then Dunbarton road. At Yoker look for brown tourist signs. Scotkart is 200 yrds from Yoker station

Opening
Daily: 12noon–10pm

Admission
Adult £12 per session (12 min),

Child £10 per session (12 min)
£1 for insurance

Contact
John Knox Street, Clydebank, Glasgow G81 1NA

t 0141 951 8900
w scotkart.co.uk
e race@scotkart.co.uk

881 Glasgow

Scottish Football Museum

2 hrs+   All year

The world's first national football museum is housed at Hampden Park, the oldest continuously used international ground in the world. It is owned by Queen's Park FC, the oldest association team in Scotland (founded 1867) and one with an unrivalled history.

* World's most impressive collection of football memorabilia, covering 140 years of football history

Location
Take junction 1 of M77, on to B768 (Titwood Road), then right on to B766 (Battlefield Road), then Kings Park Road & left into Kinghorn Drive

Opening
Daily: Mon–Sat 10am–5pm, Sun 11am–5pm

Admission
Adult £5.50, Child & Concs £2.75

Contact
Hampden Park, Glasgow G42 9BA

t 0141 616 6139
w scottishfootballmuseum.org.uk
e museuminfo@scottishfootball museum.org.uk

882 Glasgow

Tall Ship in Glasgow Harbour

1 hr+   All year

Built in 1896, the tall ship *Glenlee* circumnavigated the globe four times. Discover her rich history, depicted on board, and gain a real sense of what it was like to live and work on board in her seafaring days. Special events include pirate crafts and seafaring superstitions.

* Exhibition tells the *Glenlee* story
* Children's events throughout the year

Location
Off M8 junction 19. Follow brown thistle signs

Opening
Daily: Mar–Oct 10am–5pm; Nov–Feb 11am–4pm

Admission
Adult £4.95, Child £2.50, Concs £3.75 (Adult price includes 1 child)

Contact
100, Stobe Cross Road, Glasgow G3 8QQ

t 0141 222 2513
w thetallship.com
e info@thetallship.com

883 Glasgow

Xscape – Braehead

2 hrs+   All year

Xscape is a fantastic family day out. Try indoor free fall in the incredible fan drop, learn to ski on the real snow and test your nerve in the Skypark aerial adventure course or on the climbing wall. Alternatively, relax at the cinema or bowling alley.

* Amazing choice of cafés, restaurants & bars

Location
Junction 26 (eastbound) of M8. A new motorway junction (25a) provides dedicated westbound access roads direct to shopping centre while new eastern link road connects the A8 dual carriageway

Opening
Daily: 9am–late

Admission
Please phone for details

Contact
Kings Inch Road, Braehead, Glasgow G51 4BW

t 0871 200 3222
w xscape.co.uk
e info@xscape.co.uk

884 Kenmore

Scottish Crannog Centre

1 hr   Mar–Nov

Visit Scotland's only authentic recreation of an Iron Age loch dwelling. Discover why these ancient people built their homes out over the water, and how they lived. Guided tours, exhibits, video and ancient crafts bring the past to life.

* Shore-based exhibition with audio-visual presentation
* Tour the real thing

Location
Croft-na-Caber just S of Kenmore

Opening
Mar–Oct daily 10am–5.30pm;
Nov Sat–Sun 10am–4pm
(last tour 4.30pm)

Admission
Adult £4.95, Child £3.25, Concs £4.25

Contact
Kenmore, Loch Tay, Perthshire PH15 2HY

t 01887 830583
w crannog.co.uk
e info@crannog.co.uk

885 Kinloch Rannoch

Loch Rannoch Watersports & Quads

2 hrs+   All year

Try your hand at a variety of water-based activities, from canoeing and windsurfing to sailing, motor boating and kayaking. A comprehensive range of courses is available, run by fully qualified staff. The centre also boasts a 4-star hotel.

* Reindeer safaris at Christmas
* Quad bike & field sports centre (for ages 14+)

Location
Signed for Kinloch Rannoch off A9 N of Pitlochry

Opening
Daily: summer 9.30am–6pm
winter 10.30am–5pm

Admission
Activities priced individually

Contact
Kinloch Rannoch, Perthshire PH16 5PS

t 01882 632242
w goforth.co.uk
e lochrannoch@goforth.co.uk

886 Kircaldy

Craigencalt Ecology Centre

1 hr   All year

The Ecology Centre provides environmental education and information across a wide range of subjects. It is the home of the UK's first 'Earthship', a building created from waste and natural materials to be self-sufficient in energy and water.

* Community woodland & sustainable living display
* Workshops & events

Location
Take B923 off A921 between Burntisland & Kirkcaldy. Located beside Kinghorn Loch

Opening
Daily: sunrise–sunset

Admission
Free

Contact
Craigencalt Farm, Kinghorn, Fife KY3 9YG

t 01592 891567
w theecologycentre.org
e adminc@theecologycentre.org

887 Kirriemuir

Barrie's Birthplace

1 hr+   All year

J M Barrie, the creator of Peter Pan, was born here
in 1860, one of a handloom weaver's 10 children.
The adjacent house, No. 11, features a new Peter Pan
room where you can use your imagination and fly off
to Neverland.

* For the young at heart, adults & children alike
* Audio programme in the wash house

Location
A901/A926 in Kirriemuir, 6 miles
NW of Forfar

Opening
Sun all year 1pm–5pm;
Jun & Sep Sat–Wed 12noon–5pm;
July–Aug Mon–Sat 11am–5pm

Admission
Adult £5, Child & Concs £4

Contact
9 Brechin Road, Kirriemuir,
Angus DD8 4BX

t 01575 572646
w nts.org.uk/barrie.html
e barriesbirthplace@nts.org.uk

888 Kirriemuir

Peel Farm

1 hr+   Apr–Dec

There are many animals and birds to see at Peel Farm,
as well as a walk to enjoy along a varied and interesting
farm trail that includes a gorge and waterfall and even a
red deer park.

* Farm shop
* Antiques

Location
20 miles N of Dundee, off B951 from
Kirriemuir or B954 from Alyth

Opening
Daily: Apr–Dec 10am–5pm

Admission
Free

Contact
Lintrathen, by Kirriemuir,
Angus DD8 5JJ

t 01575 560205/560718
w peelfarm.com

889 Linlithgow

Linlithgow Palace

1 hr   All year

Set in its own park and beside Linlithgow Loch, this is
a magnificent ruin of a great royal palace. A favoured
residence of Stuart royalty, it was the birthplace of both
James V and Mary, Queen of Scots.

* North range has a fine Renaissance façade
* Oldest working fountain in Britain

Location
On A803/M9, in town centre

Opening
Daily: Apr–Sep 9.30am–6.30pm;
Oct–Mar Mon–Sat 9.30am–4.30pm,
Sun 2pm–4.30pm

Admission
Adult £4.50, Child £2, Concs £3.50

Contact
Kirkgate, Linlithgow, West Lothian
EH49 7AL

t 01506 842896
w historic-scotland.gov.uk

890 Motherwell

M&D's Theme Park

5 hrs+   Mar–Oct

Scotland's biggest theme park, M&D has a host of activities to suit all ages. Brave the Vortex or the terrifying Tornado, or for a more leisurely ride try out the pony adventures. Inside there is an extensive arcade with the latest hi-tech thrills and spills.

* 2 themed restaurant areas
* Extensive Pool Hall

Location	Admission
Leave M74 at junction 5 (signed A725 Bellshill, Coatbridge, East Kilbride, Edinburgh), then at roundabout take 4th exit (signed Strathclyde Park)	*Single unlimited wristband* £14.50
	Contact
	Strathclyde Country Park, Motherwell ML1 3RT
Opening	
Please phone for details	t 0870 112 3777
	w scotlandsthemepark.com
	e info@scotlandsthemepark.com

891 New Lanark

New Lanark World Heritage Site

2 hrs+   All year

This beautifully restored conservation village was once Britain's largest cotton-manufacturing centre and was the birthplace of Robert Owen's reforms. Now a World Heritage Site, New Lanark's award-winning visitor centre features the amazing Millennium Experience.

* Award-winning visitor centre
* Accommodation available at New Lanark Mill Hotel

Location	Contact
Off M74 junction 13, signed off all routes	New Lanark Mills, South Lanarkshire ML11 9DB
Opening	t 01555 661345
Daily: Jun–Aug 10.30am–5pm; Sep–May 11am–5pm	w newlanark.org
	e trust@newlanark.org
Admission	
Adult £5.95, Child & Concs £4.95	

892 North Queensferry

Deep Sea World

2 hrs+   All year

Explore the undersea world at the triple award-winning National Aquarium of Scotland. Situated on the banks of the Firth of Forth, below the Forth Railway Bridge, this fascinating attraction ensures a perfect day out for the whole family.

* Seal sanctuary dedicated to orphan & sick seal pups

Location	Admission
1 mile from M90 on N side of Forth Road Bridge	Please phone for details
	Contact
Opening	North Queensferry, Fife KY11 1JR
Daily: Apr–Aug 10am–6pm; Sep–Mar Mon–Fri 10am–5pm, Sat–Sun 10am–6pm (last admission 1 hr before close)	t 01383 411880
	w deepseaworld.com
	e info@deepseaworld.co.uk

893 Perth

Dewar's Centre

3 hrs+   All year

Come and brush up on your curling skills, or take a deep breath and learn to skate for the first time. Everyone is catered for – including the little ones, with Tiny Tots on Ice.

* 8-rink indoor bowling arena
* Superb catering facilities

Location	Contact
In city centre	Glover Street, Perth PH2 0TH
Opening	t 01738 624188
Daily: Please check before visiting as times vary	w dewarcentre.co.uk
	e info@curlingscotland.com
Admission	
£5.90 (under 5s free)	

894 Perth

Noah's Ark

2 hrs   All year

Noah's Ark is a specially equipped children's soft play barn for under-12s. There are three separate areas to ensure the safety of all the children. Indoor go-karting is available and you can also enjoy a game of tenpin bowling with family and friends.

* 4-star Visitor Attraction
* Ceramic studio & trampolines

Location
On W edge of Perth,
½ mile from A9

Opening
Soft play **Daily**
Please phone to confirm times

Admission
Adult free, Child (under 5) £3.75,
Child (over 5) £4.25
Karting £3.50 for 5 min,
£4 for 5 min in twin karts

Contact
Old Gallows Road,
Perth PH1 1QE

t 01738 445568

895 Pitlochry

Killiecrankie Visitor Centre

1 hr+   Apr–Oct

In 1689 the Pass of Killiecrankie echoed with the sounds of battle, when a Jacobite army defeated the government forces. The spectacular gorge is tranquil now and a fine example of mixed deciduous woodland. The visitor centre explains the battle, natural history and ranger services.

* Site of Special Scientific Interest
* Visitors can watch birds nesting via a remote camera

Location
On B8079, 3 miles N of Pitlochry

Opening
Daily: Apr–Oct 10am–5.30pm

Admission
Free. Car park £2

Contact
nr Pitlochry, Perthshire PH16 5LG

t 01796 473233
w nts.org.uk

896 Pittenweem

Kellie Castle & Garden

2 hrs   All year

This beautiful castle was started in 1360, though much of the present building dates from the C16 and early C17. Don't miss the Victorian nursery with its fascinating collection of dolls and toys. Outdoor attractions include Victorian stables and a charming walled garden.

* Fine example of domestic architecture

Location	Contact
On B9171, 3 miles from Pittenweem	Pittenweem, Fife KY10 2RF
Opening	t 01333 720271
Castle Daily: Easter & May–Sep	w nts.org.uk
1pm–5pm	e information@nts.org.uk
Garden Daily: 9.30am–5.30pm	
Admission	
Adult £8, Child & Concs £5	

897 Plean

Plean Country Park

3 hrs+   All year

This beautiful Victorian estate provides extensive woodland walks, parkland, a picnic area and great orienteering courses. There is also a fine walled garden and enchanting wildflower meadows.

* Varied events throughout the year
* Horse trails

Location	Contact
Off M9, M80 & M876, S of Stirling	Viewforth, Stirling FK8 2ET
Opening	t 01786 442541
Daily: dawn–dusk	w stirling.gov.uk/countryside
Admission	
Free	

898 St Andrews

British Golf Museum

1 hr+   All year

Ever wondered where the word golf comes from? Why there are 18 holes on a golf course? Why golfers shout 'Fore!'? Here you'll learn the answers and many more interesting facts besides. The museum tells the story of British golf from its origins to the present day.

* Regular calendar of events
* Guided walks on the Old Course (summer only)

Location	Contact
Signed from town centre	Bruce Embankment, St Andrews,
Opening	Fife KY16 9AB
Apr–Oct Mon–Sat 9.30am–5.30pm,	t 01334 460046
Sun 10am–5pm;	w britishgolfmuseum.co.uk
Nov–Mar daily 10am–4pm	e judychance@randa.org
Admission	
Adult £5, Child £2.75, Concs £4	

899 St Andrews

Scotland's Secret Bunker

1 hr+   Apr–Oct

Hidden beneath a farm house is a 24,000 sq ft secret nuclear bunker. Walk down the 150m entrance tunnel and through the 3 ton blastproof doors to explore the underground accommodation where up to 300 staff would have lived for up to three months at a time.

* Built in complete secrecy in the 1950s
* Discover how they would have survived when you wouldn't

Location	Contact
On B940, between St Andrews	Crown Buildings, Troywood,
& Anstruther	nr St Andrews, Fife KY16 8QH
Opening	t 01333 310301
Daily: Apr–Oct 10am–6pm	w secretbunker.co.uk
(last admission 5pm)	e mod@secretbunker.co.uk
Admission	
Adult £7.80, Child £4.80, Concs £6.20,	
Family ticket (2 Adult & 2 Child) £23	

900 Stirling

Bannockburn Heritage Centre

1 hr+   Mar–Oct

On the site of the famous battlefield where in 1314 Robert the Bruce routed the forces of Edward II to win freedom from English domination for the Scots, the centre contains an exhibition on the period and an audio-visual presentation of the battle.

Wars of independence exhibition
Learn about William Wallace

Location
Off M80/M9 junction 9, 2 miles
S of Stirling

Opening
Daily: Mar–Oct 10am–5.30pm

Admission
Adult £5, Child & Concs £4, Family
ticket £14

Contact
Glasgow Road, Whins of Milton,
Stirling, Stirlingshire FK7 0LJ

t 01786 812664
w nts.org.uk

901 Stirling

Blair Drummond Safari & Adventure Park

4 hrs+   Mar–Oct

See a fascinating collection of animals from all over the world, including elephants, giraffes, lions, tigers and rhinos. You can take a safari to Chimpanzee Island, watch the performing sea lion show or visit the Pet Farm.

* 3 African rhinos
* Adventure playground & giant Astraglide

Location
In Blair Drummond by junction 10 of
M9, 4 miles along A84 towards
Callander

Opening
Daily: 25 Mar–23 Oct 10am–5.30pm
(last admission 4.30pm)

Admission
Adult £9.50, Child & Concs £6

Contact
Blair Drummond, Stirling,
Stirlingshire FK9 4UR

t 01786 841456
w blairdrummond.com
e enquiries@blairdrummond.com

902 Stirling

The MacRobert Centre

2 hrs+   All year

The MacRobert Centre is a premier children's art venue and Scotland's first dedicated children's theatre. It includes projection facilities for animation and other film work produced by children, and there is a fully supervised crèche involving children in art activities.

* Ideal for children with special needs
* Evening shows for adults

Location
Off A9. Follow signs to University of Stirling

Opening
Daily: 10am–late
Please phone for details

Admission
Varies, please phone for details

Contact
University of Stirling,
Stirling FK9 4LA

t 01786 466666
w macrobert.org
e macrobert-arts@stir.ac.uk

903 Stirling

Stirling Castle

1 hr+   All year

Stirling Castle is considered by many to be the grandest of Scotland's castles, perching on a rocky outcrop. There is a medieval kitchens display and an exhibition on what life was like in the royal palace.

* Audio guides in 6 languages
* Regimental Museum of the Highlanders

Location
Off M9, in old town

Opening
Daily: Apr–Sep 9.30am–6pm;
Oct–Mar 9.30am–5pm
(last admission 45 min before close)

Admission
Adult £8.50, Child £3.50, Concs £6.50

Contact
Esplanade, Stirling,
Stirlingshire FK8 1EJ

t 01786 450000
w historic-scotland.gov.uk

904 Aberdeen

Aberdeen Maritime Museum

1 hr+   All year

Discover what it is like to live and work on a massive oil platform in the middle of the North Sea. Using models, real equipment and computer displays, the exhibitions bring the maritime experience to life. There are models of fast clipper ships and fishing displays.

* Incorporates Provost Ross's House, built in 1593
* Offers a spectacular viewpoint over the busy harbour

Location	Contact
Overlooking the harbour	Shiprow, Aberdeen AB11 5BY
Opening	t 01224 337700
Daily: Mon–Sat 10am–5pm,	w aagm.co.uk
Sun 12noon–3pm	e info@aagm.co.uk
Admission	
Free	

905 Aberdeen

Archaeolink

1 hr+   All year

This dynamic historical experience covers 10,000 years from the Stone Age to the Romans. See how people used to live and work with reconstructions of homes, stone circles and even a Roman army camp. Daily activities include metalwork, weaving and combat displays.

* Special exhibitions throughout the year
* Re-enactments & spectacular events programme

Location	Contact
Just off A96 near Aberdeen	Oyne, Insch, Aberdeen AB52 6QP
Opening	t 01464 851500
Daily: Apr–Oct 10am–5pm, Nov–Mar	w archaeolink.co.uk
11am–4pm	e info@archaeolink.co.uk
Admission	
Adult £5, Child £3.40, Concs £4.50	

906 Aberdeen

Beach Leisure Centre

4 hrs+   All year

Relax at this amazingly well-equipped leisure centre specifically geared for families. The pool has four flumes, a fountain and rapids. There's also a fitness studio, health suite with sauna and steam room, climbing wall and sports hall.

* Free crèche
* Refurbished café

Location	Contact
Next to beach at Aberdeen	Beach Promenade, Aberdeen AB24 5NR
Opening	t 01224 655401
Please phone for details	w aberdeencity.gov.uk
Admission	e info@aberdeencity.gov.uk
Facilities priced individually	

907 Aberdeen

Codona's Pleasure Fair

3 hrs+   All year

Codona's amusement park is packed with more than
30 sensational rides and attractions for all the family.
There are fun children's rides and, for the white-
knuckle fans, the giant Log Flume and 360° Looping
Star roller coaster offer unforgettable thrills.

* 100ft ferris wheel
* Dodgems, haunted house, waltzers & crazy train

Location
Travelling from the S take A90.
Coming from Inverness take A96
Inverness–Aberdeen route. Once
in Aberdeen follow signs to Aberdeen
Fun Beach

Opening
Daily: 10am–midnight
Please phone for details

Admission
Rides priced individually

Contact
Beach Boulevard,
Aberdeen AB24 5NS

t 01224 595910
w codonas.com

908 Aberdeen

Gordon Highlanders Museum

2 hrs   Apr–Oct

Relive the compelling and dramatic story of one of
the British Army's most famous regiments through
the lives of its outstanding personalities and of the
kilted soldiers of north-east Scotland.

* Tartan Day
* Interactive displays

Location
Off Queens Road, known as Highland
Tourist Route in & out of Aberdeen

Opening
Apr–Oct Tue–Sun 10.30am–4.30pm,
Sun 12.30pm–4.30pm (closed Mon),
Nov–Mar open by appointment only

Admission
Adult £3.50, Child £1.50, Concs £2.50

Contact
St Luke's, Viewfield Road,
Aberdeen AB15 7XH

t 01224 311200
w gordonhighlanders.com
e museum@gordonhighlanders.com

909 Aberdeen

Satrosphere

2 hrs   All year

Satrosphere offers fun for families and for grown-ups who love to explore, experiment and find out how the world works. Look into infinity, light up a plasma dome, step inside a bubble or make a skeleton ride a bicycle – it's all possible at Satrosphere.

* Interactive shows
* Workshops

Location
Off Beach Boulevard & Links Road
near Patio Hotel

Opening
Daily: 10am–5pm

Admission
Adult £5.75, Child & Concs £4.50

Contact
The Tramsheds,
179 Constitution Street,
Aberdeen AB24 5TU

t 01224 640340
w satrosphere.net
e satrosphere@satrosphere.net

910 Ballater

Balmoral Castle & Estate

1 hr+   Apr–Jul

See inside one of the Queen's residences, visit the ballroom and the formal and vegetable gardens, or enjoy an audio-visual display. Other activities on the estate include pony trekking, a Land Rover safari, guided walks, fishing and trailer rides.

* Access to grounds, gardens, exhibitions, shops,
  tearoom & ballroom

Location
Off A93, between Ballater & Braemar

Opening
Daily: Apr–Jul 10am–5pm
(last admission 4pm)

Admission
Adult £7, Child £3, Concs £6

Contact
Estates Office, Balmoral Estates,
Ballater, Aberdeenshire AB35 5TB

t 01339 742534
w balmoralcastle.com
e info@balmoralcastle.com

911 Ballater

The Old Royal Station, Ballater

1 hr   All year

This renovated railway station features royalty and railway exhibitions with commentary and audio-visual presentations about Royal Deeside. A Victorian carriage will soon be arriving for display in an exhibition.

* 4-star Speciality Attraction
* Restaurant

Location
In centre of Deeside village of Ballater, on A93 Aberdeen–Braemar road

Opening
Please phone for details

Admission
Free

Contact
Station Square, Ballater AB35 5AB

t 01339 755306
w visitscotland.com
e ballater@visitscotland.com

912 Drumoak

Drum Castle, Garden & Estate

2–4 hrs   Apr–Sep

The late C13 keep, fine adjoining Jacobean mansion and the additions of Victorian lairds make Drum Castle unique. The building is set in spectacular grounds, which contain a garden of historic roses, woodland trails and a children's playground.

* Old Wood of Drum is a Site of Special Scientific Interest

Location
Off A93, 3 miles W of Peterculter, 8 miles E of Banchory & 10 miles W of Aberdeen

Opening
Good Fri–Jun & Sep Wed–Thu & Sat–Mon 12.30–5pm; Jul–Aug daily 11am–5pm (last admission 45 min before close)

Admission
Please phone for details

Contact
Drumoak, Banchory, Aberdeen & Grampian AB31 5EY

t 01330 811204
w drum-castle.org.uk
e drum@nts.org.uk

913 Forres

Findhorn Heritage Icehouse

1 hr   May–Sep

Explore underground arched chambers built 150 years ago to store ice for packing salmon on the way to London. The chambers are now used to display all aspects of the salmon net-fishing industry. Visit the Heritage Centre where the history and ecology are graphically displayed.

* Junior quiz to complete
* See the unique Findhorn Class yacht

Location
From Forres take B9089 to Kinloss, then B9011 to Findhorn & follow signs

Opening
May & Sep Sat–Sun 2pm–5pm; Jun–Aug daily 2pm–5pm

Admission
Free, donations welcomed

Contact
147, Findhorn, Forres, Moray IV36 3YL

t 01309 690659
w findhornbay.net
e s.eibbor@tesco.net

914 Fraserburgh

The Museum of Scottish Lighthouses

2 hrs+   All year

The history of Scotland's lighthouses is illuminated in the country's oldest example. There are multi-screen audio-visual presentations, and a guided tour to the top of the fully restored lighthouse where visitors can enjoy panoramic views of the Buchan coast.

* Largest collection of lighthouse equipment in the UK
* First lighthouse built on top of a fortified castle

Location
In town centre

Opening
Daily: Apr–Oct, Mon–Sat, 10am–5pm, Sun, 12 noon–5pm; Jul–Aug, Mon–Sat, 10am–6pm, Sun, 11am–6pm; Nov–Mar, Mon–Sat, 10am–4pm, Sun 12 noon–4pm

Admission
Adult £5, Child £2, Concs £4

Contact
Kinnaird Head, Stevenson Road, Fraserburgh AB43 9DU

t 01346 511022
w lighthousemuseum.co.uk
e info@lighthousemuseum.org.uk

915 Huntly

Leith Hall

3 hrs+   Apr–Sep

The home of the Leith family since 1650, this mansion house contains interesting personal possessions and a military exhibition. The estate has a garden with two ponds, a bird hide, an ice house and stables.

Halloween events
Easter egg hunt

Location
On B9002, 1 mile W of Kennethmont & 34 miles NW of Aberdeen. Signed off A96

Opening
Easter weekend & May–Sep
Fri–Tue 12noon–5pm
(last admission 4.15pm)

Admission
Adult £8, Child & Concs £5

Contact
Kennethmont, Huntly,
Aberdeenshire AB54 4NQ

t 01464 831216
w nts.org.uk
e leithhall@nts.org.uk

917 Mintlaw

Aberdeenshire Farming Museum

2 hrs   Apr–Oct

Discover 200 years of farming and family life at this museum, set within a delightful country park. The C19 farm buildings house displays on Scotland's rich agricultural history. There is also a working 1950s-style farm to explore.

Collection of farming artefacts
Sensory garden

Location
1 mile W of Mintlaw on A950

Opening
Daily: May–Sep 11am–4.30pm; Apr & Oct Sat–Sun only 12noon–4.30pm
Park All year
Please phone for details

Admission
Car park fee

Contact
Aden Country Park, nr Mintlaw,
Aberdeenshire AB42 5FQ

t 01771 622807
w aberdeenshire.gov.uk/heritage

916 Macduff

Macduff Marine Aquarium

1 hr+   All year

This most northerly of Scotland's aquariums has several unique features, including the main tank, which is open to the air. There are touch tanks, a ray pool, rock pool and inshore displays with a wealth of aquatic life to admire and sometimes even touch.

* Estuary & deep-reef exhibits
* Feeding times & dive sessions

Location
Short walk from Macduff town centre, just E of harbour. Reached via A98, A947 or A96

Opening
Daily: 10am–5pm

Admission
Adult £5, Child £2.50, Concs £3

Contact
11 High Shore, Macduff,
Banffshire AB44 1SL

t 01261 833369
w marine-aquarium.org.uk
e macduff.aquarium@aberdeenshire.
gov.uk

Peterhead

Peterhead Maritime Heritage

1 hr+   Jun–Aug

This Heritage Centre offers a historic look back at the Peterhead experience of fishing and whaling, and gives a brief insight into the North Sea oil industry. An observation box with telescopes provides breathtaking views out across the bay.

* 3-star Speciality Attraction

Location
Overlooking Peterhead Bay & beside beach & marina. Reached via A90 or A950

Opening
Daily: Jun–Aug 10.30am–5pm, Sun 11.30am–5pm

Admission
Free

Contact
South Road, Peterhead, Aberdeenshire AB42 2YP

t 01779 473000
w aberdeenshire.gov.uk

Aviemore

Cairngorm Reindeer Centre

1 hr+   Feb–Dec

Travel in a cavalcade to see 50 reindeer ranging free in the Cairngorms. Under the supervision of a guide, visitors can feed, stroke and photograph the reindeer. All ages, even babies in back-carriers, can come. Book well in advance for Christmas sleigh-pulling events.

* Guided tours on the hills (weather permitting)
* Learn more about these fascinating creatures

Location
6 miles E of Aviemore

Opening
Daily: Feb–Dec 10am–5pm Tours Feb half-term, Apr & Oct–Dec 11am Tours May–Sep 11am & 2.30pm

Admission
Adult £8, Child & Concs £4

Contact
Glenmore, Aviemore, Invernessshire PH22 1QU

t 01479 861228
w reindeer-company.demon.co.uk
e info@reindeer-company.demon.co.uk

Aviemore

The Fun House

2 hrs   All year

The Fun House is a first choice for family entertainment. A wealth of activities include mini-golf, a tree house, tenpin bowling, air hockey and soft play areas. There is also a crèche for toddlers and an American Diner.

* 3-star Visitor Attraction

Location
Off B970, on a wooded riverside estate of 65 acres (on the ski road)

Opening
Daily: 10am–5pm

Admission
Please phone for details

Contact
Hilton Coylumbridge Hotel, Aviemore, Invernessshire PH22 1QN

t 01479 813081
w aviemorefunhouse.co.uk

921 Aviemore

Strathspey Steam Railway

2 hrs   May–Sep & Dec

This steam railway runs between Aviemore and Boat of Garten and on to Broomhill, near Nethy Bridge. The railway beautifully evokes the steam era of the 1950s and 1960s and runs through unspoilt countryside with fabulous mountain views.

* 3-Star Visitor Attraction

Location
Boat of Garten is off A95 between Aviemore & Grantown-on-Spey, or off B970 between Nethy Bridge & Inverdruie

Opening
Daily: end May–end Sep & selected days in Dec. Please phone for details

Admission
Adult £9.50, Child £4.75, Concs £7

Contact
Aviemore Station,
Dalfaber Road, Aviemore,
Invernessshire PH22 1PY

t 01479 810725
w strathspeyrailway.co.uk

922 Ballindalloch

Ballindalloch Castle

2 hrs+   Easter–Sep

This magnificent C16 castle, known as 'the Pearl of the North', has been the family home of the MacPherson-Grants since 1546. Through its romantic gardens flow the Rivers Spey and Avon. The 'Biggles' author Captain W E Johns lived at nearby Pitchroy Lodge.

* Ballindalloch herd of Aberdeen Angus cattle
* Golf facilities available, subject to prior arrangement

Location
14 miles NE of Grantown-on-Spey on A95

Opening
Easter–Sep Sun–Fri 10.30am–5pm

Admission
Please phone for details

Contact
Ballindalloch, Banffshire
AB37 9AX

t 01807 500206
w ballindallochcastle.co.uk
e enquiries@ballindallochcastle.co.uk

923 Balmaha

Loch Lomond National Nature Reserve

3 hrs   All year

This beautiful reserve includes five of the loch's 38 islands, each supporting oak woodland, and the mouth of the River Endrick has fen, grassland and swamp woodland. Visit Inchailloch Island in May–June for woodland wildlife and in winter–early spring for wildfowl.

* Wonderful camp & picnic site
* Remains of a C13 parish church

Location
Inchailloch is reached by ferry from Balmaha boatyard off B837

Opening
Daily: wardens present Apr–Sep

Admission
Free

Contact
Loch Lomond & Trossochs National Park, Balmaha Visitor Centre

t 01389 722600/722100
w lochlomond-trossachs.org
e info@lochlomond-trossachs.org

924 Birsay

Kirbuster Museum

1 hr+ Mar–Oct

The custodian at this folk museum describes the farming life of the past. The museum boasts the last traditional peat-burning central hearth and stone neuk bed in Northern Europe. There are also displays of farming equipment and a traditional Victorian garden.

* Putting green
* Livestock in grounds

Location
In Kirbuster, Birsay

Opening
Daily: Mar–Oct Mon–Sat 10am–1pm & 2pm–5pm, Sun 2pm–7pm

Admission
Free

Contact
Kirbuster, Birsay, Orkney KW17 2LR
t 01856 771268
m orkney.gov.uk/heritage
e museum@orkney.gov.uk

925 Carrbridge

Landmark Forest Theme Park

5–6 hrs All year

Scotland's favourite heritage park, Landmark has a wide range of fun, discovery and adventure activities for all ages in all weather, including a wild-water coaster, a red squirrel nature trail, a steam-powered sawmill and a wildforest maze.

* 4-star Speciality Attraction
* Treetop trail

Location
7 miles N of Aviemore, 23 miles S of Inverness just off A9 at Carrbridge

Opening
Daily: Apr–mid-Jul 10am–6pm; mid-Jul–mid-Aug 10am–7pm; Sep–Mar 10am–5pm

Admission
Adult £8.95, Child (under 4) free, Child (over 4) £6.90

Contact
Main Street, Carrbridge, Invernessshire PH23 3AJ

t 01479 841613
w landmark-centre.co.uk
e landmarkcentre@btconnect.com

926 Corrigal

Corrigall Farm Museum

2 hrs Mar–Oct

This museum is a fully renovated Orkney farm cottage, complete with its peat fire and box beds. A kiln, parish weaver's loom and other traditional crafts help you catch a flavour of the farming and domestic life of the Orkney people from the C18 to the C20.

* Various livestock
* Horse-drawn farm machinery

Location
Signed from main Kirkwall–Stromness road

Opening
Mar–Oct Mon–Sat 10.30am–1pm & 2pm–5pm, Sun 2pm–7pm

Admission
Free

Contact
Midhouse, Corrigall, Harray KW17

t 01856 771411
w orkney.gov.uk/heritage
e museum@orkney.gov.uk

927 Culloden

Culloden Battlefield

1 hr+   Feb–Dec

This was the site of one of the most infamous battles in Scottish history, when more than 1,500 Jacobites were killed. Today it is a poignant and haunting location. The visitor centre has a fascinating exhibition, including an audio-visual programme.

* Permanent exhibition of the type of weapons used in battle
* New £8 million visitor centre opening summer 2007

Location
On B9006, 5 miles E of Inverness

Opening
Daily: Feb & Nov–Dec 11am–4pm; Mar–May 10am–4pm; Jun–Aug 9am–6pm; Sep–Oct 9am–5.30pm

Admission
Adult £5, Child & Concs £4, Family ticket £14

Contact
The National Trust for Scotland, Culloden Moor, Inverness IV2 5EU

t 01463 790607
w nts.org.uk/culloden

928 Dornoch

Historylinks Museum

1 hr+   All year

This small museum is packed with 700 years of history – the treachery and violence of the Picts and Vikings, feuding clans, and the shameful burning of Scotland's last condemned witch.

* Activities & quizzes
* Dressing up for children

Location
In Dornoch town centre, 2 miles from A9

Opening
Easter week & Jun–Sep daily 10am–4pm; May Mon–Fri 10am–4pm; Oct–Mar Wed–Thu 10am–4pm

Admission
Adult £2, Child free, Concs £1.50

Contact
The Meadows, Dornoch, Sutherland IV25 3SF

t 01862 811275
w historylinks.org.uk
e historylinks@dsl.pipex.com

929 Drumnadrochit

Loch Ness Monster Exhibition Centre

1 hr+   All year

Through photographs, descriptions and film footage, this exhibition presents the evidence about the existence of the Loch Ness Monster. It also highlights the efforts of various search expeditions, by both individuals and respected institutions, such as Operation Deepscan.

* Travel round the loch, view places & meet locals
* Exhibition cinema in 8 languages

Location
On A82, W of Inverness

Opening
Daily: Apr–Oct 9am–9pm; Nov–Mar 9am–5pm

Admission
Adult £5, Child £3.50, Concs £3.95

Contact
Drumnadrochit, Invernessshire IV63 6TU

t 01456 450342
w lochness-centre.com
e donald@lochness-centre.com

930 Elgin

Elgin Cathedral

2 hrs   All year

The superb remains of a majestic and beautiful C13 cathedral that was almost destroyed in 1390 by Alexander Stewart, the infamous Wolf of Badenoch. You can also visit the bishop's home at Spynie Palace, 2 miles north of the town.

* Joint ticket available with Spynie Palace
* 4-star Historic Site Attraction

Location
Cathedral can be found just N of centre of Elgin by following brown tourist signs

Opening
Apr–Sep daily 9.30am–6.30pm; Oct–Mar Sat–Wed 9.30am–4.30pm

Admission
Adult £4, Child £1.60, Concs £3

Contact
Historic Scotland, Longmore House, Salisbury Place, Edinburgh EH9 1SH

t 01343 547171
w historic-scotland.gov.uk
e hs.explorer@scotland.gov.uk

931 Fochabers

WDCS Wildlife Centre

2 hrs+   Feb–Dec

A wildlife centre with exhibitions about dolphins, ospreys, otters and wildfowl. It is run by the Whale and Dolphin Conservation Society, and provides children's activities throughout the summer.

* Nature reserve adjacent
* Wildlife activity holidays

Location
On A96 at mouth of River Spey, 5 miles N of Fochabers

Opening
Feb–Mar Sat–Sun 10.30am–5pm;
Apr–Oct daily 10.30am–5pm;
Oct–Dec Sat–Sun 10.30am–5pm

Admission
Free

Contact
Fochabers, Moray IV32 7PJ

t 01343 820339
w mfwc.co.uk
e wildlifecentre@wdcs.org

932 Fort William

Vertical Descents

3 hrs+   All year

This adventure centre offers canyoning, white-water rafting, paintballing, fun yakking, adventure holidays, adrenaline sports, adventure travel, mountain biking, abseiling and a bridge swing (like a bungee with a swing). No previous experience is required.

* All necessary clothing & equipment provided

Location
Off A82, 7 miles S of Fort William

Opening
Daily. (closed Christmas hols)

Admission
£40 per person (half-day canyoning)
Activities priced individually

Contact
Inchree Falls, Inchree, Onich, nr Fort William PH33 6SE

t 01855 821593
w activities-scotland.com
e info@verticaldescents.com

933 Glencoe

Glencoe Visitor Centre

1 hr   All year

Built in 2002, this state-of-the-art eco-friendly centre is built from timber, insulated with sheep's wool and heated by burning local wood chips. The exhibition covers the ecology and geology of Glencoe, mountaineering and the history of Glencoe.

* Summer events programme
* Display on the history of mountaineering in the glen

Location
On A82, between Glasgow & Fort William

Opening
Mar daily 10am–4pm;
Apr–Aug daily 9.30am–5.30pm;
Sep–Oct daily 10am–5pm;
Nov–Feb Thu–Sun 10am–4pm

Admission
Adult £5, Child & Concs £4

Contact
Ballachulish, Argyll PH49 4HX

t 01855 811307
w glencoe.nts.org.uk
e glencoe@nts.org.uk

934 Inveraray

Inveraray Jail

1 hr+   All year

Sit and listen to trials in the 1820 courtroom. Talk to guides dressed as warders, prisoners and the matron. Visit the two prisons and experience the sounds and smells that would have accosted you then.

* View a Black Maria prison transport vehicle
* Try the crank machine, whipping table & hammocks

Location
Off A82/83 Glasgow–Campbeltown road

Opening
Daily: Apr–Oct 9.30am–6pm;
Nov–Mar 10am–5pm (last admission
1 hr before close)

Admission
Adult £6.25, Child (4–16) £3.15,
Concs £4.15, Family ticket £17.20

Contact
Church Square, Inveraray,
Argyll PA32 8TX

t 01499 302381
w inverarayjail.co.uk
e info@inverarayjail.co.uk

935 Inverness

Inverness Dolphin Cruises

1 hr+   Mar–Oct

Enjoy a 1½–hour cruise on the *Daniel Quilp* out on the Moray Firth, where you will see the most northerly resident colony of dolphins in the world, common and grey seals, porpoises, minke whales, red kites and ospreys.

* Room for 50 passengers
* Commentary from professional guide

Location
Boat leaves from Inverness harbour

Opening
Daily: Mar–end Oct. Cruises leave at
10.30am, 12noon, 1.30pm, 3pm &
4.30pm (& 6pm in Jul–Aug)

Admission
Adult £12.50, Child £9, Concs £10

Contact
Shore Street Quay, Shore Street,
Inverness IV1 1NF

t 01463 717900
w inverness-dolphin-cruises.co.uk
e info@inverness-dolphin
    cruises.co.uk

936 Inverness

Inverness Terror Tour

1 hr+   All year

Led by Davy the Ghost, this walking tour of horror and laughter takes you through the streets of Inverness. Hear gruesome stories along the way of witches, ghosts and ghastly happenings before ending at the haunted tavern, where a free drink is provided.

* Witches, ghosts, torture & murders

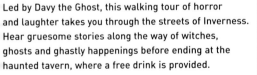

Location
Outside Tourist Information
Centre on Bridge Street

Opening
Daily: 7pm

Admission
Adult £7, Child £5, Concs £6.50

Contact
Tourist Information Centre,
Bridge Street, Inverness IV2 3BJ

t 07730 831069

937 Isle of Barra

Kisimul Castle

1 hr+   Mar–Sep

The historic restored seat of the MacNeils of Barra, chiefs of the Clan MacNeil. Located on an island, it is reached by a small boat from the village of Castlebay.

* Real & lived-in castle
* Fabulous views of Castlebay

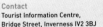

Location
In Castlebay, Isle of Barra, reached
by a small boat from Castlebay (5
min trip, weather permitting)

Opening
Daily: Mar–Sep 9.30am–6.30pm
(last admission 5.30pm)

Admission
Adult £4, Child £1.60, Concs £3

Contact
Castlebay, Isle of Barra,
Western Isles HS9 5XD

t 01871 810313
w historic-scotland.gov.uk
e hs.explorer@scotland.gsi.gov.uk

938 Isle of Lewis

The Black House Museum

1 hr   All year

Visit a traditional Isle of Lewis crofter's thatched cottage, or black house. Now a museum, it is fully furnished, complete with attached barn, byre, peat fire and stackyard. The visitor centre provides a wealth of fascinating information about Hebridean life.

* Interactive displays
* 5-star Scottish Tourism Award

Location
Off A858

Opening
Please phone for details

Admission
Adult £4.50, Child £2, Concs £3.50

Contact
Arnol, Isle of Lewis,
Western Isles HS2 9DB

t 01851 710395
w historic-scotland.gov.uk

939 Isle of Lewis

Lewis Karting Centre

Varies   All year

Arrive and drive at this outdoor go-karting centre. There are go-karts for hire for children aged eight and upwards and a Kiddie Kart section for the younger driver on a safe inflatable circuit.

* Sessions include briefing, kit & 12 minutes on the track
* Maclaren-style 2-seater coming soon

Location
4 miles S of Stornoway on A859

Opening
Please phone for details

Admission
Please phone for details

Contact
Creed Enterprise Park, Lochs Road,
Stornoway, Isle of Lewis HS2 9JN

t 01851 700222
w lewiscarclub.co.uk
e enquiries@lewiscarclub.co.uk

940 Isle of Mull

Whale Watching Trips

1 hr+   Mar–Oct

Climb aboard the *Alpha Beta* for a fun-filled trip among the Hebridean islands in search of a host of wildlife. Seek out the magnificent minke whales measuring more than 10 metres long, encounter the playful dolphins or if you're very lucky spot the awesome killer whales.

* Inter-island cruises also available

Location
Signed from Dervaig to Croig (longer trips)
Signed for Tobermory (shorter trips)

Opening
Daily: Mar–Oct from 9.45am.
Please phone for details

Admission
From £25 per person

Contact
Sea Life Surveys, Ledaig, Tobermory, Isle of Mull PA75 6NU

t 01688 302916
w sealifesurveys.com
e info@sealifesurveys.com

941 Isle of Raasay

Raasay Outdoor Centre

4 hrs+   Apr–Oct

Raasay Outdoor Centre is situated in the historic mansion of Raasay House. Try your hand at sailing around the seas of Skye, kayaking around Raasay's sheltered bays, or rock climbing and abseiling in some of the island's most beautiful locations.

* Whole range of outdoor activities
* Café & fine restaurant

Location
Isle of Raasay is a 15 min ferry journey from Isle of Skye. There is a direct bus route from Inverness & Glasgow

Opening
Daily: Apr–Oct 8am–11pm or fully residential
Please phone for details

Admission
Free (activities range from £6)

Contact
Raasay House, Isle of Raasay, by Kyle IV40 8PB

t 01478 660266
w raasay-house.co.uk

942 Isle of Skye

Bella Jane Boat Trips

3 hrs+   Mar–Oct

Bella Jane boat trips take you to the world-famous Loch Coruisk and the seal colony at the heart of the Cuillin on the Isle of Skye. During the journey you will see a wealth of sea life and enjoy breathtaking scenery. Excursions from one hour to a whole day.

* 4-star Visitor Attraction
* Aquaxplore excursions to Canna & Rum

Location
Take B8083 from Broadford to Elgol for 15 miles (45 min by car)

Opening
Daily: Mar–Oct. Trip times vary, please phone for details

Admission
£10–£20 Please book in advance

Contact
Elgol, Isle of Skye IV49 9BJ

t 0800 731 3089 (from 7.30am)
w bellajane.co.uk
e david@bellajane.co.uk

943 Isle of Skye

The Bright Water Visitor Centre

1 hr   Apr–Oct

The centre offers a unique child-friendly, interactive experience that unfolds the area's dramatic history and celebrates the wealth of local wildlife. It also commemorates Gavin Maxwell, author of *Ring of Bright Water.*

* 3-star Speciality Attraction
* Visit the Stevenson Lighthouse

Location
Take Kyleakin exit at Skye roundabout (at the end of Skye Bridge)

Opening
Apr–Oct Mon–Fri 10am–4pm

Admission
Free, donations requested

Contact
The Pier, Kyleakin, Isle of Skye IV41 8PL

t 01599 530040
w eileanban.org
e enquiries@eileanban.org

944 Isle of Skye

Family's Pride II Glassbottom Boat Trips

1 hr   Mar–Oct

Cruise around the spectacular Bay of Islands in a glassbottomed boat. See seals, birds and porpoises above deck, then step below and be mesmerised by the amazing sights of the underwater world.

* Frequent daily sailings

Location
In Broadford, Isle of Skye, 8 miles from Skye Bridge

Opening
Daily: Mar–Oct 10.30am–4.45pm

Admission
Adult £10, Child (under 12) £5

Contact
5 Scullamus, Breakish, Isle of Skye IV42 8QB

t 0800 783 2175
w glassbottomboat.co.uk

945 Kincraig

Working Sheepdogs

1 hr   All year

Participate in the working day of a Highland shepherd and his dogs. Help to shear a sheep and bottle-feed orphan lambs. Meet the friendly pups and feed the Highland cows.

* 2-star Wildlife & Nature Attraction
* Live performances

Location
On a working farm, 5 miles S of Aviemore & 5 miles N of Kingussie on B9152

Opening
Daily: demonstrations at 12noon & 4pm
Private bookings available

Admission
Please phone for details

Contact
Leault Farm,Kincraig, Invernessshire PH21 1LZ

t 01540 651310

946 Kingussie

Highland Folk Museum, Newtonmore

3 hrs   Easter–Oct

Get a fascinating glimpse into 300 years of Highland life at this recreation of a thriving C18 farming township with clockmaker's workshop and working croft. See how Highland people adapted to the harsh environment, and enjoy demonstrations of traditional skills and crafts.

* 4-star Visitor Attraction
* Vintage buses on site

Location
On A86, ¼ mile N of Newtonmore

Opening
Please phone for details

Admission
Please phone for details

Contact
Duke Street, Kingussie, Invernessshire PH21 1JG

t 01540 661307
w highlandfolk.com
e highlandfolk@highland.gov.uk

947 Kingussie

Highland Wildlife Park

3 hrs+   All year

Enjoy a wild day out in the Cairngorm National Park. Drive through the scenic main reserve then explore the rest of the park on foot. There are wolves, otters, reindeer, lynx, pine martens, capercaillie and more.

* 4-star Visitor Attraction
* Educational tours & talks

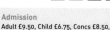

Location
7 miles S of Aviemore on B road, 2½ hrs from Edinburgh

Opening
Daily: Apr–May & Sep–Oct 10am–6pm; Jun–Aug 10am–7pm; Nov–Mar 10am–4pm (last admission 2 hrs before close). If heavy ice or snow please phone before visiting

Admission
Adult £9.50, Child £6.75, Concs £8.50, Family ticket £32.50

Contact
Kincraig, Kingussie, Invernessshire PH21 1NL

t 01540 651270
w highlandwildlifepark.org
e info@highlandwildlifepark.org

948 Kirkwall

The Orkney Museum

3 hrs   All year

Visit this C16 town-house museum to discover the history of Orkney. From prehistory to the C20, the story of Orkney is told through archaeological and social history exhibits, ranging from a Scar Viking boat burial through to a 300-year-old calculator.

* C16 Scottish vernacular architecture
* Beautiful gardens

Location	Admission
Kirkwall, Orkney, opposite St Magnus Cathedral	Free
Opening	Contact
May–Sep Mon–Sat 10.30am–5pm, Sun 2pm–5pm; Oct–Apr Mon–Sat 10.30am–12.30pm & 1.30pm–5pm	Tankerness House, Broad Street, Kirkwall, Orkney KW15 1DH
	t 01856 873191
	w orkneyheritage.com
	e museum@orkney.gov.uk

949 Kirkwall

Scapa Flow Visitor Centre & Museum

2 hrs+   All year

A British Navy base during WWI and WWII, Scapa Flow is now a museum with many interesting relics from the war days. Advance booking is required for the ferry from Houton to Lyness. Don't miss the audio-visual show in the oil rig.

* Artefacts from HMS *Hampshire*
* Display on HMS *Royal Oak*

Location	Admission
Near Lyness Pier, on island of Hoy	Free
Opening	Contact
Daily: May–Sep Mon–Sat 9am–4.30pm, Sun please phone for details; Oct–Apr Mon–Fri 9am–4.30pm	Lyness, Hoy, Kirkwall, Orkney KW16 3NT
	t 01856 791300
	w orkney.gov.uk/heritage
	e museum@orkney.gov.uk

950 Kyle of Lochalsh

Seaprobe *Atlantis*

1 hr+   Apr–Oct

Embark on Scotland's only fabulous, semi-submersible, glassbottomed boat. You can enjoy views of a WWII shipwreck, kelp forests, fish, jellyfish, sea urchins, starfish and occasional dolphins and whales. Visit seal and bird colonies, and look out for otters.

* 4-star Visitor Attraction
* Comprehensive commentary during the voyage

Location	Contact
Off A87 at Kyle of Lochalsh; boat departs from below Lochalsh Hotel. Follow the brown tourist signs	Kyle Tourist Information Centre, Old Ferry Pier, Kyle of Lochalsh IV40 8AQ
Opening	t 0800 980 4846
Daily: Easter–Oct 10am–evening	w seaprobeatlantis.com
Admission	e seaprobe@msn.com
1-hour trip Adult £12.50, Child (3–12) £6.25. Tickets available from Kyle TIC	

951 Lairg

Ferrycroft Countryside Visitor Centre

2 hrs   Apr–Oct

A hands-on family-oriented visitor centre displaying the natural and archaeological history of an area rich in beauty and wildlife. The centre guides the visitor through the changes in land use in the area from the Ice Age to the present day. There is public internet access and you can download your photos to disc.

* Indoor & outdoor play areas
* Countryside ranger

Location
Central Sutherland, on shore of Loch Shin

Opening
Daily: Apr–May & Sep–Oct 10am–4pm;
Jun–Aug 10am–5pm

Admission
Free

Contact
Lairg, Sutherland IV27 4AZ

t 01549 402160
w lairghighlands.org.uk
e ferrycroft@croftersrestaurant.fsnet.
co.uk

952 Liddle

Tomb of the Eagles

1 hr+   All year

A visit to the Tomb of the Eagles gives a valuable insight into the life of our Neolithic ancestors. Visitors are given the opportunity to handle some of the original artefacts.

* Guided tour of Bronze Age house
* Children's indoor play area

Location
South Ronaldsay, Orkney.
Overlooking Pentland Firth,
on Scottish mainland

Opening
Daily: Mar–Oct 9.30am–5.30pm;
Nov–Feb by arrangement

Admission
Please phone for details

Contact
Liddle, South Ronaldsay,
Orkney KW17 2RW

t 01856 831339
w tomboftheeagles.co.uk
e info@tomboftheeagles.co.uk

Cawdor Castle

2 hrs   May–Oct

A superb fairytale castle, complete with fortress-like tower and drawbridge. In vaults deep beneath stands an ancient and mystical holly tree and close by is a secret dungeon. Outside a series of paths wind through the Big Wood where you may catch sight of red deer.

* 9-hole golf course & gift shops
* Holiday cottages available

Location
Between Inverness & Nairn on B9090 off A96.

Opening
Daily: May–Oct 10am–5.30pm

Admission
Adults £7.30, Child £4.50, Concs £6.30
Garden only £4

Contact
Nairn IV12 5RD

t 01667 404401
w cawdorcastle.com
e info@cawdorcastle.com

Scottish Sealife & Marine Sanctuary

2½ hrs   All year

Nestling on the shore of Loch Creran, Scotland's leading marine animal rescue centre cares for abandoned seal pups and also has resident common seals and otters. The centre combines a spectacular aquarium with a busy rescue and rehabilitation facility.

* 3-star Marine Attraction
* New displays added regularly

Location
10 miles N of Oban on A828

Opening
Please phone for details

Admission
Please phone for details

Contact
Sanctuary, Barcaldine, Oban, Argyll PA37 1SE

t 01631 720386
w sealsanctuary.co.uk
e oban@sealsanctuary.co.uk

Balfour Castle

2 hrs   May–Sep

A Victorian castle surrounded by landscaped grounds and a plantation of trees. The interior is richly decorated in an Italianate style, and the grounds boast a superb Victorian walled garden. A delicious Orkney afternoon tea is included in the price.

* Victorian walled gardens
* Ferry trip included

WC

Location
2 min from Shapinsay Harbour, reached by ferry from Kirkwall on Orkney mainland, a 25 min journey

Opening
May–Sep for guided tours every Sun. Other times by prior arrangement only

Admission
Adult £18, Child £9
(includes ferry charge)

Contact
Shapinsay, Orkney KW17 2DY

t 01856 711282
w balfourcastle.co.uk
e info@balfourcastle.com

956 Spean Bridge

Monster Activities

2 hrs   All year

Go rafting on a beautiful Highland river with impressive grade-3 rapids guaranteed. A host of other activities includes canoeing, kayaking, sailing, waterskiing, mountain biking, abseiling and archery. Accredited courses are available for all ages and abilities.

* All kinds of outdoor activities on land & water
* All necessary equipment available for hire

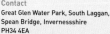

Location
On A82, between Fort William & Inverness

Opening
Daily: 9.30am–5.30pm

Admission
Depends on activity, please phone for details

Contact
Great Glen Water Park, South Laggan, Spean Bridge, Invernessshire PH34 4EA

t 01809 501340
w monsteractivities.com
e info@monsteractivities.com

957 Westray

Westray Heritage Centre

2 hrs+   May–Sep

A uniquely artistic, permanent natural history display, with annual historic exhibitions, hands-on children's models, family historic displays and crafts. The ever-expanding archive of material is available for visitors to browse through.

* 4-star Visitor Attraction

Location
On island of Westray

Opening
Daily: May–Sep 10am–12noon & 2pm–5pm
Other times by arrangement
Please phone for details

Admission
Adult £2–3, Child 50p, Concs £1.50–£2

Contact
9 Gill Pier, Westray, Orkney KW17 2DL

t 01857 677231

958 Ancrum

Harestanes Countryside Visitor Centre

2 hrs+   Apr–Oct

This visitor centre has lots of events, exhibitions and walks for all the family and the biggest play park in the Borders. Activities include children's crafts, science and nature workshops, circus skills and dance courses.

* Play park
* Exhibitions, events & activities

Location
3 miles N of Jedburgh. Well signed from A68, A698 & B6400

Opening
Daily: Apr–Oct 10am–5pm

Admission
Free

Contact
c/o Scottish Borders Council, Ancrum, Jedburgh TD8 6UQ

t 01835 830306
w scotborders.gov.uk
e harestanes@scotborders.gov.uk

959 Annan

Devil's Porridge Exhibition

1 hr   May–Oct

In 1915 the greatest munitions factory on earth was built in Gretna: 30,000 people were employed in the factory, which stretched for 9 miles and was 2 miles wide. The exhibition tells the story of this remarkable venture and the secret towns that were created to accommodate its workers.

* Learn about Britain's worst rail disaster
* Hear stories from WWII evacuees

Location
Follow A75 from Gretna, take Eastriggs turn-off & follow signs

Opening
May–Oct Mon–Sat 10am–4pm, Sun 12noon–4pm

Admission
Adults £2, Child & Concs £1

Contact
Dunedin Road, Eastriggs, nr Annan DG12 6QE

t 01461 700021
w devilsporridge.co.uk
e devils-porridge@tiscali.net

960 Ayr

Tam O'Shanter Experience

2 hrs   All year

Explore the rich Burns heritage of Alloway in this modern visitor centre set in acres of landscaped gardens. Laser-disc technology and theatrical effects bring Robbie Burns's best-loved tale to life in a special audio-visual presentation.

* 3-star Speciality Attraction
* Air-conditioned restaurant

Location
In village of Alloway, 5 miles S of Ayr town centre

Opening
Daily: Apr–Sep 10am–5.30pm; Oct–Mar 10am–5pm

Admission
Adult £5, Child & Concs £3

Contact
Murdochs Lone Alloway, Ayr, Ayrshire KA7 4PQ

t 01292 443700
w burnsheritagepark.com
e info@burnsheritagepark.com

961 Berwick-upon-Tweed

Fishwick Mains Amazing Maize Maze

2 hrs+   Jul–Sep

This fantastic themed maze is fun for all the family. Visitors are provided with a booklet of clues, riddles and puzzles to help them navigate their way through the intricate labyrinth. Each year the theme changes and so does the route!

* More than 3 miles of paths

Location
Off B6461, 5 miles W of Berwick-upon-Tweed bypass on N side of River Tweed

Opening
Daily: mid-Jul–mid-Sep 11am–6pm (last admission 4pm)

Admission
Adult £4, Child £3

Contact
nr Paxton, Berwick-upon-Tweed, Berwickshire TD15 1XQ

t 01289 386111
w fishwickmaze.com

962 Berwick-upon-Tweed

Paxton House & Country Park

2 hrs   Apr–Oct

This beautiful C18 Palladian country house has lots of activities for young people. Younger children can follow the Paxton Ted house trail and for older children there is an activity guide. Outside there is a Nature Detective trail and an adventure playground.

* 5-star historic house
* Children's summer activities

Location
On B6461, 3 miles from A1 Berwick-upon-Tweed bypass

Opening
House Daily: Apr–Oct 11am–5pm (last tour 4pm)
Garden Daily: Apr–Oct 10am–sunset

Admission
House & Garden Adult £6, Child £3
Garden only £3, £1.50

Contact
Berwick-upon-Tweed TD15 1SZ

t 01289 386291
w paxtonhouse.com
e info@paxtonhouse.com

963 Caerlaverock

WWT Caerlaverock Wetlands Centre

3 hrs+   All year

Caerlaverock has a 1,400-acre wild nature reserve with modern hides and observation towers linked by a network of screened approaches. In winter you can see thousands of barnacle geese and watch twice-daily feeds of wild swans.

* Self-catering accommodation available
* Summer nature trail

Location
9 miles SE of Dumfries along Solway Coast Heritage Trail

Opening
Daily: 10am–5pm

Admission
Adult £4.40, Child (under 4) free, Child (over 4) £2.70, Concs £3.60

Contact
Eastpark Farm, Caerlaverock, Dumfriesshire DG1 4RS

t 01387 770200
w www.org.uk
e info.caerlaverock@wwt.org.uk

964 Castle Douglas

Cream O'Galloway

3 hrs   Easter–Oct

An outdoor experience for the whole family, in which you can enjoy the adventure playground, nature trails, dog walk and beautiful scenery. There are also bicycle tracks on site and farm tours.

* 4-star Visitor Attraction
* Ice-cream factory with viewing gallery

Location
In SW of Scotland. From A75 near Gatehouse-of-Fleet take road to Sandgreen. Turn left after 1½ miles

Opening
Daily: from 10am

Admission
Adult £1.50, Child £3

Contact
Rainton, Gatehouse-of-Fleet, Castle Douglas DG7 2DR

t 01557 814040
w creamogalloway.co.uk
e info@creamogalloway.co.uk

965 Castle Douglas

Threave Garden, House & Estate

3 hrs   All year

A garden for all seasons, best known for its springtime display of daffodils. Herbaceous beds are colourful in summer and the trees and heather striking in autumn.

* Visitor centre with exhibitions
* Baronial house

Location
Off A75 near Castle Douglas

Opening
House Apr–Oct Wed–Fri & Sun
11am–3.30pm (guided tours)
Garden Daily: 9.30am–sunset

Admission
Please phone for details

Contact
Castle Douglas,
Dumfries & Galloway DG7 1RX

t 01556 502575
w nts.org.uk
e tjones@nts.org.uk

---

966 Coldingham

St Abb's Head Nature Reserve

2-4 hrs   All year

This national nature reserve is an important site for cliff-nesting seabirds in summer. Visitors can watch them wheeling and diving below the high cliffs and take guided walks with a ranger.

* Formed by an extinct volcano

Location
Off A1107, 2 miles N of Coldingham

Opening
Daily: All reasonable times

Admission
Free

Contact
Ranger's Cottage,
Northfield, St Abb's,
Eyemouth, Borders TD14 5QF

t 018907 71443
w nts.org.uk
e krideout@nts.org.uk

---

967 Creetown

Creetown Heritage Museum

1 hr   Apr–Oct

An exhibition on Creetown past and present, with historical photographs, artefacts, and audio and video presentations. Hands-on activities include exploring the Wigtown Bay nature reserve. CCTV cameras now show live and recorded pictures of red squirrels and peregrine falcons.

* 3-star Speciality Museum
* Information about the making of the cult film *The Wicker Man*

Location
500 yrds off A75 between Gatehouse-
of-Fleet & Newton Stewart

Opening
Apr–Oct Sun–Tue & Thu–Fri
11am–4pm; Easter week daily;
Jun–Aug also open Wed

Admission
Adult £2, Child & Concs £1

Contact
91 St John Street, Creetown,
Newton Stewart DG8 7JE

t 01671 820471
w creetown-heritage-museum.com

---

968 Dalbeattie

Dalbeattie Museum

1 hr   Apr–Sep

This museum gives an insight into things we used in the past. Visitors can view and handle household utensils and children's games, as well as agricultural, quarrying and bobbinmaking tools. There is also a model of the *Titanic* and an exhibition on the disaster.

* True story of First Officer Murdoch of *Titanic* fame

Location
On corner of Southwick Road
& high street in town centre

Opening
Daily: Apr–Sep Mon–Sat 10am–4pm,
Sun 2pm–4pm

Admission
Free

Contact
1 Southwick Road,
Dalbeattie DG5 4BS

t 01556 611657
e tommy.ullvele@wanadoo.co.uk

969 Dumfries

Caerlaverock Castle

1 hr+   All year

With its moat, twin-towered gate house and imposing battlements, Caerlaverock Castle is the epitome of the medieval stronghold. The castle's turbulent history owes much to its proximity to England, which brought it into border conflicts.

* Children's adventure park & nature trail
* Video presentation available

Location
8 miles SE of Dumfries on B725

Opening
Daily: Apr–Sep 9.30am–6.30pm;
Oct–Mar 9.30am–4.30pm
(last admission ¹/₂ hr before close)

Admission
Adult £4.50, Child £2, Concs £3.50

Contact
Caerlaverock, Dumfries,
Dumfriesshire DG1 4RU

t 01387 770244
w historic-scotland.gov.uk

970 Dumfries

Dumfries Museum & Camera Obscura

1 hr   All year

Set in its own gardens, Dumfries Museum & Camera Obscura is housed in a converted C18 windmill. From the camera on the top floor you can enjoy a panoramic view of Dumfries. The museum is a treasure house of the history of Dumfries & Galloway.

* Lively programme of exhibitions & events
* Museum trails & fun activities for all ages

Location
In town centre

Opening
Daily: Apr–Sep Mon–Sat 10am–5pm,
Sun 2pm–5pm; Oct–Mar Tue–Sat
10am–1pm & 2pm–5pm

Admission
Museum **Free**
Camera Obscura **Adult £1.90,**
Child & Concs 95p

Contact
Rotchell Road, Dumfries DG2 7SW

t 01387 253374
w dumgal.gov.uk/museums
e dumfriesmuseum@dumgal.gov.uk

971 Dumfries

Neverland Adventure Play Centre

1 hr   All year

Neverland is an indoor adventure play centre for children up to the age of 10. It is themed on J M Barrie's enduringly popular story of *Peter Pan*, and they can meet all their favourite characters here.

* Venue available for children's parties

Location
In town centre, reached via A75, A76
or A701

Opening
Daily: 10am–5pm

Admission
Adult free, Child £2

Contact
Park Lane, Dumfries,
Dumfriesshire DG1 2AX

t 01387 249100
w mabiefarmpark.co.uk

972 Dumfries

Old Bridge House Museum

1 hr+   Apr–Sep

Visit Dumfries's oldest house, now a museum of everyday life. You can see the family kitchen, nursery and bedroom of a Victorian home and pay a visit to an early dentist's surgery.

* 3-star Visitor Award
* Children's worksheets available

Location
At end of Old Bridge on Maxwelltown bank of River Nith

Opening
Daily: Apr–Sep Mon–Sat 10am–5pm, Sun 2pm–5pm

Admission
Free

Contact
Mill Road, Dumfries DG2 7BE

t 01387 256904
w dumgal.gov.uk/museum
e dumfriesmuseum@dumgal.gov.uk

973 Dumfries

Robert Burns Centre

1 hr   All year

Situated in an old mill building, this museum is dedicated to the history and literature of the legendary Scottish poet Robert Burns.

* 4-star Visitor Award
* Film theatre

Location
On Mill Road at Old Wear on Maxwelltown bank of River Nith

Opening
Daily: Apr–Sep Mon–Sat 10am–8pm, Sun 2pm–5pm; Oct–Mar Tue–Sat 10am–1pm, 2pm–5pm

Admission
Free

Contact
Mill Road, Dumfries DG2 7BE

t 01387 264808
w dumgal.gov.uk/museum
e dumfriesmuseum@dumgal.gov.uk

Robert Burns House

1 hr   All year

This is the house in which the famous Scottish poet Robert Burns died. It has been preserved in its original condition and contains many original artefacts and manuscripts.

* Children's worksheets available
* Original desk & chair where Burns wrote his best-known poems

Location	Admission
In Burns Street, off Shakespeare Street, next to Brooms Road car park	Free
	Contact
Opening	Burns Street, Dumfries DG1 2PS
Daily: *summer* Mon–Sat 10am–5pm, Sun 2pm–5pm *winter* Tue–Sat 10am–1pm, 2pm–5pm	t 01387 255297
	w dumgal.gov.uk/museum
	e dumfriesmuseum@dumgal.gov.uk

Shambellie House Museum of Costume

2 hrs+   Apr–Oct

Step back in time and experience Victorian and Edwardian elegance in this museum displaying original costumes in appropriate room settings. Take a fascinating look at the fashion and social etiquette of the era, before enjoying a pleasant stroll in the wooded gardens.

* Tearooms
* Regular events for families

Location	Contact
7 miles S of Dumfries on A710, Solway coast road	New Abbey, Dumfries, Dumfriesshire DG2 8HQ
Opening	t 01387 850375
Daily: Apr–Oct 10am–5pm	w nms.ac.uk
Admission	e info@nms.ac.uk
Adult £3, Child (under 12) free, Concs £2	

976 Dundonald

Dundonald Castle

1 hr   Apr–Oct

The castle's association with the Stuarts is what gives Dundonald its special importance. It was built by Robert Stuart in 1371 to mark his succession to the throne of Scotland.

* 4-star Historic Attraction
* Available for wedding ceremonies

Location
In village of Dundonald on A759, 6 miles from Ayr & 3 miles from Kilmarnock

Opening
Daily: Apr–Oct 10am–5pm

Admission
Adult £2.50, Child & Concs £1.25

Contact
Winehouse Yett, Dundonald, Ayrshire KA2 9HD

t 01563 851489
w dundonald.org.uk
e info@dundonald.org.uk

977 Eyemouth

Eyemouth Museum

1 hr   Apr–Oct

This museum has exhibitions on fishing, farming, milling, wheelwrighting and blacksmithing. One of the highlights is a large tapestry that commemorates the terrible East coast fishing disaster of 1881 in which 189 local fishermen were drowned.

* 3-star Visitor Attraction
* Exhibitions change throughout the year

Location
In centre of town

Opening
Apr–Jun & Sep daily Mon–Sat 10am–5pm, Sun 10am–1pm; Jul–Aug daily Mon–Sat 10am–5pm, Sun 10am–2pm; Oct Mon–Sat 10am–4pm

Admission
Adult £2.50, Child free, Concs £2

Contact
Auld Kirk, Manse Road, Eyemouth TD14 5JE

t 01890 750678

978 Fairlie

Kelburn Castle & Country Centre

4 hrs+   All year

Kelburn is a historic country park with a castle that dates back to the C13. There are exotic gardens, and a beautiful glen with waterfalls and deep gorges to explore. Take a tour of the castle or visit the falconry centre.

* Adventure course & pets corner
* Horse-riding available

Location
On A78 between Ayr & Greenock

Opening
Daily: Easter–Oct fully 10am–6pm; Nov–Easter (grounds & riding centre only) daily 11am–5pm

Admission
Adult £7, Child & Concs £4.50

Contact
South Offices, Fairlie, Ayrshire KA29 0BE

t 01475 568685
w kelburncountrycentre.com
e admin@kelburncountrycentre.com

979 Fenwick

Rowallan Activity Centre

2–4 hrs   All year

Whether you want to play football, learn to ride or discover the thrill of paintballing, this multifunctional indoor and outdoor centre has something for everyone.

* Crèche
* Amusement arcade

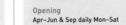

Location
From A77 take junction 7, then turn right at T junction. Turn left & follow signs for B751. Centre is 1 mile on the left

Opening
Daily: 8am–late

Admission
Free

Contact
Melklemosside, Fenwick, Ayrshire KA3 6AY

t 01560 600769
w rowallanac.com

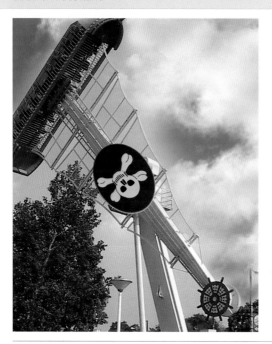

Loudoun Castle Family Theme Park

4 hrs+   Apr–Sep

A great day out for all the family is certain here, with rides and entertainment to suit all ages, in a historic setting. Live shows featuring Rory & The Gang! run throughout the day.

* Twist & Shout roller coaster
* Dougal McDougal's farm

Location
On A719 on edge of Galston

Opening
Daily: May–Jun 10am–4pm,
Jul–mid-Aug 10.30am–6pm
Also open some days in Apr & Sep,
please phone for details

Admission
Please phone for details

Contact
Galston, Ayrshire KA4 8PE

t 01563 822296
w loudouncastle.co.uk
e loudouncastle@btinternet.com

Gretna Green World Famous Blacksmith's Shop & Centre

1 hr+   All year

Visit the blacksmith's shop where many 16-year-olds married after eloping from England. The centre also has an exhibition about the history of Gretna Green, a coach museum with horse-drawn carriages, a native breeds' park with Highland cattle, and a play park.

* Old coach collection
* Juicy stories of romance, intrigue & scandal

Location
On M74, just N of border

Opening
Daily: Apr–Sep 9am–early evening;
Oct–Mar 9am–5pm

Admission
Exhibition Adult £3, Child & Concs
£2.50

Contact
Gretna Green Group Ltd,
Headless Cross, Gretna Green,
Dumfries & Galloway DG16 5EA

t 01461 338441
w gretnagreen.com
e info@gretnagreen.com

Drumlanrig's Tower

1 hr   Apr–Oct

Drumlanrig's Tower interprets Hawick's turbulent history from medieval times, using the latest audio-visual technology. The exhibition is housed in a beautifully restored period building.

* Exhibition tells the story of the house
* Display of watercolours by the artist Tom Scott

Location
In Hawick high street

Opening
Daily: Apr–Oct Mon–Sat 10am–5pm,
Sun 12noon–3pm

Admission
Adult £2.50, Child free, Concs £1.50

Contact
1 Towerknowe, Hawick TD9 9EN

t 01450 373457
w scotborders.gov.uk/museums
e museum@scotborders.gov.uk

983 Hirsel

Coldstream

4 hrs+   All year

Coldstream has interesting grounds with a museum and crafts centre. There are extensive nature trails through the woodland and grounds where you may catch a glimpse of the well-known Douglas pedigree Highland cattle. There is also a children's play area.

* Birthplace of the Coldstream Guards
* Once a rival to Gretna Green

Location
15 miles from Berwick-upon-Tweed on A698

Opening
Museum Daily: 10am–5pm
Garden & Grounds Daily: dawn–dusk

Admission
Free. Car park £2.50

Contact
Douglas & Angus Estates,
Hirsel Country Park,
Hirsel TD12 4LP

t 01573 224144
w hirselcountrypark.co.uk
e rogerdodd@btconnect.com

984 Innerleithen

Robert Smail's Printing Works

1–2 hrs   Jun–Sep

At this restored printing works visitors will discover how the industry operated at the beginning of the C20. See the printing presses in action and try your hand at old-fashioned typesetting.

* Secrets of the printing works
* Shop

Location
6 miles E of Peebles

Opening
Jun–Sep Thu–Mon 12noon–5pm,
Sun 1–5pm; also open Good
Fri–Easter Mon

Admission
Adult £5, Child & Concs £4

Contact
7–9 High Street, Innerleithen,
Borders EH44 6HA

t 01896 830206
w nts.org.uk
e smail@nts.org.uk

985 Isle of Arran

Brodick Castle, Garden & Country Park

3 hrs+   All year

With a history dating back to the Vikings, Brodick Castle offers a wonderful day of heritage, nature and relaxation. The castle boasts an impressive collection of sporting pictures and trophies, while the gardens and park offer delightful trails.

* Waymarked trails & wildlife garden
* Various events held throughout the year

Location	Admission
Take ferry from Ardrossan to Brodick for the connecting bus to castle	Please phone for details
Opening	**Contact**
Castle Daily: Apr–Oct 11am–4pm (3pm in Oct)	Isle of Arran
Country park Daily: 9.30am–sunset	t 01770 302202
	w nts.org.uk
	e brodickcastle@nts.org.uk

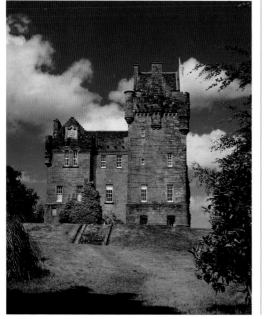

986 Jedburgh

Jedburgh Castle Jail & Museum

1 hr+   Mar–Oct

A C19 reform prison with displays interpreting the history of Jedburgh. This is one of the most haunted buildings in Scotland and has an ever-changing programme of exhibitions.

* 3-star Museum Attraction

Location	Admission
Off A68 Jedburgh road	Adult £2, Child (under-16, accompanied) & Scottish Border residents free, Concs £1.50
Opening	
Daily: Mar–Oct Mon–Sat 10am–4pm, Sun 1pm–4pm	**Contact**
	Castlegate, Jedburgh TD8 6QD
	t 01835 864750

---

987 Jedburgh

Jedforest Deer & Farm Park

3 hrs+   Easter–Oct

At this modern working farm you can see deer herds and rare breeds as well as your favourite farm animals. Enjoy the conservation area pond, wildfowl, soft play area, and picnic and barbecue area. Colour-coded nature trails wind through the woodlands.

* Bird of prey displays & tuition
* Feed the animals

Location	Contact
5 miles S of Jedburgh on A68	Mervinslaw Estate, Jedburgh, Roxburghshire TD8 6PL
Opening	t 01835 840364
Daily: Easter–Aug 10am–5.30pm; Sep–Oct 11am–4.30pm	w aboutscotland.com/jedforest/
Admission	e mervinslaw@ecosse.net
Adult £4.50, Child & Concs £2.50	

988 Jedburgh

Mary Queen of Scots Visitor Centre

1 hr   Mar–Nov

A fine C16 fortified house with period rooms set in a formal garden of pear trees. The visitor centre tells the story of the life of the tragic queen, who visited Jedburgh in 1566. Artefacts include a lock of Mary's hair and weapons from Carberry Hill battlefield.

* One of Scotland's top visitor attractions
* See some of Mary's possessions

Location
On A68 in centre of Jedburgh, SE of Selkirk

Opening
Daily: early Mar–Nov Mon–Sat 10am–4.30pm, Sun 11am–4.30pm

Admission
Adult £3, Child (under-16, accompanied) & Scottish Border residents free, Concs £2

Contact
Queen Street, Jedburgh TD8 6EN

t 01835 863331

990 Kilmarnock

Galleon Centre

2 hrs+   All year

This leisure facility has a swimming pool and ice rink, as well as a games hall that is suitable for badminton, football, basketball and table tennis. There is also a bowling hall, a comprehensive fitness suite and two bars serving a range of healthy refreshments.

* Trampolining clubs
* Swimming & skating lessons

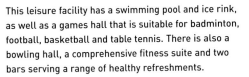

Location
In Kilmarnock town centre. Follow signs

Opening
Daily: Mon–Fri 7am–11pm, Sat 8am–6pm, Sun 9am–11pm

Admission
Adult £1.10, Child & Concs 85p
Various activities priced individually

Contact
99 Titchfield Street, Kilmarnock KA1 1QY

t 01563 524014
w galleoncentre.com
e adminoffice@galleoncentre.com

989 Kelso

Floors Castle

2 hrs   Apr–Oct

This fairytale castle is set in parkland that abounds with fauna and wildlife. Look out for oystercatchers, herons, tawny owls and red squirrels or have fun in the adventure playground, which has a flying fox, swings, a slippery dip and other fun games.

* Exhibitions & events throughout the season
* Works by well-known artists, including Matisse

Location
On edge of Kelso

Opening
Daily: Apr–Oct 11am–5pm (last admission 4.30pm)

Admission
Adult £6, Child £3.25, Concs £5

Contact
Kelso, Roxburghshire TD5 7SF

t 01573 223333
w floorscastle.com
e marketing@floorscastle.com

Kilmarnock

The Garage

2 hrs+   All year

The Garage offers entertainment and fun for all the family. There is indoor go-karting with grand prix events and computerised lap timing, and 12 lanes of bowling built for sporting as well as leisure bowlers.

* Helmets & safety suits provided
* Viewing gallery

Location	Contact
Off A77	36–40 Grange Street, Kilmarnock KA1 2DD
Opening	
Daily: 10am–midnight	t 01563 573355
	w garageleisure.co.uk
Admission	e thegarage@kilmarnock10.freestyle.
Free. Activities priced individually	co.uk

Kilmarnock

Scottish Maritime Museum

1 hr+   Apr–Oct

Irvine Harbour was once one of Glasgow's main trading ports. There are many facilities, from the Magnum Leisure Centre to bird-watching on the river estuary and an indoor boating pond. There are fine walks and rides with magnificent views of the Firth of Clyde from the beach.

* Guided tours, experimental room & test tank for kids
* Explore a large collection of vessels moored at pontoons

Location	Contact
W of Kilmarnock on A71. 10 min walk from Irvine railway station	Harbourside, Irvine, Ayrshire KA12 8QE
Opening	t 01294 278283
Daily: Apr–Oct 10am–5pm	w scottishmaritimemuseum.org/irvine
Admission	
Adult £3, Child & Concs £2, Family ticket £7	

Kilwinning

Dalgarven Mill Museum

1 hr+   All year

A country life museum in a C16 restored grain mill converted to house an extensive collection of Ayrshire memorabilia and costumes, both farming and domestic. The museum tells the story of the self-sufficient, pre-industrial rural community of Dalgarven.

* 3-star Visitor Attraction
* River beach & wildflower meadows

Location	Admission
On A737 between Kilwinning & Dalry	Please phone for details
Opening	Contact
Easter–Oct Tue–Sun 10am–5pm; Nov–Easter Tue–Fri 10am–4pm, Sat–Sun 10am–5pm	Dalgarven Mill, Dalry Road, nr Kilwinning, Ayrshire KA13 6PL
	t 01294 552448
	w dalgarvenmill.org.uk
	e admin@dalgarvenmill.org.uk

Kirkcudbright

Galloway Wildlife Conservation Park

2 hrs+   All year

This wildlife park has plenty to entertain the whole family, including South America exhibits, a play area, a pets' corner and free snake encounters (depending on the weather).

* 27–acre site
* More than 200 animals

Location
1 mile from Kirkcudbright on B727, turn up hill at Royal Hotel. Signed from A75

Opening
Daily: Mar–Oct 10am–5pm;
Nov–Feb Sat–Sun 10am–4pm

Admission
Adult £4.50, Child £2.50, Concs £3.50

Contact
Lochfergus Plantation, Kirkcudbright,
Dumfries & Galloway DG6 4XX

t 01557 331645
w gallowaywildlife.co.uk
e info@gallowaywildlife.co.uk

Kirkpatrick Fleming

Robert the Bruce's Cave

1 hr+   Easter–Nov

This world-famous ancient monument marks the site where Robert the Bruce hid in a cave during the wars of independence and was inspired by a spider's perseverance. There is an abundance of wildlife around, including red squirrels and deer.

* Camping available
* Cycling, fishing, children's park & shop

Location
Follow brown tourist signs from Gretna

Opening
Daily: Easter–Sep 9.30am–9pm;
Oct–Nov 9.30am–5pm
(closing times may vary)

Admission
Please phone for details

Contact
Cove Farm, Cove Estate,
Kirkpatrick Fleming,
Dumfries & Galloway DG11 3AT

t 01461 800285
w brucescave.co.uk
e enquiries@brucescave.com

Largs

The Viking Experience

1 hr   Feb–Nov

Travel back in time to AD825 and experience the sounds and smells of a homestead beside a Norwegian fjord. Meet resident Vikings who will tell sagas associated with Viking life and culture. Visit the longhouse with views over the fjord and see longships moored outside.

* Regular shows
* Leisure facilities, soft play centre & theatre

Location
On Largs seafront

Opening
Feb & Nov Sat 12.30pm–3.30pm,
Sun 10.30am–3.30pm;
Mar & Oct daily 10.30am–3.30pm;
Apr–Sep daily 10.30am–5.30pm

Admission
Adult £4.10, Child & Concs £3.10

Contact
Vikingar, Greenock Road,
Largs, Ayrshire KA30 8QL

t 01475 689777
w vikingar.co.uk
e info@vikingar.co.uk

Melrose

Three Hills Roman Centre & Fort

1 hr+   All year

The most important Roman military complex between Hadrian's Wall and the Antonine Wall guarded and secured the crossing of the River Tweed at Newstead in the C1 and C2. Excavations have revealed much of what went on there. See finds from 1905 to 1910 and 1989 to 1998.

* See millennium milestone & timber tower
* Viewing platforms & information boards

Location
Market Square in Melrose

Opening
Daily: Apr–Oct 10.30am–4.30pm;
Nov–Mar please phone for details

Admission
Walks Adult £3, Child free, Concs £2.50
Exhibition £1.50, £1, £1

Contact
Ormiston, Melrose TD6 9PN

t 01896 822651
w trimontium.net
e secretary@trimontium.freeserve.
co.uk

998 Newton Stewart

Galloway Red Deer Range

2 hrs   Jun–Sep

This attraction has a viewpoint near the road from which beautiful red deer can be observed in their natural habitat. Visitors to the range can also walk among the deer, photograph them and even touch them, under supervision – a memorable experience.

* Guided tours in summer
* See & hear roaring stags during the rutting season

Location
On A712, 3 miles SW of Clatteringshaws Loch

Opening
End of Jun–mid-Sep Tue & Thu 11am–2pm, Sun 11am–2.30pm
Tours Tue & Thu 11am & 2.30pm, Sun 2.30pm

Admission
Adult £3.50, Child £1.25, Concs £2.50, Family ticket £8

Contact
Red Deer Range Car Park, nr Clatteringshaws, Newton Stewart, Dumfries & Galloway DG7 3SQ
t 01671 402420
w forestry.gov.uk/gallowayforestpark
e galloway@forestry.gsi.gov.uk

999 Saltcoats

North Ayrshire Museum

1 hr   All year

Visit the refurbished North Ayrshire Museum and discover the history of this region from prehistoric times to the present day. Exhibits include maritime models and displays of archaeology.

* Rich variety of artefacts
* Industrial history

Location
Just off A78 & A738

Opening
Mon–Tue & Thu–Sat 10am–1pm & 2pm–5pm

Admission
Free

Contact
Manse Street, Saltcoats, Ayrshire KA21 5AA
t 01294 464174
w north-ayrshire.gov.uk/museums
e namuseum@north-ayrshire.gov.uk

1000 Sanquhar

Sanquhar Tolbooth Museum

1 hr   Apr–Sep

Housed in a fine C18 tolbooth, this museum charts the life of ordinary Upper Nithsdale people. Exhibits recreate life in a local jail and tell the story of the mines and the local knitting tradition.

→ Community life in times past

Location
In town centre

Opening
Apr–Sep Tue–Sat 10am–1pm
& 2pm–5pm, Sun 2pm–5pm

Admission
Free

Contact
High Street, Sanquhar,
Dumfries & Galloway DG46BN

t 01659 50186
w www.dumgal.gov.uk/museum
e dumfriesmuseum@dumgal.gov.uk

1001 Selkirk

Halliwell's House Museum

1 hr   Apr–Oct

Step back in time in Halliwell's House and discover the building's former use as a home and ironmonger's shop. It also tells the story of the historic burgh of Selkirk. The Robson Gallery has regular contemporary art exhibitions.

* Guided tours (by arrangement)
* Children's play area

Location
Just off Market Place in heart of
Selkirk. Selkirk can be reached by A7
from Galashiels

Opening
Daily: Apr–Sep Mon–Sat 10am–5pm
(5.30pm in Jul–Aug), Sun
10am–12noon; Oct Mon–Sat
10am–4pm

Admission
Free

Contact
Halliwell's Close, Market Place,
Selkirk TD7 4BL

t 01750 720096
e museums@scotborders.gov.uk

Halliwell'sHouse©

Index

@Bristol 56
Abbotsbury Swannery 87
Aberdeen Maritime Museum 337
Aberdeenshire Farming Museum 341
Abington Museum 157
Acton Scott 168
Adventure Island 121
Air Raid Shelters 245
Airport Tour Centre 272
Aldenham Country Park 122
Almond Valley Heritage Centre 317
Alnwick Castle 292
Alphabet Zoo/KK5 245
Alstone Wildlife Park 99
Althorp House 156
Alton Towers 172
Amazing Hedge Puzzle 167
Amberley Working Museum 48
The American Adventure 146
Anderton Boat Lift 242
Anglesey Sea Zoo 191
Animal Farm Adventure Park 96
Animalarium 188
Aquarium of the Lakes 256
Arbeia Roman Fort 304
Archaeolink 337
Arlington Court 68
Ash End House Children's Farm 175
Ashby-de-la-Zouch Castle 147
Ashridge Estate 122
Athelstan Museum 103
Atholl Country Life Museum 315
Atlantis 218
Auchingarrich Wildlife Centre 314
Avebury 102
Avon Heath Country Park 85
Babbacombe Model Village 78
Baconsthorpe Castle 130
Bagshaw Museum 229
Balfour Castle 353
Ballindalloch Castle 343
Balmoral Castle & Estate 339
BALTIC 301
Bamburgh Castle 293
Banham Zoo 126
Bank Boats 131
Bank of England Museum 36
Bannockburn Heritage Centre 335
Bardsea Country Park 260
Barleylands Craft Village & Farm Centre 117
Barnard Castle 286

Barnsley Metrodome 224
Barnstaple Heritage Centre 68
Barrie's Birthplace 331
Barrington Court 94
Barton House Railway 132
Bateman's 13
Bath Balloons 94
Battle Abbey & Battlefield 12
Baytree Garden Centre & Owl Centre 154
BBC Television Centre Tours 38
Beach Leisure Centre 337
The Beacon 261
Beacon Country Park 281
Beale Park 7
Beamish, The North of England
   Open-Air Museum 286
Beatles Story 277
Beatrix Potter Gallery 252
Beaulieu Abbey & National
   Motor Museum 17
Bede's World & St Paul's Church 302
Bedford Butterfly Park 111
Bedlam Paintball, Edinburgh 317
Bedlington Country Park 293
Beer Quarry Caves 68
Beeston Castle 246
Bekonscot Model Village & Railway 10
Bella Jane Boat Trips 349
Belsay Hall, Castle & Gardens 298
Belvoir Castle 149
Bempton Cliffs Nature Reserve 207
Berkeley Castle 88
Berrington Hall 167
Berwick Barracks Museum &
   Art Gallery 294
Betton Farm Visitor Centre &
   Animal Farm 218
Bicton Park Botanical Gardens 71
Big Pit National Mining Museum 197
Big Sheep & Little Cow Farm 211
Bignor Roman Villa 50
Bill Quay Farm 301
Billing Aquadrome 157
Birdland Park 89
Birmingham Botanical Gardens &
   Glasshouses 183
Bishop's Boats Seal Trips 130
Bithell Boats (Show Boats of Chester) 239
Black Country Living Museum 182
Blackbrook Zoological Park 176
Blackgang Chine Fantasy Park 24

The Black House Museum 348
Blackpool Illuminations 262
The Blackpool Piers 262
Blackpool Pleasure Beach 263
Blackpool Sands 72
Blackpool Sea Life Centre 263
Blackpool Tower & Circus 264
Blackwell, The Arts & Crafts House 249
Blair Drummond Safari & Adventure Park 335
Blakeney Point 127
Blue Planet Aquarium 240
Blue Reef Aquarium 307
Bluebell Railway 16
The Boat Museum 241
Bocketts' Farm Park 47
Bodiam Castle 12
Bodmin & Wenford Railway 58
Bolam Lake Country Park 294
Bolsover Castle 144
Bolton Abbey 220
Bolton Aquarium 265
Bolton Castle 214
Bolton Museum & Art Gallery 265
Bolton Wanderers Football Club 265
Bondville Model Village 207
Border Regiment & King's Own
   Royal Border Regiment Museum 250
Bosworth Battlefield Visitor Centre &
   Country Park 178
Bowes Museum 286
Bowood House 103
Bradford Industrial Museum &
   Horses at Work 229
Brandon Marsh Nature Centre 176
Brechin Castle Centre 314
Bredgar & Wormshill Light Railway 32
Bressingham Steam Experience &
   Gardens 128
Brewers Quay 87
Bridlington Leisure World 207
Brigantium 300
Brighton Sea Life Centre 12
The Bright Water Visitor Centre 349
Bristol Ice Rink 56
Bristol Zoo Gardens 56
British Golf Museum 334
British in India Museum 269
The British Museum 33
British Wildlife Centre 47
British Wildlife Rescue Centre 174
Brixworth Country Park 156

Brockhampton Estate 166
Brockholes Farm Visitor Centre 224
Brocklands Adventure Park 60
Brodick Castle, Garden & Country Park 364
Brontë Boats 231
Brooklands Museum 47
Brookside Miniature Railway 244
Broomey Croft Children's Farm 177
Brownsea Island National Trust 84
Buckfast Butterfly Farm &
  Dartmoor Otter Sanctuary 70
Buckingham Palace 35
Buckinghamshire County Museum &
  Roald Dahl Gallery 9
Buckinghamshire Railway Centre 9
Bucks Goat Centre 9
Bungay Castle 135
Bure Valley Railway 126
Burnby Hall Gardens 210
Burpham Court Farm Park 46
Burrs Activity Centre 265
Bury St Edmunds Abbey Gardens 136
Butlins (Skegness) 153
The Butterfly & Wildlife Park 155
Bygones 79
Cadbury World 181
The Cadies & Witchery Tours 318
Caerlaverock Castle 358
Caerphilly Castle 197
Cairngorm Reindeer Centre 342
Caithness Crystal Visitor Centre 131
Calderglen Country Park 325
Caldicot Castle & Country Park 201
California Country Park 8
Callendar House Museum 323
Calshot Castle 22
Camel Trail 59
Camelot Theme Park 267
Cannon Hall Farm 224
The Canterbury Tales 25
Capesthorne Hall 241
Captain Cook Memorial Museum 221
Cardiff Castle 197
Cardigan Heritage Centre 199
Cardigan Island Coastal Farm Park 199
Carlisle Castle 250
Carlisle Park 298
Cars of the Stars 254
Castle Eden Dene Nature Reserve 291
Castle Howard 221
Catalyst Science Discovery Centre 247
Cattle Country Adventure Park 89
Cawdor Castle 353
Cedar Farm Galleries 270
Centre for Life 303
Charlestown Shipwreck &
  Heritage Centre 65
Cheddar Gorge & Caves 97
Chedworth Roman Villa 90
Chelmsford Museum & Essex Regiment
  Museum 119

Chelsea FC Museum & Tour 35
Cherryburn 296
Cheshire Military Museum 239
Chessington World of Adventures 45
Chester Visitor Centre 239
Chester Zoo 239
Chestnut Centre Otter Haven &
  Owl Sanctuary 146
Chillingham Castle 295
Chinnor & Princes Risborough Railway 42
Chirk Castle 193
Chislehurst Caves 27
Cholderton Rare Breeds Farm Park 104
City Museum & Art Gallery 57
City of Caves 160
Clare Castle Country Park 139
Classic Boat Museum 20
Cleethorpes Humber Estuary
  Discovery Centre 151
Cliff Castle Museum 231
Clydebuilt Scottish Maritime Museum 326
Coastal Voyager 138
Codona's Pleasure Fair 338
Cogges Manor Farm Museum 43
Colchester Zoo 119
Coldstream 363
Collford Lake Park 59
Colour Museum 230
Combined Military Services Museum 120
Conisbrough Castle 224
Conkers 144
Coors Visitor Centre 173
Corfe Castle 86
Cornish Mines & Engines 65
Corrigall Farm Museum 344
Corris Craft Centre 190
Cotebrook Shire Horse Centre &
  Countryside Park 240
Cotswold Farm Park 90
Cotswold Motor Museum & Toy Collection 89
Cotswold Wildlife Park & Gardens 42
Crabble Corn Mill 27
Cragside Estate 298
Craigencalt Ecology Centre 330
Crealy Adventure Park 72
Cream O'Galloway 356
Creetown Heritage Museum 357
Cresswell Dunes 299
Crook Hall Gardens 288
Crownhill Fort 75
Croxteth Hall & Country Park 277
Cruckley Farm 208
Culloden Battlefield 345
Cumberland Pencil Museum 254
The Cutty Sark 35
Dairyland Farm World 63
Dalbeattie Museum 357
Dalemain Historic House & Garden 257
Dales Countryside Museum 212
Dalgarven Mill Museum 366
Deben Cruises 140

Deen City Farm 37
The Deep 208
Deep Sea World 332
Denby Pottery Visitor Centre 145
Denny Abbey & The Farmland Museum 117
Derby Museum of Industry & History 146
Derwent Water Marina 254
Devil's Porridge Exhibition 354
Dewa Roman Experience 240
Dewar's Centre 332
Didcot Railway Centre 42
Diggerland – Devon 71
Diggerland – Durham 288
Diggerland – Kent 32
Dinosaur Adventure Park 132
The Dinosaur Museum 82
Dinton Pastures Country Park 8
Discovery Museum 303
Discovery Point 316
The DLI Museum 288
Docker Park Farm Visitor Centre 266
Dolaucothi Gold Mines 190
Doncaster Aeroventure 225
The Donkey Sanctuary 77
Donington Grand Prix Collection 145
Dorman Museum 291
Dorset Belle Cruises 81
Dorset County Museum 82
The Dorset Teddy Bear Museum 83
Dover Castle 28
Drayton Manor Theme Park 175
Druidstone Park & Art Park 25
Drum Castle, Garden & Estate 340
Drumlanrig's Tower 362
Druridge Bay Country Park 299
Drusillas Park 13
Dudley Canal Trust 182
Dudley Zoological Gardens 182
Dumfries Museum & Camera Obscura 358
Dundonald Castle 361
Dunfermline Abbey & Palace 316
Dunstable Downs Countryside Centre &
  Whipsnade Estate 112
Dunster Castle 97
Durham Castle 289
Durlston Country Park 85
Dyrham Park 91
Eagle Heights Bird of Prey Centre 28
Earnley Butterflies & Gardens 49
East Lancashire Railway 266
Eastnor Castle 167
Eden Camp Modern History Museum 214
Eden Ostrich World 257
The Eden Project 65
Edinburgh Butterfly & Insect World 318
Edinburgh Castle 318
Edinburgh Crystal Visitor Centre 319
Edinburgh Dungeon 319
Edinburgh Zoo 319
The Edward Haughey Solway
  Aviation Museum 251

Index

Elephant Playbarn	134	
Elgin Cathedral	345	
Emberton Country Park	11	
The English School of Falconry	111	
Etruria Industrial Museum	174	
Eureka! The Museum for Children	230	
Everton Football Club	278	
Exmouth Model Railway	73	
Explosion! The Museum of Naval Firepower	19	
Eyemouth Museum	361	
Fairhaven Woodland & Water Garden	132	
Fairlands Valley Park	125	
The Falkirk Wheel	323	
Falls of Clyde Visitor Centre & Wildlife Reserve	326	
Family's Pride II Glassbottom Boat Trips	350	
The Famous Grouse Experience at Glenturret Distillery	315	
Farleigh Hungerford Castle	98	
Farmer Palmer's Farm Park	84	
Farmer Parr's Animal World	267	
Farming World	28	
Farne Islands	300	
Felbrigg Hall, Garden & Park	133	
Felinwynt Rainforest & Butterfly Centre	188	
Ferens Art Gallery	209	
Ferne Animal Sanctuary	96	
Ferrycroft Countryside Visitor Centre	352	
The Ffestiniog Railway	196	
Findhorn Heritage Icehouse	340	
Fishers Farm Park	48	
Fishwick Mains Amazing Maize Maze	355	
Flag Fen Bronze Age Centre	115	
Flambards Theme Park	61	
Flamingo Land Theme Park & Zoo	213	
Fleet Air Arm Museum	102	
Floors Castle	365	
Florence Mine Heritage Centre	251	
The Flying Fortress	50	
Folly Farm	201	
Forest Hills Watersports	314	
Formby	281	
Fort Paull	209	
Fort Victoria Marine Aquarium	25	
Fort Victoria Model Railway	25	
The Foundry Climbing Centre	226	
Four Seasons White Water Rafting	291	
Foxton Canal Museum	150	
The Fun Centre	192	
The Fun House	342	
Galleon Centre	365	
Galloway Red Deer Range	368	
Galloway Wildlife Conservation Park	367	
The Garage	366	
Gibraltar Point National Nature Reserve & Visitor Centre	154	
Gibside	304	
Gigrin Farm	190	
Gladstone Pottery Museum	173	
Glamis Castle	325	
Glasgow Police Museum	326	
Glasgow Science Centre	326	
Glasgow Ski & Snowboarding Centre	327	
Glastonbury Abbey	98	
Glencoe Visitor Centre	346	
Glendurgan Gardens	60	
Globe Theatre	38	
Go Ape! – Berkshire	6	
Go Ape! – Cumbria	252	
Go Ape! – Nottinghamshire	159	
Godstone Farm	47	
The Golden Hind	70	
Goonhilly Satellite Earth Station	61	
Gordon Highlanders Museum	338	
Grand Pier	77	
Great Central Railway	149	
Great Yarmouth Sealife Centre	128	
Green's Mill & Science Centre	161	
Greenwood Forest Park	195	
Gressenhall Museum & Workhouse	127	
Gretna Green World Famous Blacksmith's Shop & Centre	362	
Grimes Graves	127	
Groombridge Place Gardens & The Enchanted Forest	32	
Gulliver's Kingdom	147	
Gulliver's World	246	
Hack Green Secret Nuclear Bunker	242	
Haddon Hall	144	
Haigh Country Park	272	
Hall Hill Farm	290	
Halliwell's House Museum	369	
Hamerton Zoo Park	116	
Hampton Court Palace	45	
Hamsterley Forest	287	
Hanningfield Reservoir Visitor Centre	117	
Harbour Park	50	
Hardy's Animal Farm	151	
Harestanes Countryside Visitor Centre	354	
Harewood House & Bird Gardens	232	
Harlequin Puppet Theatre	194	
Harperley POW Camp	287	
Hartlepool's Maritime Experience	290	
Hastings Castle & 1066 Story	15	
Hatfield Water Park	225	
Hatton Country World	177	
The Hawk Conservancy Trust	17	
Hawkshead Trout Farm	248	
Hawkstone Park	170	
Haynes Motor Museum	100	
Hazel Brow Visitor Centre	217	
Heatherton Country Sports Park	202	
Hedingham Castle	120	
Heights of Abraham	147	
The Helicopter Museum	101	
Henblas Country Park	191	
Heritage Centre, Bellingham	293	
Hertford Museum	123	
High Lodge Forest Centre	135	
High Woods Country Park	119	
Highland Adventure Safaris	314	
Highland Folk Museum, Newtonmore	350	
Highland Wildlife Park	350	
Hill Top	248	
The Historic Dockyard, Chatham	27	
Historylinks Museum	345	
Holdenby House, Gardens & Falconry Centre	157	
Hollingworth Lake Country Park	269	
Holywell Bay Fun Park	63	
Honister Slate Mine	249	
Hoo Farm	171	
The Hop Farm	33	
The Hop Pocket Craft Centre	184	
Horseworld	58	
Horsey Windpump	129	
Horton Park Children's Farm	45	
Houghton Mill	115	
House of Marbles	73	
Houses of Parliament	41	
The House on the Hill Toy Museum	121	
Housesteads Roman Fort, Hadrian's Wall	296	
'How We Lived Then' Museum of Shops	14	
Howletts Wild Animal Park	26	
HULA Animal Rescue: South Midlands Animal Sanctuary	113	
Hull & East Riding Museum	209	
Hull Arena	209	
Hunstanton Sea Life Centre	130	
ILPH Hall Farm	133	
Imperial War Museum	36	
Imperial War Museum Duxford	114	
Ingleborough Cave	211	
Inigo Jones Slateworks	192	
INTECH-Hands-on Science & Technology Centre	24	
Inveraray Jail	347	
Inverkeithing Museum	324	
Inverness Dolphin Cruises	347	
Inverness Terror Tour	347	
Ipswich Transport Museum	136	
Irchester Country Park	158	
Ironbridge Gorge Museums	171	
Isle of Wight Steam Railway	21	
Isle of Wight Zoo	21	
Isles of Scilly Steamship Company	64	
The Jane Austen Centre	95	
Jedburgh Castle Jail & Museum	364	
Jedforest Deer & Farm Park	364	
Jewish Museum of Manchester	273	
Jodrell Bank Science Centre & Arboretum	241	
John Dony Field Centre	112	
Jorvik	221	
Keighley & Worth Valley Railway	231	
Kelburn Castle & Country Centre	361	
Kellie Castle & Garden	334	
Kelvedon Hatch Secret Nuclear Bunker	118	
Kendal Museum	253	
Kent & East Sussex Railway	32	

Keswick Climbing Wall 255
Kielder Water Leaplish Waterside Park 295
Killerton House 72
Killhope Lead Mining Museum 292
Killiecrankie Visitor Centre 333
King Arthur's Labyrinth 189
Kingsbury Water Park 179
Kingston Maurward Gardens 83
Kirbuster Museum 344
Kirby Hall 156
Kisimul Castle 347
Knightshayes Court 78
Knockhill Racing Circuit 316
Knowsley Safari Park 281
Lacock Abbey & Fox Talbot Museum 103
The Lake District Coast Aquarium 255
Lake Vyrnwy Nature Reserve 190
Lakeland Bird of Prey Centre 257
Lakeland Miniature Village 252
Lakeland Pony Trekking 261
Lakeland Wildlife Oasis 256
Lamont City Farm 327
Lancaster Castle 268
Land's End Visitor Centre 65
Landmark Forest Theme Park 344
Langham Glass 128
Lanhydrock House 59
Lappa Valley Steam Railway 64
Lapworth Museum of Geology 180
Laserquest 250
Leeds Castle 30
Legoland Windsor 7
Leighton Buzzard Railway 111
Leighton Hall 267
Leisure Lakes 270
Leith Hall 341
Lewis Karting Centre 348
Lightwater Valley 217
Lincoln Aviation Heritage Centre 155
Lindisfarne Castle 297
Lindisfarne Priory 297
Link Centre 105
Linlithgow Palace 331
Lion Salt Works 243
Liverpool Football Club Museum &
Tour Centre 278
Liverpool Planetarium 278
Livesey Museum for Children 34
Living Coasts 79
The Living Rainforest 6
Llangollen Wharf 195
Llangorse Rope & Riding Centre 189
Loch Lomond National Nature Reserve 343
Loch Ness Monster Exhibition Centre 345
Loch Rannoch Watersports & Quads 330
London Aquarium 34
London Dungeon 37
London Eye 35
London Zoo 38
Longdown Activity Farm 22
Longleat 106

Look and Sea! 50
The Look Out Discovery Centre 6
Lost Gardens of Heligan 66
Loudoun Castle Family Theme Park 362
Low Sizergh Barn 253
Lowestoft Maritime Museum 136
Lulworth Castle 86
Lundy Island 69
Lyddington Bede House 162
Lyme Park 245
M&D's Theme Park 332
Macduff Marine Aquarium 341
The MacRobert Centre 336
Madame Tussaud's 37
Magical World of Fantasy Island 152
Magna Science Adventure Centre 226
Making It! Discovery Centre 159
Manchester Art Gallery 273
Manchester Museum 274
Manning's Amusement Park 136
Maple Street British Museum
of Miniatures 124
Marwell Zoological Park 24
Mary Queen of Scots Visitor Centre 365
Megazone 323
Mersey Ferries River Explorer Cruise 282
Midland Air Museum 179
Mid-Suffolk Light Railway Museum 138
Military Aviation Museum 49
The Milky Way Adventure Park 69
Mill Green Museum & Mill 123
Millennium Galleries 227
Millennium Stadium Tours 198
Milton Keynes Museum 11
Mister Twisters, Consett 287
Model Railway Village 282
Mole Hall Wildlife Park 121
Monk Park Farm Visitor Centre 220
The Monkey Sanctuary Trust 63
Monkey World 87
Monster Activities 354
Morwellham Quay 77
Mother Shipton's Cave & Petrifying Well 214
Motoring Heritage Centre 327
Mouldsworth Motor Museum 240
Mount Edgcumbe House & Park 67
The Muckleburgh Collection 134
Muncaster Castle 258
Museum in the Park 93
Museum of Army Flying 23
Museum of Canterbury with
Rupert Bear Museum 26
Museum of Flight 317
Museum of Kent Life 31
Museum of Lakeland Life 253
Museum of Lincolnshire Life 152
Museum of London 34
Museum of Science & Industry in
Manchester 274
Museum of Scotland 320
Museum of Scottish Country Life 328

The Museum of Scottish Lighthouses 340
Museum of Transport (Glasgow) 328
Museum of Transport (Manchester) 274
Museum of Witchcraft 59
Mythstories, Museum of Myth & Fable 170
The National Cycle Collection 189
National Football Museum 270
National Gallery 41
National Glass Centre 305
The National Marine Aquarium 75
National Maritime Museum Cornwall 60
National Motorcycle Museum 183
National Museum of Photography,
Film & Television 230
National Portrait Gallery 320
National Railway Museum 222
National Sea Life Centre 180
National Seal Sanctuary 61
National Showcaves Centre for Wales 200
National Space Centre 149
National Stud 137
National Trust Fell Foot Park 260
National Waterfront Museum 202
National Waterways Museum 91
National Wildflower Centre 277
Natural History Museum 38
NCCL Galleries of Justice 160
The Needles Park 18
Nene Valley Railway 116
Neverland Adventure Play Centre 358
New Lanark World Heritage Site 332
Newark Air Museum 159
Newby Hall & Gardens 218
Newhaven Fort 16
The New Metroland 301
Newquay Zoo 64
Noah's Ark 333
Noah's Ark Zoo Farm 58
Norfolk & Suffolk Aviation Museum 135
Norfolk Motor Cycle Museum 134
Norfolk Shire Horse Centre 127
Norman Lockyer Observatory &
James Lockyer Planetarium 77
Normanby Hall Country Park 153
North Ayrshire Museum 368
North Yorkshire Moors Railway 215
Northwich Community Woodlands 243
Norwich Union Wheel of Yorkshire 222
Nottingham Castle 160
Oakwell Hall Country Park 229
Oakwood Theme Park 202
Oasis Leisure Centre 105
Oceanarium Bournemouth 81
Old Bridge House Museum 359
Old Fulling Museum of Archaeology 289
Old MacDonald's Educational Farm Park 118
The Old Royal Station, Ballater 340
Old Sarum 104
Old Trafford Museum & Tour 275
Oliver Cromwell's House 114
Ordsall Hall Museum 276

Index

Organic Garden Ryton 177
The Original Great Maze 118
The Orkney Museum 351
Ormesby Hall 215
Osborne House 17
Oswaldtwistle Mills Shopping Village 262
Oulton Park Race Circuit 246
Our Dynamic Earth 320
The Oxfordshire Museum 43
The Oxford Story 43
Paignton & Dartmouth Steam Railway 74
Paignton Zoo Environmental Park 74
Painshill Park 44
Paradise Park 16
Paradise Wildlife Park 122
Park Hall Countryside Experience 170
Park Rose Owl & Bird of Prey Centre 207
Paultons Park 20
Paxton House & Country Park 355
Peak Cavern 145
Pecorama Pleasure Gardens & Exhibition 76
Peel Farm 331
Pembrokeshire Motor Museum 200
Pendle Heritage Centre 269
Pennington Flash Country Park 268
Pennywell Farm & Wildlife Centre 70
People's History Museum 275
People's Palace 328
Peterhead Maritime Heritage 342
Pickering Castle 216
Pickering Trout Lake 216
Pier Amusements Centre 305
The Piping Centre 328
Plas Menai National Watersports Centre 192
Plas Newydd 191
Platty+ 249
The Play Barn 134
Plean Country Park 334
Pleasure Beach, Great Yarmouth 129
Pleasurewood Hills Theme Park 137
Plessey Woods Country Park 293
Poldark Mine & Heritage Complex 62
Polka Theatre 41
Polkemmet Country Park 320
Polkyth Leisure Centre 66
Pony & Quad Treks 193
Porfell Animal Land Wildlife Park 62
Port Lympne Wild Animal Park 30
Portmeirion 196
Pot-a-Doodle-Do 294
Prince Bishop River Cruiser 289
Prinknash Bird & Deer Park 92
Prior Park Landscape Garden 95
ProAdventure 196
Puzzle Wood 91
The Quad Squad 211
Quarry Bank Mill & Styal Estate 247
Quasar at Rollerworld 120
Raasay Outdoor Centre 349
Raby Castle 288
Radstock Museum 100

The RAF Museum – Cosford 169
Ragged School Museum 39
The Raptor Foundation 117
Ravenglass & Eskdale Railway 258
Rays Farm Country Matters 168
Red House Glass Cone 183
Reddish Vale Country Park 246
Redwings Rescue Centre 139
Renishaw Hall Gardens 227
Rheged – Enter into the Spirit of Cumbria 258
RHS Garden Harlow Carr 212
Richmond Castle 217
Ripley Castle 212
Rivacre Valley Local Nature Reserve 245
River Wey & Godalming Navigations & Dapdune Wharf 46
The Riviera International Centre & Waves Leisure Pool 80
Robert Burns Centre 359
Robert Burns House 360
Robert Smail's Printing Works 363
Robert the Bruce's Cave 367
Robinswood Hill Country Park 92
Rockingham Castle 150
Roman Army Museum 295
Roman Baths & Pump Rooms 95
Roman Museum 26
Romney, Hythe & Dymchurch Railway 31
Rowallan Activity Centre 361
Royal Air Force Museum 36
The Royal Armouries – Fort Nelson 18
Royal Armouries Museum 232
Royal Botanic Garden Edinburgh 321
Royal Cornwall Museum 67
Royal Gunpowder Mills 121
Royal Museum of Scotland 321
Royal Victoria Country Park 23
The Royal Yacht Britannia 321
Rufford Old Hall 271
Rumble Tumble 272
Rural Life Centre 46
Rutland County Museum 162
Rutland Water 162
Ryedale Folk Museum 212
Salt Museum 243
Saltwell Park 302
Sandal Castle 234
Sandcastle Tropical Waterworld 264
Sandford Parks Lido 90
Sanquhar Tolbooth Museum 369
Satrosphere 339
Scapa Flow Visitor Centre & Museum 351
Scarborough Castle 218
Science Museum 39
Scotch Gill Woods Local Nature Reserve 299
Scotkart 329
Scotland's Secret Bunker 334
Scottish Crannog Centre 330
Scottish Deer Centre 324
Scottish Fisheries Museum 324

Scottish Football Museum 329
Scottish Maritime Museum 366
Scottish Railway Exhibition 322
Scottish Seabird Centre 322
Scottish Sealife & Marine Sanctuary 353
Scottish Vintage Bus Museum 325
Sea Life & Marine Sanctuary 219
The Seal Sanctuary 153
Seahouses Heritage Centre 300
Seaprobe Atlantis 351
Seaquarium, Weston-super-Mare 101
Seaton Tramway 76
Seaview Wildlife Encounter 21
Secret Hills – Shropshire Hills Discovery Centre 168
Segedunum Roman Fort, Baths & Museum 308
Sellafield Visitor Centre 259
Selly Manor 181
Sensation: Dundee 316
Seven Sisters Country Park 15
Sewerby Hall & Gardens 208
Shakespeare's Birthplace 178
Shambellie House Museum of Costume 360
Shanklin Chine 22
Sheffield Cycle Speedway Club 228
Sheffield Ski Village 228
Shepreth Wildlife Park 124
Sherlock Holmes Museum 37
Sherwood Forest Country Park & Visitor Centre 158
Shibden Hall 231
Shipley Art Gallery 302
Shortwood Family Farm 166
Sizergh Castle & Garden 259
Skegness Natureland Seal Sanctuary 154
Ski Rossendale 270
Skipton Castle 220
Small Breeds Farm Park & Owl Centre 166
Smuggler's Adventure 15
Snappy's Adventure Play Centre 33
Snibston Discovery Park 148
The Snowdome 176
Snowdon Mountain Railway 195
Soldiers of Gloucestershire Museum 92
Somerset County Museum 101
Sound Cruising 75
Souter Lighthouse 305
South Creake Maize Maze 128
South Devon Railway 70
South Lakes Wild Animal Park 251
South of England Rare Breeds Centre 29
South Tyne Trail 296
South Tynedale Railway 248
Southwold Pier 138
Speke Hall, Garden & Estate 279
Spinnaker Tower 20
The Spirit of the Tattoo 323
Spirit of the West American Theme Park 66
Springfields Fun Park & Pony Centre 66
SS Great Britain 57

St Abb's Head Nature Reserve 357
St Andrews Aquarium 325
St Fagans National History Museum 198
St Leonard's Farm Park 234
Stafford Castle 174
Staintondale Shire Horse Farm
  Visitor Centre 219
Stapehill Abbey, Crafts & Gardens 88
Stapeley Water Gardens 242
Staunton Country Park 19
STEAM – Museum of the Great
  Western Railway 105
Stephenson Railway Museum 303
Stepping Stones Farm 39
Stirling Castle 336
Stockley Farm 244
Stockwood Craft Museum & Gardens 113
Stokesay Castle 169
Stondon Motor Museum 112
Stonehenge 102
Stoneywish Nature Reserve 13
Stourhead Gardens 104
Stratford Butterfly Farm 178
Strathspey Steam Railway 343
Streetlife Museum of Transport 210
Stretton Watermill 244
Stuart Line Cruises & Boat Trips 73
Studland Beach & Nature Reserve 85
Sudbury Hall & Museum of Childhood 172
Suffolk Owl Sanctuary 138
Sunderland Museum & Winter Gardens 306
Sundown Adventure Land 161
Sutton Hoo 140
Swanage Railway 86
Tales of Robin Hood 160
Talkin Tarn Country Park 250
Tall Ship in Glasgow Harbour 329
The Tamar Otter & Wildlife Centre 62
Tam O'Shanter Experience 355
Tanfield Railway 306
Tank Museum 82
Tate Liverpool 279
Tattershall Castle 155
Techniquest 199
Tehidy Country Park 60
Temple Newsam House & Farm 232
Thackray Museum 233
Thames Barrier Information &
  Learning Centre 41
ThinkTank 180
Thorne Memorial Park Miniature
  Railway 225
Thorpe Park 44
Threave Garden, House & Estate 357
Three Hills Roman Centre & Fort 367
Thrigby Hall Wildlife Gardens 129
Tiggywinkles, The Wildlife Hospital Trust 9
Tintagel Castle 67
Tiverton Museum of Mid Devon Life 78
Tolkien's Birmingham 180
Tomb of the Eagles 352

Top Gear Indoor Karting 290
Topsy Turvy World 125
Totnes Elizabethan House Museum 80
Tower Bridge Exhibition 40
Tower of London 40
Trafford Ecology Park 276
Treasure Island 14
Trethorne Leisure Farm 62
Tropical Birdland 148
Tropical Butterfly House &
  Wildlife Centre 228
Tropical World 233
Trotters World of Animals 255
Tuckers Maltings 74
Tulleys Farm 49
The Tutankhamun Exhibition 83
Twinlakes Park 150
Twycross Zoo 176
Tyne Riverside Country Park 298
Tynemouth Priory & Castle 307
Ullswater 'Steamers' 252
Upton Country Park 85
Upton Heritage Centre 184
Vale of Rheidol Railway 188
Vertical Descents 346
Verulamium Museum 124
Viaduct Fishery 101
The Viking Experience 367
Vindolanda 297
Wallington Estate 295
Walton Hall Gardens 247
Wansbeck Riverside Park 292
Warwick Castle 179
Waterhall Farm & Craft Centre 123
Waterworld 174
WDCS Wildlife Centre 346
Weald & Downland Open-Air Museum 49
Welsh Chocolate Farm 201
Welsh Highland Railway (Caernarfon) 192
Welsh International Climbing &
  Activity Centre 202
The Welsh Mountain Zoo 194
West Midland Safari & Leisure Park 184
West Somerset Railway 99
West Somerset Rural Life Museum 99
West Stow Country Park &
  Anglo-Saxon Village 140
Westbury White Horse & Bratton Camp 106
Westray Heritage Centre 354
Wetheriggs Pottery 258
Whale Watching Trips 349
Whickham Thorns Outdoor
  Activity Centre 301
Whinlatter Forest Park 255
Whipsnade Wild Animal Park 112
White Post Farm Centre 158
White Scar Cave 213
Whitley Bay Ice Rink 308
Whitworth Hall Country Park 291
Whitworth Water Ski &
  Recreation Centre 271

Wicksteed Park 157
Wildfowl & Wetlands Trust Washington 308
The Wildlife Park at Cricket St Thomas 96
Wildwood 29
Williamson Park & Butterfly House 268
Williamson Tunnels 280
Willows Farm Village 125
Wimborne Model Town & Gardens 88
Wimpole Home Farm 116
Windermere Lake Cruises 261
Windsor Castle 8
Winston Churchill's Britain at War
  Experience 40
Woburn Safari Park 113
Wollaton Hall Museum 161
Wonderland 171
Wonderland & The Cardew Tea Pottery 69
Woodchester Park & Mansion 92
Woodlands Leisure Park 80
Wookey Hole Caves & Papermill 102
Woolsthorpe Manor 151
Worcester Cathedral 184
Worden Arts & Crafts Centre 269
Working Sheepdogs 350
The World of Beatrix Potter 249
World of Glass 282
Wroxeter Roman City (Virconium) 171
Wroxham Barns 130
WWT Arundel 48
WWT Caerlaverock Wetlands Centre 356
WWT Slimbridge Wildfowl &
  Wetlands Trust 93
Wycombe Museum 10
Wykeham Lakes 219
Wyreside Ecology Centre 264
Wythenshawe Park 276
Xcite Playworld 139
Xscape – Braehead 330
Xscape – Milton Keynes 11
Yellow Duckmarine 280
York Dungeons 222
York Maze 222
York Minster 223
Yorkshire Air Museum 223
Yorkshire Museum & Gardens 223
Yorkshire Sculpture Park 234
Zorb South UK 84

Acknowledgements & picture credits

The publishers would like to acknowledge the important contribution the British Tourist Authority made to this publication through the use of images from its website, *www.britainonview.com.*

The publishers would like to thank the National Trust, the National Trust for Scotland and English Heritage, who kindly supplied photographs for use with their entries.

The publishers would also like to thank all contributors who provided information, and especially all those who kindly supplied photographs. Particular thanks go to Tony Stuchbury (www.ajsphotos.co.uk).

Compiled, edited and designed by Butler and Tanner. Edited by Libby Willis. Design and layout by Lyn Davies and Carole McDonald. Project Manager Nick Heal. Special thanks to Carl Luke, Jennie Golding and Dianne Penny.